Lecture Notes in Computer Science 11429

Commenced Publication in 1973
Founding and Former Series Editors:
Gerhard Goos, Juris Hartmanis, and Jan van Leeuwen

Advanced Research in Computing and Software Science
Subline of Lecture Notes in Computer Science

More information about this series at http://www.springer.com/series/7407

Dirk Beyer · Marieke Huisman ·
Fabrice Kordon · Bernhard Steffen (Eds.)

Tools and Algorithms for the Construction and Analysis of Systems

25 Years of TACAS: TOOLympics
Held as Part of ETAPS 2019
Prague, Czech Republic, April 6–11, 2019
Proceedings, Part III

Springer Open

Editors
Dirk Beyer
LMU Munich
Munich, Germany

Marieke Huisman
University of Twente
Enschede, The Netherlands

Fabrice Kordon
LIP6 - CNRS UMR
Paris, France

Bernhard Steffen
TU Dortmund University
Dortmund, Germany

ISSN 0302-9743   ISSN 1611-3349 (electronic)
Lecture Notes in Computer Science
ISBN 978-3-030-17501-6   ISBN 978-3-030-17502-3 (eBook)
https://doi.org/10.1007/978-3-030-17502-3

LNCS Sublibrary: SL1 – Theoretical Computer Science and General Issues

This Springer imprint is published by the registered company Springer Nature Switzerland AG
The registered company address is: Gewerbestrasse 11, 6330 Cham, Switzerland

ETAPS Foreword

Welcome to the 22nd ETAPS! This is the first time that ETAPS took place in the Czech Republic in its beautiful capital Prague.

ETAPS 2019 was the 22nd instance of the European Joint Conferences on Theory and Practice of Software. ETAPS is an annual federated conference established in 1998, and consists of five conferences: ESOP, FASE, FoSSaCS, TACAS, and POST. Each conference has its own Program Committee (PC) and its own Steering Committee (SC). The conferences cover various aspects of software systems, ranging from theoretical computer science to foundations to programming language developments, analysis tools, formal approaches to software engineering, and security.

Organizing these conferences in a coherent, highly synchronized conference program enables participation in an exciting event, offering the possibility to meet many researchers working in different directions in the field and to easily attend talks of different conferences. ETAPS 2019 featured a new program item: the Mentoring Workshop. This workshop is intended to help students early in the program with advice on research, career, and life in the fields of computing that are covered by the ETAPS conference. On the weekend before the main conference, numerous satellite workshops took place and attracted many researchers from all over the globe.

ETAPS 2019 received 436 submissions in total, 137 of which were accepted, yielding an overall acceptance rate of 31.4%. I thank all the authors for their interest in ETAPS, all the reviewers for their reviewing efforts, the PC members for their contributions, and in particular the PC (co-)chairs for their hard work in running this entire intensive process. Last but not least, my congratulations to all authors of the accepted papers!

ETAPS 2019 featured the unifying invited speakers Marsha Chechik (University of Toronto) and Kathleen Fisher (Tufts University) and the conference-specific invited speakers (FoSSaCS) Thomas Colcombet (IRIF, France) and (TACAS) Cormac Flanagan (University of California at Santa Cruz). Invited tutorials were provided by Dirk Beyer (Ludwig Maximilian University) on software verification and Cesare Tinelli (University of Iowa) on SMT and its applications. On behalf of the ETAPS 2019 attendants, I thank all the speakers for their inspiring and interesting talks!

ETAPS 2019 took place in Prague, Czech Republic, and was organized by Charles University. Charles University was founded in 1348 and was the first university in Central Europe. It currently hosts more than 50,000 students. ETAPS 2019 was further supported by the following associations and societies: ETAPS e.V., EATCS (European Association for Theoretical Computer Science), EAPLS (European Association for Programming Languages and Systems), and EASST (European Association of Software Science and Technology). The local organization team consisted of Jan Vitek and Jan Kofron (general chairs), Barbora Buhnova, Milan Ceska, Ryan Culpepper, Vojtech Horky, Paley Li, Petr Maj, Artem Pelenitsyn, and David Safranek.

The ETAPS SC consists of an Executive Board, and representatives of the individual ETAPS conferences, as well as representatives of EATCS, EAPLS, and EASST. The Executive Board consists of Gilles Barthe (Madrid), Holger Hermanns (Saarbrücken), Joost-Pieter Katoen (chair, Aachen and Twente), Gerald Lüttgen (Bamberg), Vladimiro Sassone (Southampton), Tarmo Uustalu (Reykjavik and Tallinn), and Lenore Zuck (Chicago). Other members of the SC are: Wil van der Aalst (Aachen), Dirk Beyer (Munich), Mikolaj Bojanczyk (Warsaw), Armin Biere (Linz), Luis Caires (Lisbon), Jordi Cabot (Barcelona), Jean Goubault-Larrecq (Cachan), Jurriaan Hage (Utrecht), Rainer Hähnle (Darmstadt), Reiko Heckel (Leicester), Panagiotis Katsaros (Thessaloniki), Barbara König (Duisburg), Kim G. Larsen (Aalborg), Matteo Maffei (Vienna), Tiziana Margaria (Limerick), Peter Müller (Zurich), Flemming Nielson (Copenhagen), Catuscia Palamidessi (Palaiseau), Dave Parker (Birmingham), Andrew M. Pitts (Cambridge), Dave Sands (Gothenburg), Don Sannella (Edinburgh), Alex Simpson (Ljubljana), Gabriele Taentzer (Marburg), Peter Thiemann (Freiburg), Jan Vitek (Prague), Tomas Vojnar (Brno), Heike Wehrheim (Paderborn), Anton Wijs (Eindhoven), and Lijun Zhang (Beijing).

I would like to take this opportunity to thank all speakers, attendants, organizers of the satellite workshops, and Springer for their support. I hope you all enjoy the proceedings of ETAPS 2019. Finally, a big thanks to Jan and Jan and their local organization team for all their enormous efforts enabling a fantastic ETAPS in Prague!

February 2019   Joost-Pieter Katoen
                                                        ETAPS SC Chair
                                                     ETAPS e.V. President

TACAS Preface

TACAS 2019 was the 25th edition of the International Conference on Tools and Algorithms for the Construction and Analysis of Systems conference series. TACAS 2019 was part of the 22nd European Joint Conferences on Theory and Practice of Software (ETAPS 2019). The conference was held at the Orea Hotel Pyramida in Prague, Czech Republic, during April 6–11, 2019.

Conference Description. TACAS is a forum for researchers, developers, and users interested in rigorously based tools and algorithms for the construction and analysis of systems. The conference aims to bridge the gaps between different communities with this common interest and to support them in their quest to improve the utility, reliability, flexibility, and efficiency of tools and algorithms for building systems. TACAS 2019 solicited four types of submissions:

- *Research papers*, identifying and justifying a principled advance to the theoretical foundations for the construction and analysis of systems, where applicable supported by experimental validation.
- *Case-study papers*, reporting on case studies and providing information about the system being studied, the goals of the study, the challenges the system poses to automated analysis, research methodologies and approaches used, the degree to which goals were attained, and how the results can be generalized to other problems and domains.
- *Regular tool papers*, presenting a new tool, a new tool component, or novel extensions to an existing tool, with an emphasis on design and implementation concerns, including software architecture and core data structures, practical applicability, and experimental evaluations.
- *Tool-demonstration papers* (short), focusing on the usage aspects of tools.

Paper Selection. This year, 164 papers were submitted to TACAS, among which 119 were research papers, 10 case-study papers, 24 regular tool papers, and 11 were tool-demonstration papers. After a rigorous review process, with each paper reviewed by at least three Program Committee members, followed by an online discussion, the Program Committee accepted 29 research papers, 2 case-study papers, 11 regular tool papers, and 8 tool-demonstration papers (50 papers in total).

Artifact-Evaluation Process. The main novelty of TACAS 2019 was that, for the first time, artifact evaluation was compulsory for all regular tool papers and tool demonstration papers. For research papers and case-study papers, artifact evaluation was optional. The artifact evaluation process was organized as follows:

- *Regular tool papers and tool demonstration papers.* The authors of the 35 submitted papers of these categories of papers were required to submit an artifact alongside their paper submission. Each artifact was evaluated independently by three reviewers. Out of the 35 artifact submissions, 28 were successfully evaluated, which corresponds to an acceptance rate of 80%. The AEC used a two-phase reviewing process: Reviewers first performed an initial check to see whether the artifact was technically usable and whether the accompanying instructions were consistent, followed by a full evaluation of the artifact. The main criterion for artifact acceptance was consistency with the paper, with completeness and documentation being handled in a more lenient manner as long as the artifact was useful overall. The reviewers were instructed to check whether results are consistent with what is described in the paper. Inconsistencies were to be clearly pointed out and explained by the authors. In addition to the textual reviews, reviewers also proposed a numeric value about (potentially weak) acceptance/rejection of the artifact. After the evaluation process, the results of the artifact evaluation were summarized and forwarded to the discussion of the papers, so as to enable the reviewers of the papers to take the evaluation into account. In all but three cases, tool papers whose artifacts did not pass the evaluation were rejected.

- *Research papers and case-study papers.* For this category of papers, artifact evaluation was voluntary. The authors of each of the 25 accepted papers were invited to submit an artifact immediately after the acceptance notification. Owing to the short time available for the process and acceptance of the artifact not being critical for paper acceptance, there was only one round of evaluation for this category, and every artifact was assigned to two reviewers. The artifacts were evaluated using the same criteria as for tool papers. Out of the 18 submitted artifacts of this phase, 15 were successfully evaluated (83% acceptance rate) and were awarded the TACAS 2019 AEC badge, which is added to the title page of the respective paper if desired by the authors.

TOOLympics. TOOLympics 2019 was part of the celebration of the 25th anniversary of the TACAS conference. The goal of TOOLympics is to acknowledge the achievements of the various competitions in the field of formal methods, and to understand their commonalities and differences. A total of 2^4 competitions joined TOOLympics and were presented at the event. An overview and competition reports of 11 competitions are included in the third volume of the TACAS 2019 proceedings, which are dedicated to the 25th anniversary of TACAS. The extra volume contains a review of the history of TACAS, the TOOLympics papers, and the papers of the annual Competition on Software Verification.

Competition on Software Verification. TACAS 2019 also hosted the 8th International Competition on Software Verification (SV-COMP), chaired and organized by Dirk Beyer. The competition again had high participation: 31 verification systems with developers from 14 countries were submitted for the systematic comparative evaluation, including three submissions from industry. The TACAS proceedings includes the competition report and short papers describing 11 of the participating verification systems. These papers were reviewed by a separate Program Committee (PC); each of the papers was assessed by four reviewers. Two sessions in the TACAS program (this year as part of the TOOLympics event) were reserved for the presentation of the results: the summary by the SV-COMP chair and the participating tools by the developer teams in the first session, and the open jury meeting in the second session.

Acknowledgments. We would like to thank everyone who helped to make TACAS 2019 successful. In particular, we would like to thank the authors for submitting their papers to TACAS 2019. We would also like to thank all PC members, additional reviewers, as well as all members of the artifact evaluation committee (AEC) for their detailed and informed reviews and, in the case of the PC and AEC members, also for their discussions during the virtual PC and AEC meetings. We also thank the Steering Committee for their advice. Special thanks go to the Organizing Committee of ETAPS 2019 and its general chairs, Jan Kofroň and Jan Vitek, to the chair of the ETAPS 2019 executive board, Joost-Pieter Katoen, and to the publication team at Springer.

April 2019

Tomáš Vojnar (PC Chair)
Lijun Zhang (PC Chair)
Marius Mikucionis (Tools Chair)
Radu Grosu (Use-Case Chair)
Dirk Beyer (SV-COMP Chair)
Ondřej Lengál (AEC Chair)
Ernst Moritz Hahn (AEC Chair)

Preface

The celebration of the 25th anniversary of TACAS, the International Conference on Tools and Algorithms for the Construction and Analysis of Systems, was part of the 22nd European Joint Conferences on Theory and Practice of Software (ETAPS 2019). The celebration event was held in Prague, Czech Republic, during April 6–7, 2019.

This year, the TACAS proceedings consist of three volumes, and the third volume is dedicated to the 25th anniversary of TACAS. This extra volume contains a review of the history of TACAS, the TOOLympics papers, and the papers of the annual Competition on Software Verification.

The goal of TOOLympics 2019, as part of the celebration of the 25th anniversary of the TACAS conference, was to acknowledge the achievements of the various competitions in the field of formal methods, and to understand their commonalities and differences. A total of 2^4 competitions joined TOOLympics and were presented at the event. An overview and competition reports of 11 competitions are included in the proceedings.

We would like to thank all organizers of competitions in the field of formal methods, in particular those that presented their competition as part of TOOLympics. We would also like to thank the ETAPS 2019 Organizing Committee for accommodating TOOLympics, especially its general chairs, Jan Kofroň and Jan Vitek, the chair of the ETAPS 2019 executive board, Joost-Pieter Katoen, and the team at Springer for the flexible publication schedule.

April 2019

Dirk Beyer
Marieke Huisman
Fabrice Kordon
Bernhard Steffen

A Short History of TACAS

Introduction

The International Conference on Tools and Algorithms for the Construction and Analysis of Systems (TACAS) celebrated its 25th anniversary this year. As three of the original co-founders of the meeting, we are proud of this milestone, and also a bit surprised by it! Back in the 1993–1994 timeframe, when we were formulating plans for TACAS, we had no other aspirations than to have an interesting, well-run event interested in the theory and practice of analysis and verification tools. That said, we feel something of an obligation to record the course TACAS has followed over the years. That is the purpose of this note: to give a brief history of the conference, and to highlight some of the decisions that were made as it evolved.

Pre-history

The idea for TACAS was hatched on a tennis court in Elounda, Greece, during the 1993 Computer-Aided Verification (CAV) Conference. CAV was a relatively young meeting at the time in a field (automated verification) that was experiencing explosive growth. The three of us were playing doubles with another CAV attendee, Ed Brinksma; the four of us would go on to be the founding members of the TACAS Steering Committee. Immediately after the match we fell to talking about CAV, how great it was to have a conference devoted to verification, but how some topics, especially ones devoted to software, and to system analysis and not necessarily verification, were not on the table. This conversation turned to what another meeting might look like, and thus was the seed for what became TACAS, an event addressing tools for the construction and analysis of systems. (Perhaps interestingly, our original idea of a name for the conference was Tools, Algorithms and Methodologies – TAM. We decided to drop "methodologies" from the title in order to clearly emphasize the tool aspect.)

In subsequent meetings and e-mail exchanges we fleshed out the idea of the conference. We wanted to support papers about tools on equal footing with typical research papers and to further increase the awareness of tools by making case studies and tool demonstrations part of the main conference with dedicated topical parts. At the time, other conferences we were familiar with did not have demos, or if they did, they took place during breaks and social events, meaning the audiences were small.

By scheduling demos during regular conference sessions, we were able to ensure good attendance, and by providing the typical 15 pages for (regular) tool papers and case study papers, and four pages for tool-demo papers, we also gave tool builders an opportunity to present their tool and give something citable for others who wanted to reference the work. In fact, the most highly cited TACAS paper of all time is the 2008 tool-demo paper for the Z3 SMT solver by Leonardo de Mourna and Nikolaj Bjørner, whose citation count just passed 5,000.

The Early Years

TACAS began its life as a workshop, rather than a conference, although all its proceedings were published by Springer in its *Lecture Notes in Computer Science* series.

The first meeting of TACAS took place May 19–20, 1995, in Aarhus, Denmark as a workshop to the TAPSOFT conference series. Both TAPSOFT and our TACAS workshop were hosted by the prominent BRICS research center. The workshop featured 13 accepted papers and Springer published the proceedings in its *Lecture Notes in Computer Science* (LNCS) series. The Program Committee was chaired by the four Steering Committee members (the three of us, plus Ed Brinksma) and Tiziana Margaria.

The next meeting, March 27–29, 1996, in Passau, Germany, featured 30 papers (including 11 tool-demo papers) and lasted three days, rather than two.

The final workshop instance of TACAS occurred in Enschede, The Netherlands on April 2–4, 1997, and had 28 papers.

ETAPS

In 1994 during a TAPSOFT business meeting in Aarhus, negotiations began to integrate several European software-focused conferences into a consortium of co-located meetings. The resulting amalgam was christened the Joint European Conferences on Theory and Practice of Software (ETAPS), and has become a prominent meeting in early spring in Europe since its initial iteration in 1998.

TACAS had been a workshop until 1997, but starting in 1998 it became a conference and was one of the five founding conferences of ETAPS, along with the European Symposium on Programming (ESOP), Foundations of Software Systems and Computational Structures (FoSSaCS), Fundamental Aspects of Software Engineering (FASE), and Compiler Construction (CC). This step in the development of TACAS helped cement its status as a premiere venue for system analysis and verification tools, although the increased overhead associated with coordinating its activities with four other conferences presented challenges. The increased exposure, however, did lead to a significant growth in submissions and also in accepted papers. In 1998, the first iteration of ETAPS was held in Lisbon, Portugal; the TACAS program featured 29 presentations. Figure 1 shows a group of people during the 10 years of TACAS celebration in 2004. By 2007, the 10th incarnation of ETAPS, which was held in Braga, Portugal, the program featured 57 presentations (several of these were invited contributions, while others were tool-demo papers). Negotiating this increased presence of TACAS within ETAPS required tact and diplomacy, and it is a testament to the bona fide skills of both the TACAS and ETAPS organizers that this was achievable.

Fig. 1. 10 years of TACAS celebration in 2004 in Barcelona, Spain. From left to right: Andreas Podelski, Joost-Pieter Katoen, Lenore Zuck, Bernhard Steffen, Tiziana Margaria, Ed Brinksma, Hubert Garavel, Susanne Graf, Kim Larsen, Nicolas Halbwachs, Wang Yi, and John Hatcliff

As part of becoming a conference and a part of ETAPS, TACAS also institution-alized some of the informal practices that it had used in its early, workshop-based existence. The Steering Committee structure was formalized, with the three of us and Ed Brinksma becoming the official members. (After several years of service, Ed Brinksma left the Steering Committee to pursue leadership positions in Dutch and, subsequently, German universities and research institutions. Joost-Pieter Katoen took Brinksma's place; when he then left to assume leadership of ETAPS, Holger Hermanns ascended to the TACAS Steering Committee. Lenore Zuck and, currently, Dirk Beyer have also held ad hoc positions on the Steering Committee.)

The conference also standardized its approach to Program Committee leadership, with two co-chairs being selected each year, and with a dedicated tool chair for overseeing tool submissions and demonstractions. Today, similar committee structures can be found at other conferences as well, but they were less common when TACAS adopted them.

Subsequent Developments

Since joining ETAPS, TACAS has experimented with its programmatic aspects. In recent years, the conference has started to increase the emphasis of the four paper categories by explicitly providing four categories of paper submission: regular, tool, case study, and demo. Starting in 2012, it also started to include tool competitions, most notably SV-COMP led by Dirk Beyer, which have proved popular with the community and have attracted increasing numbers of competitors. The conference has also modified its submission and reviewing processes over the years.

At ETAPS 2014 in Grenoble we celebrated the 20th anniversary of TACAS. During this celebration, awards for the most influential papers in the first 20 years of TACAS were given. The regular-paper category went to Armin Biere, Alessandro Cimatti, Edmund Clarke, and Yunshan Zhu for their 1999 paper "Symbolic Model Checking Without BDDs," and the tool-demo category went to the "Z3: An Efficient SMT Solver" presented by Leonardo de Mourna and Nikolaj Bjørner in 2008. Figure 2 shows Armin Biere, Alessandro Cimatti, and Leonardo de Mourna during the award ceremony.

Fig. 2. Most Influencial Paper Award Ceremony at the 20 Years of TACAS celebration in 2014. From left to right Rance Cleaveland, Bernhard Steffen, Armin Biere, Alessandro Cimatti, Leonardo de Mourna, Holger Hermanns, and Kim Larsen

Reflections

As we noted at the beginning of this text, we had no idea when we started TACAS in 1995 that it would become the venue that it is 25 years later. Most of the credit should go to the authors who submitted their work to the conference, to the hard work of the Program Committee chairs and members who reviewed and selected papers for presentation at the conference, to the tool-demo chairs who oversaw the selection of tool demonstrations, and to the local arrangements organizers who ensured the technical infrastructure at conference venues could handle the requirements of tool demonstrators.

That said, we do think that some of the organizational strategies adopted by TACAS have helped its success as well. Here we comment on a few of these.

- Compact Steering Committee. The TACAS Steering Committee has always had four to five members. This is in contrast to other conferences, which may have ten or more members. The small size of the TACAS committee has enabled greater participation on the part of the individual members.
- Steering Committee ⊆ Program Committee. Unusually, and because the Steering Committee is small in number, Steering Committee members serve on the Program Committee each year. This has sometimes been controversial, but it does ensure institutional memory on the PC so that decisions made one year (about the definition of double-submission, for instance) can be recalled in later years.
- PC Co-chairs. As mentioned earlier, TACAS has two people leading the Program Committee, as well as a tool chair. Originally, this decision was based on the fact that, because TACAS had multiple submission tracks (regular, tool, case study, and tool demo), the PC chairing responsibilities were more complex. Subsequently, though, our observation is that having two leaders can lead to load-sharing and also good decision-making. This is particularly fruitful for dealing with conflicts, as one chair can oversee the papers where the other has a conflict.

This LNCS volume is devoted to the TACAS 25th anniversary event, TOOLympics, which comprises contributions from 16 tool competitions. The maturity of these challenges, as well of the participating tools impressively demonstrates the progress that has been made in the past 25 years. Back in 1994 we would never have imagined the power of today's tools with SAT solvers capable of dealing with hundreds of thousands of variables, powerful SMT solvers, and complex verification tools that make careful use of the power of these solvers. The progress is really impressive, as is still the gap toward true program verification of industrial scale. This requires a better understanding of the developed methods, algorithms, and technologies, the impact of particular heuristics, and, in particular, the interdependencies between them. TOOLympics aims at fostering the required interdisciplinary, problem-oriented cooperation, and as the founders of TACAS, we look forward to observing the results of this cooperation in forthcoming editions of TACAS.

Finally, we would like to thank Alfred Hofmann and his team at Springer for the continuous support in particular during the early phases. Without this support, TACAS would never have developed in the way it did.

February 2019

Rance Cleaveland
Kim Larsen
Bernhard Steffen

Organization

Program Committee: TACAS

Parosh Aziz Abdulla	Uppsala University, Sweden
Dirk Beyer	LMU Munich, Germany
Armin Biere	Johannes Kepler University Linz, Austria
Ahmed Bouajjani	IRIF, Paris Diderot University, France
Patricia Bouyer	LSV, CNRS/ENS Cachan, Université Paris Saclay, France
Yu-Fang Chen	Academia Sinica, Taiwan
Maria Christakis	MPI-SWS, Germany
Alessandro Cimatti	Fondazione Bruno Kessler, Italy
Rance Cleaveland	University of Maryland, USA
Leonardo de Moura	Microsoft Research, USA
Parasara Sridhar Duggirala	University of North Carolina at Chapel Hill, USA
Pierre Ganty	IMDEA Software Institute, Spain
Radu Grosu	Vienna University of Technology, Austria
Orna Grumberg	Technion – Israel Institute of Technology, Israel
Klaus Havelund	NASA/Caltech Jet Propulsion Laboratory, USA
Holger Hermanns	Saarland University, Germany
Falk Howar	TU Dortmund, Germany
Marieke Huisman	University of Twente, The Netherlands
Radu Iosif	Verimag, CNRS/University of Grenoble Alpes, France
Joxan Jaffar	National University of Singapore, Singapore
Stefan Kiefer	University of Oxford, UK
Jan Kretinsky	Technical University of Munich, Germany
Salvatore La Torre	Università degli studi di Salerno, Italy
Kim Guldstrand Larsen	Aalborg University, Denmark
Anabelle McIver	Macquarie University, Australia
Roland Meyer	TU Braunschweig, Germany
Marius Mikučionis	Aalborg University, Denmark
Sebastian A. Mödersheim	Technical University of Denmark, Denmark
David Parker	University of Birmingham, UK
Corina Pasareanu	CMU/NASA Ames Research Center, USA
Sanjit Seshia	University of California, Berkeley, USA
Bernhard Steffen	TU Dortmund, Germany
Jan Strejcek	Masaryk University, Czech Republic
Zhendong Su	ETH Zurich, Switzerland
Meng Sun	Peking University, China

Michael Tautschnig   Queen Mary University of London/Amazon Web
                                     Services, UK
Tomas Vojnar (Co-chair)   Brno University of Technology, Czech Republic
Thomas Wies   New York University, USA
Lijun Zhang (Co-chair)   Institute of Software, Chinese Academy
                                     of Sciences, China
Florian Zuleger   Vienna University of Technology, Austria

Program Committee and Jury: SV-COMP

Dirk Beyer (Chair)   LMU Munich, Germany
Peter Schrammel (2LS)   University of Sussex, UK
Jera Hensel (AProVE)   RWTH Aachen, Germany
Michael Tautschnig (CBMC)   Amazon Web Services, UK
Kareem Khazem (CBMC-Path)   University College London, UK
Vadim Mutilin   ISP RAS, Russia
  (CPA-BAM-BnB)
Pavel Andrianov   ISP RAS, Russia
  (CPA-Lockator)
Marie-Christine Jakobs   LMU Munich, Germany
  (CPA-Seq)
Omar Alhawi (DepthK)   University of Manchester, UK
Vladimír Štill   Masaryk University, Czech Republic
  (DIVINE-Explicit)
Henrich Lauko (DIVINE-SMT)   Masaryk University, Czech Republic
Mikhail R. Gadelha   University of Southampton, UK
  (ESBMC-Kind)
Philipp Ruemmer (JayHorn)   Uppsala University, Sweden
Lucas Cordeiro (JBMC)   University of Manchester, UK
Cyrille Artho (JPF)   KTH, Sweden
Omar Inverso (Lazy-CSeq)   Gran Sasso Science Institute, Italy
Herbert Rocha (Map2Check)   Federal University of Roraima, Brazil
Cedric Richter (PeSCo)   University of Paderborn, Germany
Eti Chaudhary (Pinaka)   IIT Hyderabad, India
Veronika Šoková (PredatorHP)   BUT, Brno, Czechia
Franck Cassez (Skink)   Macquarie University, Australia
Zvonimir Rakamaric (SMACK)   University of Utah, USA
Willem Visser (SPF)   Stellenbosch University, South Africa
Marek Chalupa (Symbiotic)   Masaryk University, Czech Republic
Matthias Heizmann   University of Freiburg, Germany
  (UAutomizer)
Alexander Nutz (UKojak)   University of Freiburg, Germany
Daniel Dietsch (UTaipan)   University of Freiburg, Germany
Priyanka Darke (VeriAbs)   Tata Consultancy Services, India
R. K. Medicherla (VeriFuzz)   Tata Consultancy Services, India
Pritom Rajkhowa (VIAP)   Hong Kong UST, SAR China

Liangze Yin (Yogar-CBMC)   NUDT, China
Haining Feng   National University of Defense Technology, China
  (Yogar-CBMC-Par.)

Artifact Evaluation Committee (AEC)

Pranav Ashok   TU Munich, Germany
Marek Chalupa   Masaryk University, Czech Republic
Gabriele Costa   IMT Lucca, Italy
Maryam Dabaghchian   University of Utah, USA
Bui Phi Diep   Uppsala, Sweden
Daniel Dietsch   University of Freiburg, Germany
Tom van Dijk   Johannes Kepler University, Austria
Tomáš Fiedor   Brno University of Technology, Czech Republic
Daniel Fremont   UC Berkeley, USA
Ondřej Lengál (Co-chair)   Brno University of Technology, Czech Republic
Ernst Moritz Hahn (Co-chair)   Queen's University Belfast, UK
Sam Huang   University of Maryland, USA
Martin Jonáš   Masaryk University, Czech Republic
Sean Kauffman   University of Waterloo, Canada
Yong Li   Chinese Academy of Sciences, China
Le Quang Loc   Teesside University, UK
Rasool Maghareh   National University of Singapore, Singapore
Tobias Meggendorfer   TU Munich, Germany
Malte Mues   TU Dortmund, Germany
Tuan Phong Ngo   Uppsala, Sweden
Chris Novakovic   University of Birmingham, UK
Thai M. Trinh   Advanced Digital Sciences Center, Illinois
                                  at Singapore, Singapore
Wytse Oortwijn   University of Twente, The Netherlands
Aleš Smrčka   Brno University of Technology, Czech Republic
Daniel Stan   Saarland University, Germany
Ilina Stoilkovska   TU Wien, Austria
Ming-Hsien Tsai   Academia Sinica, Taiwan
Jan Tušil   Masaryk University, Czech Republic
Pedro Valero   IMDEA, Spain
Maximilian Weininger   TU Munich, Germany

Additional Reviewers

Aiswarya, C.
Albarghouthi, Aws
Aminof, Benjamin
Américo, Arthur
Ashok, Pranav
Atig, Mohamed Faouzi
Bacci, Giovanni
Bainczyk, Alexander
Barringer, Howard
Basset, Nicolas
Bensalem, Saddek
Berard, Beatrice
Besson, Frédéric
Biewer, Sebastian
Bogomolov, Sergiy
Bollig, Benedikt
Bozga, Marius
Bozzano, Marco
Brazdil, Tomas
Caulfield, Benjamin
Chaudhuri, Swarat
Cheang, Kevin
Chechik, Marsha
Chen, Yu-Fang
Chin, Wei-Ngan
Chini, Peter
Ciardo, Gianfranco
Cohen, Liron
Cordeiro, Lucas
Cyranka, Jacek
Čadek, Pavel
Darulova, Eva
Degorre, Aldric
Delbianco, Germán Andrés
Delzanno, Giorgio
Devir, Nurit
Dierl, Simon
Dragoi, Cezara
Dreossi, Tommaso
Dutra, Rafael
Eilers, Marco
El-Hokayem, Antoine
Faella, Marco

Fahrenberg, Uli
Falcone, Ylies
Fox, Gereon
Freiberger, Felix
Fremont, Daniel
Frenkel, Hadar
Friedberger, Karlheinz
Frohme, Markus
Fu, Hongfei
Furbach, Florian
Garavel, Hubert
Ghosh, Bineet
Ghosh, Shromona
Gondron, Sebastien
Gopinath, Divya
Gossen, Frederik
Goyal, Manish
Graf-Brill, Alexander
Griggio, Alberto
Gu, Tianxiao
Guatto, Adrien
Gutiérrez, Elena
Hahn, Ernst Moritz
Hansen, Mikkel
Hartmanns, Arnd
Hasani, Ramin
Havlena, Vojtěch
He, Kangli
He, Pinjia
Hess, Andreas Viktor
Heule, Marijn
Ho, Mark
Ho, Nhut Minh
Holik, Lukas
Hsu, Hung-Wei
Inverso, Omar
Irfan, Ahmed
Islam, Md. Ariful
Itzhaky, Shachar
Jakobs, Marie-Christine
Jaksic, Stefan
Jasper, Marc
Jensen, Peter Gjøl

Jonas, Martin
Kaminski, Benjamin Lucien
Karimi, Abel
Katelaan, Jens
Kauffman, Sean
Kaufmann, Isabella
Khoo, Siau-Cheng
Kiesl, Benjamin
Kim, Eric
Klauck, Michaela
Kong, Hui
Kong, Zhaodan
Kopetzki, Dawid
Krishna, Siddharth
Krämer, Julia
Kukovec, Jure
Kumar, Rahul
Köpf, Boris
Lange, Martin
Le Coent, Adrien
Lemberger, Thomas
Lengal, Ondrej
Li, Yi
Lin, Hsin-Hung
Lluch Lafuente, Alberto
Lorber, Florian
Lu, Jianchao
Lukina, Anna
Lång, Magnus
Maghareh, Rasool
Mahyar, Hamidreza
Markey, Nicolas
Mathieson, Luke
Mauritz, Malte
Mayr, Richard
Mechtaev, Sergey
Meggendorfer, Tobias
Micheli, Andrea
Michelmore, Rhiannon
Monteiro, Pedro T.
Mover, Sergio
Mu, Chunyan
Mues, Malte
Muniz, Marco
Murano, Aniello
Murtovi, Alnis

Muskalla, Sebastian
Mutluergil, Suha Orhun
Neumann, Elisabeth
Ngo, Tuan Phong
Nickovic, Dejan
Nies, Gilles
Noller, Yannic
Norman, Gethin
Nowack, Martin
Olmedo, Federico
Pani, Thomas
Petri, Gustavo
Piazza, Carla
Poli, Federico
Poulsen, Danny Bøgsted
Prabhakar, Pavithra
Quang Trung, Ta
Ranzato, Francesco
Rasmussen, Cameron
Ratasich, Denise
Ravanbakhsh, Hadi
Ray, Rajarshi
Reger, Giles
Reynolds, Andrew
Rigger, Manuel
Rodriguez, Cesar
Rothenberg, Bat-Chen
Roveri, Marco
Rydhof Hansen, René
Rüthing, Oliver
Sadeh, Gal
Saivasan, Prakash
Sanchez, Cesar
Sangnier, Arnaud
Schlichtkrull, Anders
Schwoon, Stefan
Seidl, Martina
Shi, Xiaomu
Shirmohammadi, Mahsa
Shoukry, Yasser
Sighireanu, Mihaela
Soudjani, Sadegh
Spießl, Martin
Srba, Jiri
Srivas, Mandayam
Stan, Daniel

Stoilkovska, Ilina
Stojic, Ivan
Su, Ting
Summers, Alexander J.
Tabuada, Paulo
Tacchella, Armando
Tang, Enyi
Tian, Chun
Tonetta, Stefano
Trinh, Minh-Thai
Trtík, Marek
Tsai, Ming-Hsien
Valero, Pedro
van der Berg, Freark
Vandin, Andrea

Vazquez-Chanlatte, Marcell
Viganò, Luca
Villadsen, Jørgen
Wang, Shuai
Wang, Shuling
Weininger, Maximilian
Wendler, Philipp
Wolff, Sebastian
Wüstholz, Valentin
Xu, Xiao
Zeljić, Aleksandar
Zhang, Fuyuan
Zhang, Qirun
Zhang, Xiyue

Contents – Part III

SV-COMP 2019

TOOLympics 2019

TOOLympics 2019:
An Overview of Competitions
in Formal Methods

Ezio Bartocci[1], Dirk Beyer[2], Paul E. Black[3], Grigory Fedyukovich[4],
Hubert Garavel[5], Arnd Hartmanns[6], Marieke Huisman[6], Fabrice Kordon[7],
Julian Nagele[8], Mihaela Sighireanu[9], Bernhard Steffen[10], Martin Suda[11],
Geoff Sutcliffe[12], Tjark Weber[13], and Akihisa Yamada[14]

[1] TU Wien, Vienna, Austria
[2] LMU Munich, Munich, Germany
[3] NIST, Gaithersburg, USA
[4] Princeton University, Princeton, USA
[5] Univ. Grenoble Alpes, Inria, CNRS, Grenoble INP, LIG, Grenoble, France
[6] University of Twente, Enschede, Netherlands
[7] Sorbonne Université, Paris, France
[8] Queen Mary University of London, London, UK
[9] University Paris Diderot, Paris, France
[10] TU Dortmund, Dortmund, Germany
[11] Czech Technical University in Prague, Prague, Czech Republic
[12] University of Miami, Coral Gable, USA
[13] Uppsala University, Uppsala, Sweden
[14] NII, Tokyo, Japan

Abstract. Evaluation of scientific contributions can be done in many
different ways. For the various research communities working on the
verification of systems (software, hardware, or the underlying involved
mechanisms), it is important to bring together the community and to
compare the state of the art, in order to identify progress of and new challenges in the research area. Competitions are a suitable way to do that.

The first verification competition was created in 1992 (SAT
competition), shortly followed by the CASC competition in 1996.
Since the year 2000, the number of dedicated verification competitions is steadily increasing. Many of these events now happen regularly,
gathering researchers that would like to understand how well their
research prototypes work in practice. Scientific results have to be reproducible, and powerful computers are becoming cheaper and cheaper,
thus, these competitions are becoming an important means for advancing research in verification technology.

TOOLympics 2019 is an event to celebrate the achievements of
the various competitions, and to understand their commonalities and
differences. This volume is dedicated to the presentation of the 16
competitions that joined TOOLympics as part of the celebration of the
25th anniversary of the TACAS conference.

https://tacas.info/toolympics.php

D. Beyer et al. (Eds.): TACAS 2019, Part III, LNCS 11429, pp. 3–24, 2019.
https://doi.org/10.1007/978-3-030-17502-3_1

1   Introduction

Over the last years, our society's dependency on digital systems has been steadily increasing. At the same time, we see that also the complexity of such systems is continuously growing, which increases the chances of such systems behaving unreliably, with many undesired consequences. In order to master this complexity, and to guarantee that digital systems behave as desired, software tools are designed that can be used to analyze and verify the behavior of digital systems. These tools are becoming more prominent, in academia as well as in industry. The range of these tools is enormous, and trying to understand which tool to use for which system is a major challenge. In order to get a better grip on this problem, many different competitions and challenges have been created, aiming in particular at better understanding the actual profile of the different tools that reason about systems in a given application domain.

The first competitions started in the 1990s (e.g., SAT and CASC). After the year 2000, the number of competitions has been steadily increasing, and currently we see that there is a wide range of different verification competitions. We believe there are several reasons for this increase in the number of competitions in the area of formal methods:

- increased computing power makes it feasible to apply tools to large benchmark sets,
- tools are becoming more mature,
- growing interest in the community to show practical applicability of theoretical results, in order to stimulate technology transfer,
- growing awareness that reproducibility and comparative evaluation of results is important, and
- organization and participation in verification competitions is a good way to get scientific recognition for tool development.

We notice that despite the many differences between the different competitions and challenges, there are also many similar concerns, in particular from an organizational point of view:

- How to assess adequacy of benchmark sets, and how to establish suitable input formats? And what is a suitable license for a benchmark collection?
- How to execute the challenges (on-site vs. off-site, on controlled resources vs. on individual hardware, automatic vs. interactive, etc.)?
- How to evaluate the results, e.g., in order to obtain a ranking?
- How to ensure fairness in the evaluation, e.g., how to avoid bias in the benchmark sets, how to reliably measure execution times, and how to handle incorrect or incomplete results?
- How to guarantee reproducibility of the results?
- How to achieve and measure progress of the state of the art?
- How to make the results and competing tools available so that they can be leveraged in subsequent events?

Therefore, as part of the celebration of 25 years of TACAS we organized TOOLympics, as an occasion to bring together researchers involved in competition organization. It is a goal of TOOLympics to discuss similarities and differences between the participating competitions, to facilitate cross-community communication to exchange experiences, and to discuss possible cooperation concerning benchmark libraries, competition infrastructures, publication formats, etc. We hope that the organization of TOOLympics will put forward the best practices to support competitions and challenges as useful and successful events.

In the remainder of this paper, we give an overview of all competitions participating in TOOLympics, as well as an outlook on the future of competitions. Table 1 provides references to other papers (also in this volume) providing additional perspective, context, and details about the various competitions. There are more competitions in the field, e.g., ARCH-COMP [1], ICLP Comp, MaxSAT Evaluation, Reactive Synthesis Competition [57], QBFGallery [73], and SyGuS-Competition.

2   Overview of all Participating Competitions

A competition is an event that is dedicated to fair comparative evaluation of a set of participating contributions at a given time. This section shows that such participating contributions can be of different forms: tools, result compilations, counterexamples, proofs, reasoning approaches, solutions to a problem, etc.

Table 1 categorizes the TOOLympics competitions. The first column names the competition (and the digital version of this article provides a link to the competition web site). The second column states the year of the first edition of the competition, and the third column the number of editions of the competition. The next two columns characterize the way the participating contributions are evaluated: Most of the competitions are evaluating automated tools that do not require user interaction and the experiments are executed by benchmarking environments, such as BenchExec [29], BenchKit [69], or StarExec [92]. However, some competitions require a manual evaluation, due to the nature of the competition and its evaluation criteria. The next two columns show where and when the results of the competition is determined: on-site during the event or off-site before the event takes place. Finally, the last column provides references to the reader to look up more details about each of the competitions.

The remainder of this section introduces the various competitions of TOOLympics 2019.

2.1   CASC: The CADE ATP System Competition

Organizer: Geoff Sutcliffe (Univ. of Miami, USA)
Webpage: http://www.tptp.org

The CADE ATP System Competition (CASC) [107] is held at each CADE and IJCAR conference. CASC evaluates the performance of sound, fully automatic, classical logic Automated Theorem Proving (ATP) systems. The evaluation is

Table 1. Categorization of the competitions participating in TOOLympics 2019; planned competition Rodeo not contained in the table; CHC-COMP report not yet published (slides available: https://chc-comp.github.io/2018/chc-comp18.pdf)

Competition	Year first competition	Number editions	Automated evaluation	Interactive evaluation	On-site evaluation	Off-site evaluation	Competition reports
CASC	1996	23	●		●		[97–109, 116] [78, 79, 93–96, 110–115, 117]
CHC-COMP	2018	2	●		●		
CoCo	2012	8	●		●		[3, 4, 76]
CRV	2014	4	●			●	[12–14, 41, 81, 82]
MCC	2011	9	●			●	[2, 64–68, 70–72]
QComp	2019	1	●			●	[47]
REC	2006	5	●			●	[36–39, 42]
RERS	2010	9	●	●		●	[43, 44, 48–50, 59–61]
SAT	1992	12	●			●	[5, 6, 15, 16, 58, 86]
SL-COMP	2014	3	●			●	[84, 85]
SMT-COMP	2005	13	●			●	[7–11, 33–35]
SV-COMP	2012	8	●			●	[17–23]
termCOMP	2004	16	●			●	[45, 46, 74, 118]
Test-Comp	2019	1	●			●	[24]
VerifyThis	2011	8		●	●		[27, 32, 40, 51–56]

in terms of: the number of problems solved, the number of problems solved with a solution output, and the average runtime for problems solved; in the context of: a bounded number of eligible problems, chosen from the TPTP Problem Library, and specified time limits on solution attempts. CASC is the longest running of the various logic solver competitions, with the 25th event to be held in 2020. This longevity has allowed the design of CASC to evolve into a sophisticated and stable state. Each year's experiences lead to ideas for changes and improvements, so that CASC remains a vibrant competition. CASC provides an effective public evaluation of the relative capabilities of ATP systems. Additionally, the organization of CASC is designed to stimulate ATP research, motivate development and implementation of robust ATP systems that are useful and easily deployed in applications, provide an inspiring environment for personal interaction between ATP researchers, and expose ATP systems within and beyond the ATP community.

2.2 CHC-COMP: Competition on Constrained Horn Clauses

Organizers: Grigory Fedyukovich (Princeton Univ., USA), Arie Gurfinkel (Univ. of Waterloo, Canada), and Philipp Rümmer (Uppsala Univ., Sweden)
Webpage: https://chc-comp.github.io/

Constrained Horn Clauses (CHC) is a fragment of First Order Logic (FOL) that is sufficiently expressive to describe many verification, inference, and synthesis problems including inductive invariant inference, model checking of safety properties, inference of procedure summaries, regression verification, and sequential equivalence. The CHC competition (CHC-COMP) compares state-of-the-art tools for CHC solving with respect to performance and effectiveness on a set of publicly available benchmarks. The winners among participating solvers are recognized by measuring the number of correctly solved benchmarks as well as the runtime. The results of CHC-COMP 2019 will be announced in the HCVS workshop affiliated with ETAPS.

2.3 CoCo: Confluence Competition

Organizers: Aart Middeldorp (Univ. of Innsbruck, Austria), Julian Nagele (Queen Mary Univ. of London, UK), and Kiraku Shintani (JAIST, Japan)
Webpage: http://project-coco.uibk.ac.at/

The Confluence Competition (CoCo) exists since 2012. It is an annual competition of software tools that aim to (dis)prove confluence and related (undecidable) properties of a variety of rewrite formalisms automatically. CoCo runs live in a single slot at a conference or workshop and is executed on the cross-community competition platform STAREXEC. For each category, 100 suitable problems are randomly selected from the online database of confluence problems (COPS). Participating tools must answer YES or NO within 60 s, followed by a justification that is understandable by a human expert; any other output signals that the tool could not determine the status of the problem. CoCo 2019 features new categories on commutation, confluence of string rewrite systems, and infeasibility problems.

2.4 CRV: Competition on Runtime Verification

Organizers: Ezio Bartocci (TU Wien, Austria), Yliès Falcone (Univ. Grenoble Alpes/CNRS/INRIA, France), and Giles Reger (Univ. of Manchester, UK)
Webpage: https://www.rv-competition.org/

Runtime verification (RV) is a class of lightweight scalable techniques for the analysis of system executions. We consider here specification-based analysis, where executions are checked against a property expressed in a formal specification language.

The core idea of RV is to instrument a software/hardware system so that it can emit events during its execution. These events are then processed by a monitor that is automatically generated from the specification. During the last decade, many important tools and techniques have been developed. The growing number of RV tools developed in the last decade and the lack of standard benchmark suites as well as scientific evaluation methods to validate and test new techniques have motivated the creation of a venue dedicated to comparing and evaluating RV tools in the form of a competition.

The Competition on Runtime Verification (CRV) is an annual event, held since 2014, and organized as a satellite event of the main RV conference. The competition is in general organized in different tracks: (1) offline monitoring, (2) online monitoring of C programs, and (3) online monitoring of Java programs. Over the first three years of the competition 14 different runtime verification tools competed on over 100 different benchmarks[1].

In 2017 the competition was replaced by a workshop aimed at reflecting on the experiences of the last three years and discussing future directions. A suggestion of the workshop was to held a benchmark challenge focussing on collecting new relevant benchmarks. Therefore, in 2018 a benchmark challenge was held with a track for Metric Temporal Logic (MTL) properties and an Open track. In 2019 CRV will return to a competition comparing tools, using the benchmarks from the 2018 challenge.

2.5 MCC: The Model Checking Contest

Organizers: Fabrice Kordon (Sorbonne Univ., CNRS, France), Hubert Garavel (Univ. Grenoble Alpes/INRIA/CNRS, Grenoble INP/LIG, France), Lom Messan Hillah (Univ. Paris Nanterre, CNRS, France), Francis Hulin-Hubard (CNRS, Sorbonne Univ., France), Loïg Jezequel (Univ. de Nantes, CNRS, France), and Emmanuel Paviot-Adet (Univ. de Paris, CNRS, France)
Webpage: https://mcc.lip6.fr/

Since 2011, the Model Checking Contest (MCC) is an annual competition of software tools for model checking. Tools are confronted to an increasing benchmark set gathered from the whole community (currently, 88 parameterized models totalling 951 instances) and may participate in various examinations: state space generation, computation of global properties, computation of 16 queries with regards to upper bounds in the model, evaluation of 16 reachability formulas, evaluation of 16 CTL formulas, and evaluation of 16 LTL formulas.

For each examination and each model instance, participating tools are provided with up to 3600 s of runtime and 16 GB of memory. Tool answers are analyzed and confronted to the results produced by other competing tools to detect diverging answers (which are quite rare at this stage of the competition, and lead to penalties).

---

[1] https://gitlab.inria.fr/crv14/benchmarks

For each examination, golden, silver, and bronze medals are attributed to the three best tools. CPU usage and memory consumption are reported, which is also valuable information for tool developers. Finally, numerous charts to compare pair of tools' performances, or quantile plots stating global performances are computed. Performances of tools on models (useful when they contain scaling parameters) are also provided.

2.6 QComp: The Comparison of Tools for the Analysis of Quantitative Formal Models

Organizers: Arnd Hartmanns (Univ. of Twente, Netherlands) and Tim Quatmann (RWTH Aachen Univ., Germany)
Webpage: http://qcomp.org

Quantitative formal models capture probabilistic behaviour, real-time aspects, or general continuous dynamics. A number of tools support their automatic analysis with respect to dependability or performance properties. QComp 2019 is the first competition among such tools. It focuses on stochastic formalisms from Markov chains to probabilistic timed automata specified in the JANI model exchange format, and on probabilistic reachability, expected-reward, and steady-state properties. QComp draws its benchmarks from the new Quantitative Verification Benchmark Set. Participating tools, which include probabilistic model checkers and planners as well as simulation-based tools, are evaluated in terms of performance, versatility, and usability.

2.7 REC: The Rewrite Engines Competition

Organizers: Francisco Durán (Univ. of Malaga, Spain) and Hubert Garavel (Univ. Grenoble Alpes/INRIA/CNRS, Grenoble INP/LIG, France)
Webpage: http://rec.gforge.inria.fr/

Term rewriting is a simple, yet expressive model of computation, which finds direct applications in specification and programming languages (many of which embody rewrite rules, pattern matching, and abstract data types), but also indirect applications, e.g., to express the semantics of data types or concurrent processes, to specify program transformations, to perform computer-aided verification. The Rewrite Engines Competition (REC) was created under the aegis of the Workshop on Rewriting Logic and its Applications (WRLA) to serve three main goals:

1. being a forum in which tool developers and potential users of term rewrite engines can share experience;
2. bringing together the various language features and implementation techniques used for term rewriting; and
3. comparing the available term rewriting languages and tools in their common features.

Earlier editions of the Rewrite Engines Competition have been held in 2006, 2008, 2010, and 2018.

2.8   RERS: Rigorous Examination of Reactive System

Organizers: Falk Howar (TU Dortmund, Germany), Markus Schordan (LLNL, USA), Bernhard Steffen (TU Dortmund, Germany), and Jaco van de Pol (Univ. of Aarhus, Denmark)
Webpage: http://rers-challenge.org/

Reactive systems appear everywhere, e.g., as Web services, decision support systems, or logical controllers. Their validation techniques are as diverse as their appearance and structure. They comprise various forms of static analysis, model checking, symbolic execution, and (model-based) testing, often tailored to quite extreme frame conditions. Thus it is almost impossible to compare these techniques, let alone to establish clear application profiles as a means for recommendation. Since 2010, the RERS Challenge aims at overcoming this situation by providing a forum for experimental profile evaluation based on specifically designed benchmark suites.

These benchmarks are automatically synthesized to exhibit chosen properties, and then enhanced to include dedicated dimensions of difficulty, ranging from conceptual complexity of the properties (e.g., reachability, full safety, liveness), over size of the reactive systems (a few hundred lines to millions of them), to exploited language features (arrays, arithmetic at index pointer, and parallelism). The general approach has been described in [89,90], while variants to introduce highly parallel benchmarks are discussed in [87,88,91]. RERS benchmarks have been used also by other competitions, like MCC or SV-COMP, and referenced in a number of research papers as a means of evaluation not only in the context of RERS [31,62,75,77,80,83].

In contrast to the other competitions described in this paper, RERS is problem-oriented and does not evaluate the power of specific tools but rather tool usage that ideally makes use of a number of tools and methods. The goal of RERS is to help revealing synergy potential also between seemingly quite separate technologies like, e.g., source-code-based (white-box) approaches and purely observation/testing-based (black-box) approaches. This goal is also reflected in the awarding scheme: besides the automatically evaluated questionnaires for achievements and rankings, RERS also features the Methods Combination Award for approaches that explicitly exploit cross-tool/method synergies.

2.9   Rodeo for Production Software Verification Tools
Based on Formal Methods

Organizer: Paul E. Black (NIST, USA)
Webpage: https://samate.nist.gov/FMSwVRodeo/

Formal methods are not widely used in the United States. The US government is now more interested because of the wide variety of FM-based tools that can handle production-sized software and because algorithms are orders of magnitude faster. NIST proposes to select production software for a test suite and to hold a periodic Rodeo to assess the effectiveness of tools based on formal methods that can verify large, complex software. To select software, we will develop tools to measure structural characteristics, like depth of recursion or number of states, and calibrate them on others' benchmarks. We can then scan thousands of applications to select software for the Rodeo.

2.10   SAT Competition

Organizer: Marijn Heule (Univ. of Texas at Austin, USA), Matti Järvisalo (Univ. of Helsinki, Finland), and Martin Suda (Czech Technical Univ., Czechia)
Webpage: https://www.satcompetition.org/

SAT Competition 2018 is the twelfth edition of the SAT Competition series, continuing the almost two decades of tradition in SAT competitions and related competitive events for Boolean Satisfiability (SAT) solvers. It was organized as part of the 2018 FLoC Olympic Games in conjunction with the 21th International Conference on Theory and Applications of Satisfiability Testing (SAT 2018), which took place in Oxford, UK, as part of the 2018 Federated Logic Conference (FLoC). The competition consisted of four tracks, including a main track, a "no-limits" track with very few requirements for participation, and special tracks focusing on random SAT and parallel solving. In addition to the actual solvers, each participant was required to also submit a collection of previously unseen benchmark instances, which allowed the competition to only use new benchmarks for evaluation. Where applicable, verifiable certificates were required both for the "satisfiable" and "unsatisfiable" answers; the general time limit was 5000 s per benchmark instance and the solvers were ranked using the PAR-2 scheme, which encourages solving many benchmarks but also rewards solving the benchmarks fast. A detailed overview of the competition, including summary of the results, will appear in the JSAT special issue on SAT 2018 Competitions and Evaluations.

2.11   SL-COMP: Competition of Solvers for Separation Logic

Organizer: Mihaela Sighireanu (Univ. of Paris Diderot, France)
Webpage: https://sl-comp.github.io/

SL-COMP aims at bringing together researchers interested in improving the state of the art of automated deduction methods for Separation Logic (SL). The event took place twice until now and collected more than 1K problems for different fragments of SL. The input format of problems is based on the SMT-LIB format and therefore fully typed; only one new command is added to SMT-LIB's list, the command for the declaration of the heap's type. The SMT-LIB theory of SL comes with ten logics, some of them being combinations of SL with linear arithmetic. The competition's divisions are defined by the logic fragment, the kind of decision problem (satisfiability or entailment), and the presence of quantifiers. Until now, SL-COMP has been run on the STAREXEC platform, where the benchmark set and the binaries of participant solvers are freely available. The benchmark set is also available with the competition's documentation on a public repository in GitHub.

2.12   SMT-COMP

Organizer: Matthias Heizmann (Univ. of Freiburg, Germany), Aina Niemetz (Stanford Univ., USA), Giles Reger (Univ. of Manchester, UK), and Tjark Weber (Uppsala Univ., Sweden)
Webpage: http://www.smtcomp.org

Satisfiability Modulo Theories (SMT) is a generalization of the satisfiability decision problem for propositional logic. In place of Boolean variables, SMT formulas may contain terms that are built from function and predicate symbols drawn from a number of background theories, such as arrays, integer and real arithmetic, or bit-vectors. With its rich input language, SMT has applications in software engineering, optimization, and many other areas.

The International Satisfiability Modulo Theories Competition (SMT-COMP) is an annual competition between SMT solvers. It was instituted in 2005, and is affiliated with the International Workshop on Satisfiability Modulo Theories. Solvers are submitted to the competition by their developers, and compete against each other in a number of tracks and divisions. The main goals of the competition are to promote the community-designed SMT-LIB format, to spark further advances in SMT, and to provide a useful yardstick of performance for users and developers of SMT solvers.

2.13   SV-COMP: Competition on Software Verification

Organizer: Dirk Beyer (LMU Munich, Germany)
Webpage: https://sv-comp.sosy-lab.org/

The 2019 International Competition on Software Verification (SV-COMP) is the 8th edition in a series of annual comparative evaluations of fully-automatic tools for software verification. The competition was established and first executed in 2011 and the first results were presented and published at TACAS 2012 [17]. The most important goals of the competition are the following:

1. Provide an overview of the state of the art in software-verification technology and increase visibility of the most recent software verifiers.
2. Establish a repository of software-verification tasks that is publicly available for free as standard benchmark suite for evaluating verification software[2].
3. Establish standards that make it possible to compare different verification tools, including a property language and formats for the results, especially witnesses.
4. Accelerate the transfer of new verification technology to industrial practice.

The benchmark suite for SV-COMP 2019 [23] consists of nine categories with a total of 10 522 verification tasks in C and 368 verification tasks in Java. A verification task (benchmark instance) in SV-COMP is a pair of a program M

---

[2] https://github.com/sosy-lab/sv-benchmarks

and a property ϕ, and the task for the solver (here: verifier) is to verify the statement $M \models \phi$, that is, the benchmarked verifier should return FALSE and a violation witness that describes a property violation [26, 30], or TRUE and a correctness witness that contains invariants to re-establish the correctness proof [25]. The ranking is computed according to a scoring schema that assigns a positive score (1 and 2) to correct results and a negative score (-16 and -32) to incorrect results, for tasks with and without property violations, respectively. The sum of CPU time of the successfully solved verification tasks is the tie-breaker if two verifiers have the same score. The results are also illustrated using quantile plots.[3]

The 2019 competition attracted 31 participating teams from 14 countries. This competition included Java verification for the first time, and this track had four participating verifiers. As before, the large jury (one representative of each participating team) and the organizer made sure that the competition follows high quality standards and is driven by the four important principles of (1) *fairness*, (2) *community support*, (3) *transparency*, and (4) *technical accuracy*.

2.14   termComp: The Termination and Complexity Competition

Organizer: Akihisa Yamada (National Institute of Informatics, Japan)
Steering Committee: Jürgen Giesl (RWTH Aachen Univ., Germany), Albert Rubio (Univ. Politècnica de Catalunya, Spain), Christian Sternagel (Univ. of Innsbruck, Austria), Johannes Waldmann (HTWK Leipzig, Germany), and Akihisa Yamada (National Institute of Informatics, Japan)
Webpage: http://termination-portal.org/wiki/Termination_Competition

The termination and complexity competition (termCOMP) focuses on automated termination and complexity analysis for various kinds of programming paradigms, including categories for term rewriting, integer transition systems, imperative programming, logic programming, and functional programming. It has been organized annually after a tool demonstration in 2003. In all categories, the competition also welcomes the participation of tools providing certifiable output. The goal of the competition is to demonstrate the power and advances of the state-of-the-art tools in each of these areas.

2.15   Test-Comp: Competition on Software Testing

Organizer: Dirk Beyer (LMU Munich, Germany)
Webpage: https://test-comp.sosy-lab.org/

The 2019 International Competition on Software Testing (Test-Comp) [24] is the 1st edition of a series of annual comparative evaluations of fully-automatic tools for software testing. The design of Test-Comp is very similar to the design of SV-COMP, with the major difference that the task for the solver (here: tester)

---

[3] https://sv-comp.sosy-lab.org/2019/results/

is to generate a test suite, which is validated against a coverage property, that is, the ranking is based on the coverage that the resulting test-suites achieve.

There are several new and powerful tools for automatic software testing around, but they were difficult to compare before the competition [28]. The reason had been that so far no established benchmark suite of test tasks was available and many concepts were only validated in research prototypes. Now the test-case generators support a standardized input format (for C programs as well as for coverage properties). The overall goals of the competition are:

- Provide a snapshot of the state-of-the-art in software testing to the community. This means to compare, independently from particular paper projects and specific techniques, different test-generation tools in terms of precision and performance.
- Increase the visibility and credits that tool developers receive. This means to provide a forum for presentation of tools and discussion of the latest technologies, and to give the students the opportunity to publish about the development work that they have done.
- Establish a set of benchmarks for software testing in the community. This means to create and maintain a set of programs together with coverage criteria, and to make those publicly available for researchers to be used free of charge in performance comparisons when evaluating a new technique.

2.16   VerifyThis

Organizers 2019: Carlo A. Furia (Univ. della Svizzera Italiana, Switzerland) and Claire Dross (AdaCore, France)
Steering Committee: Marieke Huisman (Univ. of Twente, Netherlands), Rosemary Monahan (National Univ. of Ireland at Maynooth, Ireland), and Peter Müller (ETH Zurich, Switzerland)
Webpage: http://www.pm.inf.ethz.ch/research/verifythis.html

The aims of the VerifyThis competition are:

- to bring together those interested in formal verification,
- to provide an engaging, hands-on, and fun opportunity for discussion, and
- to evaluate the usability of logic-based program verification tools in a controlled experiment that could be easily repeated by others.

The competition offers a number of challenges presented in natural language and pseudo code. Participants have to formalize the requirements, implement a solution, and formally verify the implementation for adherence to the specification.

There are no restrictions on the programming language and verification technology used. The correctness properties posed in problems will have the input-output behaviour of programs in focus. Solutions will be judged for correctness, completeness, and elegance.

VerifyThis is an annual event. Earlier editions were held at FoVeOos (2011), FM (2012), and since 2015 annually at ETAPS.

3   On the Future of Competitions

In this paper, we have provided an overview of the wide spectrum of different competitions and challenges. Each competition can be distinguished by its specific problem profile, characterized by analysis goals, resource and infrastructural constraints, application areas, and dedicated methodologies. Despite their differences, these competitions and challenges also have many similar concerns, related to, e.g., (1) benchmark selection, maintenance, and archiving, (2) evaluation and rating strategies, (3) publication and replicability of results, as well as (4) licensing issues.

TOOLympics aims at leveraging the potential synergy by supporting a dialogue between competition organizers about all relevant issues. Besides increasing the mutual awareness about shared concerns, this also comprises:

- the potential exchange of benchmarks (ideally supported by dedicated interchange formats), e.g., from high-level competitions like VerifyThis, SV-COMP, and RERS to more low-level competitions like SMT-COMP, CASC, or the SAT competition,
- the detection of new competition formats or the aggregation of existing competition formats to establish a better coverage of verification problem areas in a complementary fashion, and
- the exchange of ideas to motivate new participants, e.g., by lowering the entrance hurdle.

There have been a number of related initiatives with the goal of increasing awareness for the scientific method of evaluating tools in a *competition*-based fashion, like the COMPARE workshop on Comparative Empirical Evaluation of Reasoning Systems [63], the Dagstuhl seminar on Evaluating Software Verification Systems in 2014 [27], the FLoC Olympics Games 2014[4] and 2018[5], and the recent Lorentz Workshop on Advancing Verification Competitions as a Scientific Method[6]. TOOLympics aims at joining forces with all these initiatives in order to establish a comprehensive hub where tool developers, users, participants, and organizers may meet and discuss current issues, share experiences, compose benchmark libraries (ideally classified in a way that supports cross competition usage), and develop ideas for future directions of competitions.

Finally, it is important to note that competitions have resulted in significant progress in the research areas that they belong to, respectively. Typically, new techniques and theories have been developed, and tools have become much stronger and more mature. This sometimes means that a disruption in the way that the competitions are handled is needed, in order to adapt the competition to these evolutions. It is our hope that platforms such as TOOLympics facilitate and improve this process.

---

[4] https://vsl2014.at/olympics/
[5] https://www.floc2018.org/floc-olympic-games/
[6] https://www.lorentzcenter.nl/lc/web/2019/1091/info.php3?wsid=1091

References

1. Abate, A., Blom, H., Cauchi, N., Haesaert, S., Hartmanns, A., Lesser, K., Oishi, M., Sivaramakrishnan, V., Soudjani, S., Vasile, C.I., Vinod, A.P.: ARCH-COMP18 category report: Stochastic modelling. In: ARCH18. 5th International Workshop on Applied Verification of Continuous and Hybrid Systems, vol. 54, pp. 71–103 (2018). https://easychair.org/publications/open/DzD8
2. Amparore, E., Berthomieu, B., Ciardo, G., Dal Zilio, S., Gallà, F., Hillah, L.M., Hulin-Hubard, F., Jensen, P.G., Jezequel, L., Kordon, F., Le Botlan, D., Liebke, T., Meijer, J., Miner, A., Paviot-Adet, E., Srba, J., Thierry-Mieg, Y., van Dijk, T., Wolf, K.: Presentation of the 9th edition of the model checking contest. In: Proc. TACAS, Part 3, LNCS, vol. 11429, pp. 50–68. Springer, Cham (2019). https://doi.org/10.1007/978-3-030-17502-3_4
3. Aoto, T., Hamana, M., Hirokawa, N., Middeldorp, A., Nagele, J., Nishida, N., Shintani, K., Zankl, H.: Confluence Competition 2018. In: Proc. 3rd International Conference on Formal Structures for Computation and Deduction (FSCD 2018). Leibniz International Proceedings in Informatics (LIPIcs), vol. 108, pp. 32:1–32:5. Schloss Dagstuhl-Leibniz-Zentrum fuer Informatik (2018). https://doi.org/10.4230/LIPIcs.FSCD.2018.32
4. Aoto, T., Hirokawa, N., Nagele, J., Nishida, N., Zankl, H.: Confluence Competition 2015. In: Proc. 25th International Conference on Automated Deduction (CADE-25), LNCS, vol. 9195, pp. 101–104. Springer, Cham (2015). https://doi.org/10.1007/978-3-319-21401-6_5
5. Balint, A., Belov, A., Järvisalo, M., Sinz, C.: Overview and analysis of the SAT Challenge 2012 solver competition. Artif. Intell. **223**, 120–155 (2015). https://doi.org/10.1016/j.artint.2015.01.002
6. Balyo, T., Heule, M.J.H., Järvisalo, M.: SAT Competition 2016: Recent developments. In: Singh, S.P., Markovitch, S. (eds.) Proceedings of the Thirty-First AAAI Conference on Artificial Intelligence, San Francisco, California, USA, 4–9 February 2017, pp. 5061–5063. AAAI Press (2017)
7. Barrett, C., Deters, M., de Moura, L., Oliveras, A., Stump, A.: 6 years of SMT-COMP. J. Autom. Reason. **50**(3), 243–277 (2013). https://doi.org/10.1007/s10817-012-9246-5
8. Barrett, C., Deters, M., Oliveras, A., Stump, A.: Design and results of the 3rd Annual Satisfiability Modulo Theories Competition (SMT-COMP 2007). Int. J. Artif. Intell. Tools **17**(4), 569–606 (2008)
9. Barrett, C., Deters, M., Oliveras, A., Stump, A.: Design and results of the 4th Annual Satisfiability Modulo Theories Competition (SMT-COMP 2008). Technical report TR2010-931, New York University (2010)
10. Barrett, C., de Moura, L., Stump, A.: Design and results of the 1st Satisfiability Modulo Theories Competition (SMT-COMP 2005). J. Autom. Reason. **35**(4), 373–390 (2005)
11. Barrett, C., de Moura, L., Stump, A.: Design and results of the 2nd Annual Satisfiability Modulo Theories Competition (SMT-COMP 2006). Form. Methods Syst. Des. **31**, 221–239 (2007)
12. Bartocci, E., Bonakdarpour, B., Falcone, Y.: First international competition on software for runtime verification. In: Bonakdarpour, B., Smolka, S.A. (eds.) Proc. of RV 2014: The 5th International Conference on Runtime Verification, LNCS, vol. 8734, pp. 1–9. Springer, Cham (2014). https://doi.org/10.1007/978-3-319-11164-3_1

13. Bartocci, E., Falcone, Y., Bonakdarpour, B., Colombo, C., Decker, N., Havelund, K., Joshi, Y., Klaedtke, F., Milewicz, R., Reger, G., Rosu, G., Signoles, J., Thoma, D., Zalinescu, E., Zhang, Y.: First international competition on runtime verification: Rules, benchmarks, tools, and final results of CRV 2014. Int. J. Softw. Tools Technol. Transfer **21**, 31–70 (2019). https://doi.org/10.1007/s10009-017-0454-5

14. Bartocci, E., Falcone, Y., Reger, G.: International competition on runtime verification (CRV). In: Proc. TACAS, Part 3, LNCS, vol. 11429, pp. 41–49. Springer, Cham (2019). https://doi.org/10.1007/978-3-030-17502-3_3

15. Berre, D.L., Simon, L.: The essentials of the SAT 2003 Competition. In: Giunchiglia, E., Tacchella, A. (eds.) Theory and Applications of Satisfiability Testing, 6th International Conference, SAT 2003, Santa Margherita Ligure, Italy, 5–8 May 2003, Selected Revised Papers, LNCS, vol. 2919, pp. 452–467. Springer, Heidelberg (2004)

16. Berre, D.L., Simon, L.: Fifty-five solvers in Vancouver: The SAT 2004 Competition. In: Hoos, H.H., Mitchell, D.G. (eds.) Theory and Applications of Satisfiability Testing, 7th International Conference, SAT 2004, Vancouver, BC, Canada, 10–13 May 2004, Revised Selected Papers, LNCS, vol. 3542, pp. 321–344. Springer, Heidelberg (2005)

17. Beyer, D.: Competition on software verification (SV-COMP). In: Proc. TACAS, LNCS, vol. 7214, pp. 504–524. Springer, Heidelberg (2012). https://doi.org/10.1007/978-3-642-28756-5_38

18. Beyer, D.: Second competition on software verification (Summary of SV-COMP 2013). In: Proc. TACAS, LNCS, vol. 7795, pp. 594–609. Springer, Heidelberg (2013). https://doi.org/10.1007/978-3-642-36742-7_43

19. Beyer, D.: Status report on software verification (Competition summary SV-COMP 2014). In: Proc. TACAS, LNCS, vol. 8413, pp. 373–388. Springer, Heidelberg (2014). https://doi.org/10.1007/978-3-642-54862-8_25

20. Beyer, D.: Software verification and verifiable witnesses (Report on SV-COMP 2015). In: Proc. TACAS, LNCS, vol. 9035, pp. 401–416. Springer, Heidelberg (2015). https://doi.org/10.1007/978-3-662-46681-0_31

21. Beyer, D.: Reliable and reproducible competition results with BENCHEXEC and witnesses (Report on SV-COMP 2016). In: Proc. TACAS, LNCS, vol. 9636, pp. 887–904. Springer, Heidelberg (2016). https://doi.org/10.1007/978-3-662-49674-9_55

22. Beyer, D.: Software verification with validation of results (Report on SV-COMP 2017). In: Proc. TACAS, LNCS, vol. 10206, pp. 331–349. Springer, Heidelberg (2017). https://doi.org/10.1007/978-3-662-54580-5_20

23. Beyer, D.: Automatic verification of C and Java programs: SV-COMP 2019. In: Proc. TACAS, Part 3, LNCS, vol. 11429, pp. 133–155. Springer, Cham (2019). https://doi.org/10.1007/978-3-030-17502-3_9

24. Beyer, D.: International competition on software testing (Test-Comp). In: Proc. TACAS, Part 3, LNCS, vol. 11429, pp. 167–175. Springer, Cham (2019). https://doi.org/10.1007/978-3-030-17502-3_11

25. Beyer, D., Dangl, M., Dietsch, D., Heizmann, M.: Correctness witnesses: Exchanging verification results between verifiers. In: Proc. FSE, pp. 326–337. ACM (2016). https://doi.org/10.1145/2950290.2950351

26. Beyer, D., Dangl, M., Dietsch, D., Heizmann, M., Stahlbauer, A.: Witness validation and stepwise testification across software verifiers. In: Proc. FSE, pp. 721–733. ACM (2015). https://doi.org/10.1145/2786805.2786867

27. Beyer, D., Huisman, M., Klebanov, V., Monahan, R.: Evaluating software verification systems: Benchmarks and competitions (Dagstuhl reports 14171). Dagstuhl Rep. **4**(4), 1–19 (2014). https://doi.org/10.4230/DagRep.4.4.1

28. Beyer, D., Lemberger, T.: Software verification: Testing vs. model checking. In: Proc. HVC, LNCS, vol. 10629, pp. 99–114. Springer, Cham (2017). https://doi.org/10.1007/978-3-319-70389-3_7

29. Beyer, D., Löwe, S., Wendler, P.: Reliable benchmarking: Requirements and solutions. Int. J. Softw. Tools Technol. Transfer **21**(1), 1–29 (2019). https://doi.org/10.1007/s10009-017-0469-y, https://www.sosy-lab.org/research/pub/2019-STTT.Reliable_Benchmarking_Requirements_and_Solutions.pdf

30. Beyer, D., Wendler, P.: Reuse of verification results: Conditional model checking, precision reuse, and verification witnesses. In: Proc. SPIN, LNCS, vol. 7976, pp. 1–17. Springer, Heidelberg (2013). https://doi.org/10.1007/978-3-642-39176-7_1

31. Beyer, D., Stahlbauer, A.: BDD-based software verification. Int. J. Softw. Tools Technol. Transfer **16**(5), 507–518 (2014)

32. Bormer, T., Brockschmidt, M., Distefano, D., Ernst, G., Filliâtre, J.C., Grigore, R., Huisman, M., Klebanov, V., Marché, C., Monahan, R., Mostowski, W., Polikarpova, N., Scheben, C., Schellhorn, G., Tofan, B., Tschannen, J., Ulbrich, M.: The COST IC0701 verification competition 2011. In: Beckert, B., Damiani, F., Gurov, D. (eds.) International Conference on Formal Verification of Object-Oriented Systems (FoVeOOS 2011), LNCS, vol. 7421, pp. 3–21. Springer, Heidelberg (2011)

33. Cok, D.R., Déharbe, D., Weber, T.: The 2014 SMT competition. J. Satisf. Boolean Model. Comput. **9**, 207–242 (2014). https://satassociation.org/jsat/index.php/jsat/article/view/122

34. Cok, D.R., Griggio, A., Bruttomesso, R., Deters, M.: The 2012 SMT Competition (2012). http://smtcomp.sourceforge.net/2012/reports/SMTCOMP2012.pdf

35. Cok, D.R., Stump, A., Weber, T.: The 2013 evaluation of SMT-COMP and SMT-LIB. J. Autom. Reason. **55**(1), 61–90 (2015). https://doi.org/10.1007/s10817-015-9328-2

36. Denker, G., Talcott, C.L., Rosu, G., van den Brand, M., Eker, S., Serbanuta, T.F.: Rewriting logic systems. Electron. Notes Theor. Comput. Sci. **176**(4), 233–247 (2007). https://doi.org/10.1016/j.entcs.2007.06.018

37. Durán, F., Garavel, H.: The rewrite engines competitions: A RECtrospective. In: Proc. TACAS, Part 3, LNCS, vol. 11429, pp. 93–100. Springer, Cham (2019). https://doi.org/10.1007/978-3-030-17502-3_6

38. Durán, F., Roldán, M., Bach, J.C., Balland, E., van den Brand, M., Cordy, J.R., Eker, S., Engelen, L., de Jonge, M., Kalleberg, K.T., Kats, L.C.L., Moreau, P.E., Visser, E.: The third Rewrite Engines Competition. In: Ölveczky, P.C. (ed.) Proceedings of the 8th International Workshop on Rewriting Logic and Its Applications (WRLA 2010), Paphos, Cyprus, LNCS, vol. 6381, pp. 243–261. Springer, Heidelberg (2010). https://doi.org/10.1007/978-3-642-16310-4_16

39. Durán, F., Roldán, M., Balland, E., van den Brand, M., Eker, S., Kalleberg, K.T., Kats, L.C.L., Moreau, P.E., Schevchenko, R., Visser, E.: The second Rewrite Engines Competition. Electron. Notes Theor. Comput. Sci. **238**(3), 281–291 (2009). https://doi.org/10.1016/j.entcs.2009.05.025

40. Ernst, G., Huisman, M., Mostowski, W., Ulbrich, M.: VerifyThis – verification competition with a human factor. In: Proc. TACAS, Part 3, LNCS, vol. 11429, pp. 176–195. Springer, Cham (2019). https://doi.org/10.1007/978-3-030-17502-3_12

41. Falcone, Y., Nickovic, D., Reger, G., Thoma, D.: Second international competition on runtime verification CRV 2015. In: Proc. of RV 2015: The 6th International Conference on Runtime Verification, LNCS, vol. 9333, pp. 405–422. Springer, Cham (2015). https://doi.org/10.1007/978-3-319-23820-3

42. Garavel, H., Tabikh, M.A., Arrada, I.S.: Benchmarking implementations of term rewriting and pattern matching in algebraic, functional, and object-oriented languages – The 4th Rewrite Engines Competition. In: Rusu, V. (ed.) Proceedings of the 12th International Workshop on Rewriting Logic and Its Applications (WRLA 2018), Thessaloniki, Greece, LNCS, vol. 11152, pp. 1–25. Springer, Cham (2018). https://doi.org/10.1007/978-3-319-99840-4_1

43. Geske, M., Isberner, M., Steffen, B.: Rigorous examination of reactive systems. In: Bartocci, E., Majumdar, R. (eds.) Runtime Verification (2015)

44. Geske, M., Jasper, M., Steffen, B., Howar, F., Schordan, M., van de Pol, J.: RERS 2016: Parallel and sequential benchmarks with focus on LTL verification. In: ISoLA, LNCS, vol. 9953, pp. 787–803. Springer, Cham (2016)

45. Giesl, J., Mesnard, F., Rubio, A., Thiemann, R., Waldmann, J.: Termination competition (termCOMP 2015). In: Felty, A., Middeldorp, A. (eds.) CADE-25, LNCS, vol. 9195, pp. 105–108. Springer, Cham (2015). https://doi.org/10.1007/978-3-319-21401-6_6

46. Giesl, J., Rubio, A., Sternagel, C., Waldmann, J., Yamada, A.: The termination and complexity competition. In: Proc. TACAS, Part 3, LNCS, vol. 11429, pp. 156–166. Springer, Cham (2019). https://doi.org/10.1007/978-3-030-17502-3_10

47. Hahn, E.M., Hartmanns, A., Hensel, C., Klauck, M., Klein, J., Křetínský, J., Parker, D., Quatmann, T., Ruijters, E., Steinmetz, M.: The 2019 comparison of tools for the analysis of quantitative formal models. In: Proc. TACAS, Part 3, LNCS, vol. 11429, pp. 69–92. Springer, Cham (2019). https://doi.org/10.1007/978-3-030-17502-3_5

48. Howar, F., Isberner, M., Merten, M., Steffen, B., Beyer, D.: The RERS grey-box challenge 2012: Analysis of event-condition-action systems. In: Proc. ISoLA, pp. 608–614, LNCS, vol. 7609, pp. 608–614. Springer, Heidelberg (2012). https://doi.org/10.1007/978-3-642-34026-0_45

49. Howar, F., Isberner, M., Merten, M., Steffen, B., Beyer, D., Păsăreanu, C.: Rigorous examination of reactive systems. The RERS challenges 2012 and 2013. STTT 16(5), 457–464 (2014). https://doi.org/10.1007/s10009-014-0337-y

50. Howar, F., Steffen, B., Merten, M.: From ZULU to RERS. In: Margaria, T., Steffen, B. (eds.) Leveraging Applications of Formal Methods, Verification, and Validation, LNCS, vol. 6415, pp. 687–704. Springer, Heidelberg (2010)

51. Huisman, M., Klebanov, V., Monahan, R.: VerifyThis verification competition 2012 – organizer's report. Technical report 2013-01, Department of Informatics, Karlsruhe Institute of Technology (2013). http://digbib.ubka.uni-karlsruhe.de/volltexte/1000034373

52. Huisman, M., Monahan, R., Mostowski, W., Müller, P., Ulbrich, M.: VerifyThis 2017: A program verification competition. Technical report, Karlsruhe Reports in Informatics (2017)

53. Huisman, M., Monahan, R., Müller, P., Paskevich, A., Ernst, G.: VerifyThis 2018: A program verification competition. Technical report, Inria (2019)

54. Huisman, M., Monahan, R., Müller, P., Poll, E.: VerifyThis 2016: A program verification competition. Technical report TR-CTIT-16-07, Centre for Telematics and Information Technology, University of Twente, Enschede (2016)

55. Huisman, M., Klebanov, V., Monahan, R.: VerifyThis 2012. Int. J. Softw. Tools Technol. Transf. 17(6), 647–657 (2015)

56. Huisman, M., Klebanov, V., Monahan, R., Tautschnig, M.: VerifyThis 2015. A program verification competition. Int. J. Softw. Tools Technol. Transf. **19**(6), 763–771 (2017)

57. Jacobs, S., Bloem, R., Brenguier, R., Ehlers, R., Hell, T., Könighofer, R., Pérez, G.A., Raskin, J., Ryzhyk, L., Sankur, O., Seidl, M., Tentrup, L., Walker, A.: The first reactive synthesis competition (SYNTCOMP 2014). STTT **19**(3), 367–390 (2017). https://doi.org/10.1007/s10009-016-0416-3

58. Järvisalo, M., Berre, D.L., Roussel, O., Simon, L.: The international SAT solver competitions. AI Mag. **33**(1) (2012). https://doi.org/10.1609/aimag.v33i1.2395

59. Jasper, M., Fecke, M., Steffen, B., Schordan, M., Meijer, J., Pol, J.v.d., Howar, F., Siegel, S.F.: The RERS 2017 Challenge and Workshop (invited paper). In: Proceedings of the 24th ACM SIGSOFT International SPIN Symposium on Model Checking of Software, SPIN 2017, pp. 11–20. ACM (2017)

60. Jasper, M., Mues, M., Murtovi, A., Schlüter, M., Howar, F., Steffen, B., Schordan, M., Hendriks, D., Schiffelers, R., Kuppens, H., Vaandrager, F.: RERS 2019: Combining synthesis with real-world models. In: Proc. TACAS, Part 3, LNCS, vol. 11429, pp. 101–115. Springer, Cham (2019). https://doi.org/10.1007/978-3-030-17502-3_7

61. Jasper, M., Mues, M., Schlüter, M., Steffen, B., Howar, F.: RERS 2018: CTL, LTL, and reachability. In: ISoLA 2018, LNCS, vol. 11245, pp. 433–447. Springer, Cham (2018)

62. Kant, G., Laarman, A., Meijer, J., van de Pol, J., Blom, S., van Dijk, T.: LTSmin: High-performance language-independent model checking. In: Baier, C., Tinelli, C. (eds.) Tools and Algorithms for the Construction and Analysis of Systems (2015)

63. Klebanov, V., Beckert, B., Biere, A., Sutcliffe, G. (eds.) Proceedings of the 1st International Workshop on Comparative Empirical Evaluation of Reasoning Systems, Manchester, United Kingdom, 30 June 2012, CEUR Workshop Proceedings, vol. 873. CEUR-WS.org (2012). http://ceur-ws.org/Vol-873

64. Kordon, F., Garavel, H., Hillah, L.M., Hulin-Hubard, F., Amparore, E., Beccuti, M., Berthomieu, B., Ciardo, G., Dal Zilio, S., Liebke, T., Linard, A., Meijer, J., Miner, A., Srba, J., Thierry-Mieg, J., van de Pol, J., Wolf, K.: Complete Results for the 2018 Edition of the Model Checking Contest, June 2018. http://mcc.lip6.fr/2018/results.php

65. Kordon, F., Garavel, H., Hillah, L.M., Hulin-Hubard, F., Berthomieu, B., Ciardo, G., Colange, M., Dal Zilio, S., Amparore, E., Beccuti, M., Liebke, T., Meijer, J., Miner, A., Rohr, C., Srba, J., Thierry-Mieg, Y., van de Pol, J., Wolf, K.: Complete Results for the 2017 Edition of the Model Checking Contest, June 2017. http://mcc.lip6.fr/2017/results.php

66. Kordon, F., Garavel, H., Hillah, L.M., Hulin-Hubard, F., Chiardo, G., Hamez, A., Jezequel, L., Miner, A., Meijer, J., Paviot-Adet, E., Racordon, D., Rodriguez, C., Rohr, C., Srba, J., Thierry-Mieg, Y., Trinh, G., Wolf, K.: Complete Results for the 2016 Edition of the Model Checking Contest, June 2016. http://mcc.lip6.fr/2016/results.php

67. Kordon, F., Garavel, H., Hillah, L.M., Hulin-Hubard, F., Linard, A., Beccuti, M., Evangelista, S., Hamez, A., Lohmann, N., Lopez, E., Paviot-Adet, E., Rodriguez, C., Rohr, C., Srba, J.: HTML results from the Model Checking Contest @ Petri Net (2014 edition) (2014). http://mcc.lip6.fr/2014

68. Kordon, F., Garavel, H., Hillah, L.M., Hulin-Hubard, F., Linard, A., Beccuti, M., Hamez, A., Lopez-Bobeda, E., Jezequel, L., Meijer, J., Paviot-Adet, E., Rodriguez, C., Rohr, C., Srba, J., Thierry-Mieg, Y., Wolf, K.: Complete Results for the 2015 Edition of the Model Checking Contest (2015). http://mcc.lip6.fr/2015/results.php

69. Kordon, F., Hulin-Hubard, F.: BENCHKIT, a tool for massive concurrent benchmarking. In: Proc. ACSD, pp. 159–165. IEEE (2014). https://doi.org/10.1109/ACSD.2014.12

70. Kordon, F., Linard, A., Buchs, D., Colange, M., Evangelista, S., Lampka, K., Lohmann, N., Paviot-Adet, E., Thierry-Mieg, Y., Wimmel, H.: Report on the model checking contest at Petri Nets 2011. In: Transactions on Petri Nets and Other Models of Concurrency (ToPNoC) VI, LNCS, vol. 7400, pp. 169–196 (2012)

71. Kordon, F., Linard, A., Beccuti, M., Buchs, D., Fronc, L., Hillah, L., Hulin-Hubard, F., Legond-Aubry, F., Lohmann, N., Marechal, A., Paviot-Adet, E., Pommereau, F., Rodríguez, C., Rohr, C., Thierry-Mieg, Y., Wimmel, H., Wolf, K.: Model checking contest @ Petri Nets, report on the 2013 edition. CoRR abs/1309.2485 (2013). http://arxiv.org/abs/1309.2485

72. Kordon, F., Linard, A., Buchs, D., Colange, M., Evangelista, Fronc, L., Hillah, L.M., Lohmann, N., Paviot-Adet, E., Pommereau, F., Rohr, C., Thierry-Mieg, Y., Wimmel, H., Wolf, K.: Raw report on the model checking contest at Petri Nets 2012. CoRR abs/1209.2382 (2012). http://arxiv.org/abs/1209.2382

73. Lonsing, F., Seidl, M., Gelder, A.V.: The QBF gallery: Behind the scenes. Artif. Intell. **237**, 92–114 (2016). https://doi.org/10.1016/j.artint.2016.04.002

74. Marché, C., Zantema, H.: The termination competition. In: Baader, F. (ed.) Proc. RTA, LNCS, vol. 4533, pp. 303–313. Springer, Heidelberg (2007). https://doi.org/10.1007/978-3-540-73449-9_23

75. Meijer, J., van de Pol, J.: Sound black-box checking in the LearnLib. In: Dutle, A., Muñoz, C., Narkawicz, A. (eds.) NASA Formal Methods, LNCS, vol. 10811, pp. 349–366. Springer, Cham (2018)

76. Middeldorp, A., Nagele, J., Shintani, K.: Confluence competition 2019. In: Proc. TACAS, Part 3, LNCS, vol. 11429, pp. 25–40. Springer, Cham (2019). https://doi.org/10.1007/978-3-030-17502-3_2

77. Morse, J., Cordeiro, L., Nicole, D., Fischer, B.: Applying symbolic bounded model checking to the 2012 RERS greybox challenge. Int. J. Softw. Tools Technol. Transfer **16**(5), 519–529 (2014)

78. Nieuwenhuis, R.: The impact of CASC in the development of automated deduction systems. AI Commun. **15**(2–3), 77–78 (2002)

79. Pelletier, F., Sutcliffe, G., Suttner, C.: The development of CASC. AI Commun. **15**(2–3), 79–90 (2002)

80. van de Pol, J., Ruys, T.C., te Brinke, S.: Thoughtful brute-force attack of the RERS 2012 and 2013 challenges. Int. J. Softw. Tools Technol. Transfer **16**(5), 481–491 (2014)

81. Reger, G., Hallé, S., Falcone, Y.: Third international competition on runtime verification - CRV 2016. In: Proc. of RV 2016: The 16th International Conference on Runtime Verification, LNCS, vol. 10012, pp. 21–37. Springer, Cham (2016). https://doi.org/10.1007/978-3-319-46982-9

82. Reger, G., Havelund, K. (eds.) RV-CuBES 2017. An International Workshop on Competitions, Usability, Benchmarks, Evaluation, and Standardisation for Runtime Verification Tools, Kalpa Publications in Computing, vol. 3. EasyChair (2017)

83. Schordan, M., Prantl, A.: Combining static analysis and state transition graphs for verification of event-condition-action systems in the RERS 2012 and 2013 challenges. Int. J. Softw. Tools Technol. Transfer **16**(5), 493–505 (2014)

84. Sighireanu, M., Cok, D.: Report on SL-COMP 2014. JSAT **9**, 173–186 (2014)

85. Sighireanu, M., Pérez, J.A.N., Rybalchenko, A., Gorogiannis, N., Iosif, R., Reynolds, A., Serban, C., Katelaan, J., Matheja, C., Noll, T., Zuleger, F., Chin, W.N., Le, Q.L., Ta, Q.T., Le, T.C., Nguyen, T.T., Khoo, S.C., Cyprian, M., Rogalewicz, A., Vojnar, T., Enea, C., Lengal, O., Gao, C., Wu, Z.: SL-COMP: Competition of solvers for separation logic. In: Proc. TACAS, Part 3, LNCS, vol. 11429, pp. 116–132. Springer, Cham (2019). https://doi.org/10.1007/978-3-030-17502-3_8

86. Simon, L., Berre, D.L., Hirsch, E.A.: The SAT2002 competition. Ann. Math. Artif. Intell. **43**(1), 307–342 (2005). https://doi.org/10.1007/s10472-005-0424-6

87. Steffen, B., Jasper, M., Meijer, J., van de Pol, J.: Property-preserving generation of tailored benchmark Petri nets. In: 17th International Conference on Application of Concurrency to System Design (ACSD), pp. 1–8, June 2017

88. Steffen, B., Howar, F., Isberner, M., Naujokat, S., Margaria, T.: Tailored generation of concurrent benchmarks. STTT **16**(5), 543–558 (2014)

89. Steffen, B., Isberner, M., Naujokat, S., Margaria, T., Geske, M.: Property-driven benchmark generation. In: Model Checking Software - 20th International Symposium, SPIN 2013, Stony Brook, NY, USA, 8–9 July 2013. Proceedings, pp. 341–357 (2013)

90. Steffen, B., Isberner, M., Naujokat, S., Margaria, T., Geske, M.: Property-driven benchmark generation: synthesizing programs of realistic structure. Int. J. Softw. Tools Technol. Transfer **16**(5), 465–479 (2014)

91. Steffen, B., Jasper, M.: Property-preserving parallel decomposition. In: Models, Algorithms, Logics and Tools, LNCS, vol. 10460, pp. 125–145. Springer, Cham (2017)

92. Stump, A., Sutcliffe, G., Tinelli, C.: STARExEC: A cross-community infrastructure for logic solving. In: Proc. IJCAR, LNCS, vol. 8562, pp. 367–373. Springer, Cham (2014). https://doi.org/10.1007/978-3-319-08587-6_28

93. Sutcliffe, G.: The CADE-16 ATP System Competition. J. Autom. Reason. **24**(3), 371–396 (2000)

94. Sutcliffe, G.: The CADE-17 ATP System Competition. J. Autom. Reason. **27**(3), 227–250 (2001)

95. Sutcliffe, G.: The IJCAR-2004 Automated Theorem Proving Competition. AI Commun. **18**(1), 33–40 (2005)

96. Sutcliffe, G.: The CADE-20 Automated Theorem Proving Competition. AI Commun. **19**(2), 173–181 (2006)

97. Sutcliffe, G.: The 3rd IJCAR Automated Theorem Proving Competition. AI Commun. **20**(2), 117–126 (2007)

98. Sutcliffe, G.: The CADE-21 Automated Theorem Proving System Competition. AI Commun. **21**(1), 71–82 (2008)

99. Sutcliffe, G.: The 4th IJCAR Automated Theorem Proving Competition. AI Commun. **22**(1), 59–72 (2009)

100. Sutcliffe, G.: The CADE-22 Automated Theorem Proving System Competition - CASC-22. AI Commun. **23**(1), 47–60 (2010)

101. Sutcliffe, G.: The 5th IJCAR Automated Theorem Proving System Competition - CASC-J5. AI Commun. **24**(1), 75–89 (2011)

102. Sutcliffe, G.: The CADE-23 Automated Theorem Proving System Competition - CASC-23. AI Commun. **25**(1), 49–63 (2012)

103. Sutcliffe, G.: The 6th IJCAR Automated Theorem Proving System Competition - CASC-J6. AI Commun. **26**(2), 211–223 (2013)

104. Sutcliffe, G.: The CADE-24 Automated Theorem Proving System Competition - CASC-24. AI Commun. **27**(4), 405–416 (2014)

105. Sutcliffe, G.: The 7th IJCAR Automated Theorem Proving System Competition - CASC-J7. AI Commun. **28**(4), 683–692 (2015)

106. Sutcliffe, G.: The 8th IJCAR Automated Theorem Proving System Competition - CASC-J8. AI Commun. **29**(5), 607–619 (2016)

107. Sutcliffe, G.: The CADE ATP System Competition - CASC. AI Mag. **37**(2), 99–101 (2016)

108. Sutcliffe, G.: The CADE-26 Automated Theorem Proving System Competition - CASC-26. AI Commun. **30**(6), 419–432 (2017)

109. Sutcliffe, G.: The 9th IJCAR Automated Theorem Proving System Competition - CASC-29. AI Commun. **31**(6), 495–507 (2018)

110. Sutcliffe, G., Suttner, C.: The CADE-18 ATP System Competition. J. Autom. Reason. **31**(1), 23–32 (2003)

111. Sutcliffe, G., Suttner, C.: The CADE-19 ATP System Competition. AI Commun. **17**(3), 103–182 (2004)

112. Sutcliffe, G., Suttner, C.: The State of CASC. AI Commun. **19**(1), 35–48 (2006)

113. Sutcliffe, G., Suttner, C., Pelletier, F.: The IJCAR ATP System Competition. J. Autom. Reason. **28**(3), 307–320 (2002)

114. Sutcliffe, G., Suttner, C.: Special Issue: The CADE-13 ATP System Competition. J. Autom. Reason. **18**(2), 271–286 (1997)

115. Sutcliffe, G., Suttner, C.: The CADE-15 ATP System Competition. J. Autom. Reason. **23**(1), 1–23 (1999)

116. Sutcliffe, G., Urban, J.: The CADE-25 Automated Theorem Proving System Competition - CASC-25. AI Commun. **29**(3), 423–433 (2016)

117. Suttner, C., Sutcliffe, G.: The CADE-14 ATP System Competition. J. Autom. Reason. **21**(1), 99–134 (1998)

118. Waldmann, J.: Report on the termination competition 2008. In: Proc. of WST (2009)

Confluence Competition 2019

Aart Middeldorp[1]([✉])[ID], Julian Nagele[2][ID], and Kiraku Shintani[3][ID]

[1] Department of Computer Science, University of Innsbruck, Innsbruck, Austria
aart.middeldorp@uibk.ac.at
[2] School of Electronic Engineering and Computer Science,
Queen Mary University of London, London, UK
j.nagele@qmul.ac.uk
[3] School of Information Science, JAIST, Nomi, Japan
s1820017@jaist.ac.jp

Abstract. We report on the 2019 edition of the Confluence Competition, a competition of software tools that aim to prove or disprove confluence and related (undecidable) properties of rewrite systems automatically.

Keywords: Confluence · Term rewriting · Automation

1 Introduction

The Confluence Competition (CoCo)[1] is an annual competition of software tools that aim to prove or disprove confluence and related (undecidable) properties of a variety of rewrite formalisms automatically. Initiated in 2012, CoCo runs live in a single slot at a conference or workshop and is executed on the cross-community competition platform StarExec [1]. For each category, 100 suitable problems are randomly selected from the online database of confluence problems (COPS). Participating tools must answer YES or NO within 60 s, followed by a justification that is understandable by a human expert; any other output signals that the tool could not determine the status of the problem. CoCo 2019 features new categories on commutation, infeasibility problems, and confluence of string rewrite systems.

Confluence provides a general notion of determinism and has been conceived as one of the central properties of rewriting. A rewrite system $\mathcal{R}$ is a set of directed equations, so called rewrite rules, which induces a rewrite relation $\to_{\mathcal{R}}$ on terms. We provide a simple example.

Example 1. Consider the rewrite system $\mathcal{R}$ consisting of the rules

$$0 + y \to y \qquad\qquad 0 \times y \to y$$
$$\mathsf{s}(x) + y \to \mathsf{s}(x + y) \qquad\qquad \mathsf{s}(x) \times y \to (x \times y) + y$$

---

[1] http://project-coco.uibk.ac.at/.

This research is supported by FWF (Austrian Science Fund) project P27528.

D. Beyer et al. (Eds.): TACAS 2019, Part III, LNCS 11429, pp. 25–40, 2019.
https://doi.org/10.1007/978-3-030-17502-3_2

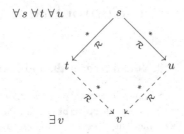

Fig. 1. Confluence.

which can be viewed as a specification of addition and multiplication over natural numbers in unary notation. Computing $2 \times (1 + 2)$ amounts to evaluating the term $s = \mathsf{s}(\mathsf{s}(0)) \times (\mathsf{s}(0) + \mathsf{s}(\mathsf{s}(0)))$. This is done by matching a subterm with the left-hand side of a rewrite rule, and if matching succeeds, replacing that subterm by the right-hand side of the rule after applying the matching substitution to its variables. For instance, the subterm $\mathsf{s}(0) + \mathsf{s}(\mathsf{s}(0))$ of s matches the left-hand side of the rule $\mathsf{s}(x) + y \to \mathsf{s}(x + y)$, with matching substitution $\{x \mapsto 0, y \mapsto \mathsf{s}(\mathsf{s}(0))\}$. Hence the subterm can be replaced by $\mathsf{s}(0 + \mathsf{s}(\mathsf{s}(0)))$. It follows that s rewrites (in a single step) to the term $t = \mathsf{s}(\mathsf{s}(0)) \times \mathsf{s}(0 + \mathsf{s}(\mathsf{s}(0)))$. Continuing this process from t eventually results in the term $\mathsf{s}(\mathsf{s}(\mathsf{s}(\mathsf{s}(\mathsf{s}(\mathsf{s}(0))))))$. This term cannot be simplified further. Such terms are called normal forms.

In the above example there are several ways to evaluate the term s. The choice does not matter since all maximal rewrite sequences terminate in the same normal form, which is readily checked. This property not only holds for the term s, but for all terms that can be constructed from the symbols in the rules. *Confluence* is the property that guarantees this. A rewrite system $\mathcal{R}$ is confluent if the inclusion $_{\mathcal{R}}^{*}\!\leftarrow \cdot \to_{\mathcal{R}}^{*} \, \subseteq \, \to_{\mathcal{R}}^{*} \cdot {}_{\mathcal{R}}^{*}\!\leftarrow$ holds. Here $\to_{\mathcal{R}}^{*}$ denotes the transitive reflexive closure of the one-step rewrite relation $\to_{\mathcal{R}}$, $_{\mathcal{R}}^{*}\!\leftarrow$ denotes the inverse of $\to_{\mathcal{R}}^{*}$, and $\cdot$ denotes relational composition. A more graphical definition of confluence is presented in Fig. 1. The precise notions of rewrite rules, associated rewrite steps, and terms to be rewritten vary from formalism to formalism.

2   Categories

In recent years the focus in confluence research has shifted towards the development of automatable techniques for confluence proofs. To stimulate these developments the Confluence Competition has been set up in 2012. Since its creation with 4 tools competing in 2 categories, CoCo has grown steadily and will feature the following 12 categories in 2019:

TRS/CPF-TRS The two original categories are about confluence of *first-order term rewriting*. CPF-TRS is a category for *certified* confluence proofs, where participating tools must generate certificates that are checked by an independent certifier.

CTRS/CPF-CTRS These two categories, introduced respectively in 2014 and 2015, are concerned (certified) confluence of *conditional term rewriting*, a formalism in which rewrite rules come equipped with conditions that are evaluated recursively using the rewrite relation.

HRS This category, introduced in 2015, deals with confluence of *higher-order rewriting*, i.e., rewriting with binders and functional variables.

GCR This category is about *ground* confluence of *many-sorted* term rewrite systems and was also introduced in 2015.

NFP/UNC/UNR These three categories, introduced in 2016, are about properties of first-order term rewrite systems related to unique normal forms, namely, *the normal form property* (NFP), *unique normal forms with respect to conversion* (UNC), and *unique normal forms with respect to reduction* (UNR).

COM This new category is about *commutation* of first-order rewrite systems.

INF This new category is about *infeasibility* problems.

SRS This new category is concerned with confluence of *string rewriting*.

The new categories are described in detail in Sect. 5. Descriptions of the other categories can be found in the CoCo 2015 [2] and 2018 [3] reports, and on the CoCo website (see Footnote 1). The underlying problem format is the topic of the next section.

3   Confluence Problems

Tools participating in CoCo are given problems from the database of *confluence problems* (COPS)[2] in a format suitable for the category in which the tools participate. Besides commutation and infeasibility problems, which are described in Sect. 5, four different formats are supported: TRS, CTRS, MSTRS, and HRS. As these formats were simplified recently, we present the official syntax below in four subsections.

In addition to the format, *tags* are used to determine suitable problems for CoCo categories. For instance, for the CTRS category, selected problems must have the `3_ctrs` and `oriented` tags. Such tags are automatically computed when problems are submitted to COPS. Detailed information on COPS, including a description of the tagging mechanism, can be found in [4].

3.1   TRS Format

The format for first-order rewrite systems comes in two versions: a basic version and an extended version. The latter contains an additional signature declaration which is used to define function symbols that do not appear in the rewrite rules.

---

[2] https://cops.uibk.ac.at/.

The basic format is a simplification of the old TPDB format,[3] according to the following grammar:

```
trs      ::= [(VAR idlist)] (RULES rulelist) [(COMMENT string)]
idlist   ::= ε | id idlist
rulelist ::= ε | rule rulelist
rule     ::= term -> term
term     ::= id | id() | id(termlist)
termlist ::= term | term, termlist
```

Here *string* is any sequence of characters and *id* is any nonempty sequence of characters not containing whitespace, the characters (,), ", ,, |, \, and the sequences ->, ==, COMMENT, VAR, and RULES. In (VAR *idlist*) the variables of the TRS are declared. If this is missing, the TRS is ground. Symbols (*id*) appearing in the (RULES *rulelist*) declaration that were not declared as variables are function symbols. If they appear multiple times, they must be used with the same number (arity) of arguments. Here is an example of the basic format, COPS #1:

```
(VAR x y)
(RULES
  f(x,y) -> x
  f(x,y) -> f(x,g(y))
  g(x) -> h(x)
  F(g(x),x) -> F(x,g(x))
  F(h(x),x) -> F(x,h(x))
)
(COMMENT
doi:10.1007/BFb0027006
[1] Example 6
submitted by: Takahito Aoto, Junichi Yoshida, and Yoshihito Toyama
)
```

In the extended format, a signature declaration specifying the set of function symbols and their arities is added. In this format, every symbol appearing in the rules must be declared as a function symbol or a variable. Formally, the *trs* declaration in the basic format is replaced by

```
trs      ::= [(VAR idlist)] (SIG funlist) (RULES rulelist)
             [(COMMENT string)]
funlist  ::= ε | fun funlist
fun      ::= (id int)
```

where *int* is a nonempty sequence of digits. An example of the extended format is provided by COPS #557:

---

[3] https://www.lri.fr/~marche/tpdb/format.html.

```
(VAR x y z)
(SIG (f 2) (a 0) (b 0) (c 0))
(RULES
  a -> b
  f(x,a) -> f(b,b)
  f(b,x) -> f(b,b)
  f(f(x,y),z) -> f(b,b)
)
(COMMENT
[111] Example 1 with additional constant c
submitted by: Franziska Rapp
)
```

3.2 CTRS Format

The format for first-order conditional rewrite systems is a simplification of the old TPDB format (see Footnote 3), according to the following grammar:

$$
\begin{array}{lcl}
\textit{ctrs} & ::= & \text{(CONDITIONTYPE } \textit{ctype}) \text{ [(VAR } \textit{idlist})] \text{ (RULES } \textit{rulelist})} \\
 & & \text{[(COMMENT } \textit{string})]} \\
\textit{ctype} & ::= & \text{SEMI-EQUATIONAL | JOIN | ORIENTED} \\
\textit{idlist} & ::= & \epsilon \text{ | } \textit{id idlist} \\
\textit{rulelist} & ::= & \epsilon \text{ | } \textit{rule rulelist} \\
\textit{rule} & ::= & \textit{term} \text{ -> } \textit{term} \text{ | } \textit{term} \text{ -> } \textit{term} \text{ '|' } \textit{condlist} \\
\textit{condlist} & ::= & \textit{cond} \text{ | } \textit{cond, condlist} \\
\textit{cond} & ::= & \textit{term} \text{ == } \textit{term} \\
\textit{term} & ::= & \textit{id} \text{ | } \textit{id}() \text{ | } \textit{id}(\textit{termlist}) \\
\textit{termlist} & ::= & \textit{term} \text{ | } \textit{term, termlist}
\end{array}
$$

The restrictions on *id* and *string* are the same as in the TRS format. The *ctype* declaration specifies the semantics of the conditions in the rewrite rules: conversion ($\leftrightarrow^*$) for semi-equational CTRSs, joinability ($\downarrow$) for join CTRSs, and reachability ($\rightarrow^*$) for oriented CTRSs. An example of the CTRS format is provided by COPS #488:

```
(CONDITIONTYPE ORIENTED)
(VAR w x y z)
(RULES
  plus(0, y) -> y
  plus(s(x), y) -> s(plus(x, y))
  fib(0) -> pair(0, s(0))
  fib(s(x)) -> pair(z, w) | fib(x) == pair(y, z), plus(y, z) == w
)
(COMMENT
doi:10.4230/LIPIcs.RTA.2015.223
[89] Example 1
submitted by: Thomas Sternagel
)
```

3.3   MSTRS Format

The format for many-sorted term rewrite systems is a modification of the TRS format, according to the following grammar:

```
trs       ::= (SIG funlist) (RULES rulelist) [(COMMENT string)]
funlist   ::= fun | fun funlist
fun       ::= (id sort)
sort      ::= idlist -> id
idlist    ::= ε | id idlist
rulelist  ::= ε | rule rulelist
rule      ::= term -> term
term      ::= id | id() | id(termlist)
termlist  ::= term | term, termlist
```

The restriction on *id* is the same as in the TRS format. Every term must be a well-typed term according the signature declared in (SIG *funlist*). Symbols (*id*) not declared in *funlist* are variables (which can take any sort). We provide an example (COPS #646):

```
(SIG
    (+      Nat Nat -> Nat)
    (s      Nat -> Nat)
    (0      -> Nat)
    (node   Nat Tree Tree -> Tree)
    (leaf   Nat -> Tree)
    (sum    Tree -> Nat)
)
(RULES
    sum(leaf(x)) -> x
    sum(node(x,yt,zt)) -> +(x,+(sum(yt),sum(zt)))
    +(x,0) -> x
    +(x,s(y)) -> s(+(x,y))
    node(x,yt,zt) -> node(x,zt,yt)
)
(COMMENT
[125] Example 13
submitted by: Takahito Aoto
)
```

3.4   HRS Format

This format deals with higher-order rewrite systems (HRSs) described by Mayr and Nipkow [5] with small modifications detailed below the typing rules. The format follows the same style as the first-order formats, adding type declarations to variables and function symbols as well as syntax for abstraction and application according to the following grammar:

```
hrs         ::= signature (RULES rulelist) [(COMMENT string)]
signature   ::= (VAR sig) (FUN sig) | (FUN sig) (VAR sig)
sig         ::= ε | id : type sig
type        ::= type -> type | id | (type)
rulelist    ::= ε | rule | rule, rulelist
rule        ::= term -> term
term        ::= id | term(termlist) | term term | \idlist.term | (term)
termlist    ::= term | term, termlist
idlist      ::= id | id idlist
```

In (FUN sig) the function symbols of the HRS are declared, while (VAR sig) declares the types of the variables that are used in the rules. An identifier must not occur in both the (FUN sig) and (VAR sig) sections, but all identifiers that occur in the (RULES rulelist) section must occur in one of them. To save parentheses the following standard conventions are used: In type, -> associates to the right. For terms, application associates to the left, while abstraction associates to the right. Moreover abstractions extend as far to the right as possible, i.e., application binds stronger than abstraction. The algebraic notation term(termlist) is syntactic sugar for nested application, i.e., t(u,...,v) is syntactic sugar for (... (t u) ...) v; note that due to left-associativity of application, s t(u,v) = (s t)(u,v) = (((s t) u) v). Finally, the expression \x ... y.s abbreviates \x. ... \y.s. Terms must be typable according to the following rules:

$$\frac{x : \sigma \in \text{VAR}}{x : \sigma} \qquad \frac{f : \sigma \in \text{FUN}}{f : \sigma} \qquad \frac{t : \sigma \to \tau \quad u : \sigma}{t\,u : \tau} \qquad \frac{x : \sigma \in \text{VAR} \quad t : \tau}{\backslash x.t : \sigma \to \tau}$$

Terms are modulo $\alpha\beta\eta$. In the interest of user-friendliness and readability we demand that the rules are given in β-normal form, but do not impose any restrictions concerning η. Note that the list of variables declared in (VAR sig) is not exhaustive, fresh variables of arbitrary type are available to construct terms. Left- and right-hand sides of a rewrite rule must be of the same base type, but we do not demand that free variables appearing on the right also occur on the left. An example of the HRS format is provided by COPS #747:

```
(FUN
  app : arrab -> a -> b
  lam : (Va -> b) -> arrab
  var : Va -> a
)
(VAR
  x : Va
  M : a -> b
  N : a
  L : arrab
)
(RULES
  app(lam(\x.M (var x)), N) -> M N,
  lam(\x.app(L, (var x))) -> L
)
(COMMENT
simply-typed lambda calculus with beta/eta in the style of [137,138]
submitted by: Makoto Hamana
)
```

4   Competition

Since 2012 a total of 17 tools participated in CoCo. Many of the tools participated in multiple categories. The proceedings of the International Workshop on Confluence[4] contain (short) descriptions of the contenders. For each category, 100 problems are randomly selected from COPS. Problem selection for CoCo 2019 is subject to the following constraints. For the TRS, CPF-TRS, NFP, UNC, and UNR categories, problems in TRS format are selected. The problems for the SRS category are further restricted to those having the srs tag. For the CTRS and CPF-CTRS categories, problems must be in CTRS format and have the tags 3_ctrs and oriented, since participating tools handle only *oriented* CTRSs of *type 3*. In an oriented CTRS the conditions in the rules are interpreted as reachability and type 3 is a syntactic restriction on the distribution of variables in rewrite rules which ensure that rewriting does not introduce fresh variables [6]. For the GCR category, eligible problems must be in TRS or MSTRS format. Being in HRS format is a prerequisite for problems to be selected for the HRS category. For the new COM and INF categories, problems must have the commutation and infeasibility tags, respectively. The respective formats are described in the next section. New in 2019 is the possibility for tool authors to submit *secret* problems just before the competition. These will be included in the selected problems.

Earlier editions of CoCo only considered problems stemming from the *literature*. This restriction was put in place to avoid bias towards one particular tool

---

[4] http://cl-informatik.uibk.ac.at/iwc/index.php.

or technique. Since both COPS and CoCo have grown and diversified considerably since their inception, this restriction has become hard to maintain in a meaningful way, while at the same time losing its importance. Consequently it has been dropped for CoCo 2019. Further selection details are available from the CoCo website.

Since 2013 CoCo is executed on the cross-community competition platform StarExec [1]. Each tool has access to a single node and is given 60 s per problem. For a given problem, tools must answer YES or NO, followed by a justification that is understandable by a human expert; any other output signals that the tool could not determine the status of the problem. The possibility in StarExec to reserve a large number of computing nodes allows to complete CoCo within a single slot of a workshop or conference. This live event of CoCo is shared with the audience via the *LiveView* [4] tool which continuously polls new results from StarExec while the competition is running. A screenshot of the LiveView of CoCo 2018 is shown in Fig. 2. New is the realtime display of YES/NO conflicts. Since all categories deal with undecidable problems, and developing software tools is error-prone, conflicts appear once a while. In the past they were identified after the live competition finished, now action by the SC can be taken before winners are announced. As can be seen from the screenshot, in last year's competition there was a YES/NO conflict in the HRS category, which led to lively discussion about the semantics of the HRS format. After each competition, the results are made available from the results page.[5]

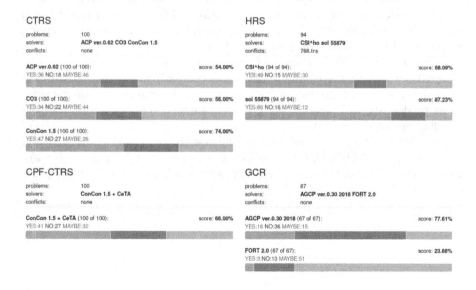

Fig. 2. Part of the LiveView of CoCo 2018 upon completion.

[5] http://project-coco.uibk.ac.at/results/.

The certification categories (CPF-TRS and CPF-CTRS) are there to ensure that tools produce correct answers. In these categories tools have to produce certified (non-)confluence proofs with their answers. The predominant approach to achieve this uses a combination of confluence prover and independent certifier. First the confluence prover analyses confluence as usual, restricting itself to criteria supported by the certifier. If it is successful the prover prints its proof in the certification problem format (CPF),[6] which is then checked by the certifier. To ensure correctness of this check, soundness of the certifier is mechanized in a proof assistant like Isabelle/HOL. So far only one certifier has participated in CoCo: CeTA.[7]

5 New Categories in 2019

5.1 Commutation

TRSs $\mathcal{R}$ and $\mathcal{S}$ *commute* if the inclusion $_\mathcal{R}^*\!\leftarrow \cdot \rightarrow_\mathcal{S}^* \subseteq \rightarrow_\mathcal{S}^* \cdot {}_\mathcal{R}^*\!\leftarrow$ holds. Commutation is an important generalization of confluence: Apart from direct applications in rewriting, e.g. for confluence,[8] standardization, normalization, and relative termination, commutation is the basis of many results in computer science, like correctness of program transformations [7], and bisimulation up-to [8].

Currently, commutation is supported by the tools CoLL [9] and FORT [10]. The former supports commutation versions of three established confluence techniques: development closedness [11], rule labeling [12], and an adaption of a confluence modulo result by Jouannaud and Kirchner [13]. The latter is a decision tool for the first-order theory of rewriting based on tree automata techniques, but restricted to left-linear right-ground TRSs.

Commutation problems consist of two TRSs $\mathcal{R}$ and $\mathcal{S}$. The question to be answered is whether these commute. To ensure compatibility of the signatures of the involved TRSs, we rename function symbols and variables in $\mathcal{S}$ on demand. Before we describe this precisely, we give an example of a commutation problem that illustrates the problem.

Consider COPS #82 (consisting of the rewrite rules $f(a) \rightarrow f(f(a))$ and $f(x) \rightarrow f(a)$) and COPS #80 (consisting of $a \rightarrow f(a,b)$ and $f(a,b) \rightarrow f(b,a)$). Since function symbol f is unary in COPS #82 and binary in COPS #80, it is renamed to f' in COPS #80:

---

[6] http://cl-informatik.uibk.ac.at/software/cpf/.

[7] http://cl-informatik.uibk.ac.at/software/ceta/.

[8] The union of confluent, pairwise commuting rewrite systems is confluent.

```
(PROBLEM COMMUTATION)
(COMMENT COPS 82 80)
(VAR x)
(RULES
  f(a) -> f(f(a))
  f(x) -> f(a)
)
(VAR )
(RULES
  a -> f'(a,b)
  f'(a,b) -> f'(b,a)
)
```

The correct answer of this commutation problem is **YES** since the critical peak of $\mathcal{R}$ and $\mathcal{S}$ makes a decreasing diagram [12]. In COPS this problem is given as

```
(PROBLEM COMMUTATION)
(COPS 82 80)
(COMMENT this comment will be removed)
```

and an inlining tool generates the earlier problem before it is passed to tools participating in the commutation category. In general, commutation problems are incorporated into COPS as follows:

```
(PROBLEM COMMUTATION)
(COPS number1  number2)
(COMMENT string)
```

where *number1* and *number2* refer to existing problems in TRS format. The (COMMENT *string*) declaration is optional. To ensure that their union is a proper TRS, the inlining tool renames function symbols in COPS #*number2* that appear as variable or as function symbol with a different arity in COPS #*number1* by adding a prime ('). The same holds for variables in COPS #*number2* that occur as function symbol in COPS #*number1*.

5.2 Infeasibility Problems

Infeasibility problems originate from different sources. Critical pairs in a conditional rewrite system are equipped with conditions. If no satisfying substitution for the variables in the conditions exists, the critical pair is harmless and can be ignored when analyzing confluence of the rewrite system in question. In this case the critical pair is said to be *infeasible* [14, Definition 7.1.8]. Sufficient conditions for infeasibility of conditional critical pairs are reported in [15,16].

Another source of infeasibility problems is the dependency graph in termination analysis of rewrite systems [17]. An edge from dependency pair $\ell_1 \to r_1$ to dependency pair $\ell_2 \to r_2$ exists in the dependency graph if two substitutions σ and τ can be found such that $r_1\sigma$ rewrites to $\ell_2\tau$. (By renaming the variables in the dependency pairs apart, a single substitution suffices.) If no substitutions exists, there is no edge, which may ease the task of proving termination of the underlying rewrite system [18,19].

We give two examples. The first one stems from the conditional critical pair between the two conditional rewrite rules in COPS #547:

```
(PROBLEM INFEASIBILITY)
(COMMENT COPS 547)
(CONDITIONTYPE ORIENTED)
(VAR x)
(RULES
  f(x) -> a | x == a
  f(x) -> b | x == b
)
(VAR x)
(CONDITION x == a, x == b)
```

The correct answer of this infeasibility problem is YES since no term in the underlying conditional rewrite system rewrites to both a and b. In COPS this problem is given as

```
(PROBLEM INFEASIBILITY)
(COPS 547)
(VAR x)
(CONDITION x == a, x == b)
(COMMENT
doi:10.4230/LIPIcs.FSCD.2016.29
[90] Example 3
submitted by: Raul Gutierrez and Salvador Lucas
)
```

and an inlining tool generates the earlier problem before it is passed to tools participating in the infeasibility category.

The second example is a special case since the condition in the infeasibility problem contains no variables:

```
(PROBLEM INFEASIBILITY)
(COMMENT COPS 47)
(VAR x)
(RULES
  F(x,x) -> A
  G(x) -> F(x,G(x))
  C -> G(C)
)
(CONDITION G(A) == A)
```

has YES as correct answer since the term G(A) does not rewrite to A. This answer can be used to conclude that the underlying rewrite system is not confluent. Again, in COPS this problem is rendered as

```
(PROBLEM INFEASIBILITY)
(COPS 47)
(CONDITION G(A) == A)
(COMMENT this comment will be removed)
```

In general, infeasibility problems are incorporated into COPS as follows:

```
(PROBLEM INFEASIBILITY)
(COPS number)
(VAR idlist)
(CONDITION condlist)
(COMMENT string)
```

where

```
condlist ::= cond | cond , condlist
    cond ::= term == term
```

has the same syntax as the conditional part of a conditional rewrite rule and *number* refers to an existing problem in CTRS or TRS format. If it is a CTRS then the semantics of == is the same as declared in the (CONDITIONTYPE *ctype*) declaration of the CTRS; if it is a TRS then the semantics of == is ORIENTED (reachability, $\to^*$). Variables declared in *idlist* are used as variables in *condlist*. The (VAR *idlist*) declaration can be omitted if the terms in *condlist* are ground. Common function symbols occurring in COPS #*number* and *condlist* have the same arity. Moreover, function symbols in COPS #*number* do not occur as variables in (VAR *idlist*) and function symbols in *condlist* do not occur as variables in COPS #*number*.

5.3 String Rewriting

String rewrite systems (SRSs) are special TRSs in which terms are strings. To ensure that the infrastructure developed for TRSs can be reused, we use the TRS format with the restriction that all function symbols are unary. So a string rule ab $\to$ ba is rendered as $a(b(x)) \to b(a(x))$ where x is a variable. A concrete example (COPS #442) is given below:

```
(VAR x)
(RULES
  f(f(x)) -> x
  f(x) -> f(f(x))
)
(COMMENT
doi:10.4230/LIPIcs.RTA.2015.257
[81] Example 1
)
```

The correct answer of this problem is YES since the addition of the redundant rules [20] f(x) -> f(f(f(x))) and f(x) -> x makes the critical pairs of the SRS development closed [11].

The SRS category has been established to stimulate further research on confluence of string rewriting. In the Termination Competition[9] there is an active community developing powerful techniques for (relative) termination of SRSs. We anticipate that these are beneficial when applied to confluence analysis.

6   Outlook

In the near future we plan to merge CoCo with COPS and CoCoWeb,[10] a convenient web interface to execute the tools that participate in CoCo without local installation, to achieve a single entry point for confluence problems, tools, and competitions. Moreover, the submission interface of COPS will be extended with functionality to support submitters of new problems as well as the CoCo SC. We anticipate that in the years ahead new categories will be added to CoCo. Natural candidates are rewriting modulo AC and nominal rewriting.

Acknowledgments. We are grateful to Nao Hirokawa for continuous support for the infrastructure of CoCo. Fabian Mitterwallner contributed to the inlining and renaming tools for the new commutation and infeasibility categories. Raúl Gutiérrez, Naoki Nishida, and Salvador Lucas contributed the initial set of infeasibility problems (COPS #818 – #936). Johannes Waldmann contributed challenging SRS problems (COPS #987 – #1036). Finally, we acknowledge the TOOLympics 2019 initiators for giving us the opportunity to present CoCo 2019.

References

1. Stump, A., Sutcliffe, G., Tinelli, C.: StarExec: a cross-community infrastructure for logic solving. In: Demri, S., Kapur, D., Weidenbach, C. (eds.) IJCAR 2014. LNCS, vol. 8562, pp. 367–373. Springer, Cham (2014). https://doi.org/10.1007/978-3-319-08587-6_28

---

[9] http://termination-portal.org/wiki/Termination_Competition.
[10] http://cocoweb.uibk.ac.at/.

2. Aoto, T., Hirokawa, N., Nagele, J., Nishida, N., Zankl, H.: Confluence competition 2015. In: Felty, A.P., Middeldorp, A. (eds.) CADE 2015. LNCS, vol. 9195, pp. 101–104. Springer, Cham (2015). https://doi.org/10.1007/978-3-319-21401-6_5
3. Aoto, T., et al.: Confluence competition 2018. In: Proceedings of 3rd International Conference on Formal Structures for Computation and Deduction. LIPIcs, vol. 108, pp. 32:1–32:5 (2018). https://doi.org/10.4230/LIPIcs.FSCD.2018.32
4. Hirokawa, N., Nagele, J., Middeldorp, A.: Cops and CoCoWeb: infrastructure for confluence tools. In: Galmiche, D., Schulz, S., Sebastiani, R. (eds.) IJCAR 2018. LNCS, vol. 10900, pp. 346–353. Springer, Cham (2018). https://doi.org/10.1007/978-3-319-94205-6_23
5. Mayr, R., Nipkow, T.: Higher-order rewrite systems and their confluence. Theor. Comput. Sci. **192**(1), 3–29 (1998). https://doi.org/10.1016/S0304-3975(97)00143-6
6. Middeldorp, A., Hamoen, E.: Completeness results for basic narrowing. Appl. Algebr. Eng. Commun. Comput. **5**, 213–253 (1994). https://doi.org/10.1007/BF01190830
7. Huet, G.: Confluent reductions: abstract properties and applications to term rewriting systems. J. ACM **27**(4), 797–821 (1980). https://doi.org/10.1145/322217.322230
8. Pous, D.: New up-to techniques for weak bisimulation. Theor. Comput. Sci. **380**(1), 164–180 (2007). https://doi.org/10.1016/j.tcs.2007.02.060
9. Shintani, K., Hirokawa, N.: CoLL: a confluence tool for left-linear term rewrite systems. In: Felty, A.P., Middeldorp, A. (eds.) CADE 2015. LNCS, vol. 9195, pp. 127–136. Springer, Cham (2015). https://doi.org/10.1007/978-3-319-21401-6_8
10. Rapp, F., Middeldorp, A.: FORT 2.0. In: Galmiche, D., Schulz, S., Sebastiani, R. (eds.) IJCAR 2018. LNCS, vol. 10900, pp. 81–88. Springer, Cham (2018). https://doi.org/10.1007/978-3-319-94205-6_6
11. van Oostrom, V.: Developing developments. Theor. Comput. Sci. **175**(1), 159–181 (1997). https://doi.org/10.1016/S0304-3975(96)00173-9
12. Aoto, T.: Automated confluence proof by decreasing diagrams based on rule-labelling. In: Proceedings of 21st RTA. LIPIcs, vol. 6, pp. 7–16 (2010). https://doi.org/10.4230/LIPIcs.RTA.2010.7
13. Jouannaud, J.P., Kirchner, H.: Completion of a set of rules modulo a set of equations. SIAM J. Comput. **15**(4), 1155–1194 (1986). https://doi.org/10.1137/0215084
14. Ohlebusch, E.: Advanced Topics in Term Rewriting. Springer, New York (2002). https://doi.org/10.1007/978-1-4757-3661-8
15. Lucas, S., Gutiérrez, R.: Use of logical models for proving infeasibility in term rewriting. Inf. Process. Lett. **136**, 90–95 (2018). https://doi.org/10.1016/j.ipl.2018.04.002
16. Sternagel, T., Middeldorp, A.: Infeasible conditional critical pairs. In: Proceedings of 4th International Workshop on Confluence, pp. 13–17 (2015)
17. Arts, T., Giesl, J.: Termination of term rewriting using dependency pairs. Theor. Comput. Sci. **236**, 133–178 (2000). https://doi.org/10.1016/S0304-3975(99)00207-8
18. Giesl, J., Thiemann, R., Schneider-Kamp, P.: Proving and disproving termination of higher-order functions. In: Gramlich, B. (ed.) FroCoS 2005. LNCS, vol. 3717, pp. 216–231. Springer, Heidelberg (2005). https://doi.org/10.1007/11559306_12

19. Middeldorp, A.: Approximating dependency graphs using tree automata techniques. In: Goré, R., Leitsch, A., Nipkow, T. (eds.) IJCAR 2001. LNCS, vol. 2083, pp. 593–610. Springer, Heidelberg (2001). https://doi.org/10.1007/3-540-45744-5_49

20. Nagele, J., Felgenhauer, B., Middeldorp, A.: Improving automatic confluence analysis of rewrite systems by redundant rules. In: Proceedings of 26th RTA. LIPIcs, vol. 36, pp. 257–268 (2015)

International Competition on Runtime Verification (CRV)

Ezio Bartocci[1(✉)], Yliès Falcone[2], and Giles Reger[3]

[1] TU Wien, Vienna, Austria
ezio.bartocci@tuwien.ac.at
[2] Univ. Grenoble Alpes, CNRS, Inria, Grenoble INP, LIG, 38000 Grenoble, France
[3] University of Manchester, Manchester, UK

Abstract. We review the first five years of the international Competition on Runtime Verification (CRV), which began in 2014. Runtime verification focuses on verifying system executions directly and is a useful lightweight technique to complement static verification techniques. The competition has gone through a number of changes since its introduction, which we highlight in this paper.

1 Introduction

Runtime verification (RV) is a class of lightweight scalable techniques for the analysis of system executions [5,7,17,18]. The field of RV is broad and encompasses many techniques. The competition has considered a significant subset of techniques concerned with the analysis of user-provided specifications, where executions are checked against a property expressed in a formal specification language. The core idea of RV is to instrument a software/hardware system so that it can emit events during its execution. The sequence of such events (the so-called trace) is then processed by a monitor that is automatically generated from the specification. One usually distinguishes online from offline monitoring, depending on whether the monitor runs with the system or post-mortem (and thus collects events from a trace).

In 2014, we observed that, in spite of the growing number of RV tools developed over the previous decade, there was a lack of standard benchmark suites as well as scientific evaluation methods to validate and test new techniques. This observation motivated the promotion of a venue[1] dedicated to comparing and evaluating RV tools in the form of a competition. The Competition on Runtime Verification (CRV) was established as a yearly event in 2014 and has been organized as a satellite event of the RV conference since then [4,6,19,32,33].

---

[1] https://www.rv-competition.org/.

This work was partially supported by the Austrian FWF-funded National Research Network RiSE/SHiNE S11405-N23 and ADynNet project (P28182).

D. Beyer et al. (Eds.): TACAS 2019, Part III, LNCS 11429, pp. 41–49, 2019.
https://doi.org/10.1007/978-3-030-17502-3_3

Over the last five years, the competition has helped to shape the development of new tools and evaluation methods but the broad objectives of the competitions remain the same. CRV aims to:

- stimulate the development of new efficient and practical runtime verification tools and the maintenance of the already developed ones;
- produce benchmark suites for runtime verification tools, by sharing case studies and programs that researchers and developers can use in the future to test and to validate their prototypes;
- discuss the metrics employed for comparing the tools;
- compare different aspects of the tools running with different benchmarks and evaluating them using different criteria;
- enhance the visibility of presented tools among different communities (verification, software engineering, distributed computing and cyber-security) involved in monitoring.

Related Work. Over the last two decades, we have witnessed the establishment of several software tool competitions [1,3,9,22–24,34] with the goal of advancing the state-of-the-art in the computer-aided verification technology.

In particular, in the area of software verification, there are three related competitions: SV-COMP [9], VerifyThis [23] and the RERS Challenge [22].

SV-COMP targets tools for software model checking, while CRV is dedicated to monitoring tools analyzing only a single program's execution using runtime and offline verification techniques. While in software model checking the verification process is separated from the program execution, runtime verification tools introduce instead an overhead for the monitored program and they consume memory resources affecting the execution of the program itself. As a consequence CRV assigns a score to both the overhead and the memory utilization. Another related series of competitions are VerifyThis [23] and the *Rigorous Examination of Reactive Systems (RERS)* challenge [22] that provide to the participants verification problems to be solved. On the contrary of CRV format, these competitions are problem centred and focus on the problem solving skills of the participants rather than on the tool characteristics and performance.

In the remainder of this paper, we discuss the early years of the competition during 2014–2016 (Sect. 2), the activities held in 2017 and 2018 that have shifted the focus of the competition (Sect. 3), and what the future holds for the competition in 2019 and beyond (Sect. 4).

2   The Early Years: 2014–2016

The early competition was organized into three different tracks: (1) offline monitoring, (2) online monitoring of C programs, and (3) online monitoring of Java programs. The competition spanned over several months before the announcement of results during the conference. The competition consisted of the following steps:

1. **Registration** collected information about participants.
2. **Benchmark Phase.** In this phase, participants submitted benchmarks to be considered for inclusion in the competition.

Table 1. Participants in CRV between 2014 and 2016.

Offline Track	Online C Track	Online Java Track
AgMon [26]	E-ACSL [14]	JavaMOP [25]
BeepBeep3 [20]	MarQ [2]	JUnitRV [13]
Breach	RiTHM-1 [29]	Larva [10]
CRL [31]	RTC [28]	MarQ [2]
LogFire [21]	RV-Monitor [27]	Mufin [12]
MonPoly [8]	TimeSquare [11]	RV-Monitor [27]
MarQ [2]		
OCLR-Check [16]		
OptySim [15]		
RiTHM-2 [29]		
RV-Monitor [27]		

3. **Clarification Phase.** The benchmarks resulting from the previous phase were made available to participants. This phase gave participants an opportunity to seek clarifications from the authors of each benchmark. Only benchmarks that had all clarifications dealt with by the end of this phase were eligible for the next phase.
4. **Monitor Phase.** In this phase, participants were asked to produce monitors for the eligible benchmarks. Monitors had to be runnable via a script on a Linux system. Monitor code should be generated from the participant's tool (therefore the tool had to be installable on a Linux system).
5. **Evaluation Phase.** Submissions from the previous phase were collected and executed, with relevant data collected to compute scores as described later. Participants were given an opportunity to test their submissions on the evaluation system. The outputs produced during the evaluation phase were made available after the competition.

Input Formats. The competition organizers fixed input formats for traces in the offline track. These were based on XML, JSON, and CSV and evolved between the first and second years of the competition based on feedback from participants. The CSV format proved the most popular for its simplicity and is now used by many RV tools. See the competition report from 2015 [19] for details.

Participants. Over the first three years of the competition 14 different RV tools competed in the competition in the different tracks. These are summarized in Table 1. One of these tools, Mufin, was written specifically in response to the competition and all tools were extended or modified to handle the challenges introduced by the competition.

Benchmarks. Benchmarks, as submitted by the participants, should adhere to requirements that ensured compliance with the later phases of the competition. This also ensured uniformity between benchmarks and was also the first step in building a benchmark repository dedicated to Runtime Verification. A benchmark contains two packages: a program/source package and a specification package. The program/source package includes the traces or the source of the program as well as scripts to compile and run it. In these early years of the competition, we chose to focus on closed, terminating and deterministic programs. The specification package includes an informal and a formal description (in some logical formalism), the instrumentation information (i.e., what in the program influences the truth-value of the specification), and the verdict (i.e., how the specification evaluates w.r.t. the program or trace).

In these three competitions, over 100 benchmarks were submitted and evaluated. All benchmarks are available from the competition website[2] organized in a repository for each year.

Evaluation Criteria/Scores. Submissions from the participants were evaluated on correctness and performance. For this purpose, we designed an algorithm that uses as inputs (i) the verdicts produced by each tool over each benchmark (ii) the execution time and memory consumption in doing so, and produces as output a score reflecting the evaluation of the tool regarding correctness and performance (the higher, the better). Correctness criteria included (i) finding the expected verdict, absence of crash, and the possibility of expressing the benchmark specification in the tool formalism. Performance criteria were based on the classical time and memory overheads (lower is better) with the addition that the score of a participant accounts for the performance of the other participants (e.g., given the execution time of a participant, more points would be given if the other participants performed poorly) using the harmonic mean. Tools were evaluated against performance, only when they produced a correct result (negative points were given to incorrect results). A benchmark score was assigned for each tool against each submitted benchmark, and the tool final score was the sum of all its benchmark scores. A participant could decide not to compete on a benchmark and would get a zero score for this benchmark.

Experimental Environment, Availability, Reproducibility, Quality. Git-based repositories and wiki pages were provided to the participants to share their benchmarks and submissions. This facilitated the communication and ensured transparency. To run the experiments, we used DataMill [30], to ensure robust

---

[2] https://www.rv-competition.org/benchmarks/.

and reproducible experiments. We selected the most powerful and general-purpose machine and evaluated all submissions on this machine. DataMill ensured flexibility and fairness in the experiments. Benchmarks could be setup and submitted via a Web interface and then be scheduled for execution. DataMill ensured that only one monitor was running on the machine at a time, in addition to a minimalist operating system, cleaned between each experiments. Execution times and memory consumption measures were obtained by averaging 10 executions. Results were available through the Web interface.

Table 2. Winners of CRV between 2014 and 2016.

Year	Offline Track	Online C Track	Online Java Track
2014	MarQ	RiTHM-1	MarQ & JavaMOP (joint)
2015	LogFire	E-ACSL	Mufin
2016	MarQ	-	Mufin

Winners. Table 2 indicates the winners in each track in each year. The detailed results are available from the competition website and associated reports [4, 6, 19]. In 2014, the scores in the Online Java track were so close that a joint winner was announced. In 2016, only one participant entered the C track and the track was not run. (We note that, more tools have been developed for monitoring Java programs thanks to the AspectJ support for instrumentation.)

Issues. The early years of the competition were successful in encouraging RV tool developers to agree on common formats but the number of participants dropped in each year with two main issues identified:

1. The amount of work required to enter was high. This was mainly due to the need to translate each benchmark into the specification language of the entered tool. Common specification languages would address this problem but there was no agreement on such languages at the time.
2. It was not clear how good the benchmarks were at differentiating tools. More work was required to understand which benchmarks were useful for evaluating RV tools.

The next two years of activities addressed these issues as described below.

3   Shifting Focus: 2017–2018

In 2017, the competition was replaced by a workshop (called RV-CuBES) [33] aimed at reflecting on the experiences of the last three years and discussing future directions. A workshop was chosen over a competition as there was strong feedback from participants in 2016 that the format of the competition should be revised (mainly to reduce the amount of work required by participants). It was decided that this was a good opportunity to reassess the format of the competition in an open setting. The workshop attracted 12 tool description papers and 5 position papers and led to useful discussion at the 2017 RV conference. A full account can be found in the associated report.

A suggestion of the workshop was to hold a benchmark challenge focusing on collecting relevant new benchmarks. Therefore, in 2018 a benchmark challenge was held with a track for Metric Temporal Logic (MTL) properties and an Open track. The purpose of the MTL track was to see what happened when participants were restricted to a single input language whilst the Open track gave full freedom on the choice of the specification language.

There were two submissions in the MTL track and seven in the Open track. The submissions in the Open track were generally in much more expressive languages than MTL and no two submissions used the same specification language. All submissions were evaluated by a panel of experts and awarded on qualities in three categories: (1) correctness and reliability (2) realism and challenge and (3) utility in evaluation. As a result of the evaluation two benchmark sets were identified for use in future competitions (see below).

4   Back to the Future

The 2019 competition is now in its initial stages and will return to a competition comparing tools, using the benchmarks from the 2018 challenge. The competition will use two specification languages: MTL and a future-time first-order temporal logic. We have chosen to fix two specification languages (with differing levels of expressiveness) to reduce the overall work for participants. Standardising the specification language of the competition has been a goal of the competition from the start and the benchmark challenge has allowed us to pick two good candidates. MTL was chosen as it can be considered a 'smallest shared' specification language in terms of expressiveness and usage. Similarly, the future-time first-order temporal logic was chosen as it can be considered a 'largest shared' specification language in terms of expressiveness and usage.

Beyond 2019, there are many opportunities to take the competition in different directions. For example, a key issue in RV is that of specifications. Thus, when organizing a competition, one may wonder whether a competition could also focus on evaluating aspects related to specifications (e.g., expressiveness, succinctness and elegance of specifications). Moreover, in so far, the competition has neglected the area of hardware monitoring, and the comparison of tools in such domains remains an open question. We note that there have been less research efforts on monitoring hardware where instrumentation aspects are more challenging. The main reasons for common specification languages not being used in the early years stemmed from two facts: (i) a main research activity in RV consists in developing new languages to have alternative representation of problems (ii) the monitoring algorithm of an RV tool is often closely coupled to the input language. Hence, a challenge is to rely on a shared specification language whilst encouraging research that explores the relationship between input language and performance or usability.

Acknowledgements. The authors would like to thank the anonymous reviewers for their helpful comments and all the colleagues involved in CRV over the last years (B. Bonakdarpour, D. Thoma, D. Nickovic, S. Hallé, K. Y. Rozier, and V. Stolz).

References

1. Barrett, C., Deters, M., de Moura, L.M., Oliveras, A., Stump, A.: 6 Years of SMT-COMP. J. Autom. Reasoning **50**(3), 243–277 (2013)
2. Barringer, H., Falcone, Y., Havelund, K., Reger, G., Rydeheard, D.: Quantified event automata: towards expressive and efficient runtime monitors. In: Giannakopoulou, D., Méry, D. (eds.) FM 2012. LNCS, vol. 7436, pp. 68–84. Springer, Heidelberg (2012). https://doi.org/10.1007/978-3-642-32759-9_9
3. Bartocci, E., et al.: TOOLympics 2019: an overview of competitions in formal methods. In: Beyer, D., Huisman, M., Kordon, F., Steffen, B. (eds.) TACAS 2019, Part III. LNCS, vol. 11429, pp. 3–24. Springer, Cham (2019)
4. Bartocci, E., Bonakdarpour, B., Falcone, Y.: First international competition on software for runtime verification. In: Bonakdarpour, B., Smolka, S.A. (eds.) RV 2014. LNCS, vol. 8734, pp. 1–9. Springer, Cham (2014). https://doi.org/10.1007/978-3-319-11164-3_1
5. Bartocci, E., Falcone, Y. (eds.): Lectures on Runtime Verification - Introductory and Advanced Topics. LNCS, vol. 10457. Springer, Cham (2018). https://doi.org/10.1007/978-3-319-75632-5
6. Bartocci, E., et al.: First international competition on runtime verification: rules, benchmarks, tools, and final results of CRV 2014. Int. J. Softw. Tools Technol. Transfer **21**, 31–70 (2019)
7. Bartocci, E., Falcone, Y., Francalanza, A., Reger, G.: Introduction to runtime verification. In: Bartocci, E., Falcone, Y. (eds.) Lectures on Runtime Verification. LNCS, vol. 10457, pp. 1–33. Springer, Cham (2018). https://doi.org/10.1007/978-3-319-75632-5_1
8. Basin, D., Harvan, M., Klaedtke, F., Zălinescu, E.: MONPOLY: monitoring usage-control policies. In: Khurshid, S., Sen, K. (eds.) RV 2011. LNCS, vol. 7186, pp. 360–364. Springer, Heidelberg (2012). https://doi.org/10.1007/978-3-642-29860-8_27
9. Beyer, D.: Software verification and verifiable witnesses - (report on SV-COMP 2015). In: Baier, C., Tinelli, C. (eds.) TACAS 2015. LNCS, vol. 9035, pp. 401–416. Springer, Heidelberg (2015). https://doi.org/10.1007/978-3-662-46681-0_31
10. Colombo, C., Pace, G.J., Schneider, G.: Larva — safer monitoring of real-time java programs (tool paper). In: Van Hung, D., Krishnan, P. (eds.) Seventh IEEE International Conference on Software Engineering and Formal Methods, SEFM 2009, Hanoi, Vietnam, 23–27 November 2009, pp. 33–37. IEEE Computer Society (2009). https://doi.org/10.1109/SEFM.2009.13. ISBN 978-0-7695-3870-9
11. DeAntoni, J., Mallet, F.: TimeSquare: treat your models with logical time. In: Furia, C.A., Nanz, S. (eds.) TOOLS 2012. LNCS, vol. 7304, pp. 34–41. Springer, Heidelberg (2012). https://doi.org/10.1007/978-3-642-30561-0_4
12. Decker, N., Harder, J., Scheffel, T., Schmitz, M., Thoma, D.: Runtime monitoring with union-find structures. In: Chechik, M., Raskin, J.-F. (eds.) TACAS 2016. LNCS, vol. 9636, pp. 868–884. Springer, Heidelberg (2016). https://doi.org/10.1007/978-3-662-49674-9_54

13. Decker, N., Leucker, M., Thoma, D.: jUnit^{RV}–adding runtime verification to jUnit. In: Brat, G., Rungta, N., Venet, A. (eds.) NFM 2013. LNCS, vol. 7871, pp. 459–464. Springer, Heidelberg (2013). https://doi.org/10.1007/978-3-642-38088-4_34

14. Delahaye, M., Kosmatov, N., Signoles, J.: Common specification language for static and dynamic analysis of C programs. In: Proceedings of SAC 2013: The 28th Annual ACM Symposium on Applied Computing, pp. 1230–1235. ACM, March 2013

15. Díaz, A., Merino, P., Salmeron, A.: Obtaining models for realistic mobile network simulations using real traces. IEEE Commun. Lett. **15**(7), 782–784 (2011)

16. Dou, W., Bianculli, D., Briand, L.: A model-driven approach to offline trace checking of temporal properties with OCL. Technical report SnT-TR-2014-5, Interdisciplinary Centre for Security, Reliability and Trust (2014)

17. Falcone, Y.: You should better enforce than verify. In: Barringer, H., et al. (eds.) RV 2010. LNCS, vol. 6418, pp. 89–105. Springer, Heidelberg (2010). https://doi.org/10.1007/978-3-642-16612-9_9

18. Falcone, Y., Havelund, K., Reger, G.: A tutorial on runtime verification. In: Broy, M., Peled, D.A., Kalus, G. (eds.) Engineering Dependable Software Systems. NATO Science for Peace and Security Series, D: Information and Communication Security, vol. 34, pp. 141–175. IOS Press (2013)

19. Falcone, Y., Ničković, D., Reger, G., Thoma, D.: Second international competition on runtime verification. In: Bartocci, E., Majumdar, R. (eds.) RV 2015. LNCS, vol. 9333, pp. 405–422. Springer, Cham (2015). https://doi.org/10.1007/978-3-319-23820-3_27

20. Hallé, S.: When RV Meets CEP. In: Falcone, Y., Sánchez, C. (eds.) RV 2016. LNCS, vol. 10012, pp. 68–91. Springer, Cham (2016). https://doi.org/10.1007/978-3-319-46982-9_6

21. Havelund, K.: Rule-based runtime verification revisited. STTT **17**(2), 143–170 (2015). https://doi.org/10.1007/s10009-014-0309-2

22. Howar, F., Isberner, M., Merten, M., Steffen, B., Beyer, D., Pasareanu, C.S.: Rigorous examination of reactive systems - the RERS challenges 2012 and 2013. STTT **16**(5), 457–464 (2014)

23. Huisman, M., Klebanov, V., Monahan, R.: Verifythis 2012 - a program verification competition. STTT **17**(6), 647–657 (2015)

24. Järvisalo, M., Berre, D.L., Roussel, O., Simon, L.: The international SAT solver competitions. AI Mag. **33**(1), 89–92 (2012)

25. Jin, D., Meredith, P.O., Lee, C., Roşu, G.: JavaMOP: efficient parametric runtime monitoring framework. In: Proceedings of ICSE 2012: The 34th International Conference on Software Engineering, Zurich, Switzerland, 2–9 June, pp. 1427–1430. IEEE Press (2012)

26. Kane, A., Fuhrman, T.E., Koopman, P.: Monitor based oracles for cyber-physical system testing: practical experience report. In: 44th Annual IEEE/IFIP International Conference on Dependable Systems and Networks, DSN 2014, Atlanta, GA, USA, 23–26 June 2014, pp. 148–155. IEEE (2014)

27. Luo, Q., et al.: RV-monitor: efficient parametric runtime verification with simultaneous properties. In: Proceedings of Runtime Verification - 5th International Conference, RV 2014, Toronto, ON, Canada, 22–25 September 2014, pp. 285–300 (2014)

28. Milewicz, R., Vanka, R., Tuck, J., Quinlan, D., Pirkelbauer, P.: Runtime checking C programs. In: Proceedings of the 30th Annual ACM Symposium on Applied Computing, pp. 2107–2114. ACM (2015)

29. Navabpour, S., et al.: RiTHM: a tool for enabling time-triggered runtime verification for C programs. In: ACM Symposium on the Foundations of Software Engineering (FSE), pp. 603–606 (2013)
30. Petkovich, J., de Oliveira, A.B., Zhang, Y., Reidemeister, T., Fischmeister, S.: Datamill: a distributed heterogeneous infrastructure for robust experimentation. Softw. Pract. Exper. **46**(10), 1411–1440 (2016)
31. Piel, A.: Reconnaissance de comportements complexes par traitement en ligne de flux d'événements. (Online event flow processing for complex behaviour recognition). Ph.D. thesis, Paris 13 University, Villetaneuse, Saint-Denis, Bobigny, France (2014)
32. Reger, G., Hallé, S., Falcone, Y.: Third international competition on runtime verification. In: Falcone, Y., Sánchez, C. (eds.) RV 2016. LNCS, vol. 10012, pp. 21–37. Springer, Cham (2016). https://doi.org/10.1007/978-3-319-46982-9_3
33. Reger, G., Havelund, K. (eds.): RV-CuBES 2017. An International Workshop on Competitions, Usability, Benchmarks, Evaluation, and Standardisation for Runtime Verification Tools. Kalpa Publications in Computing, vol. 3. EasyChair (2017)
34. Sutcliffe, G.: The 5th IJCAR automated theorem proving system competition - CASC-J5. AI Commun. **24**(1), 75–89 (2011)

Presentation of the 9th Edition
of the Model Checking Contest

Elvio Amparore[1,11], Bernard Berthomieu[2,11], Gianfranco Ciardo[3,11],
Silvano Dal Zilio[2,11], Francesco Gallà[1,11], Lom Messan Hillah[4,5,11],
Francis Hulin-Hubard[4,11], Peter Gjøl Jensen[6,11], Loïg Jezequel[7,11],
Fabrice Kordon[4,11(✉)], Didier Le Botlan[2,11], Torsten Liebke[8,11],
Jeroen Meijer[9,11], Andrew Miner[3,11], Emmanuel Paviot-Adet[4,9,11],
Jiří Srba[6,10,11], Yann Thierry-Mieg[4,11], Tom van Dijk[9,11], and Karsten Wolf[8,11]

[1] Università degli Studi di Torino, Turin, Italy
[2] LAAS-CNRS, Université de Toulouse, CNRS, INSA, Toulouse, France
[3] Department of Computer Science, Iowa State University, Ames, USA
[4] Sorbonne Université, CNRS, LIP6, 75005 Paris, France
fabrice.kordon@lip6.fr
[5] Université Paris Nanterre, 92001 Nanterre, France
[6] Department of Computer Science, Aalborg University, Aalborg, Denmark
[7] Université de Nantes, LS2N, UMR CNRS 6597, 44321 Nantes, France
[8] Institut für Informatik, Universität Rostock, 18051 Rostock, Germany
[9] Université Paris Descartes, 75005 Paris, France
[10] FI MU, Brno, Czech Republic
[11] Formal Methods and Tools, University of Twente, Enschede, The Netherlands

Abstract. The Model Checking Contest (MCC) is an annual competition of software tools for model checking. Tools must process an increasing benchmark gathered from the whole community and may participate in various examinations: state space generation, computation of global properties, computation of some upper bounds in the model, evaluation of reachability formulas, evaluation of CTL formulas, and evaluation of LTL formulas.

For each examination and each model instance, participating tools are provided with up to 3600s and 16 gigabyte of memory. Then, tool answers are analyzed and confronted to the results produced by other competing tools to detect diverging answers (which are quite rare at this stage of the competition, and lead to penalties).

For each examination, golden, silver, and bronze medals are attributed to the three best tools. CPU usage and memory consumption are reported, which is also valuable information for tool developers.

Keywords: Competition · Model checking · State space ·
Reachability formulas · CTL formulas · LTL formulas

© The Author(s) 2019
D. Beyer et al. (Eds.): TACAS 2019, Part III, LNCS 11429, pp. 50–68, 2019.
https://doi.org/10.1007/978-3-030-17502-3_4

1 Introduction

The primary goal of the Model Checking Contest (MCC) is to evaluate model-checking tools that are dedicated to the formal analysis of concurrent systems, in which several processes run simultaneously, communicate and synchronize together. The Model Checking Contest has been actively growing since its first edition in 2011, attracting key people sharing a formal methods background, but with diverse knowledge and application areas.

Table 1. All the 26 tools which participated over the 9 editions of the Model Checking Contest (the 2019 edition is not yet completed when this paper is written). Years of Involvement are noted with a colored cell.

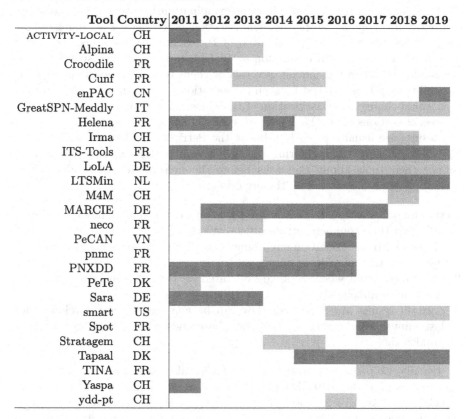

Tool	Country	2011	2012	2013	2014	2015	2016	2017	2018	2019
ACTIVITY-LOCAL	CH									
Alpina	CH									
Crocodile	FR									
Cunf	FR									
enPAC	CN									
GreatSPN-Meddly	IT									
Helena	FR									
Irma	CH									
ITS-Tools	FR									
LoLA	DE									
LTSMin	NL									
M4M	CH									
MARCIE	DE									
neco	FR									
PeCAN	VN									
pnmc	FR									
PNXDD	FR									
PeTe	DK									
Sara	DE									
smart	US									
Spot	FR									
Stratagem	CH									
Tapaal	DK									
TINA	FR									
Yaspa	CH									
ydd-pt	CH									

Contributors of models to the benchmarks, tools developers, and the organizers of the MCC are actively involved in meaningful activities that foster the growth of the MCC year after year:

- they contribute to the elaboration of the benchmark by regularly providing specifications to be processed. We currently have 88 models, many having scaling parameters for a total of 951 instances;

– they enrich their tools with new features and strategies, often using inputs from previous editions of the MCC.

So far, all editions of the MCC have been using the standardized description format for Petri nets to describe the analyzed systems: PNML [24]. PNML is an ISO/IEC standard that is suitable to describe concurrent systems. The MCC could appear as being a "Petri net-oriented" competition. However, we observe that several tools coming from other communities were able to read and exploit this input format with non-Petri net-based verification engines in a very efficient way. We observe a regular arriving of new tools together with others that participate for many years. Table 1 summarizes the participating tools over the years.

This year we propose the following examinations: state space generation, computation of global properties, computation of 16 queries with regards to upper bounds in the model, evaluation of 16 reachability formulas, evaluation of 16 CTL formulas, and evaluation of 16 LTL formulas. Since such formulas are randomly generated, having severals of them to be processed reduces the possibility of a bias induced by such a generation (e.g. a single "easy" formula that would change the classification of tools) Details on organizational issues of the recent editions of the MCC are presented in [28].

Results are usually presented during the Petri Net conference, and, for the 25th TACAS anniversary, during the TOOLympics. Developer teams usually submit their tools about 2 months before the presentation of results. Then, several phases are operated by the organizers:

1. the "qualification phase" that is processed on a reduced set of models and with a limited time confinement; its objective is to check for the interoperability of tools with the execution environment so that no mistake could result in a misuse of the tool or its results;
2. the contest itself where tools are operated on the full benchmark with the real time confinement;
3. once all results are processed, they can be analyzed by the developers for last minute validity checks, this last phase ends when results are officially published.

Usually, we present the results of the MCC[1] alongside the Petri Net conference in June. For the 2019 edition of the MCC, we are joining the TOOLympics to celebrate TACAS's 25th anniversary. The goal is also to enable discussions between organizers and participants of all the verification competitions involved in this event.

---

[1] See the full history of results on https://mcc.lip6.fr.

2   Participating Tools

This section presents a short description of all the tools which identified the MCC as a target and were able to provide a short description of their tools and the features they will experiment this year. Note that more participating tools have shown interest in the MCC, but their authors could not provide such a description. This is the case of enPAC[2] for its first participation this year.

2.1   GreatSPN

GreatSPN [3] is an open source framework[3] for modeling and analyzing Petri nets, which includes several tools accessible either through a common graphical interface [2], with a mode of interaction that was recently re-designed to support teaching [5], or through in-line commands for expert users. With GreatSPN the user can draw Petri nets (place/transition nets, colored nets and their stochastic variations) interactively, can compute (and visualize) the RG explicitly or symbolically, can analyze net properties (both qualitative and stochastic), can solve stochastic and Ordinary differential equations/Stochastic differential equations (ODE/SDE) systems, and can model-check CTL logic properties as well as performing stochastic model checking for properties defined using automata (the CSL^{TA} logic), and other advanced features. Among the various tools, the framework offers a symbolic model checker called RGMEDD. This tool generates the state space of a Petri net using Multivalued Decision Diagrams (MDD) and implements a CTL model checker with counter-example generation. The implementation of the MDD data structure is based on the highly-optimized Meddly library [7].

Main Features of GreatSPN. The symbolic model checker of GreatSPN participates in the MCC'2019 competition for StateSpace generation, deadlock search and CTL model checking for both P/T and colored nets. The model evaluation strategy consists of the following main steps:

1. *Translation phase*: a set of support tools convert the PNML model, the NUPN[4] metadata and the CTL formulas into the internal format of Great-SPN. Colored (symmetric) models are unfolded to their corresponding P/T models.
2. *Property computation phase*: several model properties are determined, including the set of minimal P-semiflows, the basis of the P-flows, the place bounds derived from the P-semiflows and the bounds derived using an ILP solver.
3. *Variable order determination*: a set of heuristics try to determine a reasonable set of (static) variable orders for the encoding of the input model. Multiple variable orders can be used at once.

---

[2] https://github.com/tvtaqa/enPAC.

[3] https://github.com/greatspn/SOURCES.

[4] NUPN [22] stands for Nested Unit Petri Nets, this is a way to carry out structural and hierarchical information about the structure of the modeled system.

4. *State space generation*: the reachability set (RS) is generated using MDDs, employing a set of different techniques (provided by the Meddly library): event saturation with chaining, on-the-fly saturation and coverability set generation (which allows to detect infinite state spaces for a class of models).
5. *Property assessment*: deadlock and CTL properties are then determined starting from the generated RS. No attempt at model reduction or formula simplification are actually implemented.

The pipeline of GreatSPN is optimized for compact MDD generation (StateSpace examinations). Currently, neither LTL nor CTL* are implemented.

Main Strength of GreatSPN. We believe that GreatSPN is fairly good in both building the state space (using the highly optimized saturation implementations of Meddly) and in finding a reasonably good variable order for the encoding a given model. In our experience, the variable order has a large impact on the tool performance. GreatSPN implements a large library of heuristics [6] to generate candidate variable orders, with about 30 base algorithms, plus several transformation heuristics (generate a new order given a starting one). This collection of algorithms allows the tool to generate a pool of orders among which a meta-heuristic can choose.

A second strength, again related to variable order, is the availability of a library of several *metrics*, i.e. heuristic functions that tries to evaluate the goodness of a variable order without building the MDD. Metrics are crucial in the design of reliable meta-heuristics.

In the two past years, GreatSPN was ranked gold for the StateSpace examination as wall as gold and bronze for the UpperBound examination.

New Features Introduced in GreatSPN for the MCC'2019. Over the last years we collected a large experience in variable order evaluation, which ended in the design of a new highly correlating metric [4] called i_{Rank} that will be used in the MCC'2019.

The i_{Rank} metric combines the count of the unique and non-productive spans of the incidence matrix (SOUPS), which accounts for places that affects many levels of the MDD, with an estimate of the number of variable dependencies to be recorded by the MDD at each single level (for a given order). This last estimate is extracted from the basis of the P-flows. The i_{Rank} metric shows very high correlation between its value and the final MDD size: on a test benchmark [4] i_{Rank} got a correlation of 0.96, while the previously best known metrics (SOUPS and PTS) had a correlation of 0.77 and 0.67, respectively. As a consequence, GreatSPN should have a very high chance of taking a good variable order as a first guess for a very large number of models. For the MCC'2019 the tool also features a new *multiple order evaluation* strategy, that selects and builds the MDD for more than one variable order, further reducing the probability of selecting a bad order.

For now the technique is sequential and single-threaded. We believe that this strategy make the tool very robust in handling general Petri net models, avoiding the risk of sticking to an unlucky (but not impossible) choice for the MDD order.

2.2   ITS-Tools

ITS-tools [34] is a model-checker supporting both multiple solution engines and multiple formalisms using an intermediate pivot called the Guarded Action Language (GAL). Both colored models and P/T models are translated to GAL. GAL models are more expressive than Petri nets, and support arithmetic and hierarchical descriptions. ITS-Tools is composed of a user-friendly front-end embedded in Eclipse, and of a command line solution back-end.

Main Features of ITS-Tools. ITS-Tools uses a powerful symbolic solution engine based on Hierarchical Set Decision Diagrams (SDD) [16]. SDD are shared decision diagrams where edges are labeled with a *set* of values. Since decision diagrams compactly represent a set, this allows to introduce hierarchy in the representation, and enables sharing of substructures of the diagram (different edges of the SDD labeled by the same set share their representation).

While this adds a new problem (find a good decomposition of the system) to the classical problem of variable ordering in DD, in many cases there exist SDD representations that are an order of magnitude smaller than the equivalent flat DD. This allows the tool to scale to very large state space sizes. The engine benefits greatly from modular decomposition of the model, either using NUPN [22] information or inferring hierarchy automatically (using Louvain decomposition). All examinations are supported on this symbolic engine.

ITS-tools further leverages two additional solution engines: LTSmin (which is also competing) and features powerful partial order reduction methods, and a SAT modulo theory (SMT) engine currently only used for reachability queries. A new component was introduced in 2018 that performs structural reductions of the input Petri net, using variants of classical pre/post agglomerations rules.

The combination of these complementary engines helps us to solve more problems from diverse categories of models.

Main Strength of ITS-Tools. The main strength of ITS-tools is its overall robustness and capacity to scale well to very large state spaces. The symbolic engine, developed over the course of a decade includes state of the art data structures and algorithms, specialized and tuned for model-checking.

For place bounds and reachability queries the combination of structural reductions with three solution engines (LTSmin+POR, SDD, SMT) covers a large set of models. For CTL, ITS-tools operate a translation to a forward CTL formula when possible, and use variants of constrained saturation to deal with EU and EG operators. ITS-Tools use a general yet precise symbolic invert to deal with predecessor relationships when translation to forward form is not feasible. The symbolic invert computes predecessor relationships, and needs to deal with models that are "lossy" (e.g. assign zero to a variable, what are the predecessor states?). It starts with an over-approximation computed by supposing that the Cartesian product of variable domains are all reachable states. If necessary (i.e. not for Petri nets) this approximation is refined by intersecting with the reachable set of states computed forward.

For LTL, ITS-tools rely on Spot [21] to translate the properties to Büchi variants, then use the LTSmin engine (with POR) or our SLAP hybrid algorithm [20] to perform the emptiness check. This algorithm leverages both the desirable on-the-fly properties of explicit techniques and the support for very large Kripke structures (state spaces) thanks to the symbolic SDD back-end. All symbolic operations benefit from state-of-the-art saturation variants when it is possible.

Over the last four editions of the MCC, ITS-Tools was always in the podium for the StateSpace examination (bronze to gold), the UpperBound examination (bronze and silver). It was 3 times in the podium (bronze and silver) for the Reachability formulas and CTL formulas (bronze and silver) as well as in the LTL formulas (bronze and silver).

New Features Introduced in ITS-Tools for the MCC'2019. Recent development in the tool focused on improving variable order choices, leveraging recent work by the GreatSPN team, and improving automatic decomposition heuristics (using Louvain modularity as a general scalable solution). Further developments concern improvements of the structural reductions, and integration of structural reductions at formula level for CTL leveraging recent work by Tapaal team.

Further information on the tool, as well as sources and installation procedure, is available from http://ddd.lip6.fr.

2.3   LoLA

LoLA (A Low Level Analyser, [36]) is a model checker for Petri nets. It supports place/transition nets as well as high-level Petri nets. Input may be given in a dedicated LoLA format (place/transition nets), or in the markup language PNML (both net classes). Supported properties include the temporal logics LTL and CTL as well as queries for upper bounds for token counts on places.

LoLA is an open source tool written in C++. It is being developed since 1998. It is available at http://service-technology.org/tools. It is purely based on command-line interaction and can be integrated as a backend tool for a modeling platform.

Main Features of LoLA. LoLA mainly uses standard explicit model checking algorithms for verification. At several stages, however, elements of Petri net theory (the state equation, invariants, siphons and traps, conflict clusters) are employed for acceleration of the algorithms. Theorems of Petri net theory are used in a portfolio approach in addition to the state space based model checking procedures wherever applicable. LoLA can apply several state space reduction methods, including partial order reduction (the stubborn set method), symmetry reduction, the sweep-line method, Karp/Miller graph construction, and bloom filtering. It has several available methods for coding markings (states).

Inputs and results can be exchanged via the UNIX standard streams. In addition, LoLA can provide results in a structured way using the JSON format.

Main Strength of LoLA. LoLA offers one of the largest collections of stubborn set dialects. For many classes of properties, a dedicated stubborn set method is applied. In addition, several classes of simple queries are solved using dedicated search routines instead of the generic model checking procedure. Assignment of a correct stubborn set dialect is based on a categorisation of the query. If more than one dialect is available, command-line parameters can be used to select one.

For symmetry reduction, LoLA automatically computes a generating set of the automorphism group of the Petri net graph representation. This way, the user does not need to exhibit the symmetries in the model in any way, and the largest possible number of symmetries is used. LoLA computes the symmetries such that the given query is preserved by the reduction.

LoLA uses a large set of rewriting rules for simplifying queries. It can detect more than 100 tautologies of the temporal logics LTL and CTL. Moreover, it uses the Petri net state equation, invariants, and traps for checking whether an atomic proposition is always true or false.

When the sweep-line method is applied, LoLA automatically computes a progress measure that is a pre-requisite for applying that method. The method can thus be applied in push-button style.

The way LoLA offers the reported features includes several original ideas and methods. Many reduction techniques can be combined, making LoLA one of the most competitive model checking tools for Petri nets.

New Features Introduced in LoLA for the MCC'2019. For the MCC'2019, LoLA will extend its portfolios for several property classes. We add an evaluation of the state equation to properties where reachability or invariance of some state predicate is sufficient or necessary for the original query. Furthermore, we shall run two state space explorations in parallel for queries where more than one stubborn set dialect is available. This way, we aim at exploiting the fact that some properties have a stubborn set dialect that performs extremely well for satisfiable queries, and another dialect that works better for unsatisfiable queries. To avoid competition between the two searches concerning memory, the search speculating for satisfaction (i.e. profiting from the on-the-fly model checking effect) gets a severe memory restriction. It will be killed upon overflow on the assigned memory thus eventually leaving all available memory to the search that speculates for violation (and needs to explore all of the reduced state space).

2.4   LTSmin

LTSmin[5] [27] has competed in the MCC since 2015. Already in the first editions, LTSmin participated in several subcategories, while since 2017 LTSmin competes in all subcategories, except for colored Petri nets, and reporting the number of fireable transitions in the marking graph.

For the MCC of this year, LTSmin only competes in the StateSpace and UpperBounds categories, as the tool is now equipped with a fully parallelized symbolic saturation algorithm for computing the state space. Otherwise the tool is relatively unchanged compared to last year, so we restrict the tool to only demonstrate the new techniques.

Main Features of LTSmin. LTSmin has been designed as a language independent model checker. This allowed us to reuse algorithms that were already used for other languages, such as Promela and mCRL2. For the MCC, we only needed to implement a PNML front-end and translate the MCC formula syntax. Improvements to the model checking algorithms, like handling integers in atomic formulas, can now in principle also be used in other languages.

LTSmin's main interface is called the Partitioned Interface to the Next-State function (PINS) [27]. Each PINS language front-end needs to implement the next-state function. It must also provide the initial state, and a dependency matrix (see below). The multi-core explicit-state and multi-core symbolic model checking back-ends of LTSmin use this information to compute the state space on-the-fly, i.e. new states and atomic predicates are only computed when necessary for the algorithm.

A key part of LTSmin are its dependency matrices. Dependency matrices must be precomputed statically by the front-end, and are extensively used during reachability analysis and model checking. An example Petri net, with its dependency matrix, is given in Fig. 1. Here transition t_1 does not depend on p_3 or p_1 in any way. Also for properties, a dependency matrix (computed by LTSmin) indicates on which variables each atomic predicate depends. For instance, the dependency matrix of some invariant is shown in Fig. 2. This invariant demonstrates LTSmin's native property syntax. A finer analysis that distinguishes read- and write-dependencies [30] pays off, in particular for 1-safe Petri nets.

Main Strength of LTSmin. LTSmin competes using the symbolic back-end pnml2lts-sym[6], handling enormous state spaces by employing decision diagrams. However, good variable orders are essential. LTSmin provides several algorithms to compute good variable orders, which operate on the transition dependency matrix, for instance Sloan's algorithm [31] for profile and wavefront reduction. LTSmin computes the marking graph symbolically and outputs its size.

---

[5] http://ltsmin.utwente.nl.
[6] http://ltsmin.utwente.nl/assets/man/pnml2lts-sym.html.

To compete in the UpperBounds category, LTSmin maintains the maximum sum of all tokens in all places over the marking graph. This can be restricted to a given set of places (using, e.g., $\texttt{-maxsum} = p_1 + p_2 + p_3$).

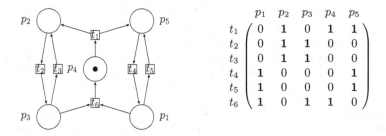

	p_1	p_2	p_3	p_4	p_5
t_1	0	1	0	1	1
t_2	0	1	1	0	0
t_3	0	1	1	0	0
t_4	1	0	0	0	1
t_5	1	0	0	0	1
t_6	1	0	1	1	0

Fig. 1. Example model: Petri net (left) and dependency matrix (right)

$$A\,G(1 \le p_2 + p_3 \land 1 \le p_5 + p_1)$$

	p_1	p_2	p_3	p_4	p_5
$1 \le p_2 + p_3$	0	1	1	0	0
$1 \le p_5 + p_1$	1	0	0	0	1

Fig. 2. Example invariant property and the dependency matrix on its atomic predicates

LTSmin is unique in the application of multi-core algorithms for symbolic model checking. In particular, both high-level algorithms (exploring the marking graph, and traversing the parse tree of the invariant), as well as low-level algorithms (decision diagram operations) are parallelized. This form of true concurrency allows LTSmin to benefit from the four CPU cores made available in the MCC, instead of a portfolio approach.

New Features Introduced in LTSmin for the MCC 2019. LTSmin is now equipped with a fully multi-core on-the-fly symbolic saturation algorithm as described in [19]. Saturation is an efficient exploration order for computing the set of reachable states symbolically. In the past, attempt to parallelize saturation only resulted in limited speedup. LTSmin now implements on-the-fly symbolic saturation using the Sylvan multi-core decision diagram package. Using the benchmarks of the MCC, we demonstrate in [19] speedups of around $3\times$ with 4 workers, which is the configuration used in the MCC. For some models we obtained superlinear speedups, even scaling to a machine with 48 cores.

2.5 SMART

SMART (Stochastic Model-checking Analyzer for Reliability and Timing) is an open-source[7] software package to study complex discrete-state systems. The SMART input language supports different types of models (non-deterministic or stochastic), described in various ways (including Petri nets, Markov chains, and Kripke structures) and with various types of queries (including temporal logic, probabilistic temporal logic, and performance measures). Models are analyzed with various back-end solution engines, including explicit and symbolic model checking, numerical solution for probabilistic model checking, and simulation.

Main Features of SMART. SMART supports Petri nets with inhibitor arcs, transition guards, and marking-dependent arc cardinalities. The input language allows users to define arrays of places and transitions, for building large Petri nets with regular structure. A specialized translation tool is used to convert PNML models into the SMART input language.

For symbolic model checking, SMART uses Multivalued Decision Diagrams (MDDs). Each Petri net place (or perhaps a set of places) is mapped to a single MDD variable. A heuristic is used to determine a variable order, as the choice of variable order is often critical to MDD efficiency. On-the-fly saturation [15] is used to generate the state space, with MDDs used to encode sets of states, and an appropriate representation used for the transition relations (either Matrix Diagrams [32] or a specialized implicit representation).

Main Strength of SMART. SMART uses MEDDLY: Multivalued and Edge-valued Decision Diagram LibrarY [7], an open-source MDD library[8], as its symbolic model checking engine. The library supports MDDs, EV^+MDDs, and EV^*MDDs natively, along with manipulation algorithms needed for CTL model checking, including saturation. Saturation is often orders of magnitude faster than a traditional breadth-first iteration for building the state space. Constrained saturation [37] can be used for efficient CTL model checking.

New Features Introduced in SMART for the MCC 2019. Gradual improvements have been made to SMART and MEDDLY over many years. The recent focus has been on eliminating bottlenecks caused by construction and storage of the Petri net transition relations, by moving to a more efficient representation utilizing implicit nodes that do not need to be updated as the state space grows. Another important area of research has been variable ordering heuristics, including the development of SOUPS (sum of unique productive spans) [33] as an estimate for the cost of transition firings.

---

[7] https://smart.cs.iastate.edu.
[8] https://asminer.github.io/meddly/.

2.6   TAPAAL

TAPAAL [18] is a tool suite for verification of Petri nets and their extensions where tokens can be associated with timing features (timed-arc Petri net model) or with colors (colored Petri nets in the style supported by MCC competition). The acronym TAPAAL stands for Timed-Arc Petri nets developed at AALborg university. The tool development started 10 years ago and the current tool release consists of a powerful GUI providing user-friendly, compositional editing of Petri nets (see screenshot at Fig. 3) and a number of standalone verification engines supporting CTL verification of colored (untimed) Petri nets, reachability analysis of timed-arc Petri nets with discrete time semantics, including a workflow analysis tool, and a continuous time verification engine. The tool suite also allows to export timed-arc Petri nets as timed automata that can be opened and verified in the tool UPPAAL [8]. TAPAAL supports the import and export of Petri nets in the PNML standard, including the parsing of queries in the XML standard introduced by the MCC competition. The currently released version 3.4.3 of TAPAAL (available at www.tapaal.net) won two gold medals in the reachability and CTL category and one silver medal in upper-bounds at MCC'18.

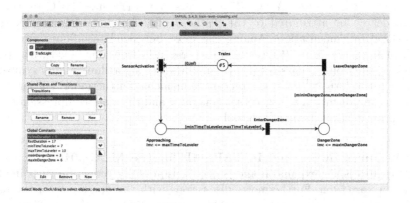

Fig. 3. Screenshot of TAPAAL GUI

Main Features of TAPAAL. The colored (untimed) verification engine of TAPAAL called verifypn [25] is the one that participates at MCC and it relies on a preprocessing of both the Petri net model as well as the verified query. The subformulas of CTL queries are recursively analysed [12] with the use of state-equations and linear programming techniques in order to discover easy-to-solve subqueries to reduce the overall query size. This allows us to answer the query on a substantial number of models without even exploring the state-space (in fact 22% of all CTL propositions in MCC'17 can be answered solely by the approximation techniques [12]), or it can reduce a CTL query into a pure reachability question on which a specialized verification method can be used (about 50% of the MCC'17 queries can be reduced to simple reachability [12]). At the same time, the Petri net model is reduced by a continuously updated set of structural reduction rules so that we can eliminate uninteresting concurrency or unimportant parts of the net (relative to the asked query).

As documented in [13], a substantial reduction in the net size can be achieved and this technique often combines well with partial order techniques based on stubborn sets that are as well implemented in TAPAAL. The tool also supports siphon-trap based algorithms for the detection of deadlock freedom. More recently a trace abstraction refinement [14] has been added to the engine and employed at MCC'18. The verification of colored Petri nets is achieved by a self-contained unfolder implemented in the `verifypn` engine in combination with over-approximation by state-equations applied for a given query on the colored net before its unfolding. Furthermore the tool employs a state-of-the-art dependency-graph technique for verification of CTL properties, utilizing the so-called certain zero optimization [17]. Another critical component is an efficient successor-generator, which paired with a compressing, time and memory-efficient state-storage data structure PTrie [26] gives `verifypn` a competitive advantage in MCC.

Main Strength of TAPAAL. The success of `verifypn` at MCC'18 can to a large degree be attributed to the plethora of techniques with an efficient, internalized implementation. Among the most beneficial techniques are over-approximation of colored Petri nets, structural reductions combined with stubborn set reductions, recursive query simplification algorithms and a symbolic method in the form of trace abstraction refinement. Furthermore, efficiency of the basic components of the successor-generator and the state-compression techniques provide a backbone of the tool.

New Features Introduced in TAPAAL for the MCC'2019. The main focus for 2019 is the expansion and generalization of net reduction-rules implemented in `verifypn`. Furthermore, discussions with the developers of the tool LoLA provided an inspiration to further optimizations for the upper-bounds category, utilizing linear over-approximation of place bounds.

2.7 TINA.tedd

TINA (TIme Petri Net Analyzer) [11] is a toolbox for the editing and analysis of various extensions of Petri nets and Time Petri nets developed at LAAS-CNRS. It provides a wide range of tools for state space generation, structural analysis, model checking, or simulation. For its third participation to the MCC, we selected a single symbolic tool from TINA, called `tedd`, to compete in the *StateSpace* category.

Main Features of TINA.tedd. We provide a new symbolic analysis tool for Petri nets that uses a mix between logic-based approaches (decision diagrams); structural reductions; and a new symbolic technique where sets of markings are represented using linear systems of equations. We give more details about the latter below.

At its core, tedd is a symbolic state-space generation tool built on top of our own implementation of Hierarchical Set Decision Diagrams (SDD) [16]. In the context of the MCC, we can use state space generation to answer all the questions from the StateSpace examination, that is computing the number of markings of an input net; its number of transitions; and the maximum number of tokens in a marking and in a place. The core capabilities of tedd, based on SDD, has shown competitive performances, on par with most of the symbolic tools present in the previous MCC contests.

The tool can accept models in the PNML format and provides a large collection of options for selecting good variable orders. A variable order module provides a rich choice of order computing algorithms based on net traversals and the structural analysis of the net (semi-flows, flows, etc.). In each case, a force [1] heuristics can be used to improve any given order. Hierarchical orders, which are a characteristic of SDD, are also available but have been seldom used so far. An order-grading method allows to choose for each model a variable ordering likely to work. Colored models are also supported using a separate tool that unfolds high-level nets into simpler PT nets. tedd also provides some limited support for reachability properties – such as finding dead states and transitions – and can be used with other decision diagrams libraries. At the moment, we provide access to a BDD library for safe nets as well as to the pnmc tool [23].

Main Strength of TINA.tedd. What sets tedd apart from other symbolic tools in the competition is the use of a novel state space generation technique based on structural reductions coupled with methods for counting sets of markings. This approach is explained in detail in [10] and was first experimented during MCC'2018, using a limited set of reductions. To the best of our knowledge, tedd is the only tool implementing such an approach.

Briefly, we enrich the notion of structural reduction (as found e.g. in [9]) by keeping track of the relationships between the reachable markings of an (initial) Petri net, N_1, and those of its reduced (final) version, N_2, using a system of linear equations with integer coefficients Q. We call Q a set of *reduction equations*.

We provide an automatic system for finding and applying structural reductions on nets. Our reductions are tailored so that the state space of N_1 can be faithfully reconstructed from that of N_2 and the reduction equations, Q. Intuitively, variables in Q include the places found in N_1 and N_2. The reduction equations provide a relation between markings of the two nets in the following sense: when setting variables in Q to values given by a marking of N_2, the set of non-negative, integer solutions to the resulting system all correspond to markings of N_1 (and reciprocally).

Reductions can be applied in succession, giving an irreducible net N_i and a final set of reduction equations Q_i. In particular, when N_i is totally reduced (N_i has an empty set of places), the state space of N_1 corresponds exactly to the solutions of system Q_i. In some sense, Q_i acts as a symbolic, "equational", representation of the reachable markings. This gives a very compact representation of the set of reachable markings that manages to preserve good complexity results for a large class of problems (e.g. finding whether a given marking is reachable, or computing the maximal possible marking for a place). This approach can also be useful when a net is only partially reduced. Then the markings of the residual net is computed symbolically (as an SDD) which, together with the reduction equations, provides a hybrid representation of the reachable markings of N.

New Features Introduced for the MCC'2019. This is the first edition of the MCC where we will experiment with an extended set of reductions improving upon those presented in [10]. With these new reductions, we are able to totally reduce about 25% of all the instances used in the previous MCC benchmarks. More generally, reductions have a positive impact on about half of the instances. In particular, based on the benchmark provided by the MCC'2018, we are able to compute results for 22 new instances for which no tool was ever able to compute a marking count during the competition.

This year, we will also use more powerful methods for counting markings in the case of totally reducible nets. Indeed, when a net is totally reduced, it is enough to compute the number of non-negative integer solutions to its system of reduction equations. There exist several methods for solving this problem, which amounts to computing the number of integer points in a convex polytope. Actually, this has been a hot topic of research in the last decade and some tools are purposely available for this task, notably `LattE` [29] and `barvinok` [35]. `TINA.tedd` is able to interface with these tools in order to compute the number of reachable markings in a net. With some adjustments, implemented in `tedd`, similar techniques can also be used for computing the number of transitions.

This approach, based on "geometric techniques", is extremely powerful when the number of variables – the number of places in the net – is low. (We restrict its use to nets with less than 50 places in the MCC.) To overcome this limitation, we have recently started experiments with our own counting method, based on a recursion-solving approach, and implemented in a dedicated package called `polycount`. The work on polycount is still preliminary though, since we cannot count transitions in all cases yet.

3   Conclusion

Through the dedication of its related communities, the Model Checking Contest has been achieving the following objectives over the past decade:

- gathering a large set of diverse, complex, and centralized benchmarks composed of concurrent systems formal descriptions;

- providing the environments and frameworks for the emergence of systematic, rigorous and reproducible means to assess model-checking tools;
- fostering the progress of the research and development efforts of model-checking tools to increase their capabilities.

Like the other existing scientific contests, the MCC also aims at identifying the theoretical approaches that are the most fruitful in practice, to possibly enable the research field to figure out which techniques, under specific conditions, best handle particular types of analyses on the systems under consideration.

As the MCC gains maturity, existing organizational challenges shift focus, and new ones appear. Among the former, is how to appropriately increase the benchmark for known models whose current instances are now easily solved, along with the way we generate temporal-logic formulas for them. Another one is creating the provisions to better balance the scoring weights between parameterized models (with regards the number of instances deduced from their scaling parameter) on the one hand, between known and surprise models on the other. Among the new challenges, is what incentives the competition could provide to keep attracting newcomers, i.e., first-time participating tools. Another one is the inclusion of some known verdicts of all previous analyses on each instance of the existing models during the past editions, and allow the competing tools to reliably access this information to speed up and increase efficiency in new analyses.

Finally, we observed a dramatic increase of the tool's confidence (and probably reliability) since this measure was introduced in 2015. Between two editions of the MCC, previous results are used as a testbench for increasing the quality of these tools and developers even exchange their tricks and algorithms. Therefore, we can state that this event benefits to the whole community.

References

1. Aloul, F.A., Markov, I.L., Sakallah, K.A.: FORCE: a fast and easy-to-implement variable-ordering heuristic. In: ACM Great Lakes Symposium on VLSI, pp. 116–119. ACM (2003)
2. Amparore, E.G.: A new GreatSPN GUI for GSPN editing and CSL^{TA} model checking. In: Norman, G., Sanders, W. (eds.) QEST 2014. LNCS, vol. 8657, pp. 170–173. Springer, Cham (2014). https://doi.org/10.1007/978-3-319-10696-0_13
3. Amparore, E.G., Balbo, G., Beccuti, M., Donatelli, S., Franceschinis, G.: 30 years of GreatSPN. In: Fiondella, L., Puliafito, A. (eds.) Principles of Performance and Reliability Modeling and Evaluation. SSRE, pp. 227–254. Springer, Cham (2016). https://doi.org/10.1007/978-3-319-30599-8_9
4. Amparore, E.G., Ciardo, G., Donatelli, S., Miner, A.: i_{Rank}: a variable order metric for DEDS subject to linear invariants. In: Tomáš, V., Zhang, L. (eds.) TACAS 2019. LNCS, vol. 11428, pp. 285–302. Springer, Cham (2019)
5. Amparore, E.G., Donatelli, S.: GreatTeach: a tool for teaching (stochastic) Petri nets. In: Khomenko, V., Roux, O.H. (eds.) PETRI NETS 2018. LNCS, vol. 10877, pp. 416–425. Springer, Cham (2018). https://doi.org/10.1007/978-3-319-91268-4_24

6. Amparore, E.G., Donatelli, S., Beccuti, M., Garbi, G., Miner, A.: Decision diagrams for Petri nets: a comparison of variable ordering algorithms. In: Koutny, M., Kristensen, L.M., Penczek, W. (eds.) Transactions on Petri Nets and Other Models of Concurrency XIII. LNCS, vol. 11090, pp. 73–92. Springer, Heidelberg (2018). https://doi.org/10.1007/978-3-662-58381-4_4

7. Babar, J., Miner, A.S.: MEDDLY: Multi-terminal and Edge-valued Decision Diagram LibrarY. In: Proceedings of QEST, pp. 195–196. IEEE Computer Society Press (2010)

8. Behrmann, G., David, A., Larsen, K.G., Pettersson, P., Yi, W.: Developing UPPAAL over 15 years. Softw. Pract. Exp. 41(2), 133–142 (2011)

9. Berthelot, G.: Transformations and decompositions of nets. In: Brauer, W., Reisig, W., Rozenberg, G. (eds.) Petri Nets: Central Models and Their Properties. LNCS, vol. 254, pp. 359–376. Springer, Berlin, Heidelberg (1987). https://doi.org/10.1007/BFb0046845

10. Berthomieu, B., Le Botlan, D., Dal Zilio, S.: Petri net reductions for counting markings. In: Gallardo, M.M., Merino, P. (eds.) SPIN 2018. LNCS, vol. 10869, pp. 65–84. Springer, Cham (2018). https://doi.org/10.1007/978-3-319-94111-0_4

11. Berthomieu, B., Ribet, P.O., Vernadat, F.: The tool TINA-construction of abstract state spaces for Petri nets and Time Petri nets. Int. J. Prod. Res. 42(14), 2741–2756 (2004)

12. Bønneland, F., Dyhr, J., Jensen, P.G., Johannsen, M., Srba, J.: Simplification of CTL formulae for efficient model checking of Petri nets. In: Khomenko, V., Roux, O.H. (eds.) PETRI NETS 2018. LNCS, vol. 10877, pp. 143–163. Springer, Cham (2018). https://doi.org/10.1007/978-3-319-91268-4_8

13. Bønneland, F., Dyhr, J., Jensen, P., Johannsen, M., Srba, J.: Stubborn versus structural reductions for Petri nets. J. Log. Algebr. Methods Program. 102, 46–63 (2019)

14. Cassez, F., Jensen, P.G., Guldstrand Larsen, K.: Refinement of trace abstraction for real-time programs. In: Hague, M., Potapov, I. (eds.) RP 2017. LNCS, vol. 10506, pp. 42–58. Springer, Cham (2017). https://doi.org/10.1007/978-3-319-67089-8_4

15. Ciardo, G., Marmorstein, R., Siminiceanu, R.: Saturation unbound. In: Garavel, H., Hatcliff, J. (eds.) TACAS 2003. LNCS, vol. 2619, pp. 379–393. Springer, Heidelberg (2003). https://doi.org/10.1007/3-540-36577-X_27

16. Couvreur, J.-M., Thierry-Mieg, Y.: Hierarchical decision diagrams to exploit model structure. In: Wang, F. (ed.) FORTE 2005. LNCS, vol. 3731, pp. 443–457. Springer, Heidelberg (2005). https://doi.org/10.1007/11562436_32

17. Dalsgaard, A., et al.: A distributed fixed-point algorithm for extended dependency graphs. Fund. Inform. 161(4), 351–381 (2018)

18. David, A., Jacobsen, L., Jacobsen, M., Jørgensen, K.Y., Møller, M.H., Srba, J.: TAPAAL 2.0: integrated development environment for timed-arc Petri nets. In: Flanagan, C., König, B. (eds.) TACAS 2012. LNCS, vol. 7214, pp. 492–497. Springer, Heidelberg (2012). https://doi.org/10.1007/978-3-642-28756-5_36

19. van Dijk, T., Meijer, J., van de Pol, J.: Multi-core on-the-fly saturation. In: Tools and Algorithms for the Construction and Analysis of Systems - 25th International Conference, TACAS. LNCS, pp. 58–75. Springer, Heidelberg (2019)

20. Duret-Lutz, A., Klai, K., Poitrenaud, D., Thierry-Mieg, Y.: Self-loop aggregation product – a new hybrid approach to on-the-fly LTL model checking. In: Bultan, T., Hsiung, P.-A. (eds.) ATVA 2011. LNCS, vol. 6996, pp. 336–350. Springer, Heidelberg (2011). https://doi.org/10.1007/978-3-642-24372-1_24

21. Duret-Lutz, A., Lewkowicz, A., Fauchille, A., Michaud, T., Renault, É., Xu, L.: Spot 2.0 – a framework for LTL and ω-automata manipulation. In: Artho, C., Legay, A., Peled, D. (eds.) ATVA 2016. LNCS, vol. 9938, pp. 122–129. Springer, Cham (2016). https://doi.org/10.1007/978-3-319-46520-3_8

22. Garavel, H.: Nested-unit Petri nets: a structural means to increase efficiency and scalability of verification on elementary nets. In: Devillers, R., Valmari, A. (eds.) PETRI NETS 2015. LNCS, vol. 9115, pp. 179–199. Springer, Cham (2015). https://doi.org/10.1007/978-3-319-19488-2_9

23. Hamez, A.: A symbolic model checker for Petri nets: pnmc. In: Koutny, M., Desel, J., Kleijn, J. (eds.) Transactions on Petri Nets and Other Models of Concurrency XI. LNCS, vol. 9930, pp. 297–306. Springer, Heidelberg (2016). https://doi.org/10.1007/978-3-662-53401-4_15

24. Hillah, L.M., Kindler, E., Kordon, F., Petrucci, L., Trèves, N.: A primer on the Petri net markup language and ISO/IEC 15909–2. Petri Net Newsl. **76**, 9–28 (2009)

25. Jensen, J.F., Nielsen, T., Oestergaard, L.K., Srba, J.: TAPAAL and reachability analysis of P/T nets. In: Koutny, M., Desel, J., Kleijn, J. (eds.) Transactions on Petri Nets and Other Models of Concurrency XI. LNCS, vol. 9930, pp. 307–318. Springer, Heidelberg (2016). https://doi.org/10.1007/978-3-662-53401-4_16

26. Jensen, P.G., Larsen, K.G., Srba, J.: PTrie: data structure for compressing and storing sets via prefix sharing. In: Hung, D., Kapur, D. (eds.) ICTAC 2017. LNCS, vol. 10580, pp. 248–265. Springer, Cham (2017). https://doi.org/10.1007/978-3-319-67729-3_15

27. Kant, G., Laarman, A., Meijer, J., van de Pol, J., Blom, S., van Dijk, T.: LTSmin: high-performance language-independent model checking. In: Baier, C., Tinelli, C. (eds.) TACAS 2015. LNCS, vol. 9035, pp. 692–707. Springer, Heidelberg (2015). https://doi.org/10.1007/978-3-662-46681-0_61

28. Kordon, F., et al.: MCC'2017 – the seventh model checking contest. In: Koutny, M., Kristensen, L.M., Penczek, W. (eds.) Transactions on Petri Nets and Other Models of Concurrency XIII. LNCS, vol. 11090, pp. 181–209. Springer, Heidelberg (2018). https://doi.org/10.1007/978-3-662-58381-4_9

29. Loera, J.A.D., Hemmecke, R., Tauzer, J., Yoshida, R.: Effective lattice point counting in rational convex polytopes. J. Symb. Comput. **38**(4), 1273–1302 (2004)

30. Meijer, J., Kant, G., Blom, S., van de Pol, J.: Read, write and copy dependencies for symbolic model checking. In: Yahav, E. (ed.) HVC 2014. LNCS, vol. 8855, pp. 204–219. Springer, Cham (2014). https://doi.org/10.1007/978-3-319-13338-6_16

31. Meijer, J., van de Pol, J.: Bandwidth and wavefront reduction for static variable ordering in symbolic reachability analysis. In: Rayadurgam, S., Tkachuk, O. (eds.) NFM 2016. LNCS, vol. 9690, pp. 255–271. Springer, Cham (2016). https://doi.org/10.1007/978-3-319-40648-0_20

32. Miner, A.S.: Implicit GSPN reachability set generation using decision diagrams. Perform. Eval. **56**(1–4), 145–165 (2004)

33. Smith, B., Ciardo, G.: SOUPS: a variable ordering metric for the saturation algorithm. In: Proceedings of the International Conference on Application of Concurrency to System Design (ACSD), pp. 1–10. IEEE Computer Society, June 2018

34. Thierry-Mieg, Y.: Symbolic model-checking using ITS-tools. In: Baier, C., Tinelli, C. (eds.) TACAS 2015. LNCS, vol. 9035, pp. 231–237. Springer, Heidelberg (2015). https://doi.org/10.1007/978-3-662-46681-0_20

35. Verdoolaege, S., Seghir, R., Beyls, K., Loechner, V., Bruynooghe, M.: Counting integer points in parametric polytopes using barvinok's rational functions. Algorithmica **48**(1), 37–66 (2007)

36. Wolf, K.: Petri net model checking with LoLA 2. In: Khomenko, V., Roux, O.H. (eds.) PETRI NETS 2018. LNCS, vol. 10877, pp. 351–362. Springer, Cham (2018). https://doi.org/10.1007/978-3-319-91268-4_18

37. Zhao, Y., Ciardo, G.: Symbolic CTL model checking of asynchronous systems using constrained saturation. In: Liu, Z., Ravn, A.P. (eds.) ATVA 2009. LNCS, vol. 5799, pp. 368–381. Springer, Heidelberg (2009). https://doi.org/10.1007/978-3-642-04761-9_27

The 2019 Comparison of Tools for the Analysis of Quantitative Formal Models
(QComp 2019 Competition Report)

Ernst Moritz Hahn[1,2] , Arnd Hartmanns[3(✉)] , Christian Hensel[4],
Michaela Klauck[5], Joachim Klein[6] , Jan Křetínský[7] , David Parker[8] ,
Tim Quatmann[4] , Enno Ruijters[3] , and Marcel Steinmetz[5]

[1] School of Electronics, Electrical Engineering and Computer Science,
Queen's University Belfast, Belfast, UK
[2] State Key Laboratory of Computer Science, Institute of Software,
Chinese Academy of Sciences, Beijing, China
[3] University of Twente, Enschede, The Netherlands
a.hartmanns@utwente.nl
[4] RWTH Aachen University, Aachen, Germany
[5] Saarland Informatics Campus, Saarland University, Saarbrücken, Germany
[6] Technische Universität Dresden, Dresden, Germany
[7] Technische Universität München, Munich, Germany
[8] University of Birmingham, Birmingham, UK

Abstract. Quantitative formal models capture probabilistic behaviour,
real-time aspects, or general continuous dynamics. A number of tools
support their automatic analysis with respect to dependability or performance properties. QComp 2019 is the first, friendly competition among
such tools. It focuses on stochastic formalisms from Markov chains to
probabilistic timed automata specified in the JANI model exchange format, and on probabilistic reachability, expected-reward, and steady-state
properties. QComp draws its benchmarks from the new Quantitative Verification Benchmark Set. Participating tools, which include probabilistic
model checkers and planners as well as simulation-based tools, are evaluated in terms of performance, versatility, and usability. In this paper, we
report on the challenges in setting up a quantitative verification competition, present the results of QComp 2019, summarise the lessons learned,
and provide an outlook on the features of the next edition of QComp.

The authors are listed in alphabetical order. This work was supported by BMBF grant
16KIS0656 (CISPA), DFG grants 383882557 (SUV), 389792660 (part of CRC 248), and
HO 2169/5-1, DFG SFB 912 (HAEC), ERC Advanced Grants 695614 (POWVER) and
781914 (FRAPPANT), Natural Science Foundation of China (NSFC) grants 61761136011
and 61532019, NWO and BetterBe B.V. grant 628.010.006, NWO VENI grant
639.021.754, and the TUM IGSSE project 10.06 (PARSEC).

D. Beyer et al. (Eds.): TACAS 2019, Part III, LNCS 11429, pp. 69–92, 2019.
https://doi.org/10.1007/978-3-030-17502-3_5

1 Introduction

Classic verification is concerned with functional, *qualitative* properties of models of systems or software: Can this assertion ever be violated? Will the server always eventually answer a request? To evaluate aspects of dependability (e.g. safety, reliability, availability or survivability) and performance (e.g. response times, throughput, or power consumption), however, *quantitative* properties must be checked on *quantitative* models that incorporate probabilities, real-time aspects, or general continuous dynamics. Over the past three decades, many modelling languages for mathematical formalisms such as Markov chains or timed automata have been specified for use by quantitative verification tools that automatically check or compute values such as expected accumulated rewards or PCTL formulae. Applications include probabilistic programs, safety-critical and fault-tolerant systems, biological processes, queueing systems, privacy, and security.

As a research field matures, developers of algorithms and tools face increasing challenges in comparing their work with the state of the art: the number of incompatible modelling languages grows, benchmarks and case studies become scattered and hard to obtain, and the tool prototypes used by others disappear. At the same time, it is hard to motivate spending effort on engineering generic, user-friendly, well-documented tools. In several areas, *tool competitions* have successfully addressed these challenges: they improve the visibility of existing tools, motivate engineering effort, and push for standardised interfaces, languages, and benchmarks. Examples include ARCH-COMP [29] for hybrid systems, the International Planning Competition [18] for planners, the SAT Competition [51] for satisfiability solvers, and SV-COMP [8] for software verification.

In this paper, we present QComp 2019: the first, friendly competition among quantitative verification tools. As the first event of its kind, its scope is intentionally limited to five stochastic formalisms based on Markov chains and to basic property types. It compares the performance, versatility, and usability of four general-purpose probabilistic model checkers, one general-purpose statistical model checker, and four specialised tools (including two probabilistic planners). All competition data is available at qcomp.org. As a friendly competition in a spirit similar to ARCH-COMP and the RERS challenge [52], QComp's focus is less on establishing a ranking among tools, but rather on gathering a community to agree on common formats, challenges, and evaluation criteria. To this end, QComp is complemented by a new collection of benchmarks, the Quantitative Verification Benchmark Set (QVBS, [46]). All models in the QVBS are available in their original modelling language as well as the JANI model exchange format [15]. While JANI is intended as the standard format for QComp, not all tools implement support for it yet and were thus executed only on those benchmarks for which they support the original modelling language.

Quantitative verification is rich in formalisms, modelling languages, types of properties, and verification approaches, of which we give an overview in Sect. 2. We summarise the selections made by QComp among all of these options as well as the overall competition design in Sect. 3. The authors of the participating tools describe the features and capabilities of their tools in Sect. 4; we then compare their usability and versatility in Sect. 5. Finally, Sect. 6 contains the technical setup and results of the performance comparison, followed by an outlook on the next edition of QComp, based on the lessons learned in this round, in Sect. 7.

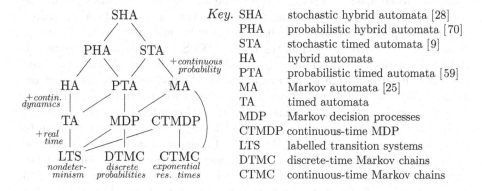

Fig. 1. The family tree of automata-based quantitative formalisms

2 The Quantitative Verification Landscape

Quantitative verification is a wide field that overlaps with safety and fault tolerance, performance evaluation, real-time systems, simulation, optimisation, and control theory. In this section, we give an overview of the formalisms, modelling languages, property types, and verification methods considered for QComp.

2.1 Semantic Formalisms

The foundation of every formal verification approach is a *formalism*: a mathematically well-defined class of objects that form the semantics of any concrete model. Most modelling languages or higher-level formalisms eventually map to some extension of automata: states (that may contain relevant structure) and transitions (that connect states, possibly with several annotations). In Fig. 1, we list the automata-based formalisms supported by JANI, and graphically show their relationships (with a higher-up formalism being an extension of the lower-level formalisms it is connected to). LTS are included as the most basic non-quantitative automata formalism; TA then add the quantity of (continuous) time, while DTMC and CTMC provide probabilistic behaviour. The list is clearly not exhaustive: for example, every formalism is a 1- or 1.5-player game, and the list could be extended by games with two or more players that capture competitive behaviour among actors with possibly conflicting goals. It also does not include higher-level formalisms such as Petri nets or dataflow that often provide extra information for verification compared to their automata semantics.

2.2   Modelling Languages

Modelling complex systems using the formalisms listed above directly would be cumbersome. Instead, domain experts use (textual or graphical) *modelling languages* to compactly describe large automata. Aside from providing a concrete human-writable and machine-readable syntax for a formalism, modelling languages typically add at least discrete variables and some form of compositionality. The current benchmarks in the QVBS were originally specified in the Galileo format [72] for fault trees, the GreatSPN format [1] for generalised stochastic Petri nets, the process algebra-based high-level modelling language Modest [36], the PGCL specification for probabilistic programs [32], PPDDL for probabilistic planning domains [77], and the lower-level guarded-command PRISM language [57]. For all benchmarks, the QVBS provides a translation to the tool-independent JSON-based JANI model exchange format [15]. The purpose of JANI is to establish a standard human-readable (though not easily human-writable) format for quantitiative verification that simplifies the implementation of new tools and fosters model exchange and tool interoperability. Many other quantitative modelling languages not yet represented in the QVBS exist such as Uppaal's XML format [7] for timed automata or those supported by Möbius [19].

2.3   Properties

Models are verified w.r.t. *properties* that specify a requirement or a query for a value of interest. The basic property types for stochastic models are probabilistic reachability (the probability to eventually reach a goal state), expected accumulated rewards (or costs; the expected reward sum until reaching a goal state), and steady-state values (the steady-state probability to be in certain states or the long-run average reward). In case of formalisms with nondeterminism, properties ask for the minimum or maximum value over all resolutions of nondeterminism. Probabilistic reachability and expected rewards can be bounded by a maximum number of transitions taken, by time, or by accumulated reward; we can then query for e.g. the maximum probability to reach a goal within a cost budget. We refer to properties that query for probabilities as *probabilistic*, to those that deal with expected rewards as *reward-based*, and to *steady-state* properties.

From these basic properties, logics can be constructed that allow the expression of *nested* quantitative requirements, e.g. that with probability 1, we must reach a state within n steps from which the probability of eventually reaching an unsafe state is less than 10^{-9}. Examples are CSL [5] for CTMC, PTCTL [59] for PTA, rPATL [17] for stochastic games, and STL [61] for hybrid systems. Another interesting class of properties are *multi-objective* tradeoffs [26], which query for Pareto-optimal strategies balancing multiple goals.

2.4   Verification Methods and Results

The two main quantitative verification approaches are probabilistic model checking and statistical model checking a.k.a. Monte Carlo simulation. Probabilistic planners use ideas similar to probabilistic model checking, but focus on heuristics and bounding methods to avoid the state space explosion problem.

Probabilistic model checking [4] is to explore a model's state space followed by or interleaved with a numeric analysis, e.g. using value iteration, to compute probabilities or reward values. It aims for results with *hard* guarantees, i.e. precise statements about the relationship between the computed result and the actual value. For example, a probabilistic model checker may guarantee that the actual probability is definitely within $\epsilon = \pm 10^{-3}$ of the reported value. Due to the need for state space exploration, these tools face the state space explosion problem and their applicability to large models is typically limited by available memory.

Statistical model checking (SMC, [49,78]) is Monte Carlo simulation on formal models: generate n executions of the model, determine how many of them satisfy the property or calculate the reward of each, and return the average as an estimate for the property's value. SMC is thus not directly applicable to models with nondeterminism and provides only statistical guarantees, for example that $\mathbb{P}(|\hat{p} - p| > \epsilon) < \delta$ where p is the (unknown) actual probability, $\hat{p}$ is the estimate, and $1 - \delta$ is the confidence that the result is ϵ-correct. As ϵ and δ decrease, n grows. SMC is attractive as it only requires constant memory independent of the size of the state space. Compared to model checking, it replaces the state space explosion problem by a runtime explosion problem when faced with rare events: it is desirable that $\epsilon \ll p$, but since n depends quadratically on ϵ for a fixed δ (e.g. in the Okamoto bound [63]), n becomes prohibitively large as p reaches around 10^{-4}. Rare event simulation [68] provides methods to tackle this problem at the cost of higher memory usage, lack of automation, or lower generality.

Probabilistic planning uses MDP heuristic search algorithms, e.g. [10,11], that try to avoid the state space explosion problem by computing values only for a small fraction of the states, just enough to answer the considered property. Heuristics—admissible approximations of the optimal values—are used to initialise the value function, which is subsequently updated until the value for the initial state has provably converged. The order of updates depends on the current values; this sometimes allows to prove states to not be part of any optimal solution *before* actually visiting all of their descendants. Such states can safely be ignored. Many heuristic search algorithms assume a specific class of MDP. To apply them to general MDP, they need to be wrapped in FRET iterations [54]: between calls to the search algorithm, FRET eliminates end components from the subgraph of the state space induced by optimal actions w.r.t. the current values. FRET-π [71] is a variant that only picks a single optimal path to the goal.

Results. The answer to a property may be a concrete number that is in some relation to the actual value (e.g. within $\pm 10^{-3}$ of the actual value). However, properties—such as PCTL formulae—may also ask qualitative questions, i.e. whether the value of interest is above or below a certain constant bound. In that case, there is an opportunity for algorithms to terminate early: they may not have computed a value close to the actual one yet, but the current approximation may already be sufficient to prove or disprove the bound. In the case of models with nondeterminism, those choices can be seen as scheduling freedom, and a user may be more interested in an optimal or sufficient *strategy* than in the actual value, i.e. in a way to resolve the nondeterministic choices to achieve the optimal or a sufficient probability or reward. Further types of quantitative results include *quantiles* [73], Pareto curves in multi-objective scenarios, and a function in terms of some model parameter in case of parametric model checking.

3   Decisions and Competition Setup

Seeing the wide range of options in quantitative verification described in the previous section, and taking into account that QComp 2019 was the first event of its kind, several decisions had to be made to limit its scope. The first was to build on JANI and the QVBS: only benchmarks available in JANI and submitted to the QVBS with a description and extensive metadata would become part of the QComp performance evaluation. We further limited the formalisms to DTMC, CTMC, MDP, MA and PTA (cf. Fig. 1). We thus included only stochastic formalisms, excluding in particular TA and HA. This is because stochastic formalisms provide more ways to exploit approximations and trade precision for runtime and memory than non-stochastic ones where verification is rather "qualitative with more complicated states". Second, we only included formalisms supported by at least two participating tools, which ruled out STA, PHA and SHA. For the same reason, we restricted to the basic properties listed at the beginning of Sect. 2.3. While many competitions focus on performance, producing an overall ranking of tools w.r.t. their total runtime over all benchmarks, QComp equally considers versatility and usability (see Sect. 5). For the performance comparison, many technical decisions (such as comparing quantitative results with an a priori fixed precision and not considering comparisons or asking for strategies) were made as explained in Sect. 6. In particular, the set of benchmarks was determined based on the wishes of the participants and announced a priori; not expecting tool authors to dubiously tweak their tools for the selected benchmarks is in line with the friendly nature of QComp 2019. The entire competition was then performed *offline*: participants submitted benchmarks and tools, the performance comparison was done by the organisers on a central server according to tool setup instructions and scripts provided by the participants, and the evaluation of versatility and usability is based on submitted tool descriptions.

4   Participating Tools

QComp is open to every tool that can check a significant subset of the models and properties of the QVBS. In particular, a participating tool need not support all model types, the JANI format, or all included kinds of properties. For example, a tool specialising in the analysis of stochastic Petri nets is not expected to solve JANI DTMC models. Nine tools were submitted to QComp

Table 1. Tool capabilities

Tool	Galileo	GreatSPN	JANI	Modest	PGCL	PPDDL	PRISM	DTMC			CTMC				MDP			MA				PTA		
								P	P_r	E	P	P_t	E	S	P	P_r	E	P	P_t	E	S	P	P_t	E
ePMC			✓				✓	✓		✓	✓	✓	✓		✓		✓							
mcsta			✓	✓				✓	✓	✓	✓	✓	✓		✓	✓	✓	✓	✓	✓		✓	✓	✓
PRISM							✓	✓		✓	✓	✓	✓	✓	✓		✓					✓	✓	✓
P-TUM							✓	✓			✓				✓									
Storm	✓	✓	✓		✓		✓	✓	✓	✓	✓	✓	✓	✓	✓	✓	✓	✓	✓	✓	✓	(✓)		(✓)
DFTRES	✓	(✓)									✓		✓					(✓)		(✓)				
modes			✓	✓				✓	✓	✓	✓	✓	✓		(✓)	(✓)	(✓)	(✓)	(✓)	(✓)		(✓)	(✓)	(✓)
MFPL			✓	✓											(✓)									
PFD		(✓)				✓									(✓)		(✓)							

2019: DFTRES [69] (by Enno Ruijters), ePMC [40] (by Ernst Moritz Hahn), mcsta [42] and modes [14] (by Arnd Hartmanns), Modest FRET-π LRTDP (by Michaela Klauck, MFPL for short), PRISM [57] (by Joachim Klein and David Parker), PRISM-TUMheuristics (by Jan Křetínský, P-TUM for short), Probabilistic Fast Downward [71] (by Marcel Steinmetz, PFD for short), and Storm [23] (by Christian Hensel). We summarise the tools' capabilities w.r.t. the supported modelling languages, formalisms, and properties in Table 1. We only include the property types most used in the QComp benchmarks; P, P_r, and P_t refer to unbounded, reward-bounded, and time-bounded reachability probabilities, respectively; E indicates expected accumulated rewards, and S steady-state probabilities. A (✓) entry signifies limited support as described in the tool-specific sections below.

4.1 Model Checkers

QComp 2019 included four general-purpose probabilistic model checkers that handle a variety of formalisms and property types as well as the more specialised PRISM-TUMheuristics tool focused on unbounded probabilistic properties.

ePMC (formerly iscasMC [40]) is mainly written in Java, with some performance-critical parts in C. It runs on 64-bit Linux, Mac OS, and Windows. ePMC particularly targets extensibility: it consists of a small core while plugins provide the ability to parse models, model-check properties of certain types, perform graph-based analyses, or integrate BDD packages [24]. In this way, ePMC can easily be extended for special purposes or experiments without affecting the stability of other parts. It supports the PRISM language and JANI as input, DTMC, CTMC, MDP, and stochastic games as formalisms, and PCTL* and reward-based properties. ePMC particularly targets the analysis of complex linear time properties [39] and the efficient analysis of stochastic parity games [41]. It has been extended to support multi-objective model checking [37] and bisimulation minimisation [38] for interval MDP. It also has experimental support for parametric Markov models [31,60]. Specialised branches of ePMC can model check quantum Markov chains [27] and epistemic properties of multi-agent systems [30]. The tool is available in source code form at github.com/liyi-david/ePMC.

mcsta is the explicit-state model checker of the Modest Toolset [42]. It is implemented in C# and works on Windows as well as on Linux and Mac OS via the Mono runtime. Built on common infrastructure in the Modest Toolset, it supports MODEST, xSADF [44] and JANI as input languages, and has access to a fast state space exploration engine that compiles models to bytecode. mcsta computes unbounded and reward-bounded reachability probabilities and expected accumulated rewards on MDP and MA, and additionally time-bounded probabilities on MA. By default, it uses value iteration and Unif+ [16]; for probabilistic reachability, it can use interval iteration [33] instead. mcsta supports PTA via digital clocks [58] and STA via a safe overapproximation [35]. It can analyse DTMC and CTMC, but treats them as (special cases of) MDP and MA, respectively, and thus cannot achieve the performance of dedicated algorithms. To deal with very large models, mcsta provides two methods to efficiently use secondary storage: by default, it makes extensive use of memory-mapped files; alternatively, given a model-specific partitioning formula, it can do a partitioned analysis [43]. For reward-bounded properties with large bounds (including time bounds in PTA), mcsta implements two unfolding-free techniques based on modified value iteration and state elimination [34]. The Modest Toolset, including mcsta, is available as a cross-platform binary package at modestchecker.net. mcsta is a command-line tool; when invoked with -?, it prints a list of all parameters with brief explanations. The download includes example MODEST models with mcsta command lines. MODEST is documented in [36] and on the toolset's website.

PRISM [57] is a probabilistic model checker for DTMC, CTMC, MDP, PTA, and variants annotated with rewards. Models are by default specified in the PRISM language, but other formats, notably PEPA [50], SBML (see sbml.org), and sparse matrix files, can be imported. Properties are specified in a language based on temporal logic which subsumes PCTL, CSL, LTL, and PCTL*; it also includes extensions for rewards, multi-objective specifications, and strategy synthesis. PRISM incorporates a wide selection of analysis techniques. Many are iterative numerical methods such as Gauss-Seidel, value iteration, interval iteration [33], and uniformisation, with multiple variants. Others include linear programming, graph-based algorithms, quantitative abstraction refinement, and symmetry reduction. Their implementations are partly symbolic (typically using binary decision diagrams) and partly explicit (often using sparse matrices). PRISM also supports statistical and parametric model checking. It can be run from a graphical user interface (featuring a model editor, simulator, and graph plotting), the command line, or Java-based APIs. It is primarily written in Java, with some C++, and works on Linux, Mac OS, and Windows. PRISM is open source under the GPL v2.0. It has been connected to many other tools using language translators, model generators, and the HOA format [3]. The tool's website at prismmodelchecker.org provides binary downloads for all major platforms, extensive documentation, tutorials, case studies, and developer resources.

PRISM-TUMheuristics is an explicit-state model checker for DTMC, CTMC, and MDP. It is implemented in Java and works cross-platform. It uses PRISM as a library for model parsing and exploration, and hence handles models in the PRISM language, with JANI support planned. It supports probabilistic reachability, safety, propositional until, and step-bounded reachability properties on MDP and DTMC as well as unbounded reachability for CTMC. At its heart, PRISM-TUMheuristics uses the ideas of [12] to only partially explore state spaces: states which are hardly reached can be omitted from computation if one is only interested in an approximate solution. Sound upper and lower bounds guide the exploration and value propagation, focusing the computation on relevant parts of the state space. Depending on the model's structure, this can yield significant speed-ups. The tool and its source code are available at prism.model.in.tum.de.

Storm [23] features the analysis of DTMC, CTMC, MDP, and MA. It supports PRISM and JANI models, dynamic fault trees [74], probabilistic programs [32], and stochastic Petri nets [1]. Storm analyses PCTL and CSL properties plus extensions of these logics with rewards, including time- and reward-bounded reachability, expected rewards, conditional probabilities, and steady-state rewards. It includes multi-objective model checking [45,65], parameter synthesis [22,64], and counterexample generation [21]. Storm allows for explicit-state and fully symbolic (binary decision diagram-based) model checking as well as mixtures of these approaches. It implements many analysis techniques, e.g. bisimulation minimisation, sound value iteration [66], Unif+ [16], learning-based exploration [12], and game-based abstraction [56]. Dedicated libraries like Eigen, Gurobi, and Z3 [62] are used to carry out sophisticated solving tasks. A command-line interface, a C++ API, and a Python API provide flexible access to the tool's features. Storm and its documentation (including detailed installation instructions) are available at stormchecker.org. It can be compiled from source (Linux and Mac OS), installed via Homebrew (Mac OS), or used from a Docker container (all platforms).

4.2 Statistical Model Checkers

Two simulation-based tools participated in QComp 2019: the DFTRES rare event simulator for fault trees, and the general-purpose statistical model checker modes.

DFTRES is the *dynamic fault tree rare event simulator* [69]: a statistical model checker for dynamic fault trees that uses importance sampling with the Path-ZVA algorithm [67]. It is implemented in Java and works cross-platform. It supports the Galileo format [72] by using DFTCalc [2] as a converter, and a subset of JANI for CTMC and MA provided any nondeterminism is spurious. Path-ZVA allows for efficient analysis of rare event models while requiring only a modest amount of memory. This algorithm is optimised for steady-state properties, but also supports probabilistic reachability (currently implemented for time-bounded properties). Simulations run in parallel on all available processor cores, resulting in a near-linear speedup on multi-core systems. DFTRES is a command-line tool; its source code is available at github.com/utwente-fmt/DFTRES, with instructions provided in a README file. Galileo format support requires the installation of DFTCalc, available at fmt.ewi.utwente.nl/tools/dftcalc, and its dependencies.

modes [14] is the Modest Toolset's statistical model checker. It shares the input languages, supported property types, fast state space exploration, cross-platform support, and documentation with mcsta. modes supports *all* formalisms that can be specified in JANI. It implements methods that address SMC's limitation to purely stochastic models and the rare event problem. On nondeterministic models, modes provides lower (upper) bounds for maximum (minimum) reachability probabilities via lightweight scheduler sampling [20]. For rare events, it implements automated importance splitting methods [13]. Simulation is easy to parallelise, and modes achieves near-linear speedup on multi-core systems and networked computer clusters. It offers multiple statistical methods including confidence intervals, the Okamoto bound [63], and the SPRT [75]. Unless overridden by the user, it automatically selects the best method per property.

4.3 Probabilistic Planners

The probabilistic planners that participated in QComp 2019 consider the analysis of maximum reachability in MDP specifically. They both incorporate FRET-π, but differ in the MDP heuristic search algorithm and the heuristic used.

Modest FRET-π LRTDP implements FRET-π with LRTDP to solve maximum probabilistic reachability on MDP. It is implemented within the Modest Toolset and motivated by an earlier performance comparison between planning algorithms usable for model checking purposes [53]. LRTDP [11] is an asynchronous heuristic search dynamic programming optimisation of value iteration that does not have to consider the entire state space and that converges faster than value iteration because not all values need to be converged (or even updated) before terminating. The tool supports the same input languages as mcsta and modes, and runs on the same platforms. Modest FRET-π LRTDP is available as a binary download at dgit.cs.uni-saarland.de that includes a detailed README file. When invoked on the command line with parameter -help, it prints a list of all command-line parameters with brief explanations.

Probabilistic Fast Downward [71] is an extension of the classical heuristic planner Fast Downward [48]. It supports expected accumulated rewards and maximum probabilistic reachability on MDP specified in PPDDL [77]. Limited JANI support is provided by a translation to PPDDL [53]. Probabilistic Fast Downward features a wide range of algorithms, including two variants of FRET [54,71] complemented by various heuristic search algorithms such as LRTDP [11], HDP [10], and other depth-first heuristic search algorithms [71]. Due to being based on Fast Downward, plenty of state-of-the-art classical planning heuristics are readily available. To make them usable for MDP, Probabilistic Fast Downward supports different methods to determinise probabilistic actions, notably the all-outcomes determinisation [76]. The code is a mixture of C++ and Python, and should compile and run on all common systems. The tool version that participated in QComp 2019 has some functionality removed but also adds performance enhancements. Both versions can be downloaded at fai.cs.uni-saarland.de, and include README files detailing how to build and run the tool. The configuration used for QComp 2019 was FRET-π with HDP [10] search and the h^1-heuristic [47] via the all-outcomes determinisation to obtain an underapproximation of the states that cannot reach the goal with positive probability.

5   Versatility and Usability Evaluation

Once a tool achieves a base level of performance, its versatility and usability may arguably become more important to its acceptance among domain experts than its performance. As versatility, we consider the support for modelling languages and formalisms, for different and complementary analysis engines, and configurability (e.g. to make runtime–precision tradeoffs). Usability is determined by the tool's documentation, the availability of a graphical interface, its installation process, supported platforms, and similar aspects. A user-friendly tool achieves consistently good performance with few non-default configuration settings.

Versatility. The five general-purpose tools—ePMC, mcsta, modes, PRISM, and Storm—support a range of modelling languages, formalisms, and properties (cf. Table 1 and Sect. 4). In terms of languages, Storm is clearly the most versatile tool. Those based on the Modest Toolset and ePMC connect to many languages via JANI. mcsta and modes implement analysis methods for *all* of the formalisms supported by JANI (cf. Fig. 1) while Storm still covers all of those considered in QComp. PRISM only lacks support for MA. However, on the formalisms that they support, PRISM and Storm implement the widest range of properties, followed by ePMC. These three tools in particular support many properties not considered in QComp 2019 such as LTL, PCTL*, multi-objective queries, and parametric model checking. PRISM and Storm also implement many algorithms for the user to choose from that provide different tradeoffs and performance characteristics; Probabilistic Fast Downward is similar in this regard when it comes to planning algorithms and heuristics. While modes is limited to deterministic MDP, MA and PTA when exact results are required as in QComp, it *can* tackle the nondeterminism via lightweight scheduler sampling to provide bounds.

Usability. The most usable among all tools is clearly PRISM: it provides extensive online documentation, a graphical user interface, and binary downloads for all platforms that only depend on Java. The Modest Toolset is less documented and contains command-line tools only, but again ships cross-platform binaries that only require the Mono runtime on non-Windows systems. All in all, the tools based on the Modest Toolset and those mainly implemented in Java (ePMC, DFTRES, PRISM, and PRISM-TUMheuristics) provide the widest platform support. Storm is notably not available for Windows, and Fast Downward partly works cross-platform but is only supported for Linux. The default way to install

Storm, and the only way to install DFTRES, ePMC, PRISM-TUMheuristics, and Probabilistic Fast Downward, is to compile from source code. Storm in particular requires a large number of dependencies in a long build process, which however is well-documented on its website. All tools come with a default analysis configuration adequate for QComp except for Probabilistic Fast Downward, which requires the explicit selection of a specific engine and heuristics. The performance evaluation results in Sect. 6.2 highlight that PRISM and Storm can benefit significantly from using non-default configuration settings tuned by experts to the individual benchmarks, with mcsta showing moderate improvements with simpler tuning.

6   Performance Evaluation

To evaluate the performance of the participating tools, they were executed on benchmark *instances*—a model, fixed values for the model's parameters, and a property—taken from the QVBS. Prior to the performance evaluation, all participants submitted a *wishlist* of (challenging) instances, from which the organisers chose a final set of 100 for the competition: 18 DTMC, 18 CTMC, 36 MDP, 20 MA and 8 PTA instances covering 40 unbounded and 22 bounded probababilistic reachability, 32 expected-reward, and 6 steady-state properties. The selection favoured models selected by multiple participants while aiming for a good balance in terms of formalisms, modelling languages, and property types. As a baseline, every tool should have a good number of supported instances included; still, some tools that were particularly restricted in terms of languages and property types (such as DFTRES and Probabilistic Fast Downward) could only check up to 10 of them. By taking *every* participant's wishlist into account, QComp naturally included instances that a certain tool would do well on (suggested by the participant who submitted the tool) as well as instances that it was not expected to perform best with (suggested by the authors of other tools).

After finalisation of the benchmark instances, participants submitted *tool packages*: installation instructions for the tool (or the tool itself) and a script to generate a JSON file (or the file itself) containing, for every instance, up to two command lines to invoke the tool. One of them was required to run the tool in its default configuration, while the other could use instance-specific parameters to tweak the tool for maximum performance. The performance evaluation was then done by the organisers on one central computer: a standard desktop machine with an Intel Core i7-920 CPU and 12 GB of RAM running 64-bit Ubuntu Linux 18.04. Tools were given 30 min per instance. The choice for a rather modest machine was intentional: the slower CPU increased the performance differentiation for moderately-challenging instances, and the moderate amount of memory allowed for some evaluation of memory efficiency by observing the number of out-of-memory results. In particular, a tool's actual memory usage is not a good measure of quality since the ideal tool will make use of all available memory to speed up the verification as much as possible on challenging instances.

6.1   The Precision Challenge

Almost all properties queried for a value, with only few asking whether a probability is equal to 1. Participants were required to submit a script that extracts the value of an instance's property from the tool output. Since quantitative verification tools can often trade precision for performance, QComp required a tool's result r_i for instance i to be within $[0.999 \cdot v_i, 1.001 \cdot v_i]$ with v_i being the instance's property's correct result—i.e. we required a relative error of at most 10^{-3}. We chose this value as a tradeoff between the advantages of model checkers (which easily achieve high precision but quickly run out of memory on large state spaces) and simulation-based tools (which easily handle large state spaces but quickly run out of time when a high precision is required).

Reference Results. Unfortunately, the actual result for a property is difficult to obtain: tools that scale to large models use inexact floating-point arithmetic, and any tool result may be affected by tool bugs. At the same time, it does not make sense to report performance data when a tool provides an incorrect result as this may be due to an error that drastically reduces or increases the analysis time. QComp 2019 adopted the following pragmatic approach: the organisers used the "most trustworthy" analysis approach available (usually an exact-arithmetic solver for small and a model checker using a sound iterative numerical method for large models) to produce reference results for all selected instances. Participants were then invited to use any other tool to try and refute the correctness of those results, and would discuss the result or benchmark in case of refutation. In the end, only one of the reference results was shown to be incorrect, and this was due to a model translation error that could be corrected before the competition.

Sound and Unsound Model Checking. Practical quantitative model checkers typically use iterative numerical algorithms relying on floating-point arithmetic. Here, certain algorithms can ensure error bounds (such as interval iteration [6,12,33] and sound value iteration [66] for probabilistic reachability, and uniformisation for time-bounded reachability in CTMC). The most common approaches, e.g. value iteration for probabilistic reachability with the standard termination criterion, however provide "good enough" results for many models encountered in practice but may also be widely off for others. It is clearly unfair to compare the runtimes of tools that provide proper precision guarantees against tools without such guarantees where the result happens to be just close enough to the reference value, perhaps even after heavy parameter tweaking to find the sweet spot between runtime and precision. For QComp 2019, since it is the first of its kind and a friendly event, participants agreed to avoid such parameter tweaking. In particular, for iterative methods with an "unsound" convergence check, all participants agreed on using a relative error threshold of $\epsilon = 10^{-6}$ for checking convergence.

6.2　Performance Results

The QComp 2019 performance evaluation produced a large amount of data, which is available at qcomp.org; we here summarise the outcomes in comparative plots. In all of them, we use a logarithmic scale for runtime.

Configurations. mcsta, modes, PRISM and Storm provided instance-specific tool parameters that significantly changed their performance characteristics. All three model checkers switched to an exact-arithmetic or sound iterative method for models with known numerical issues (i.e. the *haddad-monmege* model). Other than that, mcsta was run with some runtime checks disabled (as was modes), and its disk-based methods were disabled for models with relatively small state spaces. On PTA, it was configured to compress linear chains of states, and to use state elimination for time-bounded properties. PRISM was configured to use the best-performing of its four main analysis engines for every instance. This typically meant switching from the default "hybrid" engine to "sparse" for added speed when the state space does not result in memory issues, and to "mtbdd" for

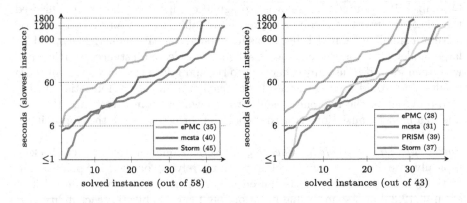

Fig. 2. Quantile plots for the general-purpose model checkers (default configuration)

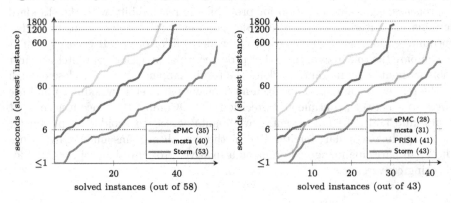

Fig. 3. Quantile plots for the general-purpose model checkers (specific configurations)

larger models with regularity. A Gauss-Seidel variant of each analysis method was used for acyclic models. Storm's specific configurations were set in a similar way to use the fastest out of its four main engines ("sparse", "hybrid", "dd", and "dd" with symbolic bisimulation minimisation) for every instance. Observe that the specific configurations of PRISM and Storm could only be obtained by testing all available engines a priori, which cannot be expected from normal users.

modes by default rejects models with nondeterminism, and runs until the required error is met with 95 % confidence, often hitting the 30-minute timeout. In the specific configurations, modes was instructed to resolve nondeterminism ad hoc, and to return the current estimate irrespective of statistical error after 28 min. It can thus solve more instances (where the nondeterminism is spurious, and where the statistical method is too strict), but risks returning incorrect results (when nondeterminism is relevant, or the error is too large).

Quantile Plots. We first compare the performance of the general-purpose model checkers by means of *quantile plots* in Figs. 2 and 3. Each plot only considers the instances that are supported by *all* of the tools shown in the plot; this is to avoid unsupported instances having a similar visual effect to timeouts and errors. 58 instances are supported by all three of ePMC, mcsta and Storm, while still 43 instances (those in the PRISM language) are also supported by PRISM. The plots' legends indicate the number of correctly solved benchmarks for each tool (i.e. where no timeouts or error occurred and the result was relatively correct up to 10^{-3}). A point $\langle x, y \rangle$ on the line of a tool in this type of plot signifies that the *individual* runtime for the x-th fastest instance solved by the tool was y seconds.

We see that PRISM and Storm are the fastest tools for *most* of the common instances in the default configuration, closely followed by mcsta. The performance of PRISM and Storm improves significantly by selecting instance-specific analysis engines, with Storm taking a clear lead. PRISM solves the largest number of instances in default configuration while Storm leads in specific configurations.

Scatter Plots. In Figs. 4, 5 and 6, we show scatter plots for all tools that compare their performance over all individual instances to the best-performing other tool for each instance. These plots provide more detailed information compared to the previous quantile plots since they compare the performance on individual instances. A point $\langle x, y \rangle$ states that the runtime of the plot's tool on one instance was x seconds while the best runtime on the same instance among all other tools was y seconds. Thus points above the solid diagonal line indicate instances where the plot's tool was the fastest; it was more than ten times faster than any other tool on points above the dotted line. Points on the vertical "TO", "ERR" and "INC" lines respectively indicate instances where the plot's tool encountered a timeout, reported an error (such as nondeterminism not being supported or a crash due to running out of memory), or returned an incorrect result (w.r.t. the relative 10^{-3} precision). Points on the horizontal "n/a" line indicate instances that none of the other tools was able to solve. The "default" plots used the default configuration for all tools, while the "specific" plots used the specific per-instance

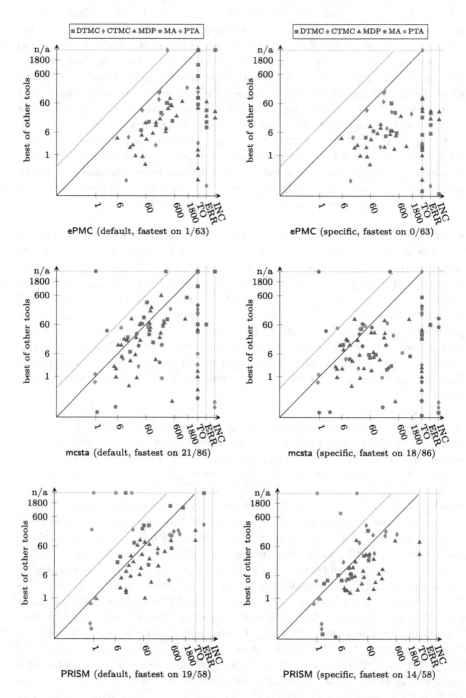

Fig. 4. Runtime of specific tools compared with the best results (1/3)

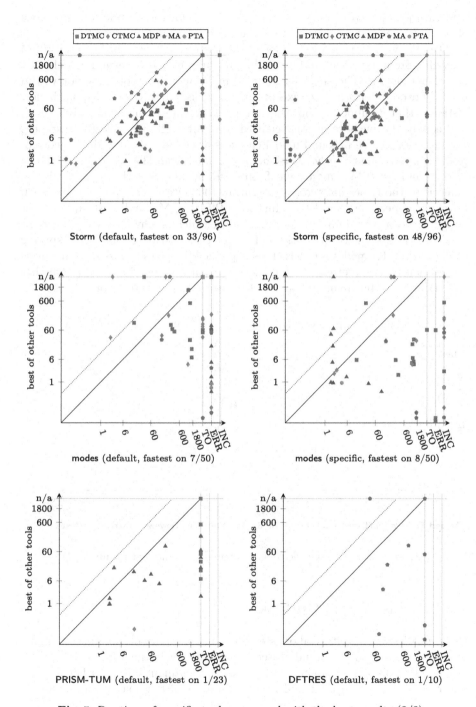

Fig. 5. Runtime of specific tools compared with the best results (2/3)

configurations for *all* tools. We do not show plots for the specific configurations of the four specialised tools since they are not significantly different.

Overall, we see that every tool is the fastest for some instances. PRISM (default), Storm (specific) and modes in particular can solve several models that no other tool can. The specialised and simulation-based tools may not win in terms of overall performance (except for Probabilistic Fast Downward, on the few instances that it supports), but they all solve certain instances uniquely—which is precisely the purpose of a specialised tool, after all. The selected instances contain a few where unsound model checkers are expected to produce incorrect results, in particular the *haddad-monmege* model from [33]; we see this clearly in the plots for ePMC, mcsta and Storm. PRISM aborts with an error when a numeric method does not "converge" within 10000 iterations, which is why such instances appear on the "ERR" line for PRISM. ePMC and mcsta do not yet implement exact or sound iterative methods, which is why they keep incorrect results in the specific configurations. The difference between default and specific configurations for modes is different, as explained; it shows that several instances are spuriously nondeterministic, and several results are good enough at a higher statistical error, but many instances also turn from errors to incorrect results.

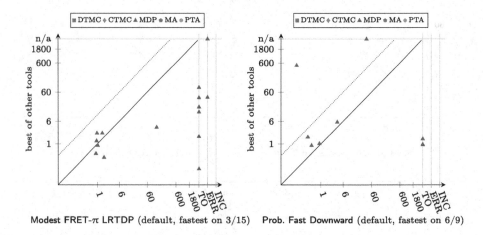

Modest FRET-π LRTDP (default, fastest on 3/15)   Prob. Fast Downward (default, fastest on 6/9)

Fig. 6. Runtime of specific tools compared with the best results (3/3)

7   Conclusion and Outlook

QComp 2019 achieved its goal of assembling a community of tool authors, motivating the collection of a standardised benchmark set in the form of the QVBS, and sparking discussions about properly comparing quantitative verifiers. It also improved JANI tool support and resulted in a set of reusable scripts for batch benchmarking and plotting. Throughout this process, some lessons for changes and requests for additions to the next instance of QComp surfaced:

- The issue that caused most discussion was the problem of how to treat tools that use "unsound" methods as explained in Sect. 6.1. In the future, we plan to provide several tracks, e.g. one where exact results up to some precision are required without per-instance tweaking of parameters, and one that allows fast but "imprecise" results with a nuanced penalty depending on the error.
- The evaluation of default and specific configurations provided important insights, but might not be continued; we expect tools to use the QComp 2019 results as a push to implement heuristics to choose good defaults automatically.
- The current versatility and usability evaluation was very informal and needs to move to clear pre-announced criteria that tool authors can plan for.
- The only addition to formalisms requested by participants is stochastic games, e.g. as in PRISM-games [55]; however, these first need standardisation and JANI support. In terms of properties, LTL is supported by several tools and will be included in the next edition of QComp. Other desirable properties include multi-objective queries, and the generation of strategies instead of just values.
- Finally, all benchmarks of QComp 2019 were known a priori. As QComp slowly transitions from a "friendly" to a more "competitive" event, the inclusion of obfuscated or a priori unknown benchmarks needs to be considered.

Acknowledgements. QComp 2019 was organised by Arnd Hartmanns and Tim Quatmann. The authors thank their tool co-developers: Yi Li (Peking University), Yong Li (Chinese Academy of Sciences), Andrea Turrini, and Lijun Zhang (Chinese Academy of Sciences and Institute of Intelligent Software) for ePMC; Pranav Ashok, Tobias Meggendorfer, and Maximilian Weininger (Technische Universität München) for PRISM-TUMheuristics; and Sebastian Junges and Matthias Volk (RWTH Aachen) for Storm.

Data Availibility. The tools used and data generated in the performance evaluation are archived and available at qcomp.org/competition/2019.

References

1. Amparore, E.G., Balbo, G., Beccuti, M., Donatelli, S., Franceschinis, G.: 30 years of GreatSPN. In: Fiondella, L., Puliafito, A. (eds.) Principles of Performance and Reliability Modeling and Evaluation. SSRE, pp. 227–254. Springer, Cham (2016). https://doi.org/10.1007/978-3-319-30599-8_9
2. Arnold, F., Belinfante, A., Van der Berg, F., Guck, D., Stoelinga, M.: DFTCALC: a tool for efficient fault tree analysis. In: Bitsch, F., Guiochet, J., Kaâniche, M. (eds.) SAFECOMP 2013. LNCS, vol. 8153, pp. 293–301. Springer, Heidelberg (2013). https://doi.org/10.1007/978-3-642-40793-2_27
3. Babiak, T., Blahoudek, F., Duret-Lutz, A., Klein, J., Kretínský, J., Müller, D., Parker, D., Strejcek, J.: The Hanoi omega-automata format. In: Kroening, D., Păsăreanu, C.S. (eds.) CAV 2015. LNCS, vol. 9206, pp. 479–486. Springer, Cham (2015). https://doi.org/10.1007/978-3-319-21690-4_31

88   E. M. Hahn et al.

4. Baier, C., Katoen, J.P.: Principles of Model Checking. MIT Press, Cambridge (2008)
5. Baier, C., Katoen, J.-P., Hermanns, H.: Approximative symbolic model checking of continuous-time Markov chains. In: Baeten, J.C.M., Mauw, S. (eds.) CONCUR 1999. LNCS, vol. 1664, pp. 146–161. Springer, Heidelberg (1999). https://doi.org/10.1007/3-540-48320-9_12
6. Baier, C., Klein, J., Leuschner, L., Parker, D., Wunderlich, S.: Ensuring the reliability of your model checker: interval iteration for Markov decision processes. In: Majumdar, R., Kunčak, V. (eds.) CAV 2017. LNCS, vol. 10426, pp. 160–180. Springer, Cham (2017). https://doi.org/10.1007/978-3-319-63387-9_8
7. Behrmann, G., David, A., Larsen, K.G., Håkansson, J., Pettersson, P., Yi, W., Hendriks, M.: UPPAAL 4.0. In: QEST, pp. 125–126. IEEE Computer Society (2006)
8. Beyer, D.: Competition on software verification. In: Flanagan, C., König, B. (eds.) TACAS 2012. LNCS, vol. 7214, pp. 504–524. Springer, Heidelberg (2012). https://doi.org/10.1007/978-3-642-28756-5_38
9. Bohnenkamp, H.C., D'Argenio, P.R., Hermanns, H., Katoen, J.P.: MODEST: a compositional modeling formalism for hard and softly timed systems. IEEE Trans. Softw. Eng. 32(10), 812–830 (2006)
10. Bonet, B., Geffner, H.: Faster heuristic search algorithms for planning with uncertainty and full feedback. In: IJCAI, pp. 1233–1238. Morgan Kaufmann (2003)
11. Bonet, B., Geffner, H.: Labeled RTDP: improving the convergence of real-time dynamic programming. In: ICAPS, pp. 12–21. AAAI (2003)
12. Brázdil, T., Chatterjee, K., Chmelik, M., Forejt, V., Kretínský, J., Kwiatkowska, M.Z., Parker, D., Ujma, M.: Verification of Markov decision processes using learning algorithms. In: Cassez, F., Raskin, J.-F. (eds.) ATVA 2014. LNCS, vol. 8837, pp. 98–114. Springer, Cham (2014). https://doi.org/10.1007/978-3-319-11936-6_8
13. Budde, C.E., D'Argenio, P.R., Hartmanns, A.: Better automated importance splitting for transient rare events. In: Larsen, K.G., Sokolsky, O., Wang, J. (eds.) SETTA 2017. LNCS, vol. 10606, pp. 42–58. Springer, Cham (2017). https://doi.org/10.1007/978-3-319-69483-2_3
14. Budde, C.E., D'Argenio, P.R., Hartmanns, A., Sedwards, S.: A statistical model checker for nondeterminism and rare events. In: Beyer, D., Huisman, M. (eds.) TACAS 2018. LNCS, vol. 10806, pp. 340–358. Springer, Cham (2018). https://doi.org/10.1007/978-3-319-89963-3_20
15. Budde, C.E., Dehnert, C., Hahn, E.M., Hartmanns, A., Junges, S., Turrini, A.: JANI: quantitative model and tool interaction. In: Legay, A., Margaria, T. (eds.) TACAS 2017. LNCS, vol. 10206, pp. 151–168. Springer, Heidelberg (2017). https://doi.org/10.1007/978-3-662-54580-5_9
16. Butkova, Y., Hatefi, H., Hermanns, H., Krčál, J.: Optimal continuous time Markov decisions. In: Finkbeiner, B., Pu, G., Zhang, L. (eds.) ATVA 2015. LNCS, vol. 9364, pp. 166–182. Springer, Cham (2015). https://doi.org/10.1007/978-3-319-24953-7_12
17. Chen, T., Forejt, V., Kwiatkowska, M.Z., Parker, D., Simaitis, A.: Automatic verification of competitive stochastic systems. FMSD 43(1), 61–92 (2013)
18. Coles, A.J., Coles, A., Olaya, A.G., Celorrio, S.J., Linares López, C., Sanner, S., Yoon, S.: A survey of the seventh international planning competition. AI Mag. 33(1), 83–88 (2012)
19. Courtney, T., Gaonkar, S., Keefe, K., Rozier, E., Sanders, W.H.: Möbius 2.3: an extensible tool for dependability, security, and performance evaluation of large and complex system models. In: DSN, pp. 353–358. IEEE Computer Society (2009)

20. D'Argenio, P.R., Hartmanns, A., Sedwards, S.: Lightweight statistical model checking in nondeterministic continuous time. In: Margaria, T., Steffen, B. (eds.) ISoLA 2018. LNCS, vol. 11245, pp. 336–353. Springer, Cham (2018). https://doi.org/10.1007/978-3-030-03421-4_22

21. Dehnert, C., Jansen, N., Wimmer, R., Ábrahám, E., Katoen, J.-P.: Fast debugging of PRISM models. In: Cassez, F., Raskin, J.-F. (eds.) ATVA 2014. LNCS, vol. 8837, pp. 146–162. Springer, Cham (2014). https://doi.org/10.1007/978-3-319-11936-6_11

22. Dehnert, C., Junges, S., Jansen, N., Corzilius, F., Volk, M., Bruintjes, H., Katoen, J., Ábrahám, E.: PROPhESY: A PRObabilistic ParamEter SYnthesis tool. In: Kroening, D., Păsăreanu, C.S. (eds.) CAV 2015. LNCS, vol. 9206, pp. 214–231. Springer, Cham (2015). https://doi.org/10.1007/978-3-319-21690-4_13

23. Dehnert, C., Junges, S., Katoen, J.-P., Volk, M.: A STORM is coming: a modern probabilistic model checker. In: Majumdar, R., Kunčak, V. (eds.) CAV 2017. LNCS, vol. 10427, pp. 592–600. Springer, Cham (2017). https://doi.org/10.1007/978-3-319-63390-9_31

24. van Dijk, T., Hahn, E.M., Jansen, D.N., Li, Y., Neele, T., Stoelinga, M., Turrini, A., Zhang, L.: A comparative study of BDD packages for probabilistic symbolic model checking. In: Li, X., Liu, Z., Yi, W. (eds.) SETTA 2015. LNCS, vol. 9409, pp. 35–51. Springer, Cham (2015). https://doi.org/10.1007/978-3-319-25942-0_3

25. Eisentraut, C., Hermanns, H., Zhang, L.: On probabilistic automata in continuous time. In: LICS, pp. 342–351. IEEE Computer Society (2010)

26. Etessami, K., Kwiatkowska, M.Z., Vardi, M.Y., Yannakakis, M.: Multi-objective model checking of Markov decision processes. LMCS **4**(4) (2008). https://doi.org/10.2168/LMCS-4(4:8)2008

27. Feng, Y., Hahn, E.M., Turrini, A., Ying, S.: Model checking omega-regular properties for quantum Markov chains. In: CONCUR. LIPIcs, vol. 85, pp. 35:1–35:16. Schloss Dagstuhl - Leibniz-Zentrum fuer Informatik (2017)

28. Fränzle, M., Hahn, E.M., Hermanns, H., Wolovick, N., Zhang, L.: Measurability and safety verification for stochastic hybrid systems. In: HSCC. ACM (2011)

29. Frehse, G., Althoff, M., Bogomolov, S., Johnson, T.T. (eds.): ARCH18. 5th International Workshop on Applied Verification of Continuous and Hybrid Systems, EPiC Series in Computing, vol. 54. EasyChair (2018)

30. Fu, C., Turrini, A., Huang, X., Song, L., Feng, Y., Zhang, L.: Model checking probabilistic epistemic logic for probabilistic multiagent systems. In: IJCAI (2018)

31. Gainer, P., Hahn, E.M., Schewe, S.: Accelerated model checking of parametric Markov chains. In: Lahiri, S.K., Wang, C. (eds.) ATVA 2018. LNCS, vol. 11138, pp. 300–316. Springer, Cham (2018). https://doi.org/10.1007/978-3-030-01090-4_18

32. Gordon, A.D., Henzinger, T.A., Nori, A.V., Rajamani, S.K.: Probabilistic programming. In: FOSE, pp. 167–181. ACM (2014)

33. Haddad, S., Monmege, B.: Interval iteration algorithm for MDPs and IMDPs. Theor. Comput. Sci. **735**, 111–131 (2018)

34. Hahn, E.M., Hartmanns, A.: A comparison of time- and reward-bounded probabilistic model checking techniques. In: Fränzle, M., Kapur, D., Zhan, N. (eds.) SETTA 2016. LNCS, vol. 9984, pp. 85–100. Springer, Cham (2016). https://doi.org/10.1007/978-3-319-47677-3_6

35. Hahn, E.M., Hartmanns, A., Hermanns, H.: Reachability and reward checking for stochastic timed automata. In: Electronic Communications of the EASST, vol. 70 (2014)

36. Hahn, E.M., Hartmanns, A., Hermanns, H., Katoen, J.P.: A compositional modelling and analysis framework for stochastic hybrid systems. FMSD **43**(2), 191–232 (2013)
37. Hahn, E.M., Hashemi, V., Hermanns, H., Lahijanian, M., Turrini, A.: Multiobjective robust strategy synthesis for interval Markov decision processes. In: Bertrand, N., Bortolussi, L. (eds.) QEST 2017. LNCS, vol. 10503, pp. 207–223. Springer, Cham (2017). https://doi.org/10.1007/978-3-319-66335-7_13
38. Hahn, E.M., Hashemi, V., Hermanns, H., Turrini, A.: Exploiting robust optimization for interval probabilistic bisimulation. In: Agha, G., Van Houdt, B. (eds.) QEST 2016. LNCS, vol. 9826, pp. 55–71. Springer, Cham (2016). https://doi.org/10.1007/978-3-319-43425-4_4
39. Hahn, E.M., Li, G., Schewe, S., Zhang, L.: Lazy determinisation for quantitative model checking. CoRR abs/1311.2928 (2013)
40. Hahn, E.M., Li, Y., Schewe, S., Turrini, A., Zhang, L.: ISCASMC: a web-based probabilistic model checker. In: Jones, C., Pihlajasaari, P., Sun, J. (eds.) FM 2014. LNCS, vol. 8442, pp. 312–317. Springer, Cham (2014). https://doi.org/10.1007/978-3-319-06410-9_22
41. Hahn, E.M., Schewe, S., Turrini, A., Zhang, L.: A simple algorithm for solving qualitative probabilistic parity games. In: Chaudhuri, S., Farzan, A. (eds.) CAV 2016. LNCS, vol. 9780, pp. 291–311. Springer, Cham (2016). https://doi.org/10.1007/978-3-319-41540-6_16
42. Hartmanns, A., Hermanns, H.: The Modest Toolset: an integrated environment for quantitative modelling and verification. In: Ábrahám, E., Havelund, K. (eds.) TACAS 2014. LNCS, vol. 8413, pp. 593–598. Springer, Heidelberg (2014). https://doi.org/10.1007/978-3-642-54862-8_51
43. Hartmanns, A., Hermanns, H.: Explicit model checking of very large MDP using partitioning and secondary storage. In: Finkbeiner, B., Pu, G., Zhang, L. (eds.) ATVA 2015. LNCS, vol. 9364, pp. 131–147. Springer, Cham (2015). https://doi.org/10.1007/978-3-319-24953-7_10
44. Hartmanns, A., Hermanns, H., Bungert, M.: Flexible support for time and costs in scenario-aware dataflow. In: EMSOFT, pp. 3:1–3:10. ACM (2016)
45. Hartmanns, A., Junges, S., Katoen, J.-P., Quatmann, T.: Multi-cost bounded reachability in MDP. In: Beyer, D., Huisman, M. (eds.) TACAS 2018. LNCS, vol. 10806, pp. 320–339. Springer, Cham (2018). https://doi.org/10.1007/978-3-319-89963-3_19
46. Hartmanns, A., Klauck, M., Parker, D., Quatmann, T., Ruijters, E.: The quantitative verification benchmark set. In: Vojnar, T., Zhang, L. (eds.) TACAS 2019. LNCS, vol. 11427, pp. 344–350. Springer, Cham (2019)
47. Haslum, P., Bonet, B., Geffner, H.: New admissible heuristics for domain-independent planning. In: AAAI/IAAI, pp. 1163–1168. AAAI/MIT Press (2005)
48. Helmert, M.: The Fast Downward planning system. J. Artif. Intell. Res. **26**, 191–246 (2006)
49. Hérault, T., Lassaigne, R., Magniette, F., Peyronnet, S.: Approximate probabilistic model checking. In: Steffen, B., Levi, G. (eds.) VMCAI 2004. LNCS, vol. 2937, pp. 73–84. Springer, Heidelberg (2004). https://doi.org/10.1007/978-3-540-24622-0_8
50. Hillston, J.: A Compositional Approach to Performance Modelling. Cambridge University Press, Cambridge (1996)
51. Järvisalo, M., Berre, D.L., Roussel, O., Simon, L.: The international SAT solver competitions. AI Mag. **33**(1), 89–92 (2012)

52. Jasper, M., Mues, M., Schlüter, M., Steffen, B., Howar, F.: RERS 2018: CTL, LTL, and reachability. In: Margaria, T., Steffen, B. (eds.) ISoLA 2018. LNCS, vol. 11245, pp. 433–447. Springer, Cham (2018). https://doi.org/10.1007/978-3-030-03421-4_27

53. Klauck, M., Steinmetz, M., Hoffmann, J., Hermanns, H.: Compiling probabilistic model checking into probabilistic planning. In: ICAPS, pp. 150–154. AAAI (2018)

54. Kolobov, A., Mausam, Weld, D.S., Geffner, H.: Heuristic search for generalized stochastic shortest path MDPs. In: ICAPS. AAAI (2011)

55. Kwiatkowska, M.Z., Parker, D., Wiltsche, C.: PRISM-games: verification and strategy synthesis for stochastic multi-player games with multiple objectives. STTT 20(2), 195–210 (2018)

56. Kwiatkowska, M.Z., Norman, G., Parker, D.: Game-based abstraction for Markov decision processes. In: QEST, pp. 157–166. IEEE Computer Society (2006)

57. Kwiatkowska, M.Z., Norman, G., Parker, D.: PRISM 4.0: verification of probabilistic real-time systems. In: Gopalakrishnan, G., Qadeer, S. (eds.) CAV 2011. LNCS, vol. 6806, pp. 585–591. Springer, Heidelberg (2011). https://doi.org/10.1007/978-3-642-22110-1_47

58. Kwiatkowska, M.Z., Norman, G., Parker, D., Sproston, J.: Performance analysis of probabilistic timed automata using digital clocks. FMSD 29(1), 33–78 (2006)

59. Kwiatkowska, M.Z., Norman, G., Segala, R., Sproston, J.: Automatic verification of real-time systems with discrete probability distributions. Theor. Comput. Sci. 282(1), 101–150 (2002)

60. Li, Y., Liu, W., Turrini, A., Hahn, E.M., Zhang, L.: An efficient synthesis algorithm for parametric Markov chains against linear time properties. CoRR abs/1605.04400 (2016)

61. Maler, O., Nickovic, D.: Monitoring temporal properties of continuous signals. In: Lakhnech, Y., Yovine, S. (eds.) FORMATS/FTRTFT -2004. LNCS, vol. 3253, pp. 152–166. Springer, Heidelberg (2004). https://doi.org/10.1007/978-3-540-30206-3_12

62. de Moura, L., Bjørner, N.: Z3: an efficient SMT solver. In: Ramakrishnan, C.R., Rehof, J. (eds.) TACAS 2008. LNCS, vol. 4963, pp. 337–340. Springer, Heidelberg (2008). https://doi.org/10.1007/978-3-540-78800-3_24

63. Okamoto, M.: Some inequalities relating to the partial sum of binomial probabilities. Ann. Inst. Stat. Math. 10(1), 29–35 (1959)

64. Quatmann, T., Dehnert, C., Jansen, N., Junges, S., Katoen, J.-P.: Parameter synthesis for Markov models: faster than ever. In: Artho, C., Legay, A., Peled, D. (eds.) ATVA 2016. LNCS, vol. 9938, pp. 50–67. Springer, Cham (2016). https://doi.org/10.1007/978-3-319-46520-3_4

65. Quatmann, T., Junges, S., Katoen, J.-P.: Markov automata with multiple objectives. In: Majumdar, R., Kunčak, V. (eds.) CAV 2017. LNCS, vol. 10426, pp. 140–159. Springer, Cham (2017). https://doi.org/10.1007/978-3-319-63387-9_7

66. Quatmann, T., Katoen, J.-P.: Sound value iteration. In: Chockler, H., Weissenbacher, G. (eds.) CAV 2018. LNCS, vol. 10981, pp. 643–661. Springer, Cham (2018). https://doi.org/10.1007/978-3-319-96145-3_37

67. Reijsbergen, D., de Boer, P.T., Scheinhardt, W., Juneja, S.: Path-ZVA: general, efficient, and automated importance sampling for highly reliable Markovian systems. TOMACS 28(3), 22:1–22:25 (2018)

68. Rubino, G., Tuffin, B.: Rare Event Simulation Using Monte Carlo Methods. Wiley, Hoboken (2009)

69. Ruijters, E., Reijsbergen, D., de Boer, P.T., Stoelinga, M.I.A.: Rare event simulation for dynamic fault trees. Reliab. Eng. Syst. Saf. **186**, 220–231 (2019). https://doi.org/10.1016/j.ress.2019.02.004

70. Sproston, J.: Decidable model checking of probabilistic hybrid automata. In: Joseph, M. (ed.) FTRTFT 2000. LNCS, vol. 1926, pp. 31–45. Springer, Heidelberg (2000). https://doi.org/10.1007/3-540-45352-0_5

71. Steinmetz, M., Hoffmann, J., Buffet, O.: Goal probability analysis in probabilistic planning: exploring and enhancing the state of the art. J. Artif. Intell. Res. **57**, 229–271 (2016)

72. Sullivan, K.J., Dugan, J.B., Coppit, D.: The Galileo fault tree analysis tool. In: FTCS-29, pp. 232–235. IEEE Computer Society (1999)

73. Ummels, M., Baier, C.: Computing quantiles in Markov reward models. In: Pfenning, F. (ed.) FoSSaCS 2013. LNCS, vol. 7794, pp. 353–368. Springer, Heidelberg (2013). https://doi.org/10.1007/978-3-642-37075-5_23

74. Volk, M., Junges, S., Katoen, J.P.: Fast dynamic fault tree analysis by model checking techniques. IEEE Trans. Ind. Inform. **14**(1), 370–379 (2018)

75. Wald, A.: Sequential tests of statistical hypotheses. Ann. Math. Stat. **16**(2), 117–186 (1945)

76. Yoon, S.W., Fern, A., Givan, R.: FF-Replan: a baseline for probabilistic planning. In: ICAPS, p. 352. AAAI (2007)

77. Younes, H.L.S., Littman, M.L., Weissman, D., Asmuth, J.: The first probabilistic track of the International Planning Competition. J. Artif. Intell. Res. **24**, 851–887 (2005)

78. Younes, H.L.S., Simmons, R.G.: Probabilistic verification of discrete event systems using acceptance sampling. In: Brinksma, E., Larsen, K.G. (eds.) CAV 2002. LNCS, vol. 2404, pp. 223–235. Springer, Heidelberg (2002). https://doi.org/10.1007/3-540-45657-0_17

The Rewrite Engines Competitions: A RECtrospective

Francisco Durán[1] and Hubert Garavel[2]([✉])

[1] Universidad de Málaga, Málaga, Spain
`duran@lcc.uma.es`
[2] Univ. Grenoble Alpes, Inria, CNRS, Grenoble INP, LIG, 38000 Grenoble, France
`hubert.garavel@inria.fr`

Abstract. Term rewriting is a simple, yet expressive model of computation, which finds direct applications in specification and programming languages (many of which embody rewrite rules, pattern matching, and abstract data types), but also indirect applications, e.g., to express the semantics of data types or concurrent processes, to specify program transformations, to perform computer-aided verification, etc. The Rewrite Engines Competition (REC) was created under the aegis of the Workshop on Rewriting Logic and its Applications (WRLA) to serve three main goals: (i) being a forum in which tool developers and potential users of term rewrite engines can share experience; (ii) bringing together the various language features and implementation techniques used for term rewriting; and (iii) comparing the available term rewriting languages and tools in their common features. The present article provides a retrospective overview of the four editions of the Rewrite Engines Competition (2006, 2008, 2010, and 2018) and traces their evolution over time.

1 Introduction

When searching Google for "rewrite engine", most of the references are about Apache web servers and rewrite engines for URLs. Such engines perform *string rewriting*, which is a particular case of *term rewriting* [1,3], a very general model of computation based on the repeated application of simplification rules. Despite its simplicity, term rewriting has shown itself a suitable paradigm for expressing fundamental concepts of logics, mathematics, and computer science (e.g., concurrency, communication, interaction, etc.).

Beyond such theoretical aspects, the ideas of term rewriting influenced the design of specification and programming languages, many of which incorporate algebraic terms and rewrite rules. Software implementations of term rewriting have been developed including, of course, rewrite engines, but also a large variety of tools for compiler construction, program transformation, and formal verification by theorem proving or model checking.

In order to evaluate and compare the various rewrite engines available, a software competition named REC (*Rewrite Engines Competition*) was created

© The Author(s) 2019
D. Beyer et al. (Eds.): TACAS 2019, Part III, LNCS 11429, pp. 93–100, 2019.
https://doi.org/10.1007/978-3-030-17502-3_6

in 2006. Organized together with WRLA (*Workshop on Rewriting Logic and its Applications*), REC provides a forum for sharing experiences among tool developers and potential users. Four editions of this competition have taken place so far: REC1 (2006), REC2 (2008), REC3 (2010), and REC4 (2018).

The present article, which is part of the TOOLympics project to celebrate the 25th anniversary of the TACAS conference by gathering numerous software competitions at ETAPS, provides a retrospective overview of past editions of the REC competition. Section 2 summarizes the developments of the competition; Sect. 3 lists all tools that have been assessed, and Sect. 4 presents the collection of benchmarks accumulated during the successive editions; finally, Sect. 5 draws perspectives for future editions of the REC competition.

2   Evolution of REC Competitions

In the mid-2000's, it became manifest that the term-rewriting community was lacking a comparative study of the different rewrite engines available. The following excerpt, quoted from [11], articulates the motivation for such a study:

> "The idea of organizing a rewrite competition arose from noticing various applications of rewriting in different areas and by different categories of researchers, many of them manifesting a genuine and explicit interest in term rewriting. We believe that many of us can benefit from such rewrite engine competitions, provided that they are fair and explicitly state what was tested in each case. For example, users of rewrite engine can more informatively select the right rewrite engine for their particular application. On the other hand, for rewrite engine developers, such events give them ideas on how to improve their tools and what to prioritize, as well as a clearer idea of how their engine compares to others."

It was not clear, however, how to conduct such a study. The abstract and general nature of term rewriting has given birth to a great diversity in software implementations. General-purpose rewrite engines differ in the various forms of rewriting they support (conditional, nondeterministic, context-sensitive, etc.). Many other rewrite engines are specialized for particular problems and embedded into programming languages, theorem provers, environments for compiler construction and program transformation, etc. (see Sect. 3 for examples).

REC1 [11] faced such doubts about the right approach to follow and decided to focus on efficiency, measured in terms of CPU time and memory use. Only two tools participated in this first edition of the competition, organized together with WRLA 2006. A collection of benchmarks, namely term rewrite systems sorted in four categories (see Sect. 4), was produced. Each benchmark was translated by hand into the input language of each participating tool, and revised by tool developers to make sure this code was optimal for their tools.

REC2 [15] expanded on the ideas of REC1, with a double goal: (i) broaden the comparison by assessing the efficiency of a larger number of rewrite engines— indeed, five tools participated in REC2; and (ii) being a showcase for the term-rewriting community, with a dedicated session at WRLA 2008, where all participating tools were presented by their developers, who exposed the features and strengths of each tool and discussed the outcomes of the competition. Tool developers actively participated in the whole process of REC2, not merely for adapting competition benchmarks to the tools, but also for exchanging views on how to organize the competition and present its results. As a result of fruitful discussions, several changes were implemented, such as the design of a common language for expressing the benchmarks (see Sect. 4 below).

REC3 [14] followed the same approach as REC2, with a greater emphasis on automation and a larger set of term-rewriting benchmarks—including problems related to program transformation, a key application area of term rewriting. The developers of all the participating tools were involved in this competition, organized together with WRLA 2010. The reported results indicate the computation time spent by each tool on each benchmark.

REC4 [17] was the result of a long-term effort undertaken in 2015 and presented at WRLA 2018. The competition's scope was broadened away from traditional rewrite engines to include functional and object-oriented languages. As a consequence, REC4 did not consider particular features implemented only in some tools, but focused instead on basic features common to all tools, namely term rewrite systems that are confluent and terminating, with free constructors and conditional rules. Tool execution and comparison of results was fully automated, making it unnecessary to include tool developers directly in the competition—although they were contacted by email, in case of problems, before the presentation of the results. A Top-5 podium was produced to indicate which tools can tackle the most problems within a given amount of time and memory.

3   Tools Assessed

So far, not fewer than 18 tools have been assessed during the REC competitions, as shown by Table 1. This table lists which tools participated in which editions of the competition. Not all tools have been assessed in all editions, as it happened, e.g., for prominent tools such as ELAN [4] and ASF+SDF [6], the development of which halted before or just after REC1.

It is worth pointing out the versatility of term rewriting and the diversity of its implementations. It is used in both specification and programming languages. These languages can be algebraic (e.g., CafeOBJ, LOTOS, Maude, mCRL2, Stratego/XT, etc.), functional (e.g., Clean, Haskell, LNT, OCaml, SML, etc.), or object-oriented (e.g., Rascal, Scala, Tom, etc.), and certain languages combine several of these traits, such as Opal, which is both algebraic and functional, or OCaml, which is both functional and object-oriented. Some languages also support higher-order programming (e.g., Haskell, OCaml), while others have built-in support for concurrency (e.g., LOTOS, LNT, Maude, mCRL2, etc.). Implementations encompass compilers and interpreters, certain languages (e.g., OCaml or Rascal) offering both, while other approaches (e.g., Tom) enable term rewrite systems to be embedded in general-purpose languages such as C or Java. Finally,

Table 1. Languages and tools considered in the Rewrite Engines Competitions

language (tool)	web site	REC1	REC2	REC3	REC4
ASF+SDF [6]	http://www.meta-environment.org	×	×	×	
CafeOBJ [12]	http://cafeobj.org				×
Clean [26]	http://clean.cs.ru.nl				×
Haskell (GHC) [22]	http://www.haskell.org				×
LNT (CADP) [8,16]	http://cadp.inria.fr				×
Lotos (CADP) [16,19]	http://cadp.inria.fr				×
Maude [9]	http://maude.cs.illinois.edu	×	×	×	×
mCRL2 [18]	http://www.mcrl2.org				×
OCaml [21]	http://www.ocaml.org				×
Opal (OCS) [25]	http://github.com/TU-Berlin/opal				×
Rascal [5]	http://www.rascal-mpl.org				×
Scala [24]	http://www.scala-lang.org				×
SML (MLton) [23]	http://www.mlton.org				×
SML (SML/NJ) [23]	http://www.smlnj.org				×
Stratego/XT [7]	http://www.metaborg.org		×	×	×
TermWare [13]	http://gradsoft.ua/index_eng.html		×		
Tom [2]	http://tom.loria.fr		×	×	×
TXL [10]	http://txl.ca			×	

some implementations (ASF/SDF, Stratego/XT, etc.) provide rich environments for language design, including support for lexical/syntactic analysis, construction and traversal of abstract syntax trees, as well as program transformations.

4   REC Benchmarks

As a byproduct of the efforts made in organizing the four REC competitions, a collection of benchmarks has been progressively accumulated[1].

REC1 [11] set up the foundations of this collection, by gathering 41 term rewrite systems, split into four distinct categories: *unconditional term rewrite systems* (in which no rewrite rule has Boolean premises), *conditional term rewrite systems* (in which some rewrite rules have Boolean premises), *rewriting modulo axioms* (in which rewriting relies on certain axioms, such as commutativity and/or associativity), and *rewriting modulo strategies* (in which rewriting is context sensitive, guided by local strategies). Several REC1 benchmarks were derived from generic benchmarks parameterized by variables (e.g., the parameter of function computing the factorial of a natural number, the length of a list to be sorted, etc.) by giving particular values to these variables. Following the terminology used for the Model Checking Contest [20], we distinguish

---

[1] These are available from http://rec.gforge.inria.fr.

between *models*, which are generic benchmarks, and *instances*, which are benchmarks derived from generic benchmarks by giving actual values to parameters; the remaining benchmarks, which are not parameterized, are counted both as models and instances.

REC2 [15] brought a significant evolution: in REC1, each benchmark was specified in the input language of each tool, which was only feasible as the number of tools was small. REC2 introduced, to express its benchmarks, a common language, which we name REC-2008 and which was inspired by the TPDB language used at that time by the Termination Competition (the Confluence Competition uses a similar language). Several tools were adapted to accept this new language REC-2008 as input; for the other tools, translation was done manually.

REC3 [14] pursued in the same vein as REC2, while increasing the number of instances. REC3 also tried to expand the scope of the competition by introducing a separate collection of benchmarks meant for program transformation and expressed in an imperative language named TIL; however, this initiative was left with no follow-through.

REC4 [17], in order to address a larger set of specification and programming languages, introduced a new language REC-2017 derived from REC-2008 with additional restrictions ensuring that benchmarks are deterministic (hence, confluent), terminating, and free from equations between constructors. Consequently, the 3rd and 4th categories (rewriting modulo equations and rewriting modulo strategies) were removed, and the 1st and 2nd categories (unconditional and conditional rewriting) were merged into a single one, as most languages do not make such a distinction. The remaining REC-2008 benchmarks were upgraded to the REC-2017 language, and many new, significantly complex benchmarks were added to the collection. To provide for an objective comparison, scripts were developed to translate REC-2017 specifications to the input languages of all tools under assessment.

Table 2 gives a quantitative overview of the evolution of the REC benchmark collection; each cells having the form "$(m)\ n$" denotes m models and n instances.

Table 2. Benchmarks considered in the Rewrite Engines Competitions

category	REC1	REC2	REC3	REC4
source language	tool-specific	REC-2008	REC-2008	REC-2017
unconditional term rewrite systems	(5) 7	(5) 12	(7) 26	(19) 43
conditional term rewrite systems	(9) 25	(8) 18	(6) 17	(24) 42
rewriting modulo equations	(4) 9	(4) 6	(4) 6	(0) 0
rewriting modulo strategies	(0) 0	(1) 1	(1) 3	(0) 0
TOTAL	(18) 41	(18) 37	(18) 52	(43) 85

5 Conclusion

Term rewriting is a fundamental topic with many applications, as illustrated by the multiplicity of term-rewriting implementations in compilers and interpreters.

The Rewrite Engines Competitions (REC), the evolutions of which have been reviewed in the present article, stimulate the research interest in this field. One main lesson to be retained from these competitions is that performance of term rewriting significantly differs across implementations: there is room for enhancements and, following the latest REC competition (2018), three developer teams already reported plans to improve their tools to take into account the REC results.

Future REC competitions should address at least two points: (i) more languages should be assessed, inviting recent tools in the competition and keeping in mind that some tools may disappear if they are no longer maintained; (ii) more benchmarks should be considered, which will require dedicated effort to develop new benchmarks, given the lack of large, computationally intensive term rewriting systems freely available on the Web, and the subtle semantic differences that exist between the various flavours of term rewrite systems.

References

1. Baader, F., Nipkow, T.: Term Rewriting and All That. Cambridge University Press, Cambridge (1998)
2. Balland, E., Brauner, P., Kopetz, R., Moreau, P.-E., Reilles, A.: Tom: Piggybacking rewriting on Java. In: Baader, F. (ed.) RTA 2007. LNCS, vol. 4533, pp. 36–47. Springer, Heidelberg (2007). https://doi.org/10.1007/978-3-540-73449-9_5
3. Bezem, M., Klop, J., de Vrijer, R., Terese (group) (eds.): Term Rewriting Systems. Cambridge Tracts in Theoretical Computer Science, vol. 55. Cambridge University Press, Cambridge (2003)
4. Borovanský, P., Kirchner, C., Kirchner, H., Moreau, P.E., Ringeissen, C.: An overview of ELAN. Electron. Notes Theor. Comput. Sci. **15**, 55–70 (1998)
5. van den Bos, J., Hills, M., Klint, P., van der Storm, T., Vinju, J.J.: Rascal: from algebraic specification to meta-programming. In: Durán, F., Rusu, V. (eds.) Proceedings of the 2nd International Workshop on Algebraic Methods in Model-based Software Engineering (AMMSE 2011), Zurich, Switzerland. Electronic Proceedings in Theoretical Computer Science, vol. 56, pp. 15–32, June 2011
6. van den Brand, M., Heering, J., Klint, P., Olivier, P.A.: Compiling language definitions: the ASF+SDF compiler. ACM Trans. Program. Lang. Syst. **24**(4), 334–368 (2002)
7. Bravenboer, M., Kalleberg, K.T., Vermaas, R., Visser, E.: Stratego/XT 0.17 – a language and toolset for program transformation. Sci. Comput. Program. **72**(1–2), 52–70 (2008)
8. Champelovier, D., Clerc, X., Garavel, H., Guerte, Y., McKinty, C., Powazny, V., Lang, F., Serwe, W., Smeding, G.: Reference Manual of the LNT to LOTOS Translator (Version 6.6), INRIA, Grenoble, France, February 2017

9. Clavel, M., Durán, F., Eker, S., Escobar, S., Lincoln, P., Martí-Oliet, N., Meseguer, J., Talcott, C.L.: Maude Manual (Version 2.7.1), July 2016

10. Cordy, J.R.: The TXL source transformation language. Sci. Comput. Program. **61**(3), 190–210 (2006)

11. Denker, G., Talcott, C.L., Rosu, G., van den Brand, M., Eker, S., Serbanuta, T.F.: Rewriting logic systems. Electron. Notes Theor. Comput. Sci. **176**(4), 233–247 (2007)

12. Diaconescu, R., Futatsugi, K.: CafeOBJ Report – The Language, Proof Techniques, and Methodologies for Object-Oriented Algebraic Specification. AMAST Series in Computing, vol. 6. World Scientific (1998)

13. Doroshenko, A.E., Shevchenko, R.: A rewriting framework for rule-based programming dynamic applications. Fundam. Inform. **72**(1–3), 95–108 (2006)

14. Durán, F., Roldán, M., Bach, J.C., Balland, E., van den Brand, M., Cordy, J.R., Eker, S., Engelen, L., de Jonge, M., Kalleberg, K.T., Kats, L.C.L., Moreau, P.E., Visser, E.: The third Rewrite Engines Competition. In: Ölveczky, P.C. (ed.) WRLA 2010. LNCS, vol. 6381, pp. 243–261. Springer, Heidelberg (2010). https://doi.org/10.1007/978-3-642-16310-4_16

15. Durán, F., Roldán, M., Balland, E., van den Brand, M., Eker, S., Kalleberg, K.T., Kats, L.C.L., Moreau, P.E., Schevchenko, R., Visser, E.: The second Rewrite Engines Competition. Electron. Notes Theor. Comput. Sci. **238**(3), 281–291 (2009)

16. Garavel, H., Lang, F., Mateescu, R., Serwe, W.: CADP 2011: a toolbox for the construction and analysis of distributed processes. Springer Int. J. Softw. Tools Technol. Transf. (STTT) **15**(2), 89–107 (2013)

17. Garavel, H., Tabikh, M.-A., Arrada, I.-S.: Benchmarking implementations of term rewriting and pattern matching in algebraic, functional, and object-oriented languages—The 4th Rewrite Engines Competition. In: Rusu, V. (ed.) WRLA 2018. LNCS, vol. 11152, pp. 1–25. Springer, Cham (2018). https://doi.org/10.1007/978-3-319-99840-4_1

18. Groote, J., Mousavi, M.: Modeling and Analysis of Communicating Systems. The MIT Press, Cambridge (2014)

19. ISO/IEC: LOTOS – A Formal Description Technique Based on the Temporal Ordering of Observational Behaviour. International Standard 8807, International Organization for Standardization – Information Processing Systems – Open Systems Interconnection, Geneva, September 1989

20. Kordon, F., Garavel, H., Hillah, L.M., Paviot-Adet, E., Jezequel, L., Rodríguez, C., Hulin-Hubard, F.: MCC'2015 – the fifth Model Checking Contest. In: Koutny, M., Desel, J., Kleijn, J. (eds.) Transactions on Petri Nets and Other Models of Concurrency XI. LNCS, vol. 9930, pp. 262–273. Springer, Heidelberg (2016). https://doi.org/10.1007/978-3-662-53401-4_12

21. Leroy, X., Doligez, D., Frisch, A., Garrigue, J., Rémy, D., Vouillon, J.: The OCaml System Release 4.04 – Documentation and User's Manual. INRIA, Paris, France, March 2016

22. Marlow, S. (ed.): Haskell 2010 Language Report, April 2010

23. Milner, R., Tofte, M., Harper, R., MacQueen, D.: Definition of Standard ML (Revised). MIT Press, Cambridge (1997)

24. Odersky, M., Altherr, P., Cremet, V., Dubochet, G., Emir, B., Haller, P., Micheloud, S., Mihaylov, N., Moors, A., Rytz, L., Schinz, M., Stenman, E., Zenger, M.: The Scala Language Specification – Version 2.11. Programming Methods Laboratory, EPFL, Switzerland, March 2016

25. Pepper, P., Lorenzen, F. (eds.): The Programming Language Opal – 6th Corrected Edition. Department of Software Engineering and Theoretical Computer Science, Technische Universität Berlin, Germany, October 2012
26. Plasmeijer, R., van Eekelen, M., van Groningen, J.: Clean Version 2.2 Language Report. Department of Software Technology, University of Nijmegen, The Netherlands, December 2011

RERS 2019: Combining Synthesis with Real-World Models

Marc Jasper[1], Malte Mues[1], Alnis Murtovi[1], Maximilian Schlüter[1],
Falk Howar[1], Bernhard Steffen[1] , Markus Schordan[2]([✉]), Dennis Hendriks[3],
Ramon Schiffelers[4], Harco Kuppens[5], and Frits W. Vaandrager[5]

[1] TU Dortmund University, Dortmund, Germany
{marc.jasper,malte.mues,alnis.murtovi,maximilian.schlueter,falk.howar,
bernhard.steffen}@tu-dortmund.de
[2] Lawrence Livermore National Laboratory, Livermore, CA, USA
schordan1@llnl.gov
[3] ESI (TNO), Eindhoven, The Netherlands
dennis.hendriks@tno.nl
[4] ASML and Eindhoven University of Technology,
Veldhoven/Eindhoven, The Netherlands
ramon.schiffelers@asml.com
[5] Radboud University, Nijmegen, The Netherlands
{H.Kuppens,F.Vaandrager}@cs.ru.nl

Abstract. This paper covers the Rigorous Examination of Reactive Systems (RERS) Challenge 2019. For the first time in the history of RERS, the challenge features industrial tracks where benchmark programs that participants need to analyze are synthesized from real-world models. These new tracks comprise LTL, CTL, and Reachability properties. In addition, we have further improved our benchmark generation infrastructure for parallel programs towards a full automation. RERS 2019 is part of TOOLympics, an event that hosts several popular challenges and competitions. In this paper, we highlight the newly added industrial tracks and our changes in response to the discussions at and results of the last RERS Challenge in Cyprus.

Keywords: Benchmark generation · Program verification · Temporal logics · LTL · CTL · Property-preservation · Obfuscation · Synthesis

1 Introduction

The Rigorous Examination of Reactive Systems (RERS) Challenge is an annual event concerned with software verification tasks—called benchmarks—on which participants can test the limits of their tools. In its now 9th iteration, the RERS Challenge continues to expand both its underlying benchmark generator infrastructure and the variety of its tracks. This year, RERS is part of

D. Beyer et al. (Eds.): TACAS 2019, Part III, LNCS 11429, pp. 101–115, 2019.
https://doi.org/10.1007/978-3-030-17502-3_7

TOOLympics [2]. As during previous years [9,12,13], RERS 2019 features tracks on sequential and parallel programs in programming/specification languages such as Java, C99, Promela [11], and (Nested-Unit) Petri nets [8,19]. Properties that participants have to analyze range from reachability queries over linear temporal logic (LTL) formulae [20] to computational tree logic (CTL) properties [6]. Participants only need to submit their "true"/"false" answers to these tasks. As a new addition in 2019, we enrich RERS with industrial tracks in which benchmarks are based on real-world models.

The main goals of RERS[1] are:

1. Encourage the combination of methods from different (and usually disconnected) research fields for better software verification results.
2. Provide a framework for an automated comparison based on differently tailored benchmarks that reveal the strengths and weaknesses of specific approaches.
3. Initiate a discussion about better benchmark generation, reaching out across the usual community barriers to provide benchmarks useful for testing and comparing a wide variety of tools.

One aspect that makes RERS unique in comparison to other competitions or challenges on software verification is its automated benchmark synthesis: The RERS generator infrastructure allows the organizers to distribute new and challenging verification tasks each year while knowing the correct solution to these tasks. Contrarily, in similar events such as the Software Verification Competition (SV-COMP) [3] which focuses on programs written in C and reachability queries, benchmarks are hand-selected by a committee and most of them are used again for subsequent challenge iterations. That the solutions to these problems are already known does not harm because, e.g. SV-COMP, does not merely focus on the answers to the posed problems, but also on details of how they are achieved. To attain this, SV-COMP features a centralized evaluation approach along with resource constraints where participants submit their tools instead of just their answers to the verification tasks. During this evaluation phase, which builds on quite an elaborate competition infrastructure, obtained counterexample traces are also evaluated automatically [4].

The situation is quite different for the Model Checking Contest (MCC) [16], a verification competition that is concerned with the analysis of Petri nets, where the correct solutions to the selected verification tasks are not always known to the competition organizers. In such cases, the MCC evaluation is often based on majority voting concerning the submissions by participants, an approach also followed by a number of other competitions despite the fact that this may penalize tools of exceptional analysis power. In contrast, the synthesis procedure of verification tasks for RERS also generates the corresponding provably correct solutions using a correctness-by-construction approach. Both SV-COMP and MCC have therefore added RERS benchmarks to their problem portfolio.

---

[1] As stated online at http://www.rers-challenge.org/2019/.

As stated above, RERS aims to foster the combination of different methods, and this includes the combination of different tools. During last year's RERS Challenge for example, one participant applied three different available tools in order to generate his submission[2] and thereby won the Method Combination Award within RERS[3]. In order to host an unmonitored and free-style challenge such as RERS on a regular basis—one where just the "true"/"false" answers need to be submitted—an automated benchmark synthesis is a must.

Potential criticism of such a synthesis approach might be that the generated verification tasks are not directly connected to any real-world problem: Their size might be realistic, however their inherent structure might be not. This criticism very much reflects a perspective where RERS benchmarks are structurally compared to handwritten code. On the other hand, being synthesized from temporal constraints, RERS benchmarks very much reflect the structure that arises in generative or requirements-driven programming. In order to be close to industrial practice, RERS 2019 also provides benchmarks via a combination of synthesis with real-world models. For this endeavor, we collaborated with ASML, a large Dutch semiconductor company.

When developing controller software, over time updates and version changes inevitably turn originally well-documented solutions into legacy software, which typically should preserve the original controller behavior. RERS 2019 addresses this phenomenon by generating legacy-like software from models via a number of property-preserving transformations that are provided by the RERS infrastructure [22]. This results in correct 'obfuscated' (legacy) implementations of the real-world models provided by ASML.

The parallel benchmarks of the last RERS challenge were built on top of well-known initial systems, dining philosophers of various sizes. As a next step towards a fully automated benchmark generation process, we created the initial system in a randomized fashion this year. The subsequent property-preserving parallel decomposition process, which may result in benchmarks of arbitrary degrees of parallelism, remained untouched [23]. For RERS 2020 we plan to use the more involved synthesis approach presented in [15] in order to be able to also guarantee benchmark hardness.

Moreover, in response to participants' requests, we implemented a generator that creates candidates for branching time properties for the parallel benchmarks. The idea is to syntactically transform available LTL properties into semantically 'close' CTL formulae. This turns out to provide interesting CTL formulae for the benchmarks systems. These formulae's validity has, of course, to be validated via model checking as the generation process is not (cannot be) semantics preserving.

In the following, the detailed observations from RERS 2018 are described in Sect. 2. Section 3 then summarizes improvements within the parallel tracks of RERS that we implemented for the 2019 challenge, before Sect. 4 introduces

---

[2] Details at http://www.rers-challenge.org/2018/index.php?page=results.

[3] The reward structure of RERS is described in previous papers such as [12].

the new industrial tracks with their dedicated benchmark construction. Our conclusions and outlook to future work can be found in Sect. 5.

2   Lessons Learned: The Sequential Tracks of RERS 2018

For RERS 2018, we received four contributions to the Sequential Reachability track and two contributions to the Sequential LTL track. Detailed results are published online.[4] The tools that participants used for the challenge are quite heterogeneous: Their profiles range from explicit-state model checking over trace abstraction techniques to a combination of active automata learning with model checking [5,10,14,18,25]. During the preparations for the new sequential and industrial tracks, we started a closer investigation on lessons we might learn from the results of the RERS 2018 challenge in addition to the valuable feedback collected during the RERS 2018 meeting in Limassol.

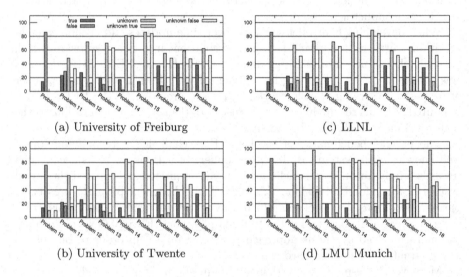

(a) University of Freiburg   (c) LLNL

(b) University of Twente   (d) LMU Munich

Fig. 1. Reachability results. (Color figure online)

In Fig. 1, the results of the participants of the reachability challenge are visualized. The blue bars indicate how many properties have not been addressed by the respective participant for a problem. Hence, these blue bars point to potential opportunities for achieving better challenge results for each tool. It is observable that the amount of green bars is decreasing with increasing problem size and difficulty. This shows that less unreachable errors are detected with increased problem size. In contrast, the purple bars still show a fair number of results for reachable errors.

---

[4] http://www.rers-challenge.org/2018/index.php?page=results.

It is obvious that showing the absence of a certain error requires a more complicated proof than demonstrating that it is reachable. Therefore, the observed result is not unexpected. To investigate this further, the blue bars are split up into the corresponding categories from which the unsolved properties originate. An orange bar shows the number of unreported reachable errors. A yellow bar shows the number of unreported unreachable errors. In most cases, the yellow bar is comparable in size to the blue bar for a problem. On the one hand, this is evidence which demonstrates that proving unreachable errors is still a hard challenge no matter which approach has been applied. On the other hand, the charts indicate that participating tools scale quite well also on the larger problems for demonstrating the existence of errors.

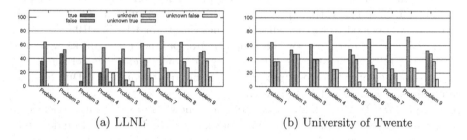

(a) LLNL   (b) University of Twente

Fig. 2. LTL results. (Color figure online)

We found a similar situation in the LTL track results reported in Fig. 2. In this figure a purple bar indicates that a LTL formula holds. This proof requires a deep understanding of major parts of the complete execution graph. This is therefore the counterpart for proving an error unreachable. As expected, it appears to be much easier for tools to disprove an LTL formula on the given examples the same way as it seems significantly easier to prove error reachability. With a few exceptions, the blue bars indicating unreported properties for a given problem are comparable in height with the orange bars for LTL formulae expected to hold on the given instance. We want to highlight that the tools which participated in RERS 2018 demonstrated a good scalability for disproving LTL formulae across the different problem sizes.

Based on the results handed in to RERS 2018, we observe some maturity in tools disproving LTL formulae and finding errors, which are both characterized by having single paths as witnesses. We appreciate this trend because a lacking scalability of verification tools was a major motivation to start the RERS challenge.

As a next step, we intend to motivate future participants to further investigate the direction of proving LTL formulae and error unreachability on systems. These properties require more complex proofs as it is not possible to verify the answer with a single violating execution path. Instead it is required to create a deeper understanding of all possible execution paths in order to give a sound answer. There is a higher chance to make a mistake and give a wrong answer resulting in a penalty.

With RERS 2019, we therefore want to encourage people to invest into corresponding verification tools by valuing that verifiable properties are more complicated to analyze than refutable ones. In the future we will award two points for each correct report of an unreachable error or a satisfied LTL formula in the competition-based ranking. The achievement reward system remains unchanged.

3   Improvements in the Parallel Tracks for RERS 2019

The initial model used for the RERS 2018 tracks on parallel programs was chosen to be the Dining Philosophers Problem in order to feature a well-known system [13]. With the goal to reflect the properties of this system as best as possible, the corresponding LTL and CTL properties were designed manually. To streamline our generation approach and minimize the amount of manual work involved, we decided to further automate these steps for RERS 2019.

In [15], a new workflow for the generation of parallel benchmarks was presented that fully automates the generation process while ensuring certain hardness guarantees of the corresponding verification/refutation tasks. Due to time constraints, we could not fully integrate this new approach into our generation pipeline for RERS 2019. Instead, we combined new and existing approaches to achieve a full automation (Fig. 3). Our workflow for RERS'19 therefore does not yet guarantee the formal hardness properties presented in [15]. On the other hand, it integrates the generation of CTL properties, an aspect that was not discussed in [15].

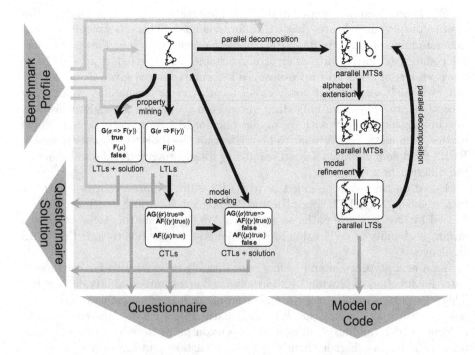

Fig. 3. Workflow of the benchmark generation for the RERS'19 parallel programs.

Input to the overall workflow (Fig. 3) is a benchmark profile that contains metadata such as the number of desired verifiable/refutable LTL/CTL properties, number of parallel components in the final code, and similar characteristics. The generation of a parallel benchmark starts with a labeled transition system (LTS). We chose to randomly generate these for RERS'19, based on parameters in the input benchmark profile. Alternatively, one could choose an existing system modeled as an LTS if its size still permits to model check it efficiently.

3.1 Property Generation

Given the initial LTS, we randomly select verifiable and refutable properties based on certain LTL patterns. This process is called property mining in Fig. 3 and was previously used to generate the parallel benchmarks of RERS'16 [9] and some of RERS'17 [12].

As a new addition to the automated workflow, we implemented a generation of CTL formulae based on the following idea:

- Syntactically transform an LTL formula ϕ_l to a CTL formula ϕ_c. This yields structurally interesting CTL properties but is not guaranteed to preserve the semantics.
- Check ϕ_c on the input model. This step compensates for the lack of property preservation of the first step.
- Possibly negate ϕ_c and then apply de Morgan-like rules to eliminate the leading negation operator in case the ratio of satisfied and violated properties does not match the desired characteristics. This works for CTL, as in contrast to LTL, formulae or their negations are guaranteed to hold (law of excluded middle).

We realized the transformation from an LTL formula to a corresponding CTL formula by prepending an **A** ('always') to every LTL operator which requires the formula to hold on every successor state. For a state to satisfy $\mathbf{AG}\,\phi$ for example, ϕ has to hold in every state on every path starting in the given state. Additionally, we introduced a diamond operator for every transition label that is not negated in the LTL formula and a box for every negated label as detailed below. The transformation was implemented as follows where the LTL formula to the left of the arrow is replaced by the CTL formula to the right of the arrow.[5]

$$\mathbf{G}\,\phi \to \mathbf{AG}\,\phi$$
$$\mathbf{F}\,\phi \to \mathbf{AF}\,\phi$$
$$\phi\,\mathbf{U}\,\psi \to \mathbf{A}(\phi\,\mathbf{U}\,\psi)$$
$$\phi\,\mathbf{W}\,\psi \to \mathbf{A}(\phi\,\mathbf{W}\,\psi)$$
$$a \to \langle a\rangle\text{true}$$
$$\neg a \to [a]\text{false}$$

---

[5] For more details on the syntax of the LTL and CTL properties, see http://rers-challenge.org/2019/index.php?page=problemDescP.

The diamond operator $\langle a \rangle \phi$ holds in a state iff the state has at least one outgoing transition labeled with an a whose target state satisfies ϕ. In this case $\langle a \rangle$true holds in a state if it has an outgoing transition labeled with a because every state satisfies 'true'. The box operator $[a]\phi$ holds in a state iff every outgoing transition labeled with an a satisfies ϕ. The negation of an atomic proposition a was replaced by $[a]$false which is only satisfied by a state which has no outgoing transitions labeled with an a.

Based on the previously mentioned steps, we can automatically generate LTL and CTL properties that are given to participants of the challenge as a questionnaire (see Fig. 3). Similarly, the corresponding solution is extracted and kept secret by the challenge organizers until the submission deadline has passed and the results of the challenge are announced.

3.2 Expansion and Translation of the Input Model

In order to synthesize challenging verification tasks and provide parallel programs, we expand the initial LTS based on property-preserving parallel decompositions [23] (see top and right-hand side of Fig. 3). The corresponding procedure works on modal transition systems (MTSs) [17], an extension of LTSs. This parallel decomposition can be iterated. During this expansion procedure, the alphabet of the initial system is extended by artificial transition labels. More details including examples can be found in [13,21].

As a last step, the final model of the now parallel program is encoded in different target languages such as Promela or as a Nested-Unit Petri net [8] in the standard PNML format[6]. The final code or model specification is presented to participants of the challenge along with the questionnaire that contains the corresponding LTL/CTL properties.

Please note the charm of verifying branching time properties: As CTL is closed under negation, proving whether a formula is satisfied or violated can in both cases be accomplished using standard model checking, and in both cases one can construct witnesses in terms of winning strategies. Thus there is not such a strong discrepancy between proving and refuting properties as in LTL.

4 Industrial Tracks

RERS 2019 includes tracks that are based on industrial embedded control systems provided by ASML. ASML is the world's leading provider of lithography systems for the semiconductor industry. Lithography systems are very complex high-tech systems that are designed to expose patterns on silicon wafers. This processing must not only be able to deliver exceptionally reliable results with an extremely high output on a 24/7 basis, it must do so while also being extremely precise. With patterns becoming smaller and smaller, ASML TWINSCAN lithography systems incorporate an increasing amount of control software to compensate for nano-scale physical effects.

---

[6] ISO/IEC 15909-2: https://www.iso.org/standard/43538.html.

To deal with the increasing amount of software, ASML employs a component-based software architecture. It consists of components that interact via explicitly specified interfaces, establishing a formalized contract between those components. Such formal interface specifications not only include syntactic signatures of the functions of an interface, but also their behavioural constraints in terms of interface protocols. Furthermore, non-functional aspects, such as timing, can be described.

Formal interface specifications enable the full potential of a component-based software architecture. They allow components to be developed, analyzed, deployed and maintained in isolation. This is achieved using enabling techniques, among which are model checking (to prove interface compliance), observers (to check interface compliance), armoring (to separate error handling from component logic) and test generation (to increase test coverage).

For newly developed components, ASML specifies the corresponding interface protocols. However, components developed in the past often do not have such interface protocol specification yet. ASML aims to obtain behavioral interface specifications for such components. Model inference techniques help to obtain such specifications in an effective way [1]. Such techniques include, for instance, static analysis exploiting information in the source code, passive learning based on execution logs, active automata learning querying the running component, and combinations of these techniques.

ASML collaborates with ESI[7] in a research project on the development of an integrated tool suite for model inference to (semi-automatically) infer interface protocols from existing software components. This tool suite is applied and validated in the industrial context of ASML. Recently, this tool suite has been applied to 218 control software components of ASML's TWINSCAN lithography machines [26]. 118 components could be learned in an hour or less. The techniques failed to successfully infer the interface protocols of the remaining 100 components.

Obtaining the best performing techniques to infer behavioral models for these components is the goal of the ASML-based industrial tracks of RERS 2019. Any model inference technique, including source code analyzers, passive learning, (model-based) testers and (test-based) modelers including active automata learning, and free-style approaches, or combinations of techniques can be used. The best submissions to the challenge might be used by ASML and ESI and incorporated into their tool suite.

4.1   ASML Components for RERS

For the RERS challenge, ASML disclosed information about roughly a hundred TWINSCAN components. We decided to select 30 among them to generate challenging benchmark problems for RERS 2019, and three additional ones that are used for training problems. Using these components allows participants to

---

[7] ESI is a TNO Joint Innovation Centre, a collaboration between the Netherlands Organisation for Applied Scientific Research (TNO), industry, and academia.

apply their tools and techniques on components of industrial size and complexity, evaluating their real-world applicability and performance.

For the disclosed components, Mealy machine (MM) models and (generated) Java and C++ source-code exist. The generation of benchmarks for the RERS challenge is based on the MM models. This allows us to open the industrial tracks also to tools that analyze C programs. The Java code of the challenge is generated by the organizers as described later in Sect. 4.4 and does not represent the originally generated Java code provided by ASML. This prevents participants from exploiting potential structural patterns in this original Java code (such structural information does not exist in legacy components). Furthermore, an execution log is provided for each component. Each execution log contains a selected number of logged traces, provided by ASML, representing behavior exhibited by either a unit or integration test.

The remainder of this section provides a brief overview of how properties are generated for these benchmarks and how code is generated using the obfuscation infrastructure from previous sequential RERS tracks. Figure 4 presents an overview of the corresponding benchmark generation workflow that is described in the following.

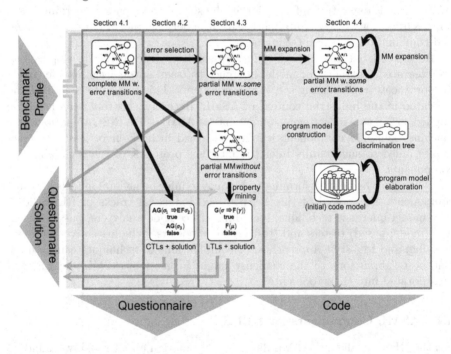

Fig. 4. Workflow of the benchmark generation for the new industrial tracks.

4.2   Generation of CTL Properties

We compute CTL formulae from Mealy machines using conformance testing algorithms. We generate a small set of traces that characterizes each state.

Using this, we can define for each state q a CTL state formula σ_q that characterizes part of its behavior. If $i_1/o_1, i_2/o_2$ is an IO sequence of state q, then formula σ_q takes the form

$$EX(i_1 \wedge EX(o_1 \wedge EX(i_2 \wedge EXo_2))).$$

These characterizing formulae are the basis for CTL properties, e.g., of the form

$$AG(\sigma_1 \vee \sigma_2 \vee \ldots \vee \sigma_n),$$
$$AG(\sigma_1 \Rightarrow EX(i \wedge EXo \wedge \sigma_2)), \text{ or}$$
$$AG(\sigma_1 \Rightarrow EF\sigma_3),$$

where i and o denote symbols from the set of inputs and outputs of the Mealy machine model, respectively. Additionally, we generate CTL formulae that do not hold in the model using the same approach.

4.3 LTL and Reachability Properties

Regarding the new ASML-based benchmarks, we used a property mining approach for the generation of LTL properties. By mining we mean that properties are extracted from the model without altering this model. As a first step, we temporarily discard all error transitions from the input Mealy machine (MM) (see Fig. 4): In line with the benchmark definition used in former editions of the RERS tracks on sequential programs, our LTL properties only constrain infinite paths. This nicely reflects the fact that controllers or protocols are typically meant to continuously run in order to react on arising input.

Having discarded all error transitions, our approach first generates random properties from relevant patterns according to [7]. A model checker is then used to determine whether or not the generated properties hold on the given input model. We iterate this process until we find a desired ratio between satisfied and violated properties. This mining approach is very similar to the previous LTL generation in RERS (cf. [22]), with the exception that no properties are used for synthesizing a MM. Because we have never altered the original MM with regard to its infinite paths, all extracted LTL properties that are satisfied characterize the input/output behavior of the given real-world model.

Similar to the former editions of RERS, the new industrial tracks also provides reachability tasks ("Is the error labeled x reachable?"). This generation process is disjoint with the LTL track generation. While we discarded all error transitions from the input model during conversion from the input model to code in the LTL track generation, we select real errors from the given input model and map them to unique error states before code generation during the reachability task generation. This way, all included errors are taken from a real system and are not synthetical. The same input models are used for the generation of the benchmarks for the reachability track and the LTL track. There are just slightly different pre-processes in place that address the handling of error transition during generation. Using real error paths is again in contrast to the benchmark synthesis of RERS that was applied during previous years where reachability tasks were artificially added to (already artificial) input models.

As depicted in the top-left corner of Fig. 4, the initial MM model is complete, meaning that each input symbol that is not supported in a certain state is represented by an error transition leading to a sink state. We randomly select some of those error transitions and reroute them so that they each lead to a distinct error state. At the same time, we introduce unreachable error states to the MM and enumerate both the reachable and unreachable error states. The resulting reachability vector is reported back to the challenge organizer as part of the Questionnaire Solution (Fig. 4). The error states are then rendered as guarded "verifier errors" in the final program (see Sect. 4.4). Unsupported transitions that were not selected for the reachability tasks are rendered as "invalid input", in line with the previous RERS tracks on sequential programs.

4.4   Obfuscation and Code Generation

The obfuscation and code generation steps are reused from the existing RERS benchmark generator of the sequential tracks. As described in Fig. 4 and in Section 11 and Section 12 of [22], the translation from the initial MM to the final code is divided into smaller steps, which are implemented as individual modules.

As shown in the right-hand side of Fig. 4, the partial MM is first expanded as done before. Additional states which are clones of existing states are added such that they are unreachable. Next, a discrimination tree is constructed using different kinds of variables as properties on the nodes and constraints on these variables on the outgoing edges of the decision tree. Based on the choice of these variables, the current complexity of the synthetic RERS benchmarks is controllable. It may range from plain encodings using only integer variables to encode the subtrees, to options with string variables, arithmetic operations and array variables in the same fashion as it was done in the past for RERS.

Next, the automaton is randomly mapped to the leaf nodes of the decision tree. The constraints collected along a path from the decision tree root to a leaf is used to encode a state of the automaton associated with that leaf. The automaton transitions are encoded based on the decision tree encoding. The now completely encoded problem is translated into the target language. While ASML normally generates C++ code from its automaton models, we decided to maintain the old RERS tradition of providing a Java and a C encoding for each problem. The underlying MM is maintained during this obfuscation and encoding step as it has been in the previous editions of RERS.

5   Conclusion and Outlook

With the addition of industrial tracks where benchmarks are based on real-world models, RERS 2019 combined the strength of automated synthesis with the relevance of actively used software. Due to these new tracks based on a collaboration with the company ASML, the variety of different tasks that participants of

RERS can address has again expanded. Independently of this new addition, we further improved our generation infrastructure and realized a fully-automated synthesis of parallel programs that feature intricate dependencies between their components.

In the future, we intend to fully integrate the approach presented in [15] into our infrastructure in order to guarantee formal hardness properties also for violated formulae. Future work might include equivalence-checking tasks between a model and its implementation, for example based on the systems provided by ASML. Furthermore, we intend to provide benchmark problems for weak bisimulation checking [24] for the RERS 2020 challenge. As a longer-term goal, we continue our work towards an open-source generator infrastructure that allows tool developers to generate their own benchmarks.

Acknowledgments. This work was partially performed under the auspices of the U.S. Department of Energy by Lawrence Livermore National Laboratory under Contract DE-AC52-07NA27344, and was supported by the LLNL-LDRD Program under Project No. 17-ERD-023. IM Release Nr. LLNL-CONF-766478.

References

1. Aslam, K., Luo, Y., Schiffelers, R.R.H., van den Brand, M.: Interface protocol inference to aid understanding legacy software components. In: Proceedings of MODELS 2018, co-located with ACM/IEEE 21st International Conference on Model Driven Engineering Languages and Systems (MODELS 2018), Copenhagen, Denmark, pp. 6–11 (2018)

2. Bartocci, E., et al.: TOOLympics 2019: an overview of competitions in formal methods. In: Beyer, D., Huisman, M., Kordon, F., Steffen, B. (eds.) TACAS 2019. LNCS, vol. 11429, pp. xx–yy. Springer, Cham (2019)

3. Beyer, D.: Competition on software verification (SV-COMP). In: Flanagan, C., König, B. (eds.) TACAS 2012. LNCS, vol. 7214, pp. 504–524. Springer, Heidelberg (2012). https://doi.org/10.1007/978-3-642-28756-5_38

4. Beyer, D.: Software verification and verifiable witnesses. In: Baier, C., Tinelli, C. (eds.) TACAS 2015. LNCS, vol. 9035, pp. 401–416. Springer, Heidelberg (2015). https://doi.org/10.1007/978-3-662-46681-0_31

5. Blom, S., van de Pol, J., Weber, M.: LTSMIN: distributed and symbolic reachability. In: Touili, T., Cook, B., Jackson, P. (eds.) CAV 2010. LNCS, vol. 6174, pp. 354–359. Springer, Heidelberg (2010). https://doi.org/10.1007/978-3-642-14295-6_31

6. Clarke, E.M., Emerson, E.A.: Design and synthesis of synchronization skeletons using branching time temporal logic. In: Kozen, D. (ed.) Logic of Programs 1981. LNCS, vol. 131, pp. 52–71. Springer, Heidelberg (1982). https://doi.org/10.1007/BFb0025774

7. Dwyer, M.B., Avrunin, G.S., Corbett, J.C.: Patterns in property specifications for finite-state verification. In: Proceedings of the 1999 International Conference on Software Engineering (IEEE Cat. No. 99CB37002), pp. 411–420, May 1999

8. Garavel, H.: Nested-unit Petri nets. J. Log. Algebraic Methods Program. **104**, 60–85 (2019)

9. Geske, M., Jasper, M., Steffen, B., Howar, F., Schordan, M., van de Pol, J.: RERS 2016: parallel and sequential benchmarks with focus on LTL verification. In: Margaria, T., Steffen, B. (eds.) ISoLA 2016. LNCS, vol. 9953, pp. 787–803. Springer, Cham (2016). https://doi.org/10.1007/978-3-319-47169-3_59

10. Heizmann, M., et al.: Ultimate Automizer with SMTInterpol. In: Piterman, N., Smolka, S.A. (eds.) TACAS 2013. LNCS, vol. 7795, pp. 641–643. Springer, Heidelberg (2013). https://doi.org/10.1007/978-3-642-36742-7_53

11. Holzmann, G.: The SPIN Model Checker: Primer and Reference Manual, 1st edn. Addison-Wesley Professional, Boston (2011)

12. Jasper, M., et al.: The RERS 2017 challenge and workshop (invited paper). In: Proceedings of the 24th ACM SIGSOFT International SPIN Symposium on Model Checking of Software, SPIN 2017, pp. 11–20. ACM (2017)

13. Jasper, M., Mues, M., Schlüter, M., Steffen, B., Howar, F.: RERS 2018: CTL, LTL, and reachability. In: Margaria, T., Steffen, B. (eds.) ISoLA 2018. LNCS, vol. 11245, pp. 433–447. Springer, Cham (2018). https://doi.org/10.1007/978-3-030-03421-4_27

14. Jasper, M., Schordan, M.: Multi-core model checking of large-scale reactive systems using different state representations. In: Margaria, T., Steffen, B. (eds.) ISoLA 2016. LNCS, vol. 9952, pp. 212–226. Springer, Cham (2016). https://doi.org/10.1007/978-3-319-47166-2_15

15. Jasper, M., Steffen, B.: Synthesizing subtle bugs with known witnesses. In: Margaria, T., Steffen, B. (eds.) ISoLA 2018. LNCS, vol. 11245, pp. 235–257. Springer, Cham (2018). https://doi.org/10.1007/978-3-030-03421-4_16

16. Kordon, F., et al.: Report on the model checking contest at Petri nets 2011. In: Jensen, K., van der Aalst, W.M., Ajmone Marsan, M., Franceschinis, G., Kleijn, J., Kristensen, L.M. (eds.) Transactions on Petri Nets and Other Models of Concurrency VI. LNCS, vol. 7400, pp. 169–196. Springer, Heidelberg (2012). https://doi.org/10.1007/978-3-642-35179-2_8

17. Larsen, K.G.: Modal specifications. In: Sifakis, J. (ed.) CAV 1989. LNCS, vol. 407, pp. 232–246. Springer, Heidelberg (1990). https://doi.org/10.1007/3-540-52148-8_19

18. Meijer, J., van de Pol, J.: Sound black-box checking in the LearnLib. In: Dutle, A., Muñoz, C., Narkawicz, A. (eds.) NFM 2018. LNCS, vol. 10811, pp. 349–366. Springer, Cham (2018). https://doi.org/10.1007/978-3-319-77935-5_24

19. Peterson, J.L.: Petri Net Theory and the Modeling of Systems. Prentice Hall PTR, Upper Saddle River (1981)

20. Pnueli, A.: The temporal logic of programs. In: 18th Annual Symposium on Foundations of Computer Science (SFCS 1977), pp. 46–57, October 1977

21. Steffen, B., Jasper, M., Meijer, J., van de Pol, J.: Property-preserving generation of tailored benchmark Petri nets. In: 17th International Conference on Application of Concurrency to System Design (ACSD), pp. 1–8, June 2017

22. Steffen, B., Isberner, M., Naujokat, S., Margaria, T., Geske, M.: Property-driven benchmark generation: synthesizing programs of realistic structure. STTT 16(5), 465–479 (2014)

23. Steffen, B., Jasper, M.: Property-preserving parallel decomposition. In: Aceto, L., Bacci, G., Bacci, G., Ingólfsdóttir, A., Legay, A., Mardare, R. (eds.) Models, Algorithms, Logics and Tools. LNCS, vol. 10460, pp. 125–145. Springer, Cham (2017). https://doi.org/10.1007/978-3-319-63121-9_7

24. Steffen, B., Jasper, M.: Generating hard benchmark problems for weak bisimulation. LNCS. Springer (2019, to appear)

25. Wonisch, D., Wehrheim, H.: Predicate analysis with block-abstraction memoization. In: Aoki, T., Taguchi, K. (eds.) ICFEM 2012. LNCS, vol. 7635, pp. 332–347. Springer, Heidelberg (2012). https://doi.org/10.1007/978-3-642-34281-3_24
26. Yang, N., et al.: Improving model inference in industry by combining active and passive learning. In: IEEE 26th International Conference on Software Analysis, Evolution, and Reengineering (SANER) (2019, to appear)

SL-COMP: Competition of Solvers for Separation Logic

Mihaela Sighireanu[2]([✉]), Juan A. Navarro Pérez[11,12P], Andrey Rybalchenko[3], Nikos Gorogiannis[4], Radu Iosif[14], Andrew Reynolds[13], Cristina Serban[14], Jens Katelaan[10], Christoph Matheja[6], Thomas Noll[6], Florian Zuleger[10], Wei-Ngan Chin[5], Quang Loc Le[9], Quang-Trung Ta[5], Ton-Chanh Le[8], Thanh-Toan Nguyen[5], Siau-Cheng Khoo[5], Michal Cyprian[1], Adam Rogalewicz[1], Tomas Vojnar[1], Constantin Enea[2], Ondrej Lengal[1], Chong Gao[7], and Zhilin Wu[7]

[1] FIT, Brno University of Technology, Brno, Czechia
[2] IRIF, University Paris Diderot and CNRS, Paris, France
mihaela.sighireanu@irif.fr
[3] Microsoft Research, Cambridge, UK
[4] Middlesex University London, London, UK
[5] National University of Singapore, Singapore, Singapore
[6] RWTH Aachen University, Aachen, Germany
[7] State Key Laboratory of Computer Science,
Chinese Academy of Sciences, Beijing, China
[8] Stevens Institute of Technology, Hoboken, USA
[9] Teesside University, Middlesbrough, UK
[10] TU Wien, Vienna, Austria
[11] University College London, London, UK
[12] Google, London, UK
[13] University of Iowa, Iowa City, USA
[14] VERIMAG, University Grenoble Alpes and CNRS,
Saint-Martin-d'Hères, France

Abstract. SL-COMP aims at bringing together researchers interested on improving the state of the art of the automated deduction methods for Separation Logic (SL). The event took place twice until now and collected more than 1K problems for different fragments of SL. The input format of problems is based on the SMT-LIB format and therefore fully typed; only one new command is added to SMT-LIB's list, the command for the declaration of the heap's type. The SMT-LIB theory of SL comes with ten logics, some of them being combinations of SL with linear arithmetics. The competition's divisions are defined by the logic fragment, the kind of decision problem (satisfiability or entailment) and the presence of quantifiers. Until now, SL-COMP has been run on the StarExec platform, where the benchmark set and the binaries of participant solvers are freely available. The benchmark set is also available with the competition's documentation on a public repository in GitHub.

© The Author(s) 2019
D. Beyer et al. (Eds.): TACAS 2019, Part III, LNCS 11429, pp. 116–132, 2019.
https://doi.org/10.1007/978-3-030-17502-3_8

1   Introduction

Separation Logic (SL) is an established and fairly popular Hoare logic for imperative, heap-manipulating programs, introduced nearly fifteen years ago by Reynolds [20,24,25]. Its high expressivity, its ability to generate compact proofs, and its support for local reasoning, and its support for local reasoning have motivated the development of tools for automatic reasoning about programs using SL. A rather exhaustive list of the past and present tools using SL may be found at [19].

These tools seek to establish memory safety properties and/or infer shape properties of the heap at a scale of millions of lines of code. They intensively use (semi-)decision procedures for checking satisfiability and entailment problems in SL. Therefore, the development of effective solvers for such problems became a challenge which led to both theoretical results on decidability and complexity of these problems for different fragments of SL and to publicly available tools. To understand the capabilities of these solvers and to motivate their improvement by comparison on a common benchmark, we initiated in 2014 the SL-COMP competition, inspired by the success of SMT-COMP for solvers on first order theories.

This paper presents the history of this competition and its organization for the round at TOOLympics 2019. Section 2 describes the main stages of the competition. Each stage is detailed in a separate section as follows: benchmark's definition in Sect. 3, the participants in Sect. 4 and the running infrastructure in Sect. 5. We conclude the paper in Sect. 6 by a discussion on the impact of the competition and its perspectives.

2   Competition's Stages

2.1   A Short History

The first edition of SL-COMP took place at FLoC 2014 Olympic Games, as an unofficial event associated with the SMT-COMP 2014 competition [31]. The organization details and the achievements of this edition are presented in details in [26]. This was an opportunity to collect from participants about 600 problems on different fragments of SL, to involve six solvers, to lay the foundations of a common input format and to set up a discussion list involving teams developing solvers or verification tools based on SL. Being attached to SMT-COMP allowed to benefit from the experience of SMT-COMP's organizer, David Cok, in setting competition's rules and the execution platform StarExec, as well as in running the competition and publishing the results.

The results of the first edition led to interesting discussions on the mailing list, mainly on the input format chosen, the layout of divisions and the frequency of running the competition. These discussions have converged in defining a working group on the input format and fixed a sparse rhythm of the competition, mainly aligned with FLoC venues.

Therefore, the second edition took place at FLoC 2018 and was associated with the first workshop on Automated Deduction for Separation Logics (ADSL). The organization of the competition followed the stages described in the next section and was disconnected from SMT-COMP. The organizer, Mihaela Sighireanu, exploited the experience acquired with the first edition in running the competition on StarExec. The competition involved ten solvers which ran on 1K problems split over ten newly defined divisions. More precisely, the benchmark set included the set of problems of the 2014 edition and new problems provided by the participants. The problems were specified in the new input format which is aligned with the latest version of SMT-LIB, as detailed in [15] and summarized in Sect. 3.2. The competition's results have been presented during a session of ADSL, which gave the opportunity of a live discussion on the different aspects of organization. The results are available on the competition web site [27].

The TOOLympics edition is a rerun of the second edition with two major changes: a new solver has been included and some benchmark instances have been fixed. The remainder of this paper will present the organization of this edition and the participants involved.

2.2   Organization Process

The competition has a short organization period, three months on average. This is possible due to the fact that material used in the competition (the benchmark set, the definition of the input format, the parsers for input and the pre-processing tools) are publicly available on StarExec and on a shared development repository [22] maintained by the participants and by the organizer.

The competition is launched by a call for benchmarks and participants which also fixes the competition timeline. The call is sent on the competition mailing list sl-comp@googlegroups.com.

New solvers are invited to send a short presentation (up to two pages) including the team, the sub-fragment of SL dealt, the main bibliography and the website. In addition, each solver has a corresponding person in the team, which is responsible of preparing the solver for running the competition. This preparation ensures that the input format is supported and that the solver is registered in the execution platform in the divisions of the competition it asked to compete. The organizer creates a subspace on the execution platform for each participant and assigns the permission to the solver's correspondent for this space. She may help the incomer to prepare the solver by providing insights on the use of the execution platform, the input format and the pre-processors from the competition's input format to the solver's format.

The benchmark problems are collected from the community and participants. Until now, we did not limit the number of benchmark instances proposed by participants in each category in order to improve our benchmark set. However, this may change in the future, as discussed on Sect. 3. The benchmark set may change during the competition due to reaction of competitors, but it is fixed starting with the pre-final run.

The competition is run in three steps. The first step is a training period where the solver's correspondent runs the solver on the execution platform and the existing benchmark set. During this step, the benchmark set may be changed as well as the solver's binary. The second step is a pre-final run, launched by the organizer using the binaries of solvers published on the execution platform. The results of this pre-final run are available for all solvers' representatives, which may allow to compare results and have a first view on competitors' achievements. The organizer contacts each correspondent to be sure that the results of this run are accepted. The last step is the final run, which determines the final result. The binaries of solvers submitted to the final run may be different from the ones used in the pre-final run.

The final run of the competition takes place one week before the event at which the competition's results are presented. However, the results are available as soon as possible on the competition's web site.

3   Benchmark Set

The current competition's benchmark set contains more than 1K problems, (precisely 1286 problems), which cover several fragments of Separation Logic. 25% of these problems are satisfiability checking problems. This section outlines the main features of this benchmark set, including the fragments covered, the input format, and the divisions established for this edition. A detailed description of the input theory and format is [15].

3.1   Separation Logic Theory

The input theory is a multi-sorted second order logic over a signature $\Sigma = (\Sigma^s, \Sigma^f)$, where the set of sorts Σ^s includes two (non necessarily disjoint) subsets of sorts representing locations of the heap, Σ^s_{Loc}, respectively heap's data, Σ^s_{Data}. For each sort Loc in Σ^s_{Loc}, the set of operations includes a constant symbol $\mathsf{nil}^{\mathsf{Loc}}$ modeling the null location. The heap's type τ is an injection from location sorts in Σ^s_{Loc} to data sorts in Σ^s_{Data}. We also assume that the signature Σ includes the Boolean signature and an equality function for each sort.

Let *Vars* be a countable set of first-order variables, each $x^\sigma \in$ *Vars* having an associated sort σ. The *Ground Separation Logic* SL^g is the set of formulae generated by the following syntax:

$$\varphi := \phi \mid \mathsf{emp} \mid \mathsf{t} \mapsto \mathsf{u} \mid \varphi_1 * \varphi_2 \mid \varphi_1 -\!\!* \varphi_2 \mid \neg\varphi_1 \mid \varphi_1 \wedge \varphi_2 \mid \exists x^\sigma . \varphi_1(x) \quad (1)$$

where ϕ is a Σ-formula, and t, u are Σ-terms of sorts in Σ^s_{Loc} and Σ^s_{Data} respectively, such that they are related by the heap's type τ. As usual, we write $\forall x^\sigma . \varphi(x)$ for $\neg\exists x^\sigma . \neg\varphi(x)$. We omit specifying the sorts of variables and functions when they are clear from the context.

The special atomic formulas of SL^g are the so-called *spatial atoms*: emp specifies an empty heap, $\mathsf{t} \mapsto \mathsf{u}$ specifies a heap consisting of one allocated cell whose address is t and whose value is u. The operator "$*$" is the separating conjunction denoting that the sub-heaps specified by its operands have disjoint locations. The operator "$-\!\!*$" is the separating implication operator, also called magic wand. A formula containing only spatial atoms combined using separating conjunction and implication is called *spatial*. Formulas without spatial atoms and separating operators are called *pure*.

The full separation logic SL contains formulas with spatial predicate atoms of the form $P^{\sigma_1 \cdots \sigma_n}(t_1, \ldots, t_n)$, where each t_i is a first-order term of sort σ_i, for $i = 1, \ldots, n$. The predicates $P^{\sigma_1 \cdots \sigma_n}$ belong to a finite set $\mathbb{P}$ of second-order variables and have associated a tuple of parameter sorts $\sigma_1, \ldots, \sigma_n \in \Sigma^s$. Second-order variables $P^{\sigma_1 \cdots \sigma_n} \in \mathbb{P}$ are defined using a set of rules of the form:

$$P(x_1, \ldots, x_n) \leftarrow \phi_P(x_1, \ldots, x_n), \tag{2}$$

where ϕ_P is a formula possibly containing predicate atoms and having free variables in $x_1, \ldots, x_n$. The semantics of predicate atoms is defined by the least fixed point of the function defined by these rules.

An example of a formula specifying a heap with at least two singly linked list cells at locations x and y is:

$$x \mapsto \mathsf{node}(1, y) \; * \; y \mapsto \mathsf{node}(1, z) \; * \; \mathsf{ls}(z, \mathsf{nil}) \; \wedge \; z \neq x \tag{3}$$

where $\Sigma^s = \{\mathsf{Int}, \mathsf{Loc}, \mathsf{Data}\}$ and the function node has parameters of sort Int and Loc and its type is Data. The predicate ls is defined by the following rules:

$$\mathsf{ls}(h, f) \leftarrow h = f \wedge \mathsf{emp} \tag{4}$$
$$\mathsf{ls}(h, f) \leftarrow \exists x, i \, . \, h \neq f \; \wedge \; x \mapsto \mathsf{node}(i, x) \; * \; \mathsf{ls}(x, f) \tag{5}$$

and specifies a possible empty heap storing a singly linked list of Data starting at the location denoted by h and whose last cell contains the location denoted by f. More complex examples of formulas and predicate definitions are provided in [15, 26].

3.2 Input Format

The input format of the competition has been changed between the first and the second edition, but it was always based on the SMT-LIB format [2]. The syntax and semantics of this format were discussed and agreed in the public mailing group.

Signature encoding: Following this format, the new functions of SL theory are declared in a "theory" file SepLogicTyped.smt2 as follows:

```
(theory SepLogicTyped

 :funs ((emp Bool)
        (sep Bool Bool Bool :left-assoc)
```

```
(wand Bool Bool Bool :right-assoc)
(par (L D) (pto L D Bool))
(par (L) (nil L))
)
)
```

Observe that `pto` and `nil` are polymorphic functions, with sort parameters L (for location sort) and D (for data sort). There is no restriction on the choice of location and data sorts. However, each problem shall fix them using a special command, not included in SMT-LIB, `declare-heap`. For example, to encode the example given in Eq. 3, we declare an uninterpreted sort `Loc` and a sort `Data` as a datatype as follows:

```
(declare-sort Loc 0)
```

```
(declare-datatype Data ((node (d Int) (next  U))))
```

```
(declare-heap (Loc Data))
```

The last declaration fixes the type of the heap model.

The predicate definitions are written into SMT-LIB format using the recursive function definition introduced in version 2.6. For instance, the definition of the list segment from Eqs. 4 and 5 is written into SMT-LIB as follows (based on the above declarations of Loc and Data):

```
(define-fun-rec ls ((h Loc) (f Loc)) Bool
   (or (and emp (= h f))
       (exists ((x Loc) (d Int))
             (and (distinct h f) (sep (pto h (node d x)) (ls x f)))))
   )
)
```

Problem format: Each benchmark file is organized as follows:

- Preamble information required by the SMT-LIB format: the sub-logic of SL theory (see Sect. 3.3), the team which proposed the problem, the kind (crafted, application, etc.) and the status (sat or unsat) of the problem.
- A list of declarations for the sorts for locations and data, for the type of the heap (the `declare-heap` command), for the second order predicates, and for the free variables used in the problem's formulae. Notice that the input format is strongly typed. At the end of the declarations, a checking command `check-unsat` may appear to trigger for some solvers the checking for models of predicate declarations.
- One or two assertions (command `assert`) introducing the formulas used in the satisfiability respectively entailment problem.
- The file ends with a checking satisfiability command `check-unsat`. Notice that checking the validity of the entailment $A \Rightarrow B$ is encoded by satisfiability checking of its negation $A \wedge \neg B$.

3.3   Divisions

The main difficulty that faces automatic reasoning using SL is that the logic, due to its expressiveness, does not have very nice decidability properties [1]. For this reason, most program verification tools use incomplete heuristics to solve the satisfiability and entailment problems in SL or restrict the logic employed to decidable fragments. Overviews of decidable results for SL are available in [8,26].

Each benchmark instance of SL-COMP refers to one of the sub-logics of the multi-sorted Separation Logic. These sub-logics identify fragments which are handled by at least two participants or have been identified to be of interest during the discussion for the organization of the round.

The sub-logics are named using groups of letters, in a way similar to SMT-LIB format. These letters have been chosen to evoke the restrictions used by the sub-logics:

- QF for the restriction to quantifier free formulas;
- SH for the so-called "symbolic heap fragment" where formulas are restricted to (Boolean and separating) conjunctions of atoms and do not contain magic wand; moreover, pure atoms are only equality or dis-equality atoms;
- LS where the only predicate allowed is the acyclic list segment, ls, defined in Eqs. 4 and 5;
- ID for the fragment with user defined predicates;
- LID for the fragment of linear user defined predicates, i.e., only one recursive call for all rules of a predicate is allowed;
- B for the ground fragment allowing any Boolean combination of atoms.

Moreover, the existing fragments defined in SMT-LIB are used to further restrict the theory signature. For example, LIA denotes the signature for linear integer arithmetics.

Table 1. Divisions at SL-COMP and the participants enrolled

Division	size	Solvers enrolled
qf_bsl_sat	46	CVC4-SL
qf_bsllia_sat	24	CVC4-SL
qf_shid_entl	312	Cyclist-SL, Harrsh, S2S, Sleek, Slide, Songbird, Spen
qf_shid_sat	99	Harrsh, S2S, Sleek, SLSat
qf_shidlia_entl	75	ComSPEN, S2S
qf_shidlia_sat	33	ComSPEN, S2S
qf_shlid_entl	60	ComSPEN, Cyclist-SL, Harrsh, S2S, Spen
qf_shls_entl	296	Asterix, ComSPEN, Cyclist-SL, Harrsh, S2S, Spen
qf_shls_sat	110	Asterix, ComSPEN, Cyclist-SL, Harrsh, S2S, Spen
shid_entl	73	Cyclist-SL, S2S, Sleek, Songbird
shidlia_entl	181	S2S, Songbird

The current round of the competition has eleven divisions, named by concatenation of the name of the logic and the kind of problem solved (sat or entl). Table 1 provides the names of these divisions and the number of problems in each division:

- qf_bsl_sat and qf_bsllia_sat divisions include satisfiability problems for quantifier free formulas in the ground logic using respectively none or LIA logic for pure formulas.
- qf_shid_entl and qf_shid_sat divisions include entailment respectively satisfiability problems for the symbolic heap fragment with user defined predicates.
- qf_shidlia_entl and qf_shidlia_sat divisions include entailment respectively satisfiability problems for the quantifier free, symbolic heap fragment with user defined predicates and linear arithmetics included in pure formulas even in the predicate definitions.
- qf_shlid_entl division includes a subset of problems of division qf_shid_entl where the predicates are "linear" and compositional [10]. This fragment is of interest because the entailment problem has an efficient decision procedure.
- qf_shls_entl and qf_shls_sat divisions include entailment respectively satisfiability problems for the quantifier free symbolic heap fragment with only ls predicate atoms.
- shid_entl division contains entailment problems for quantified formulas in the symbolic heap fragment with general predicate definitions and no other logic theories than Boolean.
- shidlia_entl divisions extends the problems in shid_entl with constraints from linear integer arithmetics.

3.4 Selection Process

The benchmark set was built mainly from the contributions of participants. Some of these problems come from academic software analysis or verification tools based on SL (e.g., SMALLFOOT [30], Hip [5]). We did not received any problem issued from industrial tools. The problems were collected in the input format submitted by the participants and then translated into the input format of the competition. With the objective of increasing the size of the benchmark set, we did not limit the number of problems submitted by a participant. In this way, the edition 2018 has seen an increase of 100% in the size of the benchmark set. However in the future we could consider a change in the regulations to find a fair balance between teams. By using the meta-information in the preamble of each file, we are able to track the team which proposed the problem.

Notice that each problem has been examined by the organizer to ensure that the input format is respected and that it passed the parsing and type checking. However, the organizer accepts the status of the problem proposed until it is signaled incorrect by another team. In this case, a round of discussion is initiated to find an agreement on the status included in the file. Notice that the status (sat or unsat) shall be known because it is important for the computation of the final result. The status of each problem was checked before the competition using at least two solvers and it did not change during the competition.

4 Participants

Eleven solvers are enrolled for this edition of the competition after its public announcement. Table 1 summarizes the enrollment of each solver in the divisions presented in the previous section.

4.1 ASTERIX

ASTERIX is presented in details in [21]. It was submitted by Juan Navarro Perez (at the time at University College London, UK, now at Google) and Andrey Rybalchenko (at the time at TU Munich, Germany, now at Microsoft Research Cambridge, UK). The solver deals with the satisfiability and entailment checking in the QF_SHLS fragment. For this, it implements a model-based approach. The procedure relies on SMT solving technology (Z3 solver is used) to untangle potential aliasing between program variables. It has at its core a matching function that checks whether a concrete valuation is a model of the input formula and, if so, generalizes it to a larger class of models where the formula is also valid.

ASTERIX was the winner of divisions qf_shls_sat and qf_shls_entl for both editions.

4.2 ComSPEN

The theoretical bases of ComSPEN have been presented in [11]. The development team is composed of Taolue Chen (University of London, UK), Chong Gao and Zhilin Wu (State Key Laboratory of Computer Science, Institute of Software, Chinese Academy of Sciences).

The solver deals with both satisfiability and entailment problems in a fragment included in logic QF_SHIDLIA and which extends QF_SHLID with integer linear arithmetics in predicate definitions. The underlaying technique for satisfiability checking of a formula φ is to define an abstraction, $Abs(\varphi)$, where Boolean variables are introduced to encode the spatial part of φ, together with quantifier-free formulae to represent the transitive closure of the data constraints in the predicate atoms. Checking satisfiability of φ is then reduced to checking satisfiability of $Abs(\varphi)$, which can be solved by the state-of-the-art SMT solvers (e.g., Z3), with an NP upper-bound. For the entailment problem $\varphi \vdash \psi$, if φ and ψ are satisfiable, the procedure builds graphs for each formula and tries to build a graph isomorphism between them.

ComSPEN is implemented in C++. It uses the libraries Z3 and boost. The input format is the SPEN's format, which requires a pre-processor for the competition's input format. Results are not available for ComSPEN because the 2019 edition is the first one for it.

4.3   CYCLIST-SL

CYCLIST-SL [4,7] was submitted by Nikos Gorogiannis (Middlesex University London, UK) in 2014. The solver deals with the entailment checking for the `QF_SLID` fragment. It is an instantiation of the theorem prover CYCLIST-SL for the case of Separation Logic with inductive definitions. The solver builds derivation trees and uses induction to cut infinite paths in these trees that satisfy some soundness condition. For the Separation Logic, CYCLIST-SL replaces the rule of weakening used in first-order theorem provers with the frame rule of SL.

CYCLIST-SL won the division `qf_slid_entl` in 2014 and was at the second place in the same division in 2018.

4.4   CVC4-SL

CVC4 has a decision procedure described in [23] for the fragment `QF_BSL`. The solver CVC4-SL has been submitted by Andrew Reynolds (The University of Iowa, USA). Although this fragment is not supported by other solvers, two divisions were created for it because this fragment is the only one including the separating wand operator. CVC4-SL [6] participated in the 2018 edition and trivially won the two divisions.

4.5   HARRSH

HARRSH [17] was submitted by Jens Katelaan (TU Wien, Austria), the development team including Florian Zuleger from the same institute and Christoph Matheja and Thomas Noll (RWTH Aachen University, Germany). HARRSH deals with the fragment `QF_SHID` for both satisfiability and entailment checking. The decision procedures use a novel automaton model, so-called heap automata [16], which works directly on the structure of symbolic heaps. A heap automaton examines a SID bottom-up, starting from the non-recursive base case. At each stage of this analysis, a heap automaton remembers a fixed amount of information. Heap automata enjoy a variety of closure properties (intersection, union and complementation).

HARRSH is licensed under the MIT license and available on GitHub [12]. HARRSH was implemented in Scala and runs on the JVM. HARRSH has its own input format, but also supports both CYCLIST-SL input format and the SL-COMP input format. Many SL-COMP entailment problems violate the syntactic restrictions of predicate definitions required by HARRSH. For this reason, the solver comes with a preprocessor that is able to transform many (but not all) benchmark's problems in the division `qf_shid_entl` into equivalent, HARRSH compatible specifications.

HARRSH entered SL-COMP in 2018 and competed in divisions `qf_shls_sat` and `qf_shid_sat` with encouraging results. Compared to all other participants, HARRSH has the disadvantage that it runs on the JVM: On simple problems, more than 99% of the runtime of HARRSH is spent starting and shutting down the JVM.

4.6 S2S

S2S is a solver submitted by Quang Loc Le (Teesside University, Middlesbrough, UK). It supports separation logic extended with string and arithmetic constraints, which correspond to all divisions of SL-COMP except ones based on QF_BSL. The solver is built around a generic framework to construct a forest of disjoint cyclic reduction trees for an input, either an entailment or a satisfiability problem. The implementation is done in Ocaml, from scratch. It contains three main components: front end with parsers, the proof systems and backend with SMT solvers (Z3). For the front end, the solver supports several formats, including the one of SL-COMP. The solver implements three concrete cyclic proof systems. The first system is a satisfiability solver in separation logic with general inductive predicates and arithmetic (fragment SLIDLIA). The second one is an entailment solver in the same fragment of separation logic above. Its implementation is the extension of a cyclic proof system with lemma synthesis [18]. The last system is a satisfiability solver for string logics. In all these three systems, any input of the leaf node evaluation method could be transformed into Presburger arithmetic and discharged efficiently by Z3.

In SL-COMP'2018, S2S won division qf_shlid_entl and qf_shidlia_sat.

4.7 SLEEK

SLEEK [5,28] participated in all editions of SL-COMP, the submitters at edition 2018 being Benjamin Lee and Wei-Ngan Chin (NUS, Singapore). The solver deals with the satisfiability and entailment checking for the QF_SHID fragment. It is an (incomplete but) automatic prover, that builds a proof tree for the input problem by using the classical inference rules and the frame rule of SL. It also uses a database of lemmas for the inductive definitions in order to discharge the proof obligations on the spatial formulas. The proof obligations on pure formulas are discharged by external provers like CVC4, Mona, or Z3.

SLEEK was the winner of the division qf_shid_entl in edition 2014, and was in the third position in the same division in edition 2018.

4.8 SLIDE

SLIDE [14,29] was submitted by Adam Rogalewicz (FIT, Brno University of Technology, Czechia), the development team including Michal Cyprian and Tomas Vojnar from the same institute and Radu Iosif (Verimag, University Grenoble Alpes & CNRS, France). The solver deals with the entailment problem in the decidable sub-fragment of QF_SLID defined in [13]. The main principle of SLIDE is a reduction of entailment problems in SL into inclusion problems of tree automata. For the problems in the fragment identified in [13], the decision procedure implemented in SLIDE is EXPTIME-hard. More precisely, the proof method for checking $\varphi \Rightarrow \psi$ relies on converting φ and ψ into two tree automata A_φ resp. A_ψ, and checking the tree language inclusion of the automaton A_φ in the automaton A_ψ.

SLIDE takes an input in its own input format, which can be generated by the dedicated SL-COMP preprocessor. The reduction from the system of predicates into tree automata and the join operator is implemented in Python3. The result of the reduction are input files for the VATA tree automata library, which is used as a backend for the inclusion tests.

SLIDE participated in both past editions of SL-COMP. In 2018 edition, SLIDE solved 61 of 312 problems in division `qf_shid_entl`, 7 of 60 problems in division `qf_shlid_entl`, and 15 of 73 problems in division `shid_entl`. The number of solved problems is related to the fact that SLIDE is a prototype implementation, where our primary goal was to show the advantages of automata techniques. In order to cover more problems, one have to implement a new top-level parser, which would split the input entailment query into a set of subsequent queries, for which the automata-based technique can be used.

4.9 SLSAT

SLSAT [3] was submitted at SL-COMP'2014 by Nikos Gorogiannis (Middlesex University London, UK) and Juan Navarro Perez (at the time at UCL, UK, now at Google). The solver deals with the satisfiability problem for the `QF_SLID` fragment. The decision procedure is based on a fixed point computation of a constraint, called the "base" of an inductive predicate definition. This constraint is a conjunction of equalities and dis-equalities between a set of free variables built also by the fixed point computation from the set of inductive definitions.

SLSAT was at the second position in division `qf_slid_sat` in edition 2014, and won this division at edition 2018.

4.10 SONGBIRD

SONGBIRD [32] was submitted by Quang-Trung Ta (National University of Singapore) and the development team includes Ton-Chanh Le (Stevens Institute of Technology, USA), Thanh-Toan Nguyen, Siau-Cheng Khoo, and Wei-Ngan Chin (National University of Singapore, Singapore). SONGBIRD targets `SHIDLIA` fragment. It employs mathematical induction to prove entailments involving user-defined predicates. In addition, SONGBIRD is also equipped with powerful proof techniques, which include a mutual induction proof system [35] and a lemma synthesis framework [36].

SONGBIRD is implemented in OCaml and uses Z3 as the underlying SMT solver for the first-order logic formula which contains equality and linear arithmetic constraints. The input syntax of SONGBIRD is described in [32].

SONGBIRD integrated SL-COMP at the 2018 edition, and was the first in four divisions: `qf_shid_entl`, `qf_shidlia_entl`, `shid_entl`, `shidlia_entl`. It can also solve 100% of the problems in other two divisions `qf_shls_entl` and `qf_shls_sat`, but the runtime is slower than the best provers of these divisions.

4.11 SPEN

SPEN [9,33] was submitted by Mihaela Sighireanu (IRIF, University Paris Diderot & CNRS, France) and the development team includes Constantin Enea from the same institute, Ondrej Lengal and Tomas Vojnar (FIT, Brno University of Technology, Czechia). The solver deals with satisfiability and entailment problems for the fragments `QF_SHLID` and `QF_SHLS`. The decision procedures call the MiniSAT solver on a Boolean abstraction of the SL formulas to check their satisfiability and to "normalize" the formulas by inferring its implicit (dis)equalities. The core of the algorithm checking if $\varphi \Rightarrow \psi$ is valid searches a mapping from the atoms of ψ to sub-formulas of φ. This search uses the membership test in tree automata to recognize in sub-formulas of φ some unfolding of the inductive definitions used in ψ.

SPEN is written in C and C++ and is open source [33]. It is based on the VATA library for tree automata. SPEN won the division `qf_shlid_entl` at edition 2014 and was in the second position in divisions `qf_shls_entl` and `qf_shls_sat` in both editions.

5 Running the Competition

SL-COMP uses the StarExec platform [34] and requires several features provided by this platform. The pre-processing phase allows to translate each problem into the input format of the solver without time penalties. It is used by most of the solvers and some pre-processors are provided by SL-COMP's organizer, freely available on the competition GitHub repository [22]. The competition did not use the scrambling of benchmark's problems because the names used for inductive definitions defined in the files of some divisions are important for the solvers. Each benchmark file includes only one problem. The incremental feature was not used and is not supported by most of the competing solvers.

StarExec imposes a time and space limit on each attempt of a solver to solve a given problem. For the 2014 edition, the CPU time was limited to 2400 s and the memory (RAM) limit was 100 GB. To gain some time in running the competition, the 2018 edition used by default a timeout of 600 s and 4 GB of memory; if the time was exceeded, timeouts of 2400 then 3600 were tried. Even with these bigger timeouts, some jobs did have CPU timeout or reached the memory limit. To simplify the running, the new edition will use a memory limit of 100 GB and a timeout of 3600 s.

The participants trained their solvers on the platform and provided feedback where the expected result of a problem did not match their result. Several benchmark's problems and solvers were fixed during this period. One training run was executed before the official run to provide insights about the global results and to do a final check of the benchmark set.

The participants at each divisions are ordered according to the rules fixed for SMT-COMP'14 edition. The best solver is the one with, in order: (a) the least number of incorrect answers, (b) the largest number of correctly solved problems, and (c) the smallest time taken in solving the correctly solved problems.

Note that solvers are allowed to respond "unknown" or to time-out on a given benchmark's problem without penalty (other than not being able to count that problem as a success).

StarExec requires that a public version of a solver be made available on StarExec as a condition of participating in a competition. This allows users of StarExec to rerun a competition if so desired. More importantly, it allows users to upload a new set of problems of interest in their application domain and to try the various solvers against those problems. This feature was very useful for SL-COMP at edition 2018, because some solvers reused the binaries submitted in 2014. The results of the competition are provided on the competition web page with a link to the CSV files generated by StarExec. We are also archiving the results of previous editions in the GitHub.

6   Impact and Perspectives

The SL-COMP initiative fulfilled its goals: an interesting suite of SL problems is publicly available in a common format and the maturity of solvers submitted for this competition has been proven.

Moreover, we achieved to propose a common format for SL which is based on a mature and maintained format for first-order theories, SMT-LIB. This format reveals the features required by the existing solvers, e.g., the strong typing of formulas, the kind of inductive definitions handled, etc.

The participation at SL-COMP allowed to measure solvers against competitors and therefore to improve solvers during the competition and in meantime. Moreover, the existing benchmark set includes challenging problems for the competitors because about half (6 over 11) of the divisions are completely solved. Five divisions include problems not yet dealt: qf_bsl_sat has 2 problems (5%), qf_shid_entl has 11 problems (4%), qf_shid_sat has 26 problems (27%), shid_entl has 3 problems (5%) and shid_sat has 29 problems (17%).

A community interested in such tools has been identified and informed about the status of the existing solvers. This community could benefit from improving the tools built on the top of decision procedures for SL.

The SMT-COMP community discovered the status of the solvers for SL and became interested in this theory, as is demonstrated by the participation of CVC4, one of the most complete solver of SMT-COMP.

We expect that the 2019 edition of SL-COMP will enforce these results.

The perspectives mainly concern improvement of the organization process as the size of the competition (number of solvers and benchmark set) increases.

First of all, we are trying to reach a consensus for a good cadence of this competition. Yearly competitions could be very exciting for the first years, but may focus on engineering improvements rather than fundamental work. We feel that a good cadence is alternating a competition year with a year of benchmark set evaluation and improvement.

With the experience of the current competition, the benchmark set has to be improved also. As mentioned above, we have to balance the number of problems coming from the same team in each division in order to reach a fair comparison criterium. For each problem, it would be interesting to attach a coefficient which is taken into account in the scoring system and thus obtain a better evaluation of each solver. A classic way to assign a difficulty level is to take into account the size of the formulas and of the inductive definitions used in the problem.

Finally, we should intensify the exchanges with related competitions in software verification and automated proving. Such competitions may benefit from SL-COMP results in terms of automation, and may provide interesting benchmark sets. For this, the results of SL-COMP should be made available in forms that allows to understood the state of the art of SL solvers and the contribution of each participating solver to this state of the art. We should also provide, in addition to the StarExec platform, other means to reproduce the results of each edition. For example, virtual machines may be archived with the sources and binaries of participants for each edition of the competition.

References

1. Antonopoulos, T., Gorogiannis, N., Haase, C., Kanovich, M., Ouaknine, J.: Foundations for decision problems in separation logic with general inductive predicates. In: Muscholl, A. (ed.) FoSSaCS 2014. LNCS, vol. 8412, pp. 411–425. Springer, Heidelberg (2014). https://doi.org/10.1007/978-3-642-54830-7_27
2. Barrett, C., Stump, A., Tinelli, C.: The Satisfiability Modulo Theories Library (SMT-LIB) (2018). www.SMT-LIB.org
3. Brotherston, J., Fuhs, C., Navarro Pérez, J.A., Gorogiannis, N.: A decision procedure for satisfiability in separation logic with inductive predicates. In: CSL-LICS, pp. 25:1–25:10. ACM (2014)
4. Brotherston, J., Gorogiannis, N., Petersen, R.L.: A generic cyclic theorem prover. In: Jhala, R., Igarashi, A. (eds.) APLAS 2012. LNCS, vol. 7705, pp. 350–367. Springer, Heidelberg (2012). https://doi.org/10.1007/978-3-642-35182-2_25
5. Chin, W.-N., David, C., Nguyen, H.H., Qin, S.: Automated verification of shape, size and bag properties via user-defined predicates in separation logic. Sci. Comput. Program. **77**(9), 1006–1036 (2012)
6. CVC4-SL. http://cvc4.cs.stanford.edu/wiki/Separation_Logic
7. CYCLIST. https://github.com/ngorogiannis/cyclist
8. Demri, S., Deters, M.: Separation logics and modalities: a survey. J. Appl. Non-Classical Logics **25**(1), 50–99 (2015)
9. Enea, C., Lengál, O., Sighireanu, M., Vojnar, T.: Compositional entailment checking for a fragment of separation logic. In: Garrigue, J. (ed.) APLAS 2014. LNCS, vol. 8858, pp. 314–333. Springer, Cham (2014). https://doi.org/10.1007/978-3-319-12736-1_17
10. Enea, C., Sighireanu, M., Wu, Z.: On automated lemma generation for separation logic with inductive definitions. In: Finkbeiner, B., Pu, G., Zhang, L. (eds.) ATVA 2015. LNCS, vol. 9364, pp. 80–96. Springer, Cham (2015). https://doi.org/10.1007/978-3-319-24953-7_7
11. Gu, X., Chen, T., Wu, Z.: A complete decision procedure for linearly compositional separation logic with data constraints. In: Olivetti, N., Tiwari, A. (eds.) IJCAR 2016. LNCS (LNAI), vol. 9706, pp. 532–549. Springer, Cham (2016). https://doi.org/10.1007/978-3-319-40229-1_36

12. Harrsh. https://github.com/katelaan/harrsh
13. Iosif, R., Rogalewicz, A., Simacek, J.: The tree width of separation logic with recursive definitions. In: Bonacina, M.P. (ed.) CADE 2013. LNCS (LNAI), vol. 7898, pp. 21–38. Springer, Heidelberg (2013). https://doi.org/10.1007/978-3-642-38574-2_2
14. Iosif, R., Rogalewicz, A., Vojnar, T.: Deciding entailments in inductive separation logic with tree automata. In: Cassez, F., Raskin, J.-F. (eds.) ATVA 2014. LNCS, vol. 8837, pp. 201–218. Springer, Cham (2014). https://doi.org/10.1007/978-3-319-11936-6_15
15. Iosif, R., Serban, C., Reynolds, A., Sighireanu, M.: Encoding separation logic in smt-lib v2.5. (2018). https://github.com/sl-comp/SL-COMP18/input/Docs
16. Jansen, C., Katelaan, J., Matheja, C., Noll, T., Zuleger, F.: Unified reasoning about robustness properties of symbolic-heap separation logic. In: Yang, H. (ed.) ESOP 2017. LNCS, vol. 10201, pp. 611–638. Springer, Heidelberg (2017). https://doi.org/10.1007/978-3-662-54434-1_23
17. Katelaan, J., Matheja, C., Noll, T., Zuleger, F.: Harrsh: a tool for unied reasoning about symbolic-heap separation logic. In: Barthe, G., Korovin, K., Schulz, S., Suda, M., Sutcliffe, G., Veanes, M., (eds.) LPAR-22 Workshop and Short Paper Proceedings. Kalpa Publications in Computing, vol. 9, pp. 23–36. EasyChair (2018)
18. Le, Q.L., Sun, J., Qin, S.: Frame inference for inductive entailment proofs in separation logic. In: Beyer, D., Huisman, M. (eds.) TACAS 2018. LNCS, vol. 10805, pp. 41–60. Springer, Cham (2018). https://doi.org/10.1007/978-3-319-89960-2_3
19. O'Hearn, P.: Separation logic. http://www0.cs.ucl.ac.uk/staff/p.ohearn/SeparationLogic/Separation_Logic/SL_Home.html
20. O'Hearn, P., Reynolds, J., Yang, H.: Local reasoning about programs that alter data structures. In: Fribourg, L. (ed.) CSL 2001. LNCS, vol. 2142, pp. 1–19. Springer, Heidelberg (2001). https://doi.org/10.1007/3-540-44802-0_1
21. Navarro Pérez, J.A., Rybalchenko, A.: Separation logic modulo theories. In: Shan, C. (ed.) APLAS 2013. LNCS, vol. 8301, pp. 90–106. Springer, Cham (2013). https://doi.org/10.1007/978-3-319-03542-0_7
22. SL-COMP Repository. https://github.com/sl-comp
23. Reynolds, A., Iosif, R., Serban, C., King, T.: A decision procedure for separation logic in SMT. In: Artho, C., Legay, A., Peled, D. (eds.) ATVA 2016. LNCS, vol. 9938, pp. 244–261. Springer, Cham (2016). https://doi.org/10.1007/978-3-319-46520-3_16
24. Reynolds, J.C.: Intuitionistic reasoning about shared mutable data structure. In: Oxford-Microsoft Symposium in Honour of Sir Tony Hoare. Palgrave Macmillan, Basingstoke (1999). Publication date November 2000
25. Reynolds, J.C.: Separation logic: a logic for shared mutable data structures. In: LICS, pp. 55–74. IEEE Computer Society (2002)
26. Sighireanu, M., Cok, D.: Report on SL-COMP 2014. JSAT **9**, 173–186 (2014)
27. SL-COMP 2018. https://www.irif.fr/~sighirea/sl-comp/18/
28. SLEEK. http://loris-7.ddns.comp.nus.edu.sg/~project/s2/beta/
29. SLIDE. http://www.fit.vutbr.cz/research/groups/verifit/tools/slide/
30. SmallFoot. http://www0.cs.ucl.ac.uk/staff/p.ohearn/smallfoot/
31. SMT-COMP. http://smtcomp.sourceforge.org
32. Songbird. https://songbird-prover.github.io/
33. SPEN. https://www.github.com/mihasighi/spen
34. StarExec. http://www.starexec.org

35. Ta, Q.-T., Le, T.C., Khoo, S.-C., Chin, W.-N.: Automated mutual explicit induction proof in separation logic. In: Fitzgerald, J., Heitmeyer, C., Gnesi, S., Philippou, A. (eds.) FM 2016. LNCS, vol. 9995, pp. 659–676. Springer, Cham (2016). https://doi.org/10.1007/978-3-319-48989-6_40
36. Ta, Q.-T., Le, T.C., Khoo, S.-C., Chin, W.-N.: Automated lemma synthesis in symbolic-heap separation logic. Proc. ACM Program. Lang. **2**(POPL), 9:1–9:29 (2017)

Automatic Verification of C and Java Programs: SV-COMP 2019

Dirk Beyer[ID]

LMU Munich, Munich, Germany

Abstract. This report describes the 2019 Competition on Software Verification (SV-COMP), the 8th edition of a series of comparative evaluations of fully automatic software verifiers for C programs, and now also for Java programs. The competition provides a snapshot of the current state of the art in the area, and has a strong focus on replicability of its results. The repository of benchmark verification tasks now supports a new, more flexible format for task definitions (based on YAML), which was a precondition for conveniently benchmarking Java programs in the same controlled competition setting that was successfully applied in the previous years. The competition was based on 10 522 verification tasks for C programs and 368 verification tasks for Java programs. Each verification task consisted of a program and a property (reachability, memory safety, overflows, termination). SV-COMP 2019 had 31 participating verification systems from 14 countries.

1 Introduction

Software verification is an increasingly important research area, and the annual Competition on Software Verification (SV-COMP)[1] is the showcase of the state of the art in the area, in particular, of the effectiveness and efficiency that is currently achieved by tool implementations of the most recent ideas, concepts, and algorithms for fully automatic verification. Every year, the SV-COMP project consists of two parts: (1) The collection of verification tasks and their partitioning into categories has to take place before the actual experiments start, and requires quality-assurance work on the source code in order to ensure a high-quality evaluation. It is important that the SV-COMP verification tasks reflect what the research and development community considers interesting and challenging for evaluating the effectivity (soundness and completeness) and efficiency (performance) of state-of-the-art verification tools. (2) The actual experiments of the comparative evaluation of the relevant tool implementations is performed by the organizer of SV-COMP. Since SV-COMP shall stimulate and showcase new technology, it is necessary to explore and define standards for a reliable and reproducible execution of such a competition: we use BENCHEXEC [19], a modern framework for reliable benchmarking and resource measurement, to run the experiments, and verification witnesses [14,15] to validate the verification results.

---

[1] https://sv-comp.sosy-lab.org

© The Author(s) 2019
D. Beyer et al. (Eds.): TACAS 2019, Part III, LNCS 11429, pp. 133–155, 2019.
https://doi.org/10.1007/978-3-030-17502-3_9

As for every edition, this SV-COMP report describes the (updated) rules and definitions, presents the competition results, and discusses other interesting facts about the execution of the competition experiments. Also, we need to measure the success of SV-COMP by evaluating whether the main objectives of the competition are achieved (cf. [10]):

1. provide an overview of the state of the art in software-verification technology and increase visibility of the most recent software verifiers,
2. establish a repository of software-verification tasks that is publicly available for free use as standard benchmark suite for evaluating verification software,
3. establish standards that make it possible to compare different verification tools, including a property language and formats for the results, and
4. accelerate the transfer of new verification technology to industrial practice.

As for (1), there were 31 participating software systems from 14 countries, representing a broad spectrum of technologies (cf. Table 5). SV-COMP is considered an important event in the research community, and increasingly also in industry. As for (2), the total set of verification tasks written in C increased in size from 8 908 tasks to 10 522 tasks from 2017 to 2019, and in addition, 368 tasks written in Java were added for 2019. Still, SV-COMP has an ongoing focus on collecting and constructing verification tasks to ensure even more diversity, as witnessed by the issue tracker[2] and by the pull requests[3] in the GitHub project. As for (3), the largest step forward was to establish a exchangeable standard format for verification witnesses. This means that verification results are fully counted only if they can be independently validated. As for (4), we continuously receive positive feedback from industry. Colleagues from industry reported to us that they observe SV-COMP in order to know about the newest and best available verification tools. Moreover, since SV-COMP 2017 there are also a few participating systems from industry.

Related Competitions. It is well-understood that competitions are an important evaluation method, and there are other competitions in the field of software verification: RERS[4] [40] and VerifyThis[5] [41]. While SV-COMP performs replicable experiments in a *controlled* environment (dedicated resources, resource limits), the RERS Challenges give more room for exploring combinations of interactive with automatic approaches without limits on the resources, and the VerifyThis Competition focuses on evaluating approaches and ideas rather than on *fully automatic* verification. The termination competition termCOMP[6] [33] concentrates on termination but considers a broader range of systems, including logic and functional programs. This year, SV-COMP is part of TOOLympics [6]. A more comprehensive list of other competitions is provided in the report on

---

[2] https://github.com/sosy-lab/sv-benchmarks/issues
[3] https://github.com/sosy-lab/sv-benchmarks/pulls
[4] http://rers-challenge.org
[5] http://etaps2016.verifythis.org
[6] http://termination-portal.org/wiki/Termination_Competition

SV-COMP 2014 [9]. There are other large benchmark collections as well (e.g., by SPEC[7]), but the `sv-benchmark` suite[8] is (a) free of charge and (b) tailored to the state of the art in software verification. There is a certain flow of benchmark sets between benchmark repositories: For example, the `sv-benchmark` suite contains programs that were used in RERS[9] or in termCOMP[10] before.

2 Procedure

The overall competition organization did not change in comparison to the past editions [7–12]. SV-COMP is an open competition, where all verification tasks are known before the submission of the participating verifiers, which is necessary due to the complexity of the C language. During the *benchmark submission* phase, new verification tasks were collected, classified, and added to the existing benchmark suite (i.e., SV-COMP uses an accumulating benchmark suite), during the *training* phase, the teams inspected the verification tasks and trained their verifiers (also, the verification tasks received fixes and quality improvement), and during the *evaluation* phase, verification runs were preformed with all competition candidates, and the system descriptions were reviewed by the competition jury. The participants received the results of their verifier directly via e-mail, and after a few days of inspection, the results were publicly announced on the competition web site. The *Competition Jury* consisted again of the chair and one member of each participating team. Team representatives of the jury are listed in Table 4.

3 Definitions, Formats, and Rules

License Requirements. Starting 2018, SV-COMP required that the verifier must be publicly available for download and has a license that

(i) allows replication and evaluation by anybody (including results publication),
(ii) does not restrict the usage of the verifier output (log files, witnesses), and
(iii) allows any kind of (re-)distribution of the unmodified verifier archive.

Verification Tasks. The definition of verification tasks was not changed and we refer to previous reports for more details [9,12]. The validation of the results based on verification witnesses [14,15] was done exactly as in the previous years (2017, 2018), mandatory for *both* answers TRUE or FALSE; the only change was that an additional new, execution-based witness validator [16] was used. A few categories were excluded from validation if the validators did not sufficiently support a certain kind of program or property.

Categories, Properties, Scoring Schema, and Ranking. The categories are listed in Tables 6 and 7 and described in detail on the competition web site.[11]

---

[7] https://www.spec.org
[8] https://github.com/sosy-lab/sv-benchmarks
[9] https://github.com/sosy-lab/sv-benchmarks/blob/svcomp19/c/eca-rers2012/README.txt
[10] https://github.com/sosy-lab/sv-benchmarks/blob/svcomp19/c/termination-restricted-15/README.txt
[11] https://sv-comp.sosy-lab.org/2019/benchmarks.php

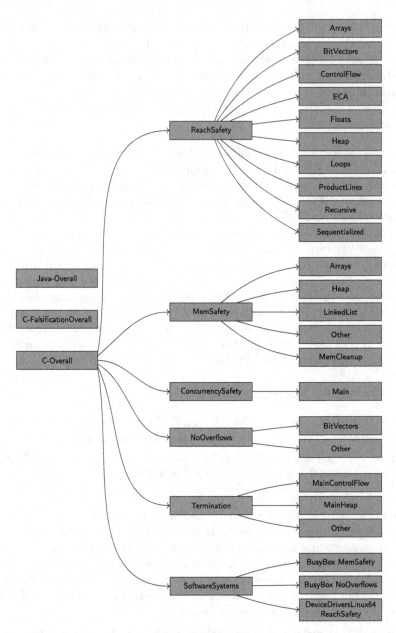

Fig. 1. Category structure for SV-COMP 2019; category *C-FalsificationOverall* contains all verification tasks of *C-Overall* without *Termination*; *Java-Overall* contains all Java verification tasks

Table 1. Properties used in SV-COMP 2019 (`G valid-memcleanup` is new)

Formula	Interpretation
`G ! call(foo())`	A call to function `foo` is not reachable on any finite execution.
`G valid-free`	All memory deallocations are valid (counterexample: invalid free). More precisely: There exists no finite execution of the program on which an invalid memory deallocation occurs.
`G valid-deref`	All pointer dereferences are valid (counterexample: invalid dereference). More precisely: There exists no finite execution of the program on which an invalid pointer dereference occurs.
`G valid-memtrack`	All allocated memory is tracked, i.e., pointed to or deallocated (counterexample: memory leak). More precisely: There exists no finite execution of the program on which the program lost track of some previously allocated memory.
`G valid-memcleanup`	All allocated memory is deallocated before the program terminates. In addition to valid-memtrack: There exists no finite execution of the program on which the program terminates but still points to allocated memory. (Comparison to Valgrind: This property can be violated even if Valgrind reports 'still reachable'.)
`F end`	All program executions are finite and end on proposition `end`, which marks all program exits (counterexample: infinite loop). More precisely: There exists no execution of the program on which the program never terminates.

Table 2. Scoring schema for SV-COMP 2019 (unchanged since 2017 [12])

Reported result	Points	Description
UNKNOWN	0	Failure to compute verification result
FALSE correct	+1	Violation of property in program was correctly found and a validator confirmed the result based on a witness
FALSE incorrect	−16	Violation reported but property holds (false alarm)
TRUE correct	+2	Program correctly reported to satisfy property and a validator confirmed the result based on a witness
TRUE correct unconfirmed	+1	Program correctly reported to satisfy property, but the witness was not confirmed by a validator
TRUE incorrect	−32	Incorrect program reported as correct (wrong proof)

Figure 1 shows the category composition. For the definition of the properties and the property format, we refer to the 2015 competition report [10]. All specifications are available in the directory `c/properties/` of the benchmark repository. Table 1 lists the properties and their syntactical representation as overview. Property `G valid-memcleanup` was used for the first time in SV-COMP 2019.

The scoring schema is identical for SV-COMP 2017–2019: Table 2 provides the overview and Fig. 2 visually illustrates the score assignment for one property. The scoring schema still contains the special rule for unconfirmed correct results for

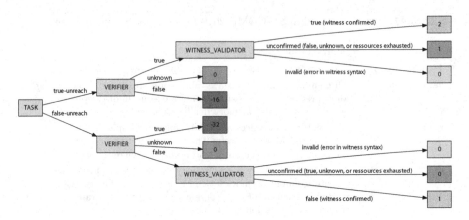

Fig. 2. Visualization of the scoring schema for the reachability property

expected result TRUE that was introduced in the transitioning phase: one point is assigned if the answer matches the expected result but the witness was not confirmed. Starting with SV-COMP 2020, the single-point rule will be dropped, i.e., points are only assigned if the results got validated or no validator was available.

The ranking was again decided based on the sum of points (normalized for meta categories) and for equal sum of points according to success run time, which is the total CPU time over all verification tasks for which the verifier reported a correct verification result. *Opt-out from Categories* and *Score Normalization for Meta Categories* was done as described previously [8] (page 597).

4   New Format for Task Definitions

Technically, we need a verification task (a pair of a program and a specification to verify) to feed as input to the verifier, and an expected result against which we check the answer that the verifier returns. We changed the format of how these tasks are specified for SV-COMP 2019: The C track is still based on the old format, while the Java track already uses the new format.

Recap: Old Format. Previously, the above-mentioned three components were specified in the file name of the program. For example, consider the file name `c/ntdrivers/floppy_true-unreach-call_true-valid-memsafety.i.cil.c`, which encodes the program, the specification (consisting of two properties), and two expected results (one for each property) in the following way:

- **Program:** The program file is identified using the file name `floppy_true-unreach-call_true-valid-memsafety.i.cil.c` in directory `c/ntdrivers/`. The original program was named as `floppy` (see [17]).
- **Specification:** The program comes with a specification that consists of two properties `unreach-call` and `valid-memsafety` thus, the two verification tasks (`floppy`, `unreach-call`) and (`floppy`, `valid-memsafety`) are defined.
- **Expected results:** The expected result for both verification tasks is `true`.

```
1  format_version: '1.0'                    '
2
3  # old file name: floppy_true—unreach—call_true—valid—memsafety.i.cil.c
4  input_files: 'floppy.i.cil—3.c'
5
6  properties:
7    — property_file: ../properties/unreach—call.prp
8      expected_verdict: true
9    — property_file: ../properties/valid—memsafety.prp
10     expected_verdict: true
```

Fig. 3. Example task definition for program `floppy.i.cil-3.c`

This format was used for eight years of SV-COMP, because it is easy to understand and use. However, whenever a new property should be added to the specification of a given program, the program's file name needs to be changed, which has negative impact on traceability and maintenance. From SV-COMP 2020 onwards, the repository will use the following new format for all tracks.

Explicit Task-Definition Files. All the above-discussed information is stored in an extra file that contains a structured definition of the verification tasks for a program. For each program, the repository contains the program file and a task-definition file. The above program is available under the name `floppy.i.cil-3.c` and comes with its task-definition file `floppy.i.cil-3.yml`. Figure 3 shows this task definition.

The task definition uses the YAML format as underlying structured data format. It contains a version id of the format (line 1) and can contain comments (line 3). The field `input_files` specifies the input program (example: 'floppy.i.cil-3.c'), which is either one file or a list of files. The field `properties` lists all properties of the specification for this program. Each property has a field `property_file` that specifies the property file (example: `../properties/unreach-call.prp`) and a field `expected_verdict` that specifies the expected result (example: `true`).

5   Including Java Programs

The first seven editions of SV-COMP considered only programs written in C. In 2019, the competition was extended to include a Java track. Some of the Java programs existed already in the repository, and many other Java programs were contributed by the community [29]. Currently, most of the programs are from the regression-test suites from the verifiers that participate in the Java track; the goal is to substantially increase the benchmark set over the next years.

In principle, the same definitions and rules as for the C track apply, but some technical details need to be slightly adapted for Java programs. Most prominently, the classes of a Java program cannot be inlined into one Java file, which is solved by using the new task-definition format, which allows lists of input files. This required an extension of BENCHEXEC that is present in version 1.17[12] and higher.

---

[12] https://github.com/sosy-lab/benchexec/releases/tag/1.17

```
CHECK( init(main()), LTL(G ! call(__VERIFIER_error())) )
```

(a) Property **c/properties/unreach-call.prp**

```
CHECK( init(Main.main()), LTL(G assert) )
```

(b) Property **java/properties/assert.prp**

Fig. 4. Standard reachability property in comparison for C and for Java

The property for reachability is also slightly different, as shown in Fig. 4: The function call to the start of the program is `Main.main()` instead of `main()`, and the verifiers check that proposition `assert` is always true, instead of checking that `__VERIFIER_error()` is never called. The new proposition `assert` is false where a Java assert statement fails, i.e., the exception `AssertionError` is thrown.

The rules for the C track specify a function `__VERIFIER_nondet_X()` for each type `X` from the set {`bool`, `char`, `int`, `float`, `double`, `loff_t`, `long`, `pchar`, `pointer`, `pthread_t`, `sector_t`, `short`, `size_t`, `u32`, `uchar`, `uint`, `ulong`, `unsigned`, `ushort`} (no side effects, `pointer` for `void *`, etc.) that all return an arbitrary, nondeterministic value ('input' value) of the respective type that may differ for different invocations. Similarly for the Java track: we use a Java class named `org.sosy_lab.sv_benchmarks.Verifier` with the following parameterless static methods: `nondetBoolean`, `nondetByte`, `nondetChar`, `nondetShort`, `nondetInt`, `nondetLong`, `nondetFloat`, `nondetDouble`, and `nondetString`. Each of those methods creates a value of the respective type using functionality from `java.util.Random`. The earlier proposal [29] to use the array of arguments that is passed to the main method to obtain nondeterministic values was not followed. The SV-COMP community found that the explicitly defined methods are better for the competition, and also closer to practice.

Finally, the static method `assume(boolean)` in the same class can be used to assume a certain value range. The implementation halts using `Runtime.getRuntime().halt(1)`. It was proposed [29] to omit this method but in the end the community decided to include it.

6   Reproducibility

It is important that all SV-COMP experiments can be independently replicated, and that the results can be reproduced. Therefore, all major components that are used for the competition need to be publicly available. Figure 5 gives an overview over the components that contribute to the reproducible setup of SV-COMP, and Table 3 provides the details. We refer to a previous report [11] for a description of all components of the SV-COMP organization and how it is ensured that all parts are publicly available for maximal replicability.

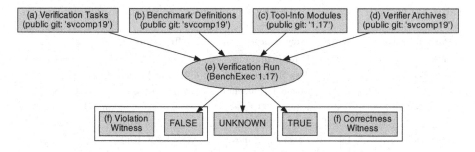

Fig. 5. Setup: SV-COMP components and the execution flow

Table 3. Publicly available components for replicating SV-COMP 2019

Component	Fig. 5	Repository	Version
Verification Tasks	(a)	github.com/sosy-lab/sv-benchmarks	svcomp19
Benchmark Definitions	(b)	github.com/sosy-lab/sv-comp	svcomp19
Tool-Info Modules	(c)	github.com/sosy-lab/benchexec	1.17
Verifier Archives	(d)	gitlab.com/sosy-lab/sv-comp/archives-2019	svcomp19
Benchmarking	(e)	github.com/sosy-lab/benchexec	1.17
Witness Format	(f)	github.com/sosy-lab/sv-witnesses	svcomp19

Since SV-COMP 2018, we use a more transparent way of making the verifier archives publicly available. All verifier archives are now stored in a public Git repository. We chose GitLab to host the repository for the verifier archives due to its generous repository size limit of 10 GB (we could not use GitHub, because it has a strict size limit of 100 MB per file, and recommends to keep the repository under 1 GB). An overview table with information about all participating systems is provided in Table 4 and on the competition web site[13].

In addition to providing the components to replicate the experiments, SV-COMP also makes the raw results available in the XML-based exchange format in which BenchExec [20] delivers the data, and also publishes all verification witnesses [13].

7   Results and Discussion

For the eighth time, the competition experiments represent the state of the art in fully automatic software-verification tools. The report shows the improvements compared to last year, in terms of effectiveness (number of verification tasks that can be solved, correctness of the results, as accumulated in the score) and efficiency (resource consumption in terms of CPU time). The results that are presented in this article were inspected and approved by the participating teams.

---

[13] https://sv-comp.sosy-lab.org/2019/systems.php

Table 4. Competition candidates with tool references and representing jury members

Participant	Ref.	Jury member	Affiliation
2LS	[49,61]	Peter Schrammel	U. of Sussex, UK
APROVE	[34,38]	Jera Hensel	RWTH Aachen, Germany
CBMC	[46]	Michael Tautschnig	Amazon Web Services, UK
CBMC-PATH	[44]	Kareem Khazem	U. College London, UK
CPA-BAM-BNB	[1,64]	Vadim Mutilin	ISP RAS, Russia
CPA-LOCKATOR	[2]	Pavel Andrianov	ISP RAS, Russia
CPA-SEQ	[18,30]	Marie-Christine Jakobs	LMU Munich, Germany
DEPTHK	[58,60]	Omar Alhawi	U. of Manchester, UK
DIVINE-EXPLICIT	[5,62]	Vladimír Štill	Masaryk U., Czechia
DIVINE-SMT	[47,48]	Henrich Lauko	Masaryk U., Czechia
ESBMC-KIND	[31,32]	Mikhail R. Gadelha	U. of Southampton, UK
JAYHORN	[42,43]	Philipp Rümmer	Uppsala U., Sweden
JBMC	[27,28]	Lucas Cordeiro	U. of Manchester, UK
JPF	[3,63]	Cyrille Artho	KTH, Sweden
LAZY-CSEQ	[50]	Omar Inverso	Gran Sasso Science Inst., Italy
MAP2CHECK	[57,59]	Herbert Rocha	Federal U. of Roraima, Brazil
PESCO	[56]	Cedric Richter	U. of Paderborn, Germany
PINAKA	[24]	Eti Chaudhary	IIT Hyderabad, India
PREDATORHP	[39,45]	Veronika Šoková	BUT, Brno, Czechia
SKINK	[21]	Franck Cassez	Macquarie U., Australia
SMACK	[36,55]	Zvonimir Rakamaric	U. of Utah, USA
SPF	[51,53]	Willem Visser	Stellenbosch U., South Africa
SYMBIOTIC	[22,23]	Marek Chalupa	Masaryk U., Czechia
UAUTOMIZER	[37]	Matthias Heizmann	U. of Freiburg, Germany
UKOJAK	[52]	Alexander Nutz	U. of Freiburg, Germany
UTAIPAN	[35]	Daniel Dietsch	U. of Freiburg, Germany
VERIABS	[25]	Priyanka Darke	Tata Consultancy Services, India
VERIFUZZ	[26]	R. K. Medicherla	Tata Consultancy Services, India
VIAP	[54]	Pritom Rajkhowa	Hong Kong UST, China
YOGAR-CBMC	[65,66]	Liangze Yin	Nat. U. of Defense Techn., China
YOGAR-CBMC-PAR.	[67]	Haining Feng	Nat. U. of Defense Techn., China

Participating Verifiers. Table 4 provides an overview of the participating verification systems and Table 5 lists the features and technologies that are used in the verification tools.

Computing Resources. The resource limits were the same as in the previous competitions [11]: Each verification run was limited to 8 processing units (cores), 15 GB of memory, and 15 min of CPU time. The witness validation was limited to 2 processing units, 7 GB of memory, and 1.5 min of CPU time for violation witnesses and 15 min of CPU time for correctness witnesses. The machines for running the experiments are part of a compute cluster that consists of 168 machines;

Table 5. Technologies and features that the competition candidates offer

Participant	CEGAR	Predicate Abstraction	Symbolic Execution	Bounded Model Checking	k-Induction	Property-Directed Reach.	Explicit-Value Analysis	Numeric. Interval Analysis	Shape Analysis	Separation Logic	Bit-Precise Analysis	ARG-Based Analysis	Lazy Abstraction	Interpolation	Automata-Based Analysis	Concurrency Support	Ranking Functions	Evolutionary Algorithms
2LS				✓	✓		✓				✓						✓	
APROVE			✓				✓	✓		✓	✓						✓	
CBMC				✓							✓					✓		
CBMC-PATH				✓							✓					✓		
CPA-BAM-BNB	✓	✓					✓				✓	✓	✓	✓				
CPA-LOCKATOR	✓	✓					✓				✓	✓	✓	✓		✓		
CPA-SEQ	✓	✓		✓	✓		✓	✓	✓		✓	✓	✓	✓		✓	✓	✓
DEPTHK				✓	✓						✓							
DIVINE-EXPLICIT							✓				✓					✓		
DIVINE-SMT							✓				✓					✓		
ESBMC-KIND				✓	✓						✓					✓		
JAYHORN	✓	✓				✓	✓						✓	✓				
JBMC				✓							✓					✓		
JPF				✓			✓	✓			✓					✓		
LAZY-CSEQ				✓							✓					✓		
MAP2CHECK				✓							✓							
PESCO	✓	✓		✓	✓		✓	✓	✓		✓	✓	✓	✓		✓	✓	
PINAKA			✓	✓							✓							
PREDATORHP									✓									
SKINK	✓						✓							✓	✓			
SMACK	✓			✓		✓					✓		✓			✓		
SPF			✓						✓							✓		
SYMBIOTIC			✓					✓			✓							
UAUTOMIZER	✓	✓									✓		✓	✓	✓		✓	
UKOJAK	✓	✓									✓		✓	✓				
UTAIPAN	✓	✓									✓		✓	✓	✓			
VERIABS	✓			✓	✓		✓	✓										
VERIFUZZ				✓			✓											✓
VIAP																		
YOGAR-CBMC	✓			✓							✓		✓			✓		
YOGAR-CBMC-PAR.	✓			✓							✓		✓			✓		

each verification run was executed on an otherwise completely unloaded, dedicated machine, in order to achieve precise measurements. Each machine had one Intel Xeon E3-1230 v5 CPU, with 8 processing units each, a frequency of 3.4 GHz, 33 GB of RAM, and a GNU/Linux operating system (x86_64-linux, Ubuntu 18.04 with Linux kernel 4.15). We used BENCHEXEC [19] to measure and control computing resources (CPU time, memory, CPU energy) and VERIFIERCLOUD[14] to distribute, install, run, and clean-up verification runs, and to collect the results.

One complete verification execution of the competition consisted of 418 benchmarks (each verifier on each selected category according to the opt-outs), summing up to 178 674 verification runs. The total consumed CPU time was 461 days for one complete competition run for verification (without validation). Witness-based result validation required 2 645 benchmarks (combinations of verifier, category with witness validation, and a set of validators) summing up to 517 175 validation runs. Each tool was executed several times, in order to make sure no installation issues occur during the execution. Including pre-runs, the infrastructure managed a total of 5 880 071 runs and consumed 15 years and 182 days of CPU time.

Quantitative Results. Table 6 presents the quantitative overview over all tools and all categories. The head row mentions the category, the maximal score for the category, and the number of verification tasks. The tools are listed in alphabetical order; every table row lists the scores of one verifier. We indicate the top three candidates by formatting their scores in bold face and in larger font size. An empty table cell means that the verifier opted-out from the respective main category (perhaps participating in subcategories only, restricting the evaluation to a specific topic). More information (including interactive tables, quantile plots for every category, and also the raw data in XML format) is available on the competition web site.[15]

Table 7 reports the top three verifiers for each category. The run time (column 'CPU Time') refers to successfully solved verification tasks (column 'Solved Tasks'). The columns 'False Alarms' and 'Wrong Proofs' report the number of verification tasks for which the verifier reported wrong results: reporting an error path when the property holds (incorrect FALSE) and claiming that the program fulfills the property although it actually contains a bug (incorrect TRUE), respectively.

Discussion of Scoring Schema. The verification community considers computation of correctness proofs to be more difficult than computing error paths: according to Table 2, an answer TRUE yields 2 points (confirmed witness) and 1 point (unconfirmed witness), while an answer FALSE yields 1 point (confirmed witness). This can have consequences for the final ranking, as discussed in the report of SV-COMP 2016 [11]. The data from SV-COMP 2019 draw a different picture.

Table 8 shows the mean and median values for resource consumption regarding CPU time and energy consumption: the first column lists the five best verifiers of category *C-Overall*, the second to fifth columns report the CPU time and CPU energy (mean and median) for results TRUE, and the sixth to ninth

---

[14] https://vcloud.sosy-lab.org
[15] https://sv-comp.sosy-lab.org/2019/results

Table 6. Quantitative overview over all results; empty cells mark opt-outs

Verifier	ReachSafety 6296 points 3831 tasks	MemSafety 649 points 434 tasks	ConcurrencySafety 1344 points 1082 tasks	NoOverflows 574 points 359 tasks	Termination 3529 points 2007 tasks	SoftwareSystems 4955 points 2809 tasks	C-FalsificationOverall 3843 points 8515 tasks	C-Overall 16663 points 10522 tasks	Java-Overall 532 points 368 tasks
2LS	2397	129	0	280	1279	119	733	4174	
APROVE					2476				
CBMC	2781	60	613	227	827	0	1432	4341	
CBMC-PATH	1657	-59	-150	192	535	-151	81	1587	
CPA-BAM-BNB						1185			
CPA-LOCKATOR			-441						
CPA-SEQ	4299	349	996	431	1785	1073	2823	9329	
DEPTHK	986	-113	420	39	37	-1182	129	159	
DIVINE-explicit	1413	25	493	0	0	2	200	1547	
DIVINE-SMT	1778	-158	339	0	0	0	-339	726	
ESBMC-kind	3404	-208	404	224	826	714	1916	3636	
JAYHORN									247
JBMC									470
JPF									290
LAZY-CSEQ			1245						
MAP2CHECK		38		8					
PESCO	4239						2313	8466	
PINAKA				218	561				
PREDATORHP		416							
SKINK									
SMACK									
SPF									365
SYMBIOTIC	3143	426	0	331	1153	555	1828	6129	
UAUTOMIZER	3264	-163	270	449	3001	1020	1050	6727	
UKOJAK	2195	-211	0	396	0	818	1060	2595	
UTAIPAN	3012	-91	271	438	0	962	1024	4188	
VERIABS	4638					1061			
VERIFUZZ	1132			123					
VIAP									
YOGAR-CBMC			1277						
YOGAR-CBMC-PAR									

Table 7. Overview of the top-three verifiers for each category (CPU time in h, rounded to two significant digits)

Rank	Verifier	Score	CPU Time	Solved Tasks	False Alarms	Wrong Proofs
ReachSafety						
1	VERIABS	**4638**	110	2 811		
2	CPA-SEQ	4299	60	2 519		
3	PESCO	4239	58	2 431	2	
MemSafety						
1	SYMBIOTIC	**426**	.030	299		
2	PREDATORHP	416	.61	296		
3	CPA-SEQ	349	.55	256		
ConcurrencySafety						
1	YOGAR-CBMC	**1277**	.31	1 026		
2	LAZY-CSEQ	1245	3.0	1 006		
3	CPA-SEQ	996	13	830		
NoOverflows						
1	UAUTOMIZER	**449**	.94	306		
2	UTAIPAN	438	.96	302		
3	CPA-SEQ	431	.59	283		
Termination						
1	UAUTOMIZER	**3001**	13	1 662		
2	APROVE	2476	33	1 004		
3	CPA-SEQ	1785	15	1 319		
SoftwareSystems						
1	CPA-BAM-BNB	**1185**	9.1	1 572		7
2	CPA-SEQ	1073	28	1 447		
3	VERIABS	1061	24	1 407		
C-FalsificationOverall						
1	CPA-SEQ	**2823**	40	2 129		
2	PESCO	2313	53	2 105	8	
3	ESBMC-KIND	1916	15	1 753	14	
C-Overall						
1	CPA-SEQ	**9329**	120	6 654		
2	PESCO	8466	120	6 466	8	1
3	UAUTOMIZER	6727	85	5 454	5	10
Java-Overall						
1	JBMC	**470**	2.7	331		
2	SPF	365	.27	337	4	2
3	JPF	290	.15	331		6

Table 8. Necessary effort to compute results FALSE versus TRUE (measurement values rounded to two significant digits)

Result	TRUE				FALSE			
	CPU Time (s)		CPU Energy (J)		CPU Time (s)		CPU Energy (J)	
	mean	median	mean	median	mean	median	mean	median
CPA-SEQ	67	9.5	690	82	58	14	560	120
PESCO	56	19	540	160	77	26	680	220
UAUTOMIZER	56	17	540	140	58	19	570	180
SYMBIOTIC	4.8	.25	57	2.9	19	.45	210	5.5
CBMC	8.6	.20	91	2.3	21	.24	180	2.8

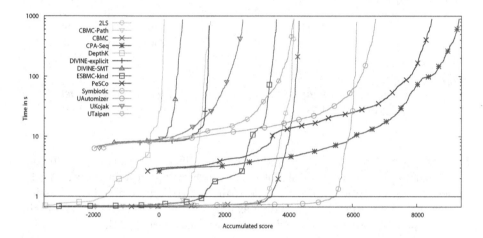

Fig. 6. Quantile functions for category *C-Overall*. Each quantile function illustrates the quantile (x-coordinate) of the scores obtained by correct verification runs below a certain run time (y-coordinate). More details were given previously [8]. A logarithmic scale is used for the time range from 1 s to 1000 s, and a linear scale is used for the time range between 0 s and 1 s.

columns for results FALSE. The mean and median are taken over successfully solved verification tasks; the CPU time is reported in seconds and the CPU energy in joule (BENCHEXEC reads and accumulates the energy measurements of Intel CPUs using the tool CPU Energy Meter[16]).

Score-Based Quantile Functions for Quality Assessment. We use score-based quantile functions [8] because these visualizations make it easier to understand the results of the comparative evaluation. The web site[15] includes such a plot for each category; as example, we show the plot for category *C-Overall*

---

[16] https://github.com/sosy-lab/cpu-energy-meter

Table 9. Alternative rankings; quality is given in score points (sp), CPU time in hours (h), energy in kilojoule (kJ), wrong results in errors (E), rank measures in errors per score point (E/sp), joule per score point (J/sp), and score points (sp)

Rank	Verifier	Quality (sp)	CPU Time (h)	CPU Energy (kJ)	Solved Tasks	Wrong Results (E)	Rank Measure
Correct Verifiers							(E/sp)
1	CPA-SEQ	9 329	120	4 300	2 811	0	.0000
2	SYMBIOTIC	6 129	9.7	390	2 519	0	.0000
3	PESCO	8 466	120	3 900	2 431	9	.0011
worst							.3836
Green Verifiers							(J/sp)
1	SYMBIOTIC	6 129	9.7	390	299	0	64
2	CBMC	4 341	11	380	296	14	88
3	DIVINE-EXPLICIT	1 547	4.4	180	256	10	120
worst							4 200
New Verifiers							(sp)
1	PESCO	8 466	120	3 900	1 026	9	8 466
2	CBMC-PATH	1 587	8.9	380	1 006	69	1 587

(all verification tasks) in Fig. 6. A total of 13 verifiers participated in category *C-Overall*, for which the quantile plot shows the overall performance over all categories (scores for meta categories are normalized [8]). A more detailed discussion of score-based quantile plots, including examples of what insights one can obtain from the plots, is provided in previous competition reports [8,11].

Alternative Rankings. The community suggested to report a couple of alternative rankings that honor different aspects of the verification process as complement to the official SV-COMP ranking. Table 9 is similar to Table 7, but contains the alternative ranking categories *Correct*, *Green*, and *New Verifiers*. Column 'Quality' gives the score in score points, column 'CPU Time' the CPU usage of successful runs in hours, column 'CPU Energy' the CPU usage of successful runs in kilojoule, column 'Solved Tasks' the number of correct results, column 'Wrong results' the sum of false alarms and wrong proofs in number of errors, and column 'Rank Measure' gives the measure to determine the alternative rank.

Correct Verifiers—Low Failure Rate. The right-most columns of Table 7 report that the verifiers achieve a high degree of correctness (all top three verifiers in the C track have less than 1% wrong results). The winners of category *C-Overall* and *Java-Overall* produced not a single wrong answer.

The first category in Table 9 uses a failure rate as rank measure: $\frac{\text{number of incorrect results}}{\text{total score}}$, the number of errors per score point (E/sp). We use E as unit for number of incorrect results and sp as unit for total score. The total score is used as tie-breaker to distinguish the rank of error-free verifiers.

Table 10. Confirmation rate of verification witnesses in SV-COMP 2019

Result	TRUE			FALSE		
	Total	Confirmed	Unconf.	Total	Confirmed	Unconf.
CPA-SEQ	4 417	3 968	90 %	449	2 859	2 686	94 %	173
PESCO	4 176	3 814	91 %	362	2 823	2 652	94 %	171
UAUTOMIZER	4 244	4 199	99 %	45	1 523	1 255	82 %	268
SYMBIOTIC	2 430	2 381	98 %	49	1 451	1 214	84 %	237
CBMC	1 813	1 702	94 %	111	1 975	1 248	63 %	727
UTAIPAN	3 015	2 936	97 %	79	915	653	71 %	262
2LS	2 072	2 045	99 %	27	1 419	945	67 %	474
ESBMC-KIND	3 679	3 556	97 %	123	2 141	1 753	82 %	388
UKOJAK	2 070	2 038	98 %	32	553	548	99 %	5
CBMC-PATH	1 206	1 162	96 %	44	897	670	75 %	727
DIVINE-EXPLICIT	693	673	97 %	20	768	353	46 %	415
DIVINE-SMT	645	626	97 %	19	943	601	64 %	342
DEPTHK	612	602	98 %	10	1 938	1 370	71 %	568

Green Verifiers—Low Energy Consumption. Since a large part of the cost of verification is given by the energy consumption, it might be important to also consider the energy efficiency. The second category in Table 9 uses the energy consumption per score point as rank measure: $\frac{\text{total CPU energy}}{\text{total score}}$, with the unit J/sp.

New Verifiers—High Quality. To acknowledge the achievements of verifiers that participate for the first time in SV-COMP, the third category in Table 9 uses the quality in score points as rank measure, that is, the official SV-COMP rank measure, but the subject systems reduced to verifiers that participate for the first time. The Java track consists exclusively of new verifiers, so the new-verifiers ranking is the same as the official ranking.

Verifiable Witnesses. For SV-COMP, it is not sufficient to answer with just TRUE or FALSE: each answer should be accompanied by a verification witness. All verifiers in categories that required witness validation support the common exchange format for violation and correctness witnesses. We used four independently developed witness-based result validators [14–16].

The majority of witnesses that the verifiers produced can be confirmed by the results-validation process. Interestingly, the confirmation rate for the TRUE results is significantly higher than for the FALSE results. Table 10 shows the confirmed versus unconfirmed results: the first column lists the verifiers of category *C-Overall*, the three columns for result TRUE reports the total, confirmed, and unconfirmed number of verification tasks for which the verifier answered with TRUE, respectively, and the three columns for result FALSE reports the total, confirmed, and unconfirmed number of verification tasks for which the verifier answered with FALSE, respectively. More information (for all verifiers) is given in

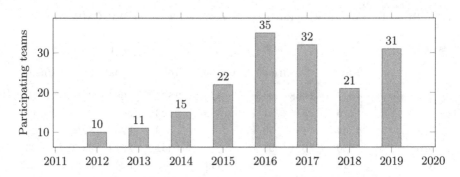

Fig. 7. Number of participating teams for each year

the detailed tables on the competition web site[15], cf. also the report on the demo category for correctness witnesses from SV-COMP 2016 [11]. Result validation is an important topic also in other competitions (e.g., in the SAT competition [4]).

8   Conclusion

SV-COMP 2019, the 8th edition of the Competition on Software Verification, attracted 31 participating teams from 14 countries (see Fig. 7 for the development). SV-COMP continues to offer the broadest overview of the state of the art in automatic software verification. For the first time, the competition included Java verification; this track had four participating verifiers. The competition does not only execute the verifiers and collect results, but also tries to validate the verification results, based on the latest versions of four independently developed results validators. The number of verification tasks was increased to 10 522 in C and to 368 in Java. As before, the large jury and the organizer made sure that the competition follows the high quality standards of the TACAS conference, in particular with respect to the important principles of fairness, community support, and transparency.

References

1. Andrianov, P., Friedberger, K., Mandrykin, M.U., Mutilin, V.S., Volkov, A.: CPA-BAM-BnB: Block-abstraction memoization and region-based memory models for predicate abstractions (competition contribution). In: Proc. TACAS, LNCS, vol. 10206, pp. 355–359. Springer, Heidelberg (2017). https://doi.org/10.1007/978-3-662-54580-5_22
2. Andrianov, P., Mutilin, V., Khoroshilov, A.: Predicate abstraction based configurable method for data race detection in Linux kernel. In: Proc. TMPA, CCIS, vol. 779, pp. 11–23. Springer, Cham (2018). https://doi.org/10.1007/978-3-319-71734-0_2

3. Artho, C., Visser, W.: Java Pathfinder at SV-COMP 2019 (competition contribution). In: Proc. TACAS, LNCS, vol. 11429, pp. 224–228. Springer, Cham (2019). https://doi.org/10.1007/978-3-030-17502-3_18

4. Balyo, T., Heule, M.J.H., Järvisalo, M.: SAT Competition 2016: Recent developments. In: Proc. AI, pp. 5061–5063. AAAI Press (2017)

5. Baranová, Z., Barnat, J., Kejstová, K., Kučera, T., Lauko, H., Mrázek, J., Ročkai, P., Štill, V.: Model checking of C and C++ with DIVINE 4. In: Proc. ATVA, LNCS, vol. 10482, pp. 201–207. Springer, Cham (2017)

6. Bartocci, E., Beyer, D., Black, P.E., Fedyukovich, G., Garavel, H., Hartmanns, A., Huisman, M., Kordon, F., Nagele, J., Sighireanu, M., Steffen, B., Suda, M., Sutcliffe, G., Weber, T., Yamada, A.: TOOLympics 2019: An overview of competitions in formal methods. In: Proc. TACAS, Part 3, LNCS, vol. 11429, pp. 3–24. Springer, Cham (2019). https://doi.org/10.1007/978-3-030-17502-3_1

7. Beyer, D.: Competition on software verification (SV-COMP). In: Proc. TACAS, LNCS, vol. 7214, pp. 504–524. Springer, Heidelberg (2012). https://doi.org/10.1007/978-3-642-28756-5_38

8. Beyer, D.: Second competition on software verification (Summary of SV-COMP 2013). In: Proc. TACAS, LNCS, vol. 7795, pp. 594–609. Springer, Heidelberg (2013). https://doi.org/10.1007/978-3-642-36742-7_43

9. Beyer, D.: Status report on software verification (Competition summary SV-COMP 2014). In: Proc. TACAS, LNCS, vol. 8413, pp. 373–388. Springer, Heidelberg (2014). https://doi.org/10.1007/978-3-642-54862-8_25

10. Beyer, D.: Software verification and verifiable witnesses (Report on SV-COMP 2015). In: Proc. TACAS, LNCS, vol. 9035, pp. 401–416. Springer, Heidelberg (2015). https://doi.org/10.1007/978-3-662-46681-0_31

11. Beyer, D.: Reliable and reproducible competition results with BENCHEXEC and witnesses (Report on SV-COMP 2016). In: Proc. TACAS, LNCS, vol. 9636, pp. 887–904. Springer, Heidelberg (2016). https://doi.org/10.1007/978-3-662-49674-9_55

12. Beyer, D.: Software verification with validation of results (Report on SV-COMP 2017). In: Proc. TACAS, LNCS, vol. 10206, pp. 331–349. Springer, Heidelberg (2017). https://doi.org/10.1007/978-3-662-54580-5_20

13. Beyer, D.: Verification witnesses from SV-COMP 2019 verification tools. Zenodo (2019). https://doi.org/10.5281/zenodo.2559175

14. Beyer, D., Dangl, M., Dietsch, D., Heizmann, M.: Correctness witnesses: Exchanging verification results between verifiers. In: Proc. FSE, pp. 326–337. ACM (2016). https://doi.org/10.1145/2950290.2950351

15. Beyer, D., Dangl, M., Dietsch, D., Heizmann, M., Stahlbauer, A.: Witness validation and stepwise testification across software verifiers. In: Proc. FSE, pp. 721–733. ACM (2015). https://doi.org/10.1145/2786805.2786867

16. Beyer, D., Dangl, M., Lemberger, T., Tautschnig, M.: Tests from witnesses: Execution-based validation of verification results. In: Proc. TAP, LNCS, vol. 10889, pp. 3–23. Springer, Cham (2018). https://doi.org/10.1007/978-3-319-92994-1_1

17. Beyer, D., Henzinger, T.A., Jhala, R., Majumdar, R.: The software model checker Blast. Int. J. Softw. Tools Technol. Transfer 9(5–6), 505–525 (2007). https://doi.org/10.1007/s10009-007-0044-z

18. Beyer, D., Keremoglu, M.E.: CPACHECKER: A tool for configurable software verification. In: Proc. CAV, LNCS, vol. 6806, pp. 184–190. Springer, Heidelberg (2011). https://doi.org/10.1007/978-3-642-22110-1_16

19. Beyer, D., Löwe, S., Wendler, P.: Benchmarking and resource measurement. In: Proc. SPIN, LNCS, vol. 9232, pp. 160–178. Springer, Cham (2015). https://doi.org/10.1007/978-3-319-23404-5_12

20. Beyer, D., Löwe, S., Wendler, P.: Reliable benchmarking: Requirements and solutions. Int. J. Softw. Tools Technol. Transfer **21**(1), 1–29 (2019). https://doi.org/10.1007/s10009-017-0469-y

21. Cassez, F., Sloane, A.M., Roberts, M., Pigram, M., Suvanpong, P., de Aledo Marugán, P.G.: Skink: Static analysis of programs in LLVM intermediate representation (competition contribution). In: Proc. TACAS, LNCS, vol. 10206, pp. 380–384. Springer, Heidelberg (2017). https://doi.org/10.1007/978-3-662-54580-5_27

22. Chalupa, M., Strejcek, J., Vitovská, M.: Joint forces for memory safety checking. In: Proc. SPIN, LNCS, vol. 10869, pp. 115–132. Springer, Cham (2018). https://doi.org/10.1007/978-3-319-94111-0_7

23. Chalupa, M., Vitovská, M., Strejcek, J.: Symbiotic 5: Boosted instrumentation (competition contribution). In: Proc. TACAS, LNCS, vol. 10806, pp. 442–446. Springer, Cham (2018). https://doi.org/10.1007/978-3-319-89963-3_29

24. Chaudhary, E., Joshi, S.: Pinaka: Symbolic execution meets incremental solving (competition contribution). In: Proc. TACAS, LNCS, vol. 11429, pp. 234–238. Springer, Cham (2019). https://doi.org/10.1007/978-3-030-17502-3_20

25. Chimdyalwar, B., Darke, P., Chauhan, A., Shah, P., Kumar, S., Venkatesh, R.: VeriAbs: Verification by abstraction (competition contribution). In: Proc. TACAS, LNCS, vol. 10206, pp. 404–408. Springer, Heidelberg (2017). https://doi.org/10.1007/978-3-662-54580-5_32

26. Chowdhury, A.B., Medicherla, R.K., Venkatesh, R.: VeriFuzz: Program aware fuzzing (competition contribution). In: Proc. TACAS, LNCS, vol. 11429, pp. 244–249. Springer, Cham (2019). https://doi.org/10.1007/978-3-030-17502-3_22

27. Cordeiro, L.C., Kesseli, P., Kröning, D., Schrammel, P., Trtík, M.: JBMC: A bounded model checking tool for verifying Java bytecode. In: Proc. CAV, LNCS, vol. 10981, pp. 183–190. Springer, Cham (2018). https://doi.org/10.1007/978-3-319-96145-3_10

28. Cordeiro, L., Kröning, D., Schrammel, P.: JBMC: Bounded model checking for Java bytecode (competition contribution). In: Proc. TACAS, LNCS, vol. 11429, pp. 219–223. Springer, Cham (2019). https://doi.org/10.1007/978-3-030-17502-3_17

29. Cordeiro, L.C., Kröning, D., Schrammel, P.: Benchmarking of Java verification tools at the software verification competition (SV-COMP). CoRR abs/1809.03739 (2018)

30. Dangl, M., Löwe, S., Wendler, P.: CPACHECKER with support for recursive programs and floating-point arithmetic (competition contribution). In: Proc. TACAS, LNCS, vol. 9035, pp. 423–425. Springer, Heidelberg (2015). https://doi.org/10.1007/978-3-662-46681-0_34

31. Gadelha, M.R., Monteiro, F.R., Cordeiro, L.C., Nicole, D.A.: ESBMC v6.0: Verifying C programs using k-induction and invariant inference (competition contribution). In: Proc. TACAS, LNCS, vol. 11429, pp.209–213. Springer, Cham (2019). https://doi.org/10.1007/978-3-030-17502-3_15

32. Gadelha, M.Y., Ismail, H.I., Cordeiro, L.C.: Handling loops in bounded model checking of C programs via k-induction. Int. J. Softw. Tools Technol. Transfer **19**(1), 97–114 (2017). https://doi.org/10.1007/s10009-015-0407-9

33. Giesl, J., Mesnard, F., Rubio, A., Thiemann, R., Waldmann, J.: Termination competition (termCOMP 2015). In: Proc. CADE, LNCS, vol. 9195, pp. 105–108. Springer, Cham (2015). https://doi.org/10.1007/978-3-319-21401-6_6

34. Giesl, J., Aschermann, C., Brockschmidt, M., Emmes, F., Frohn, F., Fuhs, C., Hensel, J., Otto, C., Plücker, M., Schneider-Kamp, P., Ströder, T., Swiderski, S., Thiemann, R.: Analyzing program termination and complexity automatically with aprove. J. Autom. Reason. **58**(1), 3–31 (2017)

35. Greitschus, M., Dietsch, D., Heizmann, M., Nutz, A., Schätzle, C., Schilling, C., Schüssele, F., Podelski, A.: Ultimate Taipan: Trace abstraction and abstract interpretation (competition contribution). In: Proc. TACAS, LNCS, vol. 10206, pp. 399–403. Springer, Heidelberg (2017). https://doi.org/10.1007/978-3-662-54580-5_31

36. Haran, A., Carter, M., Emmi, M., Lal, A., Qadeer, S., Rakamarić, Z.: SMACK+Corral: A modular verifier (competition contribution). In: Proc. TACAS, LNCS, vol. 9035, pp. 451–454. Springer, Heidelberg (2015)

37. Heizmann, M., Chen, Y., Dietsch, D., Greitschus, M., Nutz, A., Musa, B., Schätzle, C., Schilling, C., Schüssele, F., Podelski, A.: Ultimate Automizer with an on-demand construction of Floyd-Hoare automata (competition contribution). In: Proc. TACAS, LNCS, vol. 10206, pp. 394–398. Springer, Heidelberg (2017). https://doi.org/10.1007/978-3-662-54580-5_30

38. Hensel, J., Emrich, F., Frohn, F., Ströder, T., Giesl, J.: AProVE: Proving and disproving termination of memory-manipulating C programs (competition contribution). In: Proc. TACAS, LNCS, vol. 10206, pp. 350–354. Springer, Heidelberg (2017). https://doi.org/10.1007/978-3-662-54580-5_21

39. Holík, L., Kotoun, M., Peringer, P., Šoková, V., Trtík, M., Vojnar, T.: Predator shape analysis tool suite. In: Hardware and Software: Verification and Testing, LNCS, vol. 10028, pp. 202–209. Springer, Cham (2016) https://doi.org/10.1007/978-3-319-49052-6

40. Howar, F., Isberner, M., Merten, M., Steffen, B., Beyer, D.: The RERS greybox challenge 2012: Analysis of event-condition-action systems. In: Proc. ISoLA, LNCS, vol. 7609, pp. 608–614. Springer, Heidelberg (2012). https://doi.org/10.1007/978-3-642-34026-0_45

41. Huisman, M., Klebanov, V., Monahan, R.: VerifyThis 2012 - A program verification competition. STTT 17(6), 647–657 (2015). https://doi.org/10.1007/s10009-015-0396-8

42. Kahsai, T., Rümmer, P., Sanchez, H., Schäf, M.: JayHorn: A framework for verifying Java programs. In: Proc. CAV, LNCS, vol. 9779, pp. 352–358. Springer, Cham (2016). https://doi.org/10.1007/978-3-319-41528-4_19

43. Kahsai, T., Rümmer, P., Schäf, M.: JayHorn: A Java model checker (competition contribution). In: Proc. TACAS, LNCS, vol. 11429, pp. 214–218. Springer, Cham (2019). https://doi.org/10.1007/978-3-030-17502-3_16

44. Khazem, K., Tautschnig, M.: CBMC Path: A symbolic execution retrofit of the C bounded model checker (competition contribution). In: Proc. TACAS, LNCS, vol. 11429, pp. 199–203. Springer, Cham (2019). https://doi.org/10.1007/978-3-030-17502-3_13

45. Kotoun, M., Peringer, P., Soková, V., Vojnar, T.: Optimized Predators and the SV-COMP heap and memory safety benchmark (competition contribution). In: Proc. TACAS, LNCS, vol. 9636, pp. 942–945. Springer, Heidelberg (2016)

46. Kröning, D., Tautschnig, M.: CBMC: C bounded model checker (competition contribution). In: Proc. TACAS, LNCS, vol. 8413, pp. 389–391. Springer, Heidelberg (2014)

47. Lauko, H., Ročkai, P., Barnat, J.: Symbolic computation via program transformation. In: Proc. ICTAC, LNCS, vol. 11187, pp. 313–332. Springer, Cham (2018)

48. Lauko, H., Štill, V., Ročkai, P., Barnat, J.: Extending DIVINE with symbolic verification using SMT (competition contribution). In: Proc. TACAS, LNCS, vol. 11429, pp. 204–208. Springer, Cham (2019). https://doi.org/10.1007/978-3-030-17502-3_14

49. Malik, V., Hruska, M., Schrammel, P., Vojnar, T.: 2LS: Heap analysis and memory safety (competition contribution). Tech. Rep. abs/1903.00712, CoRR (2019)

50. Nguyen, T.L., Inverso, O., Fischer, B., La Torre, S., Parlato, G.: Lazy-CSeq 2.0: Combining lazy sequentialization with abstract interpretation (competition contribution). In: Proc. TACAS, LNCS, vol. 10206, pp. 375–379. Springer, Heidelberg (2017). https://doi.org/10.1007/978-3-662-54580-5_26

51. Noller, Y., Pasareanu, C., Le, B.D., Visser, W., Fromherz, A.: Symbolic Pathfinder for SV-COMP (competition contribution). In: Proc. TACAS, LNCS, vol. 11429, pp. 239–243. Springer, Cham (2019). https://doi.org/10.1007/978-3-030-17502-3_21

52. Nutz, A., Dietsch, D., Mohamed, M.M., Podelski, A.: ULTIMATE KOJAK with memory safety checks (competition contribution). In: Proc. TACAS, LNCS, vol. 9035, pp. 458–460. Springer, Heidelberg (2015). https://doi.org/10.1007/978-3-662-46681-0_44

53. Pasareanu, C.S., Visser, W., Bushnell, D.H., Geldenhuys, J., Mehlitz, P.C., Rungta, N.: Symbolic PathFinder: integrating symbolic execution with model checking for Java bytecode analysis. Autom. Softw. Eng. **20**(3), 391–425 (2013)

54. Rajkhowa, P., Lin, F.: VIAP 1.1: Automated system for verifying integer assignment programs with loops (competition contribution). In: Proc. TACAS, LNCS, vol. 11429, pp. 250–255. Springer, Cham (2019). https://doi.org/10.1007/978-3-030-17502-3_23

55. Rakamarić, Z., Emmi, M.: SMACK: Decoupling source language details from verifier implementations. In: Proc. CAV, LNCS, vol. 8559, pp. 106–113. Springer, Cham (2014). https://doi.org/10.1007/978-3-319-08867-9_7

56. Richter, C., Wehrheim, H.: PeSCo: Predicting sequential combinations of verifiers (competition contribution). In: Proc. TACAS, LNCS, vol. 11429, pp. 229–233. Springer, Cham (2019). https://doi.org/10.1007/978-3-030-17502-3_19

57. Rocha, H., Barreto, R.S., Cordeiro, L.C.: Memory management test-case generation of C programs using bounded model checking. In: Proc. SEFM, LNCS, vol. 9276, pp. 251–267. Springer, Cham (2015). https://doi.org/10.1007/978-3-319-22969-0_18

58. Rocha, H., Ismail, H., Cordeiro, L.C., Barreto, R.S.: Model checking embedded C software using k-induction and invariants. In: Proc. SBESC, pp. 90–95. IEEE (2015). https://doi.org/10.1109/SBESC.2015.24

59. Rocha, H.O., Barreto, R.S., Cordeiro, L.C.: Hunting memory bugs in C programs with Map2Check (competition contribution). In: Proc. TACAS, LNCS, vol. 9636, pp. 934–937. Springer, Heidelberg (2016)

60. Rocha, W., Rocha, H., Ismail, H., Cordeiro, L.C., Fischer, B.: DepthK: A k-induction verifier based on invariant inference for C programs (competition contribution). In: Proc. TACAS, LNCS, vol. 10206, pp. 360–364. Springer, Heidelberg (2017). https://doi.org/10.1007/978-3-662-54580-5_23

61. Schrammel, P., Kröning, D.: 2LS for program analysis (competition contribution). In: Proc. TACAS, LNCS, vol. 9636, pp. 905–907. Springer, Heidelberg (2016). https://doi.org/10.1007/978-3-662-49674-9_56

62. Štill, V., Ročkai, P., Barnat, J.: DIVINE: Explicit-state LTL model checker (competition contribution). In: Proc. TACAS, LNCS, vol. 9636, pp. 920–922. Springer, Heidelberg (2016)

63. Visser, W., Havelund, K., Brat, G., Park, S., Lerda, F.: Model checking programs. Autom. Softw. Eng. **10**(2), 203–232 (2003)
64. Volkov, A.R., Mandrykin, M.U.: Predicate abstractions memory modeling method with separation into disjoint regions. Proc. Inst. Syst. Program. (ISPRAS) **29**, 203–216 (2017). https://doi.org/10.15514/ISPRAS-2017-29(4)-13
65. Yin, L., Dong, W., Liu, W., Li, Y., Wang, J.: YOGAR-CBMC: CBMC with scheduling constraint based abstraction refinement (competition contribution). In: Proc. TACAS, LNCS, vol. 10806, pp. 422–426. Springer, Cham (2018)
66. Yin, L., Dong, W., Liu, W., Wang, J.: On scheduling constraint abstraction for multi-threaded program verification. IEEE Trans. Softw. Eng. https://doi.org/10.1109/TSE.2018.2864122
67. Yin, L., Dong, W., Liu, W., Wang, J.: Parallel refinement for multi-threaded program verification. In: Proc. ICSE. IEEE (2019)

The Termination and Complexity Competition

Jürgen Giesl[1][✉], Albert Rubio[2][✉], Christian Sternagel[3][✉],
Johannes Waldmann[4][✉], and Akihisa Yamada[5][✉]

[1] LuFG Informatik 2, RWTH Aachen University, Aachen, Germany
giesl@informatik.rwth-aachen.de
[2] Universitat Politècnica de Catalunya, Barcelona, Spain
albert@cs.upc.edu
[3] Department of Computer Science, University of Innsbruck, Innsbruck, Austria
christian.sternagel@uibk.ac.at
[4] Institut für Informatik, HTWK Leipzig, Leipzig, Germany
johannes.waldmann@htwk-leipzig.de
[5] NII, Tokyo, Japan
akihisayamada@nii.ac.jp

Abstract. The termination and complexity competition (termCOMP) focuses on automated termination and complexity analysis for various kinds of programming paradigms, including categories for term rewriting, integer transition systems, imperative programming, logic programming, and functional programming. In all categories, the competition also welcomes the participation of tools providing certifiable output. The goal of the competition is to demonstrate the power and advances of the state-of-the-art tools in each of these areas.

1 Introduction

Termination and complexity analysis have attracted a lot of research since the early days of computer science. In particular, termination for the rewriting model of computation is essential for methods in equational reasoning: the word problem [18] asks for convertibility with respect to a rewrite system, and some instances can be solved by a completion procedure where termination needs to be checked in each step [34]. Term rewriting is the basis of functional programming [42], which, in turn, is the basis of automated theorem proving [13]. As early examples for the importance of termination in other domains and models of computation we mention that completion is used in symbolic computation for the construction of Gröbner Bases

A. Rubio—This author is supported by the Spanish MINECO under the grant TIN2015-69175-C4-3-R (project LoBaSS).
C. Sternagel—This author is supported by the Austrian Science Fund (FWF) Project P27502.
A. Yamada—This author is supported by ERATO HASUO Metamathematics for Systems Design Project (No. JPMJER1603), JST.

D. Beyer et al. (Eds.): TACAS 2019, Part III, LNCS 11429, pp. 156–166, 2019.
https://doi.org/10.1007/978-3-030-17502-3_10

for polynomial ideals [15], and that boundedness of Petri Nets can be modeled by termination of vector addition systems, which is decidable [33].

Both termination and complexity (or resource consumption) are very relevant properties for many computation systems and keep being the focus of interest in newly emerging technologies. For instance, complexity analyzers are applied to analyze large Java programs in order to detect vulnerabilities [45].

Another particularly interesting example are smart contracts in blockchains, which are becoming very popular. Providing tools for analyzing their termination and bounding their resource consumption is critical [2]. For example, transactions that run out-of-gas in the Ethereum blockchain platform throw an exception, their effect is reverted, and the gas consumed up to that point is lost.

Deciding the (uniform) termination problem is to determine whether a given program has only finite executions for all possible inputs. Termination is a well-known undecidable property for programs written in any Turing complete language, and any complexity analyzer must include termination analysis as well. Despite this challenging undecidable scenario, powerful automatic tools for many different formalisms are available nowadays.

History of termCOMP. After a tool demonstration at the Termination Workshop 2003 (Valencia) organized by Albert Rubio, the community decided to hold an annual termination competition and to collect benchmarks in order to spur the development of tools and new termination techniques. Since 2004 the competition, known as termCOMP, has been organized annually, with usually between 10 and 20 tools participating in the different categories on termination, complexity, and/or certification. The actual organizers of the competition have been Claude Marché (from 2004 to 2007), René Thiemann (from 2008 to 2013), Johannes Waldmann (from 2014 to 2017), and Akihisa Yamada (since 2018). Recent competitions have been executed live during the main conferences of the field (at FLoC 2018, FSCD 2017, WST 2016, CADE 2015, VSL 2014, RDP 2013, IJCAR 2012, RTA 2011, and FLoC 2010). Information on all termination and complexity competitions is available from http://termination-portal.org/.

Computational resources for the execution of the competition have been provided by LRI, Université Paris-Sud (from 2004 to 2007) and by the University of Innsbruck (from 2008 to 2013). Since 2014, the competition runs on StarExec, a cross-community service at the University of Iowa for the evaluation of automated tools based on formal reasoning. It provides a single piece of storage and computing infrastructure to the communities in computational logic developing such tools [48].

From 2014 to 2017, competition results were presented using a separate web application star-exec-presenter developed at HTWK Leipzig [40], giving both an aggregated view of results, as well as detailed results per category. Additionally, it provides options for sorting and selecting subsets of benchmarks and solvers according to various criteria, as well as for comparing results of various competitions and/or test runs. This helps to estimate progress and to detect inconsistencies. Since 2018, starexec-master [50] (the successor of star-exec-presenter) is in use (see Fig. 1 in Sect. 2).

Competition Benchmarks. The benchmarks used to run the competition on are collected in the *Termination Problem Data Base* (TPDB for short), which was originally created by Claude Marché, Albert Rubio, and Hans Zantema, and later on maintained, extended, and reorganized by René Thiemann, Johannes Waldmann, and Akihisa Yamada. Many researchers have contributed with new benchmarks over the years. The current version of TPDB (10.6) contains a total of 43,112 benchmarks and extends over 674 MByte (uncompressed).

The termination competitions started with categories on termination of string rewrite systems (SRSs) and term rewrite systems (TRSs). Apart from standard rewriting, there were also categories based on adding strategies and extensions like equational, innermost, or context-sensitive rewriting. Further categories were introduced afterwards, including, for instance, higher-order rewriting (since 2010) and cycle rewriting (since 2015). Categories on complexity analysis of rewrite systems were added in 2008.

Regarding analysis tools for programming languages, a category on termination of logic programs was already part of the competition in 2004. Categories for other programming paradigms were introduced later: since 2007 there is a category for functional (Haskell) programs, since 2009 termination of Java programs is also considered, and since 2014 C programs are handled as well. Moreover, back-end languages like integer transition systems (ITSs) or integer term rewriting are part of termCOMP since 2014. Last but not least, complexity analysis categories for some of these languages have also been included recently.

Finally, the first certification categories on rewriting were included in 2007 and have been extended to some other languages and formalisms over the years.

Overview. In the remainder of this paper we will

- describe the organization of termCOMP in its 2019 edition (Sect. 2),
- give a detailed account of the categories in the used benchmark collection (Sect. 3),
- and give an overview on the tools and techniques at the previous termCOMP 2018 (Sect. 4).

2   Organization of the Competition

In 2019 we plan to run the competition on StarExec again. Each tool will be run on all benchmarks of the categories it is registered for, with a wall-clock timeout of 300 s per example. Tools are expected to give an answer in the first line of their standard output, followed by a justification for their answer.

In termination categories, the expected answers are YES (indicating termination), NO (indicating nontermination), and MAYBE (indicating that the tool had to give up). Each YES or NO answer will score one point, unless it turns out to be incorrect. Each incorrect answer scores −10 points.

In complexity categories, an answer specifies either or both upper- and lower-bound (worst-case) complexity. The score of an answer is the sum of the scores for the upper-bound and lower-bound, each of which depends on the number of other participants. Details of the answer format and scoring scheme are available at http://cbr.uibk.ac.at/competition/rules.php.

In contrast to previous years, we will not run the competition live but before the TACAS conference takes place. We reserve about two weeks for resolving technical issues, analyzing conflicting answers, and debugging. If participants fail to agree on the treatment of conflicts, the steering committee will finally decide which answer will be penalized.

The competition results will be presented using the **starexec-master** web front end [50], see Fig. 1.

Termination of Rewriting

category	ranking
TRS Standard 30034	APROVE 1283; NaTT 1018; ttt2-1.17+nonreach 998; muterm 5.18 832; Wanda 619;
TRS Standard Certified 30038	APROVE 1200; ttt2-1.17+nonreach 925;
SRS Standard 30035	MultumNonMulta3.12_29June2018A 976; APROVE 971; ttt2-1.17+nonreach 744; NaTT 203; muterm 5.18 136;
SRS Standard Certified 30039	APROVE 838; ttt2-1.17+nonreach 592;
TRS Relative 30036	NaTT 62; APROVE 56; ttt2-1.17+nonreach 39;
TRS Relative Certified 30040	APROVE 50; ttt2-1.17+nonreach 42;
SRS Relative 30037	MultumNonMulta3.12_29June2018A 142; APROVE 90; ttt2-1.17+nonreach 24; NaTT 7;
SRS Relative Certified 30041	APROVE 90; ttt2-1.17+nonreach 28;
TRS Equational 30042	APROVE 64; muterm 5.18 63; NaTT 46;
TRS Equational Certified 30043	APROVE 63; NaTT 25;
TRS Conditional 30044	muterm 5.18 101; APROVE 84;
TRS Context Sensitive 30045	muterm 5.18 101; APROVE 97;
TRS Innermost 30046	APROVE 296; muterm 5.18 208;
HRS (union beta) 30047	sol 37957 219; Wanda 165; SizeChangeTool 93;

Termination of Programs

category	ranking
C 30048	APROVE 292; UltimateAutomizer 0;
C Integer 30049	APROVE 316; VeryMax-termCOMP17 315; UltimateAutomizer 0;
Integer Transition Systems 30050	VeryMax-termCOMP17 1025; irankfinder v1 524; Ctrl 450;
Integer TRS Innermost 30051	APROVE 102; Ctrl 85;

Complexity Analysis

category	ranking
Complexity: ITS 30054	APROVE 1688; CoFloCo 2018 648;
Complexity: C Integer 30055	CoFloCo 2018 518; APROVE 476;
Runtime Complexity: TRS 30091	APROVE 2209; tct 2018-07-13 1303;
Runtime Complexity: TRS Innermost 30092	APROVE 1787; tct 2018-07-13 998;
Runtime Complexity: TRS Innermost Certified 30094	tct 2018-07-13 407; APROVE 388;

Fig. 1. The **starexec-master** web front end summarizing the 2018 competition

3   Categories

Benchmarks are grouped in the TPDB according to the underlying computational model (rewriting or programming) and to the aim of the analysis (termination or complexity). This organization results in the following three *meta categories* since **termCOMP** 2014: *termination of rewriting*, *termination of programs*, and *complexity analysis*. (A further split of *complexity analysis* into two meta categories *"complexity of rewriting"* and *"complexity of programs"* might be considered in the future if there are categories concerning the complexity of several different programming languages.)

Roughly speaking, the two termination meta categories cover, on the one hand, termination of different flavors of rewriting according to various strategies (*termination of rewriting*), and on the other hand, termination of actual programming languages as well as related formalisms (*termination of programs*).

Which categories of a given meta category are actually run during a competition depends on the registered participants. Any category with at least two participants is run as part of its associated meta category. Of course, it is desirable to have as many participants as possible and therefore all developers of termination and complexity analysis tools are strongly encouraged to participate in the competition. In addition, as a special case, all those categories having only a single participant are collected into the auxiliary *demonstration* meta category. (While *demonstration* categories are not considered for computing scores and are thus not part of a competition in terms of awards or medals, this at least allows us to make unique tools visible to the outside world.)

Independent of their respective meta categories, there are several categories that come also in a special *certified* variant (marked by ☑ below). Before 2007, the standard approach of participating tools was to give some textual justification for their answers. However, there was no consensus on the format or the amount of detail for such justifications. Automated termination and complexity tools are rather complex programs. They are typically tuned for efficiency using sophisticated data structures and often have short release cycles facilitating the quick integration of new techniques. So, why should we trust such tools? *Certification* is the answer to this question. Tools that participate in certified categories are required to produce their justifications in a common format, the *certification problem format*, or CPF [46] for short. Justifications in this format are usually called *certificates*. To make sure that certificates are correct, certified categories employ a *certifier*—an automated tool that is able to rigorously validate a given certificate. For recent editions of termCOMP this certifier is CeTA [6,49], short for "certified tool assertions". Its reliability is due to the fact that its correctness has been established using the proof assistant Isabelle/HOL [43]. In the past, other certifiers like CoLoR/Rainbow [11] and CiME/Coccinelle [17], formalized in Coq [8], were used as well.

3.1 Termination of Rewriting

There are many different flavors of term rewriting and strategies for applying rewrite rules. Many of those have their own categories.

For standard term rewrite systems, there are categories for plain rewriting (TRS Standard ☑), relative rewriting (TRS Relative ☑), rewriting modulo equational theories (TRS Equational ☑), conditional term rewriting (TRS Conditional), context-sensitive rewriting (TRS Context Sensitive), innermost rewriting (TRS Innermost ☑), and outermost rewriting (TRS Outermost ☑). There is also a category for higher-order rewriting systems (HRS (union beta)).

Concerning string rewrite systems, there are categories for plain rewriting (SRS Standard ☑), relative rewriting (SRS Relative ☑), and cycle rewriting (Cycle Rewriting).

3.2 Termination of Programs

Regarding programming languages and related formalisms, there are categories for C programs (C), C programs restricted to integers (C Integer), Java Bytecode (Java Bytecode), Prolog programs (Prolog), Haskell programs (Haskell), integer transition systems (Integer Transition Systems), and innermost rewriting with integer term rewrite systems (Integer TRS Innermost). Concerning termination of C programs, there is an "overlap" with the *SV-COMP* competition,[1] where however the focus of the two competitions is different, since *SV-COMP* considers all kinds of verification tasks for C programs, whereas termCOMP considers termination of all kinds of programming languages. Usually, *SV-COMP* runs in winter and termCOMP runs in summer, such that in each of the competitions the new current state-of-the-art of C termination analysis is represented.

3.3 Complexity Analysis

With respect to complexity analysis, there are categories for integer transition systems (Complexity: ITS), C programs restricted to integers (Complexity: C Integer), runtime complexity of term rewrite systems (Runtime Complexity: TRS ☑), runtime complexity of innermost rewriting (Runtime Complexity: TRS Innermost ☑), and derivational complexity of term rewrite systems (Derivational Complexity: TRS ☑).

4 Tools and Techniques

In this section, we give an overview on the tools that participated in the last edition, termCOMP 2018, of the competition and highlight the main techniques used by these tools.

4.1 Termination of Rewriting

In 2018, eight tools participated in categories devoted to term rewriting. On the one hand, some tools are specifically designed for certain variants of rewriting (e.g., MultumNonMulta only handles string rewrite systems, whereas Wanda, SOL, and SizeChangeTool are mainly designed for higher-order rewriting). On the other hand, the tools AProVE, $\text{T}_\text{T}\text{T}_2$, NaTT, and MU-TERM participated in categories for many different variants of term rewrite systems. To prove termination of TRSs, the tools use both classical reduction orderings as well as more recent powerful improvements like dependency pairs [3], matrix interpretations [20], match-bounds [26], etc. To generate the required orderings automatically, the tools typically apply existing SAT and SMT solvers.

More precisely, AProVE [27] and $\text{T}_\text{T}\text{T}_2$ [39] implement the dependency pair framework [28,30] which performs termination proofs in a modular way and allows the tool to apply different termination techniques for each sub-proof.

---

[1] See https://sv-comp.sosy-lab.org.

NaTT [51] combines the dependency pair framework with the weighted path order [52]. MU-TERM [1] is particularly suitable for TRSs with modified reduction relations (like innermost, context-sensitive, equational, or conditional rewriting). The goal of the tool MultumNonMulta [31] is to demonstrate the power of a few selected methods based on matrix interpretations for termination analysis of string rewrite systems. WANDA [35] implements higher-order termination techniques based on dependency pairs [38] and higher-order orderings [32], and applies an external first-order termination tool (AProVE) as a back-end [25]. The tool SOL [29] uses an extended notion of reducibility [9] for termination proofs of rules derived from second-order algebraic theories. Finally, SizeChangeTool [10] extends the size-change termination principle [41] to higher-order rewriting.

4.2   Termination of Programs

In 2018, two tools (AProVE and UltimateAutomizer) participated in the category for termination of full C programs (which may include low-level memory operations). For C programs that only operate on integers, in addition to the two tools above, the tool VeryMax participated as well. The categories for termination of other programming languages (Java, Haskell, and Prolog) were only run as a demonstration, since in that year, only the tool AProVE analyzed their termination.

For all of these programming languages, AProVE uses an approach to transform the original program into a simple back-end language (an integer transition system or a combination of ITSs and TRSs) and to prove termination of the resulting back-end system instead [47]. In contrast, the tool UltimateAutomizer [16] uses a generalization of program paths to Büchi Automata in order to remove terminating paths. VeryMax [12] is based on a framework which allows to combine conditional termination proofs obtained using Max-SMT solvers in order to generate an (unconditional) termination proof of the program.

Termination of ITSs was analyzed by the tools VeryMax, iRankFinder, and Ctrl. Moreover, Ctrl and AProVE also analyzed termination of systems that combine ITSs and TRSs. Here, iRankFinder [19] generates lexicographic combinations of ranking functions and ranks transitions incrementally [7]. Ctrl [37] and AProVE prove termination of TRSs extended by built-in integers by suitable adaptions of termination techniques for ordinary TRSs [24, 36].

4.3   Complexity Analysis

Complexity of ITSs and of C programs on integers was analyzed by CoFloCo and AProVE, where AProVE applies two integrated sub-tools KoAT and LoAT to infer upper and lower runtime bounds for integer programs, respectively. The tool CoFloCo [21] uses a modeling with cost relations to infer amortized cost bounds, whereas KoAT [14] infers both upper runtime and size bounds for parts of the program in an alternating way. Lower bounds on the worst-case runtime are inferred by LoAT [23] by simplifying programs using an adaption of ranking functions for lower bounds, and by a subsequent inference of asymptotic lower bounds for the resulting simplified programs.

Runtime complexity of TRSs was analyzed by AProVE and T$_C$T. While runtime complexity only considers evaluations that start with basic terms (where "algorithms" are applied to "data objects"), T$_C$T also analyzed derivational complexity of arbitrary evaluations in corresponding demonstration categories. For complexity analysis, both AProVE and T$_C$T [5] use techniques which originate from termination analysis of TRSs and which are adapted in order to infer upper bounds on the number of evaluation steps [4,44]. Moreover, the tools also infer lower bounds on the (worst-case) runtime using an extension of the concept of *loops* in order to detect rules that are guaranteed to result in certain asymptotic lower bounds [22].

5   Conclusion

In this short paper, we gave a brief summary of the termination and complexity competition (termCOMP), described its organization and its different categories, and presented an overview on recent tools that participated in the competition. The competition is always open to introduce new categories in order to reflect the continuing development in the area. It also welcomes the submission of new termination and complexity problems, especially problems that come from applications. Thus, it strives to remain the main competition in the field of automated termination and complexity analysis.

References

1. Alarcón, B., Gutiérrez, R., Lucas, S., Navarro-Marset, R.: Proving termination properties with MU-TERM. In: Johnson, M., Pavlovic, D. (eds.) AMAST 2010. LNCS, vol. 6486, pp. 201–208. Springer, Heidelberg (2011). https://doi.org/10.1007/978-3-642-17796-5_12
2. Albert, E., Gordillo, P., Rubio, A., Sergey, I.: GASTAP: a gas analyzer for smart contracts. CoRR abs/1811.10403 (2018). https://arxiv.org/abs/1811.10403
3. Arts, T., Giesl, J.: Termination of term rewriting using dependency pairs. Theoret. Comput. Sci. **236**(1–2), 133–178 (2000). https://doi.org/10.1016/S0304-3975(99)00207-8
4. Avanzini, M., Moser, G.: A combination framework for complexity. Inf. Comput. **248**, 22–55 (2016). https://doi.org/10.1016/j.ic.2015.12.007
5. Avanzini, M., Moser, G., Schaper, M.: T$_C$T Tyrolean complexity tool. In: Chechik, M., Raskin, J.-F. (eds.) TACAS 2016. LNCS, vol. 9636, pp. 407–423. Springer, Heidelberg (2016). https://doi.org/10.1007/978-3-662-49674-9_24
6. Avanzini, M., Sternagel, C., Thiemann, R.: Certification of complexity proofs using CeTA. In: Fernández, M. (ed.) RTA 2015, LIPIcs, vol. 36, pp. 23–39 (2015). https://doi.org/10.4230/LIPIcs.RTA.2015.23
7. Ben-Amram, A.M., Genaim, S.: On multiphase-linear ranking functions. In: Majumdar, R., Kunčak, V. (eds.) CAV 2017. LNCS, vol. 10427, pp. 601–620. Springer, Cham (2017). https://doi.org/10.1007/978-3-319-63390-9_32

8. Bertot, Y., Castéran, P.: Interactive Theorem Proving and Program Development-Coq'Art: The Calculus of Inductive Constructions. Springer, Heidelberg (2004). https://doi.org/10.1007/978-3-662-07964-5

9. Blanqui, F.: Termination of rewrite relations on λ-terms based on Girard's notion of reducibility. Theoret. Comput. Sci. **611**, 50–86 (2016). https://doi.org/10.1016/j.tcs.2015.07.045

10. Blanqui, F., Genestier, G.: Termination of $\lambda\Pi$ modulo rewriting using the size-change principle. In: Lucas, S. (ed.) WST 2018, pp. 10–14 (2018). http://wst2018.webs.upv.es/wst2018proceedings.pdf

11. Blanqui, F., Koprowski, A.: CoLoR: a Coq library on well-founded rewrite relations and its application to the automated verification of termination certificates. Math. Struct. Comput. Sci. **21**(4), 827–859 (2011). https://doi.org/10.1017/S0960129511000120

12. Borralleras, C., Brockschmidt, M., Larraz, D., Oliveras, A., Rodríguez-Carbonell, E., Rubio, A.: Proving termination through conditional termination. In: Legay, A., Margaria, T. (eds.) TACAS 2017. LNCS, vol. 10205, pp. 99–117. Springer, Heidelberg (2017). https://doi.org/10.1007/978-3-662-54577-5_6

13. Boyer, R.S., Moore, J.S.: Proving theorems about LISP functions. J. ACM **22**(1), 129–144 (1975). https://doi.org/10.1145/321864.321875

14. Brockschmidt, M., Emmes, F., Falke, S., Fuhs, C., Giesl, J.: Analyzing runtime and size complexity of integer programs. ACM Trans. Program. Lang. Syst. **38**(4), 13:1–13:50 (2016). http://dl.acm.org/citation.cfm?id=2866575

15. Buchberger, B.: Ein algorithmisches Kriterium für die Lösbarkeit eines algebraischen Gleichungssystems. Aequationes Math. **4**, 373–383 (1970). http://eudml.org/doc/136098

16. Chen, Y., et al.: Advanced automata-based algorithms for program termination checking. In: Foster, J.S., Grossman, D. (eds.) PLDI 2018, pp. 135–150 (2018). https://doi.org/10.1145/3192366.3192405

17. Contejean, E., Courtieu, P., Forest, J., Pons, O., Urbain, X.: Automated certified proofs with CiME3. In: Schmidt-Schauß, M. (ed.) RTA 2011, LIPIcs, vol. 10, pp. 21–30 (2011). https://doi.org/10.4230/LIPIcs.RTA.2011.21

18. Dehn, M.: Über unendliche diskontinuierliche Gruppen. Math. Ann. **71**(1), 116–144 (1911)

19. Doménech, J.J., Genaim, S.: iRankFinder. In: Lucas, S. (ed.) WST 2018, p. 83 (2018). http://wst2018.webs.upv.es/wst2018proceedings.pdf

20. Endrullis, J., Waldmann, J., Zantema, H.: Matrix interpretations for proving termination of term rewriting. J. Autom. Reasoning **40**(2–3), 195–220 (2008). https://doi.org/10.1007/s10817-007-9087-9

21. Flores-Montoya, A.: Upper and lower amortized cost bounds of programs expressed as cost relations. In: Fitzgerald, J., Heitmeyer, C., Gnesi, S., Philippou, A. (eds.) FM 2016. LNCS, vol. 9995, pp. 254–273. Springer, Cham (2016). https://doi.org/10.1007/978-3-319-48989-6_16

22. Frohn, F., Giesl, J., Hensel, J., Aschermann, C., Ströder, T.: Lower bounds for runtime complexity of term rewriting. J. Autom. Reasoning **59**(1), 121–163 (2017). https://doi.org/10.1007/s10817-016-9397-x

23. Frohn, F., Naaf, M., Hensel, J., Brockschmidt, M., Giesl, J.: Lower runtime bounds for integer programs. In: Olivetti, N., Tiwari, A. (eds.) IJCAR 2016. LNCS (LNAI), vol. 9706, pp. 550–567. Springer, Cham (2016). https://doi.org/10.1007/978-3-319-40229-1_37

24. Fuhs, C., Giesl, J., Plücker, M., Schneider-Kamp, P., Falke, S.: Proving termination of integer term rewriting. In: Treinen, R. (ed.) RTA 2009. LNCS, vol. 5595, pp. 32–47. Springer, Heidelberg (2009). https://doi.org/10.1007/978-3-642-02348-4_3

25. Fuhs, C., Kop, C.: Harnessing first order termination provers using higher order dependency pairs. In: Tinelli, C., Sofronie-Stokkermans, V. (eds.) FroCoS 2011. LNCS (LNAI), vol. 6989, pp. 147–162. Springer, Heidelberg (2011). https://doi.org/10.1007/978-3-642-24364-6_11

26. Geser, A., Hofbauer, D., Waldmann, J.: Match-bounded string rewriting systems. Appl. Algebra Eng. Commun. Comput. **15**(3–4), 149–171 (2004). https://doi.org/10.1007/s00200-004-0162-8

27. Giesl, J., et al.: Analyzing program termination and complexity automatically with AProVE. J. Autom. Reasoning **58**(1), 3–31 (2017). https://doi.org/10.1007/s10817-016-9388-y

28. Giesl, J., Thiemann, R., Schneider-Kamp, P., Falke, S.: Mechanizing and improving dependency pairs. J. Autom. Reasoning **37**(3), 155–203 (2006). https://doi.org/10.1007/s10817-006-9057-7

29. Hamana, M.: How to prove your calculus is decidable: practical applications of second-order algebraic theories and computation. Proc. ACM Program. Lang. **1**(ICFP), 22:1–22:28 (2017). https://doi.org/10.1145/3110266

30. Hirokawa, N., Middeldorp, A.: Automating the dependency pair method. Inf. Comput. **199**(1–2), 172–199 (2005). https://doi.org/10.1016/j.ic.2004.10.004

31. Hofbauer, D.: MultumNonMulta at TermComp 2018. In: Lucas, S. (ed.) WST 2018, p. 80 (2018). http://wst2018.webs.upv.es/wst2018proceedings.pdf

32. Jouannaud, J., Rubio, A.: Polymorphic higher-order recursive path orderings. J. ACM **54**(1), 2:1–2:48 (2007). https://doi.org/10.1145/1206035.1206037

33. Karp, R.M., Miller, R.E.: Parallel program schemata. J. Comput. Syst. Sci. **3**(2), 147–195 (1969)

34. Knuth, D.E., Bendix, P.: Simple word problems in universal algebras. In: Leech, J. (ed.) Computational Problems in Abstract Algebra, pp. 263–297 (1970)

35. Kop, C.: Higher order termination. Ph.D. thesis, VU University Amsterdam (2012). https://www.cs.ru.nl/~cynthiakop/phdthesis.pdf

36. Kop, C., Nishida, N.: Term rewriting with logical constraints. In: Fontaine, P., Ringeissen, C., Schmidt, R.A. (eds.) FroCoS 2013. LNCS (LNAI), vol. 8152, pp. 343–358. Springer, Heidelberg (2013). https://doi.org/10.1007/978-3-642-40885-4_24

37. Kop, C., Nishida, N.: Constrained term rewriting tooL. In: Davis, M., Fehnker, A., McIver, A., Voronkov, A. (eds.) LPAR 2015. LNCS, vol. 9450, pp. 549–557. Springer, Heidelberg (2015). https://doi.org/10.1007/978-3-662-48899-7_38

38. Kop, C., van Raamsdonk, F.: Dynamic dependency pairs for algebraic functional systems. Logical Methods Comput. Sci. **8**(2) (2012). https://doi.org/10.2168/LMCS-8(2:10)2012

39. Korp, M., Sternagel, C., Zankl, H., Middeldorp, A.: Tyrolean termination tool 2. In: Treinen, R. (ed.) RTA 2009. LNCS, vol. 5595, pp. 295–304. Springer, Heidelberg (2009). https://doi.org/10.1007/978-3-642-02348-4_21

40. von der Krone, S., Muhl, R., Waldmann, J.: star-exec-presenter (Software) (2014). https://github.com/jwaldmann/star-exec-presenter/

41. Lee, C.S., Jones, N.D., Ben-Amram, A.M.: The size-change principle for program termination. In: Hankin, C., Schmidt, D. (eds.) POPL 2001, pp. 81–92 (2001). https://doi.org/10.1145/360204.360210

42. McCarthy, J.: Recursive functions of symbolic expressions and their computation by machine, part I. Commun. ACM **3**(4), 184–195 (1960). https://doi.org/10.1145/367177.367199
43. Nipkow, T., Wenzel, M., Paulson, L.C. (eds.): Isabelle/HOL - A Proof Assistant for Higher-Order Logic. LNCS, vol. 2283. Springer, Heidelberg (2002). https://doi.org/10.1007/3-540-45949-9
44. Noschinski, L., Emmes, F., Giesl, J.: Analyzing innermost runtime complexity of term rewriting by dependency pairs. J. Autom. Reasoning **51**(1), 27–56 (2013). https://doi.org/10.1007/s10817-013-9277-6
45. Space/Time Analysis for Cybersecurity (STAC). https://www.darpa.mil/program/space-time-analysis-for-cybersecurity
46. Sternagel, C., Thiemann, R.: The certification problem format. In: Benzmüller, C., Woltzenlogel Paleo, B. (eds.) UITP 2014. EPTCS, vol. 167, pp. 61–72 (2014). https://doi.org/10.4204/EPTCS.167.8
47. Ströder, T., et al.: Automatically proving termination and memory safety for programs with pointer arithmetic. J. Autom. Reasoning **58**(1), 33–65 (2017). https://doi.org/10.1007/s10817-016-9389-x
48. Stump, A., Sutcliffe, G., Tinelli, C.: StarExec: a cross-community infrastructure for logic solving. In: Demri, S., Kapur, D., Weidenbach, C. (eds.) IJCAR 2014. LNCS (LNAI), vol. 8562, pp. 367–373. Springer, Cham (2014). https://doi.org/10.1007/978-3-319-08587-6_28
49. Thiemann, R., Sternagel, C.: Certification of termination proofs using CeTA. In: Berghofer, S., Nipkow, T., Urban, C., Wenzel, M. (eds.) TPHOLs 2009. LNCS, vol. 5674, pp. 452–468. Springer, Heidelberg (2009). https://doi.org/10.1007/978-3-642-03359-9_31
50. Yamada, A.: starexec-master (Software) (2018). https://github.com/AkihisaYamada/starexec-master
51. Yamada, A., Kusakari, K., Sakabe, T.: Nagoya termination tool. In: Dowek, G. (ed.) RTA 2014. LNCS, vol. 8560, pp. 466–475. Springer, Cham (2014). https://doi.org/10.1007/978-3-319-08918-8_32
52. Yamada, A., Kusakari, K., Sakabe, T.: A unified ordering for termination proving. Sci. Comput. Program. **111**, 110–134 (2015). https://doi.org/10.1016/j.scico.2014.07.009

International Competition on Software Testing (Test-Comp)

Dirk Beyer[iD]

LMU Munich, Munich, Germany

Abstract. Tool competitions are a special form of comparative evaluation, where each tool has a team of developers or supporters associated that makes sure the tool is properly configured to show its best possible performance. Tool competitions have been a driving force for the development of mature tools that represent the state of the art in several research areas. This paper describes the International Competition on Software Testing (Test-Comp), a comparative evaluation of automatic tools for software test generation. Test-Comp 2019 is presented as part of TOOLympics 2019, a satellite event of the conference TACAS.

1 Introduction

Software testing is as old as software development itself, because the easiest way to find out if the software works is to test it. In the last few decades the tremendous breakthrough of theorem provers and satisfiability-modulo-theory (SMT) solvers have led to the development of efficient tools for automatic test-case generation. For example, symbolic execution and the idea to use it for test-case generation [14] exists for more than 40 years, efficient implementations (e.g., KLEE [8]) had to wait for the availability of mature constraint solvers. On the other hand, with the advent of automatic software model checking, the opportunity to extract test cases from counterexamples arose (see BLAST [5] and JPF [16]). In the following years, many techniques from the areas of model checking and program analysis were adapted for the purpose of test-case generation and several strong hybrid combinations have been developed [9].

There are several powerful software test generators available [9], but they are very difficult to compare. For example, a recent study [6] first had to develop a framework that supports to run test-generation tools on the same program source code and to deliver test cases in a common format for validation. Furthermore, there is no widely distributed benchmark suite available and neither input programs nor output test suites follow a standard format. In software verification, the competition SV-COMP [4] helped to overcome the problem: the competition community developed standards for defining nondeterministic functions and a language to write specifications (so far for C and Java programs) and established a standard exchange format for the output (witnesses). The competition also helped to adequately give credits to PhD students and PostDocs for their engineering efforts and technical contributions.

D. Beyer et al. (Eds.): TACAS 2019, Part III, LNCS 11429, pp. 167–175, 2019.
https://doi.org/10.1007/978-3-030-17502-3_11

A competition event with high visibility can foster the transfer of theoretical and conceptual advancements in software testing into practical tools, and would also give credits and benefits to students who spend considerable amounts of time developing testing algorithms and software packages (achieving a high rank in the testing competition improves the CV).

Test-Comp is designed to compare automatic state-of-the-art software testers with respect to effectiveness and efficiency. This comprises a preparation phase in which a set of benchmark programs is collected and classified (according to application domain, kind of bug to find, coverage criterion to fulfill, theories needed), in order to derive competition categories. After the preparation phase, the tools are submitted, installed, and applied to the set of benchmark instances.

Test-Comp uses the benchmarking framework BENCHEXEC [7], which is already successfully used in other competitions, most prominently, all competitions that run on the STAREXEC infrastructure [15]. Similar to SV-COMP, the test generators in Test-Comp are applied to programs in a fully automatic way. The results are collected via the BENCHEXEC results format, and transformed into tables and plots in several formats.

Competition Goals. In summary, the goals of Test-Comp are the following:

- Provide a snapshot of the state-of-the-art in software testing to the community. This means to compare, independently from particular paper projects and specific techniques, different test-generation tools in terms of effectiveness and performance.
- Increase the visibility and credits that tool developers receive. This means to provide a forum for presentation of tools and discussion of the latest technologies, and to give the students the opportunity to publish about the development work that they have done.
- Establish a set of benchmarks for software testing in the community. This means to create and maintain a set of programs together with coverage criteria, and to make those publicly available for researchers to be used in performance comparisons when evaluating a new technique.
- Establish standards for software test generation. This means, most prominently, to develop a standard for marking input values in programs, define an exchange format for test suites, and agree on a specification language for test-coverage criteria.

Related Competitions. In other areas, there are several established competitions. For example, there are three competitions in the area of software verification: (i) a competition on automatic verifiers under controlled resources (SV-COMP [3]), (ii) a competition on verifiers with arbitrary environments (RERS [12]), and (iii) a competition on (interactive) verification (VerifyThis [13]). In software testing, there are several competition-like events, for example, the IEEE International Contest on Software Testing, the Software Testing World Cup, and the Israel Software Testing World Cup. Those contests are organized as on-site events, where teams of people interact with certain testing platforms in order to achieve a certain coverage of the software under test.

There is no comparative evaluation of automatic test-generation tools in a controlled environment. Test-Comp is meant to close this gap. The results of the first edition of Test-Comp will be presented as part of the TOOLympics 2019 event [1], where 16 competitions in the area of formal methods are presented.

2   Organizational Classification

The competition Test-Comp is designed according to the model of SV-COMP [2], the International Competition on Software Verification. Test-Comp shares the following organizational principles:

- **Automatic:** The tools are executed in a fully automated environment, without any user interaction.
- **Off-site:** The competition takes place independently from a conference location, in order to flexibly allow organizational changes.
- **Reproducible:** The experiments are controlled and reproducible, that is, the resources are limited, controlled, measured, and logged.
- **Jury:** The jury is the advisory board of the competition, is responsible for qualification decisions on tools and benchmarks, and serves as program committee for the reviewing and selection of papers to be published.
- **Training:** The competition flow includes a training phase during which the participants get a chance to train their tools on the potential benchmark instances and during which the organizer ensures a smooth competition run.

3   Competition Schedule

Schedule. A typical Test-Comp schedule has the following deadlines and phases:

- **Call for Participation:** The organizer announces the competition on the mailing list.[1]
- **Registration of Participation / Training Phase:** The tool developers register for participation and submit a first version of their tool together with documentation to the competition. The tool can later be updated and is used for pre-runs by the organizer and for qualification assessment by the jury. Preliminary results are reported to the tool developers, and made available to the jury.
- **Final-Version Submission / Evaluation Phase:** The tool developers submit the final versions of their tool. The benchmarks are executed using the submitted tools and the experimental results are reported to the authors. Final results are reported to the tool developers for inspection and approval.
- **Results Announced:** The organizer announces the results on the competition web site.
- **Publication:** The competition organizer writes the competition report, the tool developers write the tool description and participation reports. The jury reviews the papers and the competition report.

---

[1] https://groups.google.com/forum/#!forum/test-comp

4   Participating Tools

The following tools for automatic software test generation participate in the first edition of Test-Comp (the list provides the tester name, the representing jury member, the affiliation, and the URL of the project web site):

- CoVeriTest, Marie-Christine Jakobs, LMU Munich, Germany
  https://cpachecker.sosy-lab.org/
- CPA/Tiger-MGP, Sebastian Ruland, TU Darmstadt, Germany
  https://www.es.tu-darmstadt.de/testcomp19
- ESBMC-bkind, Rafael Menezes, Federal University of Amazonas, Brazil
  http://www.esbmc.org/
- ESBMC-falsif, Mikhail Gadelha, University of Southampton, UK
  http://www.esbmc.org/
- FairFuzz, Caroline Lemieux, University of California at Berkeley, USA
  https://github.com/carolemieux/afl-rb
- KLEE, Cristian Cadar, Imperial College London, UK
  http://klee.github.io/
- PRTest, Thomas Lemberger, LMU Munich, Germany
  https://github.com/sosy-lab/tbf
- Symbiotic, Martina Vitovská, Masaryk University, Czechia
  https://github.com/staticafi/symbiotic
- VeriFuzz, Raveendra Kumar Medicherla, Tata Consultancy Services, India
  https://www.tcs.com/creating-a-system-of-systems

5   Rules and Definitions

Test Task. A *test task* is a pair of an input program (program under test) and a test specification. A *test run* is a non-interactive execution of a test generator on a single test task, in order to generate a test suite according to the test specification. A *test suite* is a sequence of test cases, given as a directory of files according to the format for exchangeable test-suites.[2]

Execution of a Test Generator. Figure 1 illustrates the process of executing one test generator on the benchmark suite. One test run for a test generator gets as input (i) a program from the benchmark suite and (ii) a test specification (find bug, or coverage criterion), and returns as output a test suite (i.e., a set of test vectors). The test generator is contributed by the competition participant. The test runs are executed centrally by the competition organizer. The test validator takes as input the test suite from the test generator and validates it by executing the program on all test cases: for bug finding it checks if the bug is exposed and for coverage it reports the coverage using the GNU tool gcov.[3]

---

[2] Test-suite format: https://gitlab.com/sosy-lab/software/test-format/
[3] https://gcc.gnu.org/onlinedocs/gcc/Gcov.html

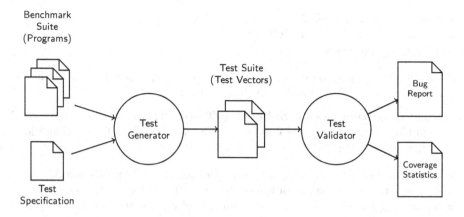

Fig. 1. Flow of the Test-Comp execution for one test generator

Table 1. Coverage specifications used in Test-Comp 2019

Formula	Interpretation
COVER EDGES(@CALL(__VERIFIER_error))	The test suite contains at least one test that executes function __VERIFIER_error.
COVER EDGES(@DECISIONEDGE)	The test suite contains tests such that all branches of the program are executed.

Test Specification. The specification for testing a program is given to the test generator as input file (either properties/coverage-error-call.prp or properties/coverage-branches.prp for Test-Comp 2019).

The definition init(main()) is used to define the initial states of the program by a call of function main (with no parameters). The definition FQL(f) specifies that coverage definition f should be achieved. The FQL (FShell query language [11]) coverage definition COVER EDGES(@DECISIONEDGE) means that all branches should be covered, COVER EDGES(@BASICBLOCKENTRY) means that all statements should be covered, and COVER EDGES(@CALL(__VERIFIER_error)) means that function __VERIFIER_error should be called. A complete specification looks like: COVER(init(main()), FQL(COVER EDGES(@DECISIONEDGE))).

Table 1 lists the two FQL formulas that are used in test specifications of Test-Comp 2019. The first describes a formula that is typically used for bug finding: the test generator should find a test case that executes a certain error function. The second describes a formula that is used to obtain a standard test suite for quality assurance: the test generator should find a test suite for branch coverage.

Setup. The competition runs on an otherwise unloaded, dedicated compute cluster composed of 168 machines with Intel Xeon E3-1230 v5 CPUs, with 8 processing units each, a frequency of 3.4 GHz, and 33 GB memory. Each test run will be started on such a machine with a GNU/Linux operating system (x86_64-linux, Ubuntu 18.04); there are three resource limits for each test run:

- a memory limit of 15 GB (14.6 GiB) of RAM,
- a runtime limit of 15 min of CPU time, and
- a limit to 8 processing units of a CPU.

Further technical parameters of the competition machines are available in the repository that also contains the benchmark definitions.[4]

License Requirements for Submitted Tester Archives. The testers need to be publicly available for download as binary archive under a license that allows the following (cf. [4]):

- replication and evaluation by anybody (including results publication),
- no restriction on the usage of the verifier output (log files, witnesses), and
- any kind of (re-)distribution of the unmodified verifier archive.

Qualification. Before a tool or person can participate in the competition, the jury evaluates the following qualification criteria.

Tool. A test tool is qualified to participate as competition candidate if the tool is (a) publicly available for download and fulfills the above license requirements, (b) works on the GNU/Linux platform (more specifically, it must run on an x86_64 machine), (c) is installable with user privileges (no root access required, except for required standard Ubuntu packages) and without hard-coded absolute paths for access to libraries and non-standard external tools, (d) succeeds for more than 50 % of all training programs to parse the input and start the test process (a tool crash during the test-generation phase does not disqualify), and (e) produces test suites that adhere to the exchange format (see above).

Person. A person (participant) is qualified as competition contributor for a competition candidate if the person (a) is a contributing designer/developer of the submitted competition candidate (witnessed by occurrence of the person's name on the tool's project web page, a tool paper, or in the revision logs) or (b) is authorized by the competition organizer (after the designer/developer was contacted about the participation).

6   Categories and Scoring Schema

Error Coverage. The first category is to show the abilities to discover bugs. The programs in the benchmark set contain programs that contain a bug.

Evaluation by scores and runtime. Every run will be started by a batch script, which produces for every tool and every test task (a C program) one of the following scores:

+1 point:	program under test is executed on all generated test cases and the bug is found (i.e., specified function was called)
0 points:	all other cases

---

[4] https://gitlab.com/sosy-lab/test-comp/bench-defs/

The participating test-generation tools are ranked according to the sum of points. Tools with the same sum of points are ranked according to success-runtime. The success-runtime for a tool is the total CPU time over all benchmarks for which the tool reported a correct verification result.

Branch Coverage. The second category is to cover as many branches as possible. The coverage criterion was chosen because many test-generation tools support this standard criterion by default. Other coverage criteria can be reduced to branch coverage by transformation [10].

Evaluation by scores and runtime. Every run will be started by a batch script, which produces for every tool and every test task (a C program) the coverage (as reported by `gcov`; value between 0 and 1) of branches of the program that are covered by the generated test cases. The score is the returned coverage.

$+c$ points:	program under test is executed on all generated tests and c is the coverage value as measured with the tool `gcov`
0 points:	all other cases

The participating verification tools are ranked according to the cumulative coverage. Tools with the same coverage are ranked according to success-runtime. The success-runtime for a tool is the total CPU time over all benchmarks for which the tool reported a correct verification result.

7   Benchmark Programs

The first edition of Test-Comp is based on programs written in the programming language C. The input programs are taken from the largest and most diverse open-source repository of software verification tasks[5], which is also used by SV-COMP [4]. We selected all programs for which the following properties were satisfied (cf. issue on GitHub[6]):

1. compiles with `gcc`, if a harness for the special methods is provided,
2. should contain at least one call to a nondeterministic function,
3. does not rely on nondeterministic pointers,
4. does not have expected result 'false' for property 'termination', and
5. has expected result 'false' for property 'unreach-call' (only for category *Error Coverage*).

This selection yields a total of 2 356 test tasks, namely 636 test tasks for category *Error Coverage* and 1 720 test tasks for category *Code Coverage*.[7] The final set of benchmark programs might be obfuscated in order to avoid overfitting.

---

[5] https://github.com/sosy-lab/sv-benchmarks
[6] https://github.com/sosy-lab/sv-benchmarks/pull/774
[7] https://test-comp.sosy-lab.org/2019/benchmarks.php

8   Conclusion and Future Plans

This report gave an overview of the organizational aspects of the International Competition on Software Testing (Test-Comp). The competition attracted nine participating teams from six countries. At the time of writing of this article, the execution of the benchmarks of the first edition of Test-Comp was just finished. Unfortunately, the results could not be processed on time for publication. The feedback from the testing community was positive, and the competition on software testing will be held annually from now on. The plan for next year is to extend the competition to more categories of programs and to more tools.

References

1. Bartocci, E., Beyer, D., Black, P.E., Fedyukovich, G., Garavel, H., Hartmanns, A., Huisman, M., Kordon, F., Nagele, J., Sighireanu, M., Steffen, B., Suda, M., Sutcliffe, G., Weber, T., Yamada, A.: TOOLympics 2019: An overview of competitions in formal methods. In: Proc. TACAS, Part 3, LNCS, vol. 11429, pp. 3–24. Springer, Cham (2019). https://doi.org/10.1007/978-3-030-17502-3_1
2. Beyer, D.: Competition on software verification (SV-COMP). In: Proc. TACAS, LNCS, vol. 7214, pp. 504–524. Springer, Heidelberg (2012). https://doi.org/10.1007/978-3-642-28756-5_38
3. Beyer, D.: Software verification with validation of results (Report on SV-COMP 2017). In: Proc. TACAS, LNCS, vol. 10206, pp. 331–349. Springer, Heidelberg (2017). https://doi.org/10.1007/978-3-662-54580-5_20
4. Beyer, D.: Automatic verification of C and Java programs: SV-COMP 2019. In: Proc. TACAS, Part 3, LNCS, vol. 11429, pp. 133–155. Springer, Cham (2019). https://doi.org/10.1007/978-3-030-17502-3_9
5. Beyer, D., Chlipala, A.J., Henzinger, T.A., Jhala, R., Majumdar, R.: Generating tests from counterexamples. In: Proc. ICSE, pp. 326–335. IEEE (2004). https://doi.org/10.1109/ICSE.2004.1317455
6. Beyer, D., Lemberger, T.: Software verification: Testing vs. model checking. In: Proc. HVC, LNCS, vol. 10629, pp. 99–114. Springer, Cham (2017). https://doi.org/10.1007/978-3-319-70389-3_7
7. Beyer, D., Löwe, S., Wendler, P.: Reliable benchmarking: Requirements and solutions. Int. J. Softw. Tools Technol. Transfer **21**(1), 1–29 (2019). https://doi.org/10.1007/s10009-017-0469-y
8. Cadar, C., Dunbar, D., Engler, D.R.: KLEE: Unassisted and automatic generation of high-coverage tests for complex systems programs. In: Proc. OSDI, pp. 209–224. USENIX Association (2008)
9. Godefroid, P., Sen, K.: Combining model checking and testing. In: Handbook of Model Checking, pp. 613–649. Springer, Cham (2018). https://doi.org/10.1007/978-3-319-10575-8_19
10. Harman, M.: We need a testability transformation semantics. In: Proc. SEFM, LNCS, vol. 10886, pp. 3–17. Springer, Cham (2018). https://doi.org/10.1007/978-3-319-92970-5_1
11. Holzer, A., Schallhart, C., Tautschnig, M., Veith, H.: How did you specify your test suite. In: Proc. ASE, pp. 407–416. ACM (2010). https://doi.org/10.1145/1858996.1859084

12. Howar, F., Isberner, M., Merten, M., Steffen, B., Beyer, D., Păsăreanu, C.S.: Rigorous examination of reactive systems. The RERS challenges 2012 and 2013. Int. J. Softw. Tools Technol. Transfer **16**(5), 457–464 (2014). https://doi.org/10.1007/s10009-014-0337-y

13. Huisman, M., Klebanov, V., Monahan, R.: VerifyThis 2012 - A program verification competition. STTT **17**(6), 647–657 (2015). https://doi.org/10.1007/s10009-015-0396-8

14. King, J.C.: Symbolic execution and program testing. Commun. ACM **19**(7), 385–394 (1976). https://doi.org/10.1145/360248.360252

15. Stump, A., Sutcliffe, G., Tinelli, C.: StarExec: A cross-community infrastructure for logic solving. In: Proc. IJCAR, LNCS, vol. 8562, pp. 367–373. Springer, Cham (2014). https://doi.org/10.1007/978-3-319-08587-6_28

16. Visser, W., Păsăreanu, C.S., Khurshid, S.: Test input generation with Java PathFinder. In: Proc. ISSTA, pp. 97–107. ACM (2004). https://doi.org/10.1145/1007512.1007526

VerifyThis – Verification Competition with a Human Factor

Gidon Ernst[1], Marieke Huisman[2(✉)], Wojciech Mostowski[3],
and Mattias Ulbrich[4]

[1] University of Melbourne, Melbourne, Australia
gidon.ernst@unimelb.edu.au
[2] University of Twente, Enschede, The Netherlands
m.huisman@utwente.nl
[3] Halmstad University, Halmstad, Sweden
wojciech.mostowski@hh.se
[4] Karlsruhe Institute of Technology, Karlsruhe, Germany
mattias.ulbrich@kit.edu

Abstract. VerifyThis is a series of competitions that aims to evaluate the current state of deductive tools to prove functional correctness of programs. Such proofs typically require human creativity, and hence it is not possible to measure the performance of tools independently of the skills of its user. Similarly, solutions can be judged by humans only. In this paper, we discuss the role of the human in the competition setup and explore possible future changes to the current format. Regarding the impact of VerifyThis on deductive verification research, a survey conducted among the previous participants shows that the event is a key enabler for gaining insight into other approaches, and that it fosters collaboration and exchange.

Keywords: VerifyThis · Program verification ·
Specification languages · Tool development · Competition

1 Introduction

The VerifyThis program verification is held in 2019 for the 8th time; earlier editions were held at FoVeOOS 2011 [6], FM 2012 [15,20], Dagstuhl (April 2014) [4], and ETAPS 2015–2018 [16–18,21], the next event takes place as part of TOOLympics at ETAPS 2019 [2]. On the VerifyThis webpage[1] the aim of the competition is formulated as follows:

- *to bring together those interested in formal verification, and to provide an engaging, hands-on, and fun opportunity for discussion, and*

---

[1] See http://www.pm.inf.ethz.ch/research/verifythis.html.

Author names are in alphabetic order.

D. Beyer et al. (Eds.): TACAS 2019, Part III, LNCS 11429, pp. 176–195, 2019.
https://doi.org/10.1007/978-3-030-17502-3_12

- to evaluate the usability of logic-based program verification tools in a controlled experiment that could be easily repeated by others.

The competition will offer a number of challenges presented in natural language and pseudo code. Participants have to formalize the requirements, implement a solution, and formally verify the implementation for adherence to the specification.

There are no restrictions on the programming language and verification technology used. The correctness properties posed in problems will have the input-output behaviour of programs in focus. Solutions will be judged for correctness, completeness, and elegance.

What we would like to emphasise up-front is that VerifyThis is different from most other competitions of formal method tools at TOOLympics[2] at ETAPS 2019, see the TOOLympics proceedings [2] (this volume) for more details on each of them. Typically, the other events run a (large) number of benchmarks as batch jobs to determine the winner from values that are obtained from the invocations (like the runtimes or the number of successes) in a fully mechanised way.[3] Moreover, often they target both proving and *disproving* examples. There are also other TOOLympics competitions in which software verification tools are compared: SV-COMP [3] and RERS [23], which are both off-site events focussing on automatically checkable system properties that do not require user input.

In contrast, VerifyThis deliberately takes the user into the loop, and only considers proving correctness. VerifyThis challenges are developed under the assumption that there is currently no technique available out there that can run the problem in a widely accepted input specification format out of the box. Part of the challenge – and in many cases also the key to a successful solution – is to find a suitable logical encoding of the desired property, and to come up with smartly-encoded sufficiently strong annotations, i.e., specification engineering. Understanding the problem is essential for solving the challenges, the human factor can thus definitely not be removed.

In this paper, we discuss the current set-up of the competition, and our experiences from the past editions (Sect. 2). In addition, we also critically reflect on the current organisation, and discuss whether it still matches the competition's aims. For this purpose, we have investigated feedback and experiences from earlier participants (Sect. 3). From the participants' feedback and our experiences, we conclude that VerifyThis indeed is an engaging and fun experience. However, it is less clear whether the current setup indeed evaluates the capabilities of the tools used, or if also other things are measured. Therefore, in Sect. 4 we make several suggestions of possible changes to the setup that could make the measuring aspects of the competition more precise.

---

[2] https://tacas.info/toolympics.php.

[3] A notable exception are the *evaluation-based rewards* of the RERS [23] competition where submitted approaches and solutions are reviewed and ranked by the challenge organisers.

2   Previous Editions

The format of the competition has been rather stable since its first edition (see [19] for the reflections of the organisers after the first VerifyThis edition), with fine-tuning changes made whenever it was felt that this was appropriate. In this section we discuss: who are the organisers, how do we define the challenges, who are participating, what side events do we organise, and what are the results of the competition.

Organisers. The first editions of VerifyThis were run by the same group of organisers (Marieke Huisman, Rosemary Monahan, and Vladimir Klebanov (until 2014), and Peter Müller (since 2015)). Since 2016, this part of the organisation has changed a bit. The original organisers created a steering committee, which invites a new pair of organisers every year. They work in close collaboration with one or more steering committee members to define the challenges, and are fully responsible for judging the solutions. There are several advantages to the approach: it ensures that there are sufficient fresh ideas, it avoids a repeated bias on a single technique, it widens the community, and it allows the steering committee members to also participate themselves. The two organisers are always selected with the following criteria in mind: they should be familiar with the area of program verification; at least one of them should have been participating in an earlier edition of VerifyThis; and they should be from different groups, in order to involve the community as a whole as much as possible.

Challenges. To involve the community in the competition since 2012 a call for challenges has been published widely – and the submitted challenges regularly form the basis for one of the challenges set during the competition.

There is a wide variety of program verification tools used by the participants, and no particular input programming (or specification) language has been set. Therefore, problems are either presented in a standard well-known programming language or in pseudo code, and no obligatory formal specification is given, neither in logics nor in a particular specification language. If a natural language specification is given, it is formulated as precisely as possible, showcasing the problem with exemplary situations. Good challenges move the participants out of their comfort zone: they do not immediately know how to solve it, and will have to think about how to use their tool to actually solve the challenge.

Challenges are inherently "real". If a person is expected to look into a problem and understand it, the problem cannot be a generated routine that only exposes a challenge for verification tools, but it must have a sensible purpose beyond verification. Typical problems are algorithmically challenging routines, which are (possibly simplified) real-world snippets from larger code bases.

The competition typically consists of three challenges and the participants have 90 minutes to work on each one. The first is usually a relatively simple warm-up challenge – often involving a computation on the elements of an array. The other two challenges are typically more involved. Often one of them is about a complicated heap-based data structure that for example requires reasoning about operations on a binary tree. Since 2015, the third challenge typically deals with concurrency – however, as not all tools participating in the competition support reasoning about concurrency, the challenge is always set up in such a way that it also has a sequential version. As an illustration of the kind of effort required at VerifyThis, a solved, automatically provable by most tools solution to the warm-up challenge from the FoVeOOS'11 competition [6] is shown in Fig. 1.

The maximum element property of the following array traversing procedure has to be shown:

```
int max(int[] a) {
  int x = 0, y = |a| - 1;
  while(x != y)
    if(a[x] <= a[y]) x++; else y--;
  return x;
}
```

where $|\cdot|$ stands for array length. Under the assumption (precondition) of a non-null and non-empty input array a, i.e. $a \neq \text{null} \wedge |a| > 0$, the procedure correctness assertion (postcondition) can be expressed as $\forall_{0 \leq i < |a|} \ a[i] \leq a[r]$, where r is the procedure result. The required **while** loop invariants to show this property are $0 \leq x \leq y < |a|$, $\forall_{0 \leq i \leq x} \ a[i] \leq a[x] \vee a[i] \leq a[y]$ and $\forall_{y < j < |a|} \ a[j] \leq a[x] \vee a[j] \leq a[y]$ with the $y - x$ termination measure. Teams express the procedure and specification in their tool's specific notation, in particular, the loop invariants can take different equivalent forms, many of which are more compact, yet might be more difficult to read, see [6] for the complete range of solutions.

Fig. 1. Search by elimination VerifyThis challenge from FoVeOOS'11 competition.

At the end of the 90 minutes, all teams are asked to submit their solutions (also if they are only partial) to the organisers by email. These are the versions that will be judged. However, teams sometimes also send a more complete version later, as a kind of evidence how close they were to the full solution. This happens in particular if somebody completes the challenges in the break right after the challenge was finished.

The full collection of earlier challenges (with links to polished solutions) is available from the VerifyThis webpage. This collection also serves as a benchmark set (beyond the competitions) in the program verification community, in particular because it enables comparison in verification efforts and approaches for different verification tools.

Participants & Tools. Over the years, the number of participants in VerifyThis has grown slightly. The very first editions of the competition had about 6 to 8 teams participating; the more recent ones had 10 to 12 teams participating. Most teams are "developer teams", i.e., their members are actively working on the development of the tool (sometimes even during the competition). However, we have also had several non-developer teams participating, and in particular Dafny [28] is widely used. We specifically encourage participation of students/PhD candidates. The most remarkable participation was a Dafny team at

ETAPS 2016 which was formed by Bachelor students from the Technical University of Eindhoven (where ETAPS was located that year). They had read about the competition, and then taught themselves the basics of Dafny to participate in the competition. Many of the participants joined the competition multiple times: in general they find the competition quite engaging, and will try to come back the next year.

Most of the tools are deductive program verifiers, which have explicit support for imperative programming constructs (in contrast to theorem provers for mathematical logic) and explicit support for assertion languages of various flavours. There are major differences in the way proofs are developed and checked, in the degree of automation, and the programming and specification features. Nevertheless, the common aim of these deductive tools is full-functional correctness proofs. We have also had several tools used in the competition that fall outside of this classification, such as the bounded model checkers CIVL [32] and CMBC [27], the model checker mCRL2 [9], the interactive theorem prover Isabelle [30], and the termination prover AProVE [13].

Table 1 below gives an overview of all the tools that participated in the competition, the number of times a team participated using the tool, and how many times a team using the tool actually won a first prize or first student prize.

Side Events. As VerifyThis is an on-site competition, it means that it also provides an opportunity for the program verification community to meet and exchange ideas, establish and improve personal contacts, and to see, experience and learn from each other's tools. To encourage this exchange, we organise several side events around the competition.

Since several years, before the competition itself starts, we therefore have an invited tutorial on one of the program verification tools. So far, we have tutorials about Dafny (Rustan Leino), Why3 (Jean-Christophe Filliâtre), and Viper (Alexander J. Summers). We encourage the presenter to explain the main characteristics of the tool, and to provide a challenge for the audience, so they get hands-on experience with the tool. This tutorials are open to non-competition participants as well, though typically it attracts only a few extra attendees.

Furthermore, on the evening of the competition, we organise a dinner for all participants, where they can talk about their experiences during the day. Usually, almost all participants join for the dinner, and there is a good, bonding atmosphere.

Finally, the next day the judges (usually, the organisers who set the challenges) talk with all teams privately to evaluate their solutions. The versions submitted by email form the basis for the discussion, and participants are given the chance to explain their formalisation and which parts of the challenges they have solved. Judges ask for clarifications and general questions (cf. Sect. 4.2). Experience has shown that for the judges these discussions are very helpful for understanding the solutions and the taken approaches, and thus for judging them. As teams use different tools, without the explanation, the solutions are much harder to understand and assess, and the judges might miss aspects of the solutions.

Table 1. Overview of tools with teams participating in VerifyThis[a]

Tool	# of teams participating	# of prizes won Overall/Student/Feature
AProVE [13]	1	
AutoProof [35]	1	
CBMC [27]	1	
CIVL [32]	3	F:1
Dafny [28]	12	
ESC/Java [8]	1	
F* [34]	1	
Frama-C [24]	2	
Isabelle [30]	1	O:1
jStar [10]	1	
KeY [1]	7	
KIV [11]	5	S:3
mCRL2 [9]	2	F:1
MoCHi [26]	1	
PAT [33]	1	
Spark/Ada/GNATprove [14]	1	F:1
VCC [7]	1	
VerCors [5]	5	
VeriFast [22]	4	O:2
Viper [29]	2	F:1
Why3 [12]	9	O:2, S:4, F:1

[a]Please note that prizes have not been awarded every year, and sometimes two prizes have been awarded in a single category.

In parallel, the participants meet among themselves and present their solutions amongst each other. As all participants have been intensively thinking about the same problem the day before, these discussions really help to gain insights into how other program verification tools work, and their relative strengths and weaknesses. This session occasionally is also attended by other conference participants.

Competition Results. In most editions of VerifyThis prizes have been awarded (see Table 1 for an overview). The prizes that are usually awarded are:

- best overall team,
- best student team, and
- distinguished tool feature.

Occasionally, the judges have decided to award a second prize in some category, or to hand out two prizes (this happened in particular in the category of distinguished tool feature). Thanks to our sponsors, we usually have been able to hand out not only a certificate, but also a financial reward. No further order on the participating teams is given.

In addition, in some years we have also had a prize for the best submitted challenge, or the tool used by most teams. However, even though related to the competition, these prizes are not for the competition effort itself, and are not further discussed here.

Judging is done by considering the following aspects of the submitted solution:

– How close is the solution to a complete solution, i.e., how much work will it be to finish verification of the code w.r.t. the implementation?
– Did the team capture all the relevant properties to be verified in the specification?
– How understandable and accessible are the specifications?

In general, the judges do not penalise the use of auxiliary annotations such as loop invariants or intermediate assertions. Because of the time constraint, a tool requiring many auxiliary annotations, already has a drawback. Often the judges find it relatively straightforward to decide about a winner (and are relieved that no further ordering on teams is required). In some cases, the decision required more discussion, and careful re-examining of the submitted solutions.

3   The Impact of VerifyThis

In order to asses the impact of VerifyThis we conducted an online survey among all previous participants. The survey consisted of three parts: (1) General questions, such as number of times participated, the current position, participation as student and/or developer, (2) an assessment of recent advances and the state-of-the-art of deductive verification tools relative to several categories of tool qualities and features, and (3) the participant's personal take-away from the competition, including the impact it had on his/her research and career, as well as feedback to the organisers. The questionnaire is included in Appendix A.

For the second part, we asked the participants more specifically for their opinion about: which progress in recent years they considered most important, which aspects could have the most impact if they were improved, and how this is reflected in the development of the participants' own verification tools. We were interested specifically in the following categories, with an additional possibility of submitting free form responses.

– Expressiveness and ease of use of specification languages
– Proof automation and guidance
– Integration with static analysis techniques (e.g. invariant inference)
– Verification debugging and counterexample generation
– Specification and proof refactoring

Position	# responses	developer
PhD/MSc student	5	0
Postdoc	3	3
Academic	6	5
Industry	2	2
Overall	16	10

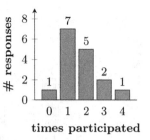

Fig. 2. Background of participants who took part in our questionnaire

Results. We received 16 responses from the approximately 80 previous participants that we contacted. Figure 2 shows the distribution of their current positions, respectively, whether they are tool developers, and how many times they have participated. Note that there is one response of a person having not participated in the competition itself (but presumably in the side events).

Figure 3 shows the responses on the current state of verification tools w.r.t. the five categories, ranked on a scale with four items. Based on the responses, the participants agree that advances in all of these categories have been made, and significantly so in expressiveness, automation, and debugging. However, no participant felt that a major breakthrough had been achieved in any of the categories. Additional remarkable improvements that were mentioned in the free-form responses were proof support for safety and liveness properties, the automation of separation logic, and integration of tools into development environments.

Regarding potential impact if major breakthroughs *were* to be achieved, the most common answer was proof automation, followed by debugging capabilities, and further advances in the expressiveness of specification languages. Integration of static analysis into deductive tools was typically considered of minor importance. The free-form answers furthermore mentioned ease of use and graphical interfaces, maturity and predictability of tools, integration into development process and existing codebases. One answer suggested to address different properties separately, i.e., separate functional specifications from canonical concerns such as memory safety and race-freedom.

Participants who are also developers indicated a number of improvements to their tools related to all of the above categories, partly in response to the experience of the competition. The majority of completely new features was related to expressiveness of specification languages, and one mention of each proof automation and debugging, respectively. One free-form answer mentioned, however, that major investments into all of the categories are planned.

Another result from the survey is that verification challenges serve as benchmarks or regression tests of the tools, with five answers indicating 9 or more challenges to be used in this way, and seven answers indicating between 3 and 6 challenges used.

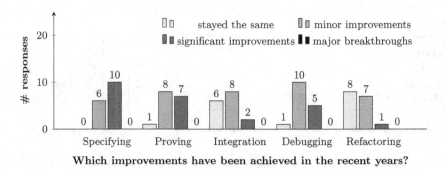

Which improvements have been achieved in the recent years?

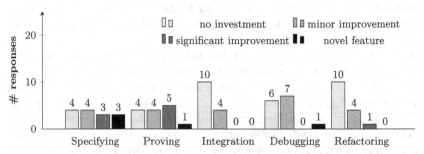

Which tool aspects would have the most impact if improved?

Which features were improved or implemented as response to the competition?

Fig. 3. Participants' assessment on the current state of deductive verification tools

All participants of the survey stated that they had enjoyed solving the challenges, and almost all indicated they particularly liked the exchange between colleagues and learning about how other tools tackle challenges. The participants were less excited about the Jury discussions (9 answers) and the presentation sessions (7 answers with a suggestion that these should be more formally organized). An additional free-form response appreciated the publications associated with the competitions that summarize the results and discuss the solutions.

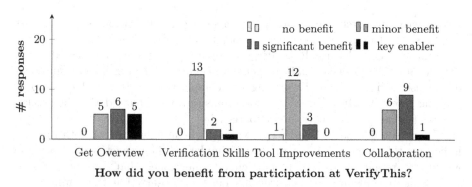

Fig. 4. Participants' personal benefit from the VerifyThis events

Participating in the competition lead to personal take-away regarding the following aspects: getting an overview and learning about state-of-the-art techniques and tools, improving one's own ability in specification and verification, improving one's own tools for day-to-day use, and establishing academic contacts or collaborative research. The results are shown in Fig. 4: The most common and greatest benefit, as indicated by the participants, is thereby to obtain a better insight into other approaches.

We have received several suggestions to improve future instalments. Some answers were related to potential off-line participation (reminiscent of VSComp [25]), potentially for a subset of the challenges to facilitate participation. One response suggested to release a "prepare for this" exercise beforehand, and one response suggested to release a more difficult off-line challenge. There was the suggestion to release partial information on the nature of the challenges in advance, i.e., which tool and library features would be helpful, to ease preparation. We were also encouraged to increase the variety of verification problems.

Discussion. The feedback from the participants sheds some light into the mostly academic perspective on the state-of-the-art and recent advances in deductive verification tools.

The response rate of 20% was less than what we had hoped for. However, clearly many of the younger participants of the earlier instalments are likely to have completed their degrees and thus moved to another institution or industry.

Since the answers to the three tool-related questions had the same format, we can attempt to investigate how well current research is aligned with those aspects that are thought to be critical. Of the 66 data points for the question on improvements made to the tools, there were 34 indications of "no investment" to a particular aspect, and of these the majority of 26 answers is related to integration with static analysis, debugging, and proof maintenance. While the latter two features have been identified to have critical importance in industrial context [31], they seem to be less important in academic verification projects, which are often at a smaller scale w.r.t. the software being built, as well as the team involved. Integration with static analysis, on the other hand, is arguably a less active research area, and from personal communication we can report scepticism on the usefulness of e.g., automatically inferred invariants.

Similarly, considering the *motivation* of improving the tools' capabilities, almost all of the answers relate to *personal benefit* to the developers (and academic users), i.e., related to solving the competitions better and to support ongoing research. Only three (free-form) answers were related to other stakeholders (industry, customers, non-experts).

The personal impact of VerifyThis was overwhelmingly positive, with 7 replies indicating that participation was the key enabler for the respective category. We would also remark that 7 of 11 participants mentioned that improvements to their tools were inspired by features of other tools observed at the competition.

Outlook. The more general question with respect to the impact of VerifyThis is in which way can VerifyThis be understood as a controlled experiment? Which measurements can be taken for a systematic better assessment of the potential and improvements of modern verification tools over time? Given the diversity in approaches, tools, and levels of experience of the participants in relation to their (relatively) small numbers of participants and the great effort to develop challenges and solutions, it is not likely that events like VerifyThis can arrive at statistically sound scientific conclusions any time soon.

However, it is possible to keep track of some descriptive measures, similarly to the data obtained by this survey, as a proxy that would provide an ongoing and semi-rigorous evaluation that is independent of the individual challenges and VerifyThis instalments. We therefore plan to conduct similar surveys on a routine basis as part of the competition event. This will provide a more thorough, up-to-date, and ongoing assessment of the field, in addition to the results reported here.

4   The Human Factor

The feedback from Sect. 3 is very encouraging and suggests that VerifyThis has succeeded as a community event, i.e., having achieved its first goal. However, it is much less clear in which sense the current format of the competition including the evaluation and summarization done in the corresponding publications, constitutes to an experimental assessment of the usability of verification tools, i.e., the quality of user guidance, and feedback in case of failed verification attempts, to tackle real verification problems? How do we even measure this?

As mentioned before, the crucial aspect in this discussion is that VerifyThis takes the human into the loop. In fact, there are several ways in which the outcome of a task depends on the person(s) performing the task, i.e., where the *human factor* becomes visible, namely, through the abilities of the participants during the competition to solve the challenge using their respective tools, as well as through the ability of the judges to compensate for the varying tool contexts and the need to be objective about the quality of (often partial) solutions.

4.1   The Human Factor in the Competition

Most competitions in the area of formal methods are *unsupervised*, i.e., fully automated tools are run on a batch of challenges without human interaction and the ranking is determined from the results that they produce (and, possibly, their runtimes/memory consumption). VerifyThis is a supervised competition since challenges are not submitted to a fully automatic analysis.

One aspect in the success of solving a particular problem, at a high-level, is the experience of a competition participant with respect to the problem's characteristics (e.g., whether it involves pointer structures, concurrency, ...). This determines how hard or easy one may find it to come up with suitable invariants, for example, or to employ clever approaches that lend themselves to an elegant solution, mathematically.

As an example, even a seemingly trivial property like sortedness can be formalised in different ways, either stating that any element is not greater than its successor ($a[i] \leq a[i+1]$ for all $i < |a| - 1$), or stating that any element is not greater than all succeeding elements ($a[i] \leq a[j]$ for all $i < j < |a|$). Note that in order to derive the second formulation from the first one, an explicit induction is needed, and hence the second one is strictly more "powerful" when one may assume, e.g., a sorted input. Depending on the challenge, choosing the right encoding may be the enabling key to a successful verification. In general, finding the ideal encoding, the ideal function contract or the ideal loop invariant can require a considerable amount of creativity and ingenuity.

Another aspect is that such intuition must be formalized into a concrete representation of the specification within the confines of the deductive verification tool. This task is usually more than a straightforward logical encoding of natural language properties. Not only could logical choices (as the one above) critically affect whether the automation can find a proof (at all resp. within a reasonable time limit). Even benign things like the order of conjuncts can make a significant difference. As a consequence, effective use of a verification tool may require significant and detailed knowledge of the internal mechanics of the tool itself and the verification infrastructure it is built on.

The central question regarding the goal of the VerifyThis competition is, hence, whether it is

- a competition in which humans compete about their capabilities to perform difficult verification tasks verification, *or*
- a competition in which the capabilities, strengths or weaknesses of the participating verification tools come to light.

The conciliatory answer to this is that VerifyThis combines both, as these characters are inherently entangled by the nature of the field itself: Deductive program verification for challenging, algorithmic problems with heavyweight properties is far from begin a push-button technology–and probably always will be for sufficiently complex challenges. Human and tool must play together to succeed. Moreover, in all but trivial cases, a challenge will not be solved in one go, but requires an iterative process towards the final solution. The design of the Veri-fyThis competition reflects these aspects and thus mirrors reality in this respect. The human factor is not added *per se* as an on-top feature to the competition, but arises as an integral part of the specification and verification process. Furthermore, the human factor brings to light the qualities of a verification tool in the interactive process. For instance,

- usability and intuitiveness, in particular of the provided error messages,
- degree of automation,
- responsiveness (how easy is it to try a slightly changed specification),
- facilities to debug failed verification attempts, e.g. by producing counterexamples for failing specifications,
- the quality of counterexamples and their presentation,
- and the quality of a tool's specification libraries

all manifest themselves through the human factor. To measure these aspects, the human operator needs to be involved in the process and its evaluation. The in-vitro character of the competition emphasizes the human factor since it takes much experience to successfully interact with the tool under the tight time constraints.

How can the competition and the challenges be designed to control the influence of the human factor?

Ideally, one would like to separate the abilities of the human expert from the usability and performance of a tool when assessing the solution of a challenge. Due to the mentioned entanglement, this is difficult. Even worse, missing experience or unfamiliarity with a particular part of the verification system or type of specification, may be a showstopper for a team during the competition time. Several ideas for the design of the competition have emerged that would allow one to control the role of the human in the process, in particular by reducing its impact.

Reduce the need for human creativity: If crucial proof-guiding annotations (e.g. invariants) cannot be found, a solution to a challenge may become stuck in early stages. To mitigate this factor, the challenge description could contain logical formulations of such annotations. These hints could also be provided in a closed envelope, to be opened at the discretion of the team only, or half way through the time available for the challenge. This challenge scheme where part of the solution is given away, suggests itself particularly for the warm-up challenge where the solution is usually not so particular to the applied verification technology.

As an alternative, instead of an algorithm-driven challenge, we could provide a specification and ask to provide a verifiable implementation.

Reduce the need for experience: Experience with program verification in general and with a particular verification tool have a prominent impact on the results of the competition. To lessen this effect, one of the challenges could be solved by ad-hoc teams composed during the competition. This has the potential to bring together different experience levels and tool expertises, and would also provide a great opportunity for knowledge transfer.

Decouple tools from their users: Verification tools may have a tendency to be (over)fitted to the specification and verification style of their developers. To lighten this bias, we could do a cross-validation experiment, where teams are asked to reproduce a solution of another team, in their own specification methodology using their own technique.

Another possible cross-validation experiment is to reserve one of the challenges as a competition of tool A vs. tool B (judged separately). This can be incorporated into the tutorial session, where both these tools could be presented but the audience is leveraged for a more systematical evaluation. Such an effort could also be done off-line, similarly to the Isabelle competition[4].

4.2 The Human Factor in the Judging

There is a second human factor involved with supervised competitions: Judging cannot be automated to the same degree as it can with unsupervised competitions. For the latter, ranking schemes can still be biased for particular tools or approaches, but at least the criteria are defined a priori. Manually crafted solutions are usually not comparable by pre-definable metrics, and require careful examination. Therefore, for the judges, the most intensive activity of the competition with substantial time urgency is the evaluation process to arrive at the prize decision: the complete judging for all the teams and their solutions takes just one (long) day. This activity is certainly receptive to the judges' subjective views and tastes, and thus another human factor.

The judges have to consider all the possible specification and verification aspects in the solutions – parts that have been done, parts that could have been done, and parts that were only completed to a certain degree, as well as the automation level and tool support aspects. At the same time, the teams being interviewed concentrate on the best and completed parts of their solution. Both sides also tend to have a technology specific view – the teams look at the solution and possible improvements from the point of view of their tool and method, while the judges, even though staying impartial, would have their own expertise and tool bias. This is especially true considering that the judging committee is now different every competition instance and coming with their own expertise, expectations, and often first time experience approach.

Defining objective criteria: In this context, one of the ideas that we would like to implement in the future instalment of the competition to reduce the biases and to optimize the judging process is a challenge solution form that the teams should fill in along with the submission. The form would include generic questions about the solution completeness, e.g.,

- "Have you specified the main functional property?",
- "To what degree were you able to prove it?",
- "Have you specified/proved the termination/memory safety/non-interference/... properties?",

---

[4] See https://competition.isabelle.systems.

- "Are the proofs automatic? If not, what is the user interaction effort?",
- "Is the incompleteness of your solution due to insufficient proof guidance (e.g., too weak invariants), or due to tool or method shortcomings?",
- "Estimate how much time you would need to complete the task?", etc.

Systematic judging process: Such questions would also give the teams the chance to preliminary self-evaluate the solution before the discussion and prepare some answers up-front. To not occupy the challenge solving time, this form can be easily filled in between the challenge closing time and the judging, nevertheless it should be obligatory.

A structured interview after the competition also helps to mitigate the human factor and use it to our advantage: By explicitly querying about the usability and interaction support of the tool (e.g., guided by the usability issues listed in Sect. 4.1), both weaknesses and strengths can be learned by inspecting the impact of the human factor during the competition. This feedback can then again help developers to improve the user experience of their tools. One question that was typically asked previously during judging was "which tool feature did you find most helpful", in order to determine the corresponding prize.

Another possibility is to integrate the judging and the team presentations into a single event. This opens up the opportunity to involve all participants in the judgement process through consensus (e.g. a voting or scoring scheme), thereby avoiding potential bias of the judges on the competition's outcome.

These suggestions can help in answering questions related to completeness of solutions and usability of the tool. It still remains difficult to check whether a given solution does in fact formalize the requirements adequately, i.e., whether it is a *correct* solution. Answering this question is highly non-trivial as it involves not only understanding the specification language of the tool, but also its meta-theory and verification approach and what is, semantically, implied by proving a particular statement. An example for this was last year's third concurrency challenge, which involved a lock-free data structure [17]: How fine-grained is the concurrency model of the tool? How do the synchronization primitives work? Such aspects can be illuminated in the dialogue between the judges and the participants only.

Finally, one criterion where the human factor is intentionally brought into the judging process is "elegance". While elegance affects the ranking much less than completeness and correctness of solutions, it may serve as a tie-breaker, and is often recognized by singling out certain solutions in the competition reports.

5   Conclusion

We set out to reflect on the organisation of VerifyThis, discussed the competition's format and impact to come up with several concrete ideas to improve future events.

The survey in Sect. 3 showed that VerifyThis leads to an intense exchange between participants, allowing them to gain a unique overview of the state-of-the-art and establishing academic collaboration. The personal contact between the participants is thereby a major strength of VerifyThis. VerifyThis has also led to concrete improvements to the verification tools including a few completely novel features.

In Sect. 4 we illustrated that the human factor in the competition is inherent both in solving the challenges as well as in the judging. Human interaction (e.g., by providing a suitable encoding in the specification or by providing auxiliary annotations) is indispensable in deductive program verification of sophisticated properties. The human factor can thus not be fully eliminated from the competition – nor should it be. The discussion led to a few suggestions responding to the involved human factor: We identified a number of possible modifications of the modalities of the challenges regarding the composition of the teams and the design of the challenges. To mitigate the influence of the human factor in the judging, we suggest to aid the process by questionnaires filled out by the participants themselves.

Finally, we think it is important to widen our reach for a more diverse set of tools that implement different approaches, such as software model checkers and tools to synthesise specifications and programs that are correct by construction, as attempted in Dagstuhl in 2014 [4].

The VerifyThis competition enriches the portfolio of the TOOLympics as it differs from other competitions by explicitly incorporating the tool's user into the process.

Acknowledgement. We thank Microsoft Research, Amazon Web Services, Galois, and Formal Methods Europe for their support and generous sponsorship of VerifyThis over the last years. We thank Rosemary Monahan for suggestions to improve the competition format and feedback on the manuscript.

A   Survey Questions

As part of the celebration 20's anniversary of TACAS, we are writing an article on the VerifyThis competition. In contrast to previous publications on the series (which emphasized the practical technical aspects), we would now like to focus on the higher-level perspective that relates the competition to the field, the community, as well as your personal view.

A.1   General Questions

- How many times have you participated? [1–6]
- What is your current position? [Undergraduate, PhD/MSc, Postdoc, Academic, Other...]
- Have you participated as a student? [Yes, No, Both]
- Have you participated as a tool developer? [Yes, No]

A.2   Tool Improvement

– Which improvements in deductive verification tools do you think have been achieved in the recent years?
  Scale: [Stayed the same, Minor improvements, Significant improvements, Major breakthroughs that have or will change the field]
  Categories:
  - Expressiveness and ease of use of specification languages
  - Proof automation and guidance
  - Integration with static analysis techniques (invariant inference, shape analysis, ...)
  - Verification debugging and counterexample generation
  - Specification and proof refactoring
– Which tool aspects do you think could have the most impact if they were improved?
  Scale: [No impact/irrelevant, Minor impact, Significant impact, Major breakthroughs that would change the field]
  Categories: (as above)
– Are there any other future improvements that you think need to happen?
– If you are a developer: Which changes to the tool were improved or implemented as response to the experience at the competition?
  Scale: [No investment, Minor improvements, Significant improvements, Novel feature previously not present]
  Categories: (as above)
– Are there any other future improvements that you would like to add to your tool?
– If you are a developer: What was the motivation for adding new features?
  - Missing feature required solve certain competition challenges
  - For research unrelated to the competition
  - Improvements to the verification process
  - Other: ...

A.3   Personal Take-Away

– How did you benefit from participation?
  Scale: [Did not benefit, Minor benefit, Significant benefit, Major benefit that was primarily enabled through participating at VerifyThis]
  Categories
  - Learn about state-of-the-art techniques and tools
  - Improve own ability in specification and verification
  - Improve own tool in day-to-day use
  - Establish academic contacts or collaborative research
– How many of the VerifyThis challenges from the past serve currently as a benchmark/test in the development of your tool?

- Which aspects of the event did you particularly enjoy?
  - The challenge problems & solving them
  - Presentation sessions among the participants
  - Discussions with the jury
  - Exchange with colleagues
  - Leaning how other approaches tackle things
  - Other: ...
- How could future instalments be improved?

References

1. Ahrendt, W., Beckert, B., Bubel, R., Hähnle, R., Schmitt, P.H., Ulbrich, M. (eds.): Deductive Software Verification - The KeY Book: From Theory to Practice. LNCS, vol. 10001. Springer, Cham (2016). https://doi.org/10.1007/978-3-319-49812-6
2. Bartocci, E., et al.: TOOLympics 2019: an overview of competitions in formal methods. In: Beyer, D., Huisman, M., Kordon, F., Steffen, B. (eds.) TACAS 2019. LNCS, vol. 11429, pp. 3–24. Springer, Cham (2019)
3. Beyer, D.: Automatic verification of C and Java programs: SV-COMP 2019. In: Beyer, D., Huisman, M., Kordon, F., Steffen, B. (eds.) TACAS 2019. LNCS, vol. 11429, pp. 133–155. Springer, Cham (2019)
4. Beyer, D., Huisman, M., Klebanov, V., Monahan, R.: Evaluating software verification systems: benchmarks and competitions (Dagstuhl Reports 14171). Dagstuhl Rep. **4**(4), 1–19 (2014)
5. Blom, S., Darabi, S., Huisman, M., Oortwijn, W.: The VerCors tool set: verification of parallel and concurrent software. In: Polikarpova, N., Schneider, S. (eds.) IFM 2017. LNCS, vol. 10510, pp. 102–110. Springer, Cham (2017). https://doi.org/10.1007/978-3-319-66845-1_7
6. Bormer, T., et al.: The COST IC0701 verification competition 2011. In: Beckert, B., Damiani, F., Gurov, D. (eds.) FoVeOOS 2011. LNCS, vol. 7421, pp. 3–21. Springer, Heidelberg (2012). https://doi.org/10.1007/978-3-642-31762-0_2
7. Cohen, E., et al.: VCC: a practical system for verifying concurrent C. In: Berghofer, S., Nipkow, T., Urban, C., Wenzel, M. (eds.) TPHOLs 2009. LNCS, vol. 5674, pp. 23–42. Springer, Heidelberg (2009). https://doi.org/10.1007/978-3-642-03359-9_2
8. Cok, D.R., Kiniry, J.R.: ESC/Java2: uniting ESC/Java and JML. In: Barthe, G., Burdy, L., Huisman, M., Lanet, J.-L., Muntean, T. (eds.) CASSIS 2004. LNCS, vol. 3362, pp. 108–128. Springer, Heidelberg (2005). https://doi.org/10.1007/978-3-540-30569-9_6
9. Cranen, S., et al.: An overview of the mCRL2 toolset and its recent advances. In: Piterman, N., Smolka, S.A. (eds.) TACAS 2013. LNCS, vol. 7795, pp. 199–213. Springer, Heidelberg (2013). https://doi.org/10.1007/978-3-642-36742-7_15
10. DiStefano, D., Parkinson, M.: jStar: towards practical verification for Java. In: ACM Conference on Object-Oriented Programming Systems, Languages, and Applications, pp. 213–226. ACM Press (2008)
11. Ernst, G., Pfähler, J., Schellhorn, G., Haneberg, D., Reif, W.: KIV: overview and VerifyThis competition. Int. J. Softw. Tools Technol. Transfer **17**(6), 677–694 (2015)
12. Filliâtre, J.-C., Paskevich, A.: Why3 — where programs meet provers. In: Felleisen, M., Gardner, P. (eds.) ESOP 2013. LNCS, vol. 7792, pp. 125–128. Springer, Heidelberg (2013). https://doi.org/10.1007/978-3-642-37036-6_8

13. Giesl, J., et al.: Proving termination of programs automatically with AProVE. In: Demri, S., Kapur, D., Weidenbach, C. (eds.) IJCAR 2014. LNCS (LNAI), vol. 8562, pp. 184–191. Springer, Cham (2014). https://doi.org/10.1007/978-3-319-08587-6_13

14. Hoang, D., Moy, Y., Wallenburg, A., Chapman, R.: SPARK 2014 and GNATprove - a competition report from builders of an industrial-strength verifying compiler. STTT **17**(6), 695–707 (2015)

15. Huisman, M., Klebanov, V., Monahan, R.: VerifyThis verification competition 2012 - organizer's report. Technical report 2013-01, Department of Informatics, Karlsruhe Institute of Technology (2013). http://digbib.ubka.uni-karlsruhe.de/volltexte/1000034373

16. Huisman, M., Monahan, R., Mostowski, W., Müller, P., Ulbrich, M.: VerifyThis 2017: a program verification competition. Technical report, Karlsruhe Reports in Informatics (2017)

17. Huisman, M., Monahan, R., Müller, P., Paskevich, A., Ernst, G.: VerifyThis 2018: a program verification competition. Technical report, Inria (2019)

18. Huisman, M., Monahan, R., Müller, P., Poll, E.: VerifyThis 2016: a program verification competition. Technical report TR-CTIT-16-07, Centre for Telematics and Information Technology, University of Twente, Enschede (2016)

19. Huisman, M., Klebanov, V., Monahan, R.: On the organisation of program verification competitions. In: Klebanov, V., Beckert, B., Biere, A., Sutcliffe, G. (eds.) 1st International Workshop on Comparative Empirical Evaluation of Reasoning Systems (COMPARE 2012). CEUR Workshop Proceedings, vol. 873. CEUR-WS.org (2012)

20. Huisman, M., Klebanov, V., Monahan, R.: VerifyThis 2012. Int. J. Softw. Tools Technol. Transf. **17**(6), 647–657 (2015)

21. Huisman, M., Klebanov, V., Monahan, R., Tautschnig, M.: VerifyThis 2015. A program verification competition. Int. J. Softw. Tools Technol. Transf. **19**(6), 763–771 (2017)

22. Jacobs, B., Smans, J., Piessens, F.: Solving the VerifyThis 2012 challenges with VeriFast. STTT **17**(6), 659–676 (2015)

23. Jasper, M., et al.: RERS 2019: combining synthesis with real-world models. In: Beyer, D., Huisman, M., Kordon, F., Steffen, B. (eds.) TACAS 2019. LNCS, vol. 11429, pp. 101–115. Springer, Cham (2019)

24. Kirchner, F., Kosmatov, N., Prevosto, V., Signoles, J., Yakobowski, B.: Frama-C: a software analysis perspective. Formal Asp. Comput. **27**(3), 573–609 (2015)

25. Klebanov, V., et al.: The 1st verified software competition: experience report. In: Butler, M., Schulte, W. (eds.) FM 2011. LNCS, vol. 6664, pp. 154–168. Springer, Heidelberg (2011). https://doi.org/10.1007/978-3-642-21437-0_14

26. Kobayashi, N., Sato, R., Unno, H.: Predicate abstraction and CEGAR for higher-order model checking. In: Hall, M.W., Padua, D.A. (eds.) 32nd ACM SIGPLAN Conference on Programming Language Design and Implementation (PLDI 2011), pp. 222–233. ACM (2011)

27. Kroening, D., Tautschnig, M.: CBMC – C bounded model checker - (competition contribution). In: Ábrahám, E., Havelund, K. (eds.) TACAS 2014. LNCS, vol. 8413, pp. 389–391. Springer, Heidelberg (2014). https://doi.org/10.1007/978-3-642-54862-8_26

28. Leino, K.R.M.: Dafny: an automatic program verifier for functional correctness. In: Clarke, E.M., Voronkov, A. (eds.) LPAR 2010. LNCS (LNAI), vol. 6355, pp. 348–370. Springer, Heidelberg (2010). https://doi.org/10.1007/978-3-642-17511-4_20

29. Müller, P., Schwerhoff, M., Summers, A.J.: Viper: a verification infrastructure for permission-based reasoning. In: Jobstmann, B., Leino, K.R.M. (eds.) VMCAI 2016. LNCS, vol. 9583, pp. 41–62. Springer, Heidelberg (2016). https://doi.org/10.1007/978-3-662-49122-5_2

30. Nipkow, T., Wenzel, M., Paulson, L.C. (eds.): Isabelle/HOL: A Proof Assistant for Higher-Order Logic. LNCS, vol. 2283. Springer, Heidelberg (2002). https://doi.org/10.1007/3-540-45949-9

31. O'Hearn, P.W.: Continuous reasoning: scaling the impact of formal methods. In: Proceedings of the 33rd Annual ACM/IEEE Symposium on Logic in Computer Science, pp. 13–25. ACM (2018)

32. Siegel, S.F., et al.: CIVL: the concurrency intermediate verification language. Technical report UD-CIS-2014/001, Department of Computer and Information Sciences, University of Delaware (2014)

33. Sun, J., Liu, Y., Dong, J.S., Pang, J.: PAT: towards flexible verification under fairness. In: Bouajjani, A., Maler, O. (eds.) CAV 2009. LNCS, vol. 5643, pp. 709–714. Springer, Heidelberg (2009). https://doi.org/10.1007/978-3-642-02658-4_59

34. Swamy, N., Chen, J., Fournet, C., Strub, P., Bhargavan, K., Yang, J.: Secure distributed programming with value-dependent types. J. Funct. Program. **23**(4), 402–451 (2013)

35. Tschannen, J., Furia, C.A., Nordio, M., Polikarpova, N.: AutoProof: auto-active functional verification of object-oriented programs. In: Baier, C., Tinelli, C. (eds.) TACAS 2015. LNCS, vol. 9035, pp. 566–580. Springer, Heidelberg (2015). https://doi.org/10.1007/978-3-662-46681-0_53

SV-COMP 2019

CBMC Path: A Symbolic Execution Retrofit of the C Bounded Model Checker
(Competition Contribution)

Kareem Khazem[1]([envelope]) and Michael Tautschnig[2]

[1] University College London, London, UK
karkhaz@karkhaz.com
[2] Queen Mary University of London, London, UK

Abstract. We gave CBMC the ability to explore and model check single program paths, as opposed to its default whole-program model-checking behaviour. This means that CBMC, when invoked with the `--paths` flag, symbolically executes one program path at a time—saving unexplored paths for later—and attempts to prove properties for only that path. By doing this repeatedly for each path that CBMC encounters, CBMC can detect property violations in a scalable and incremental way.

Implementing single-path exploration raises the question of which order the paths should be explored in. Our implementation makes it easy for researchers to implement and investigate alternative path exploration strategies. Our competition contribution uses a breadth-first strategy, where diverging paths are each pushed onto a queue at program decision points, and the path to explore next is gotten by dequeueing the oldest path to have been added.

1 Overview

CBMC Path is an extension to the C Bounded Model Checker. The original CBMC tool was first described in [1] and is also competing in this year's SV-COMP (as previously described in [3]). CBMC symbolically executes C programs up to a user-defined loop unrolling bound. It generates a bit-precise encoding of the unrolled program, annotated with assertions that are the negation of properties the user wishes to verify. Such an encoding is satisfiable if the original program violates the properties. Thus, CBMC can be used to demonstrate that bugs occur when the program is run up to the unwinding bound for some input.

The original CBMC tool generates a single formula describing the disjunction of all program paths, dispatching this entire formula off to a SAT solver. The solver thus decides whether a bug exists at any point in the entire program. In contrast, CBMC Path dispatches the formula for a *single program path* to the SAT solver, checking whether that path violates any properties before continuing to execute and dispatch subsequent program paths. As with CBMC, the SAT solver used in CBMC Path for SV-COMP is MiniSat 2.2.0 [2].

K. Khazem—Juror.

D. Beyer et al. (Eds.): TACAS 2019, Part III, LNCS 11429, pp. 199–203, 2019.
https://doi.org/10.1007/978-3-030-17502-3_13

The intermediate representation that CBMC uses has no control-flow structures. Instead, GOTO statements explicitly define control flow. Furthermore, all functions in the intermediate representation have a single return point, at the end of the function. Thus, program paths that diverge—either due to an explicit conditional in the original code or an unrolled loop—eventually reunite at a later point in code. The treatment of these join points is an important difference between CBMC and CBMC Path.

CBMC Path is merged into the main CBMC codebase; users activate it by passing the `--paths` flag to CBMC in addition to the other options that they wish to use. Since it is a fairly focussed change to the codebase, we describe only the aspects that differ from CBMC's default mode in this report.

2 Architecture

The changes that CBMC Path makes to the original codebase are confined to the symbolic execution phase. There are three main changes, illustrated in Fig. 1:

- the symbolic execution (symex) state, including the path taken so far, can now be saved. This means that the symex process as a whole can be paused and subsequently resumed from a saved state.
- The symex code now has the option to avoid merging two divergent program paths at their join point. When combined with the above point, this means that CBMC Path can save both divergent paths at their branch point, execute one of the paths, and then continue executing past the join point without considering the other branch at all.
- The top-level symex code now maintains a worklist of symex states (partially-executed paths), rather than a single state that lives through execution of the entire target program. The top-level symex code includes a loop that repeatedly pops the worklist and executes the popped state until it reaches a branch point (conditional goto), at which point the states corresponding to each branch are pushed onto the worklist. When combined with the above two points, this means that control returns to the top-level each time a pair of divergent paths in the target program are saved onto the worklist. The top-level code then decides which path to continue executing, and pops that path from the worklist.

Program paths are thus pushed to and popped from the worklist until one of the paths has been executed to the end of the program; at this point, the top-level code dispatches its formula to the SAT solver, before continuing to execute the remaining paths.

The decision of which path should be resumed can be expressed as a list-popping strategy. We have so far implemented the last-in, first-out (LIFO) and first-in, first-out (FIFO) disciplines. LIFO explores the program depth-first, completing a single path before starting to explore any others; this strategy uses memory efficiently (since only a single full path is maintained in memory), but takes far longer to cover a variety of program paths. FIFO expands the explored-instruction frontier of all program paths in a round-robin manner; this achieves excellent coverage at the (considerable) expense of keeping all paths in memory until each of them reaches the end of the program. The user can choose the strategy as an argument to the --paths option. For SV-COMP, we chose to use FIFO for all benchmarks, since the modest size of the benchmarks means that memory use was rarely a problem. The strategy system is designed to be easily extensible to encourage researchers to experiment with the different trade-offs of more sophisticated path-popping strategies.

3 Motivation, Strengths, and Weaknesses

CBMC Path shares many of the strengths and weaknesses that CBMC has compared to other tools, which are discussed in the CBMC system report. In this section, we focus on a comparison with CBMC.

CBMC Path is aimed at users wishing to discover bugs quickly and efficiently, while being not so suited to proving program correctness. By only model-checking individual program paths, each SAT solver call returns much more quickly, ensuring that bugs along those paths are discovered without having to wait for the rest of the program to be encoded and checked. In addition, CBMC Path can be parsimonious in its memory usage, since the formulas dispatched to the solver are much smaller. These qualities make CBMC Path complementary to whole-program bug-finding or correctness-proving tools. The intended use-case is that CBMC Path is used to quickly find bugs of the low-hanging fruit variety, so that users can avoid model-checking the entire program only to discover an error residing a few lines into the program entry-point.

The overhead of saving and resuming paths, and of multiple calls to the SAT solver, means that CBMC Path will always take significantly longer to check

```
1        if (x > y)
2            GOTO 3;
3        GOTO 2;
4    3:  ret = 1;
5        GOTO 1;
6    2:  ret = 0;
7    1:  return;
```

Fig. 1. The program above (in CBMC's intermediate representation) illustrates the difference between CBMC's and CBMC Path's exploration strategies. CBMC executes all seven lines. At the join point (line 7), CBMC creates a disjunction representing both paths. In contrast, at line 1, CBMC Path pauses symbolic execution and saves two paths onto the top-level worklist: one path whose program counter is line 3, and another whose program counter is line 4. The top-level workloop then chooses a path from the worklist to resume executing.

an entire program than CBMC does. Proving absence of property violations always requires checking the entire program, so CBMC is expected to outperform CBMC Path on most SV-COMP benchmarks. On the other hand, CBMC Path usually has a lower maximum memory use than CBMC when using the LIFO strategy, since both the in-memory symbolic state and the formulas dispatched to the solver are smaller at all times. This means that CBMC Path can still be useful for proving correctness, specifically when used on large programs that require more-than-available system memory under CBMC. CBMC Path is most useful when used for finding bugs, since it will often find a property violation before CBMC has had a chance to fully explore the program. In addition, the user experience is often more encouraging using CBMC Path, since results are displayed incrementally. This is an important contrast to tools which terminate due to memory exhaustion before displaying any results at all. We view CBMC Path as complimentary to CBMC, and hope that developers use them both to their respective strengths.

This year (CBMC Path's SV-COMP debut), CBMC outperformed CBMC Path on most benchmarks. For small SV-COMP benchmarks, the time that CBMC spends in the solver for the entire program is less than the path pushing and popping overhead. We hope to introduce more sophisticated path strategies that will mitigate this overhead for future competitions.

4   Tool Setup

The competition submission is based on CBMC version 5.10, with additional patches. The archive of the competition binary is available at https://gitlab.com/sosy-lab/sv-comp/archives-2019/raw/svcomp19/2019/cbmc-path.zip.

To process a benchmark FOO.c (with properties in FOO.prp), the wrapper cbmc-path.py should be invoked as follows:

```
cbmc-path.py --graphml-cex witness.cex \
             --propertyfile FOO.prp --32 FOO.c
```

for all categories with a 32-bit memory model; for those with a 64-bit memory model, --32 should be replaced by --64.

Participation. CBMC Path competes in all categories.

Output. The last line of output produced by cbmc is one of TRUE, FALSE, FALSE(no-overflow), FALSE(valid-free), FALSE(valid-deref), or FALSE(valid-memtrack). Absence of such a final line is treated as UNKNOWN by the wrapper script.

5   Software Project

CBMC Path is fully merged into the original CBMC codebase. It is maintained by Daniel Kroening with patches supplied by the community. It is made publicly available under a BSD-style license. The source code and binaries for popular platforms are available at http://www.cprover.org/cbmc.

Acknowledgements. We would like to thank the reviewers for their feedback and Mark R. Tuttle for his assistance with this work.

References

1. Clarke, E., Kroening, D., Lerda, F.: A tool for checking ANSI-C programs. In: Jensen, K., Podelski, A. (eds.) TACAS 2004. LNCS, vol. 2988, pp. 168–176. Springer, Heidelberg (2004). https://doi.org/10.1007/978-3-540-24730-2_15
2. Eén, N., Sörensson, N.: An extensible SAT-solver. In: Giunchiglia, E., Tacchella, A. (eds.) SAT 2003. LNCS, vol. 2919, pp. 502–518. Springer, Heidelberg (2004). https://doi.org/10.1007/978-3-540-24605-3_37
3. Kroening, D., Tautschnig, M.: CBMC – C bounded model checker - (competition contribution). In: Ábrahám, E., Havelund, K. (eds.) TACAS 2014. LNCS, vol. 8413, pp. 389–391. Springer, Heidelberg (2014). https://doi.org/10.1007/978-3-642-54862-8_26

Extending **DIVINE** with Symbolic Verification Using SMT
(Competition Contribution)

Henrich Lauko[(✉)], Vladimír Štill, Petr Ročkai, and Jiří Barnat

Faculty of Informatics, Masaryk University, Brno, Czech Republic
xlauko@mail.muni.cz, divine@fi.muni.cz

Abstract. DIVINE is an LLVM-based verification tool focusing on analysis of real-world C and C++ programs. Such programs often interact with their environment, for example via inputs from users or network. When these programs are analyzed, it is desirable that the verification tool can deal with inputs symbolically and analyze runs for all inputs. In DIVINE, it is now possible to deal with input data via symbolic computation instrumented into the original program at the level of LLVM bitcode. Such an instrumented program maintains symbolic values internally and operates directly on them. Instrumentation allows us to enhance the tool with support for symbolic data without substantial modifications of the tool itself. Namely, this competition contribution uses SMT formulae for representation of input data.

1 Verification Approach and Software Architecture

DIVINE is an explicit-state model checker primarily designed to detect bugs in multithreaded programs [6]. Testing of multithreaded programs is a known hard problem because of nondeterminism in the execution caused by thread interleavings. To deal with control flow nondeterminism, DIVINE exhaustively explores all relevant executions of the multithreaded program. Unfortunately, this explicit approach fails to deal with data nondeterminism caused by communication with the environment. In order to verify a program with inputs, DIVINE would need to examine all the possible inputs of the program. This would cause enormous state-space explosion and would be unmanageable in reasonable time and space.

The traditional way to cope with input values during verification is to represent them symbolically – i.e., to perform symbolic execution on the program. In DIVINE it would be sufficient to extend the LLVM interpreter to work with input values symbolically and adapt the exploration algorithm to work with symbolic states, similarly as other tools do [2,3,5]. However, this would make the core of the verification procedure more complicated and possibly slow it

This work has been partially supported by the Czech Science Foundation grant No. 18-02177S and by Red Hat, Inc.

H. Lauko—SV-COMP jury member.

D. Beyer et al. (Eds.): TACAS 2019, Part III, LNCS 11429, pp. 204–208, 2019.
https://doi.org/10.1007/978-3-030-17502-3_14

down, introduce bugs and/or reduce maintainability and extensibility. Hence, we have decided to shift the responsibility for symbolic values from the verifier to the verified program [4]. Instead of (re-)interpreting instructions symbolically, we translate symbolic instructions into equivalent explicit code which performs the computation symbolically. The transformation performs a dependency analysis on symbolic values of the program and translates symbolic instructions. By providing a set of symbolic operations as a library, we obtain a program that manipulates symbolic values. The method is further described in Fig. 1.

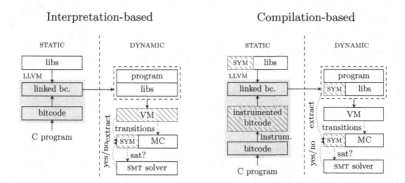

Fig. 1. Comparison of interpretation-based approach and compilation-based approaches. All manipulations of symbolic values are denoted by red color. In both cases, the virtual machine generates transitions in the state space and passes them to the model checker (MC), which performs safety analysis. In the compilation-based approach, symbolic operations are instrumented into the program, while in the interpretation-based one, they are the responsibility of the VM. (Color figure online)

In order to maintain efficiency we do not transform the entire program, but only the parts that might come into contact with symbolic values. As shown in Fig. 2, the program is analyzed starting from **input** points, and all downstream operations are augmented (s_add, s_eq), but concrete computation remains unchanged (fun). The transformed program uses a special operation called lift, which takes a concrete value and returns a symbolic one. The result of lifting * represents an arbitrary input value.

In comparison to standard programs, a program with symbolic values might not have deterministic control flow. When a program contains a branch which depends on a symbolic value, both outcomes might be possible.[1] To capture such behavior in the transformed program, we introduce a nondeterministic choice and execute both branches. We take advantage of the fact that DIVINE is already capable of handling nondeterminism. Further, in the taken path we constrain values by extending a path condition (see Fig. 3).

---

[1] Given a symbolic value x and a branch with condition x < 5, the condition can be both true and false. The program makes a nondeterministic choice and extends the path condition with $x < 5$ or $x \geq 5$ respectively.

```
a:int  ← input()
b:int  ← fun(7)
c:int  ← add(a, b)
d:bool ← eq(a, b)
```

```
a:s_int ← lift(*)
b:int   ← fun(7)
c:s_int ← s_add(a, lift(b))
d:s_bool ← s_eq(a, lift(b))
```

Fig. 2. Transformation to the program working with symbolic values (right).

```
a:s_int ← lift(*)
b:s_int ← lift(*)
c:s_int ← s_add(a, b)
if nondet()
    assume(c < 5)
    d:s_int ← s_mul(c, 3)
```

Fig. 3. The transformed program builds term trees that represent symbolic values. The boxes correspond to symbolic variables while the circles are the concrete representation of terms. Question marks denote unconstrained nullary symbols. Gray boxes represent path condition constraints.

In the program, symbolic data are represented as term trees – see Fig. 3. Exploring the state space, DIVINE extracts term trees from program states in the model checking algorithm, and checks for the feasibility by querying SMT solver (Z3) for satisfiability of extracted path condition. Moreover, DIVINE needs to recognize when it has reached a repeated state. This can not be done by a simple comparison of states, because different symbolic states may represent the same set of concrete states. Hence, to check equality of states, we also utilize the SMT solver. To precisely model program arithmetic, we use the bitvector theory.

2   Strengths and Weaknesses

In comparison to bounded model checkers, DIVINE's strength is sound verification – it explores a whole state-space and uses formulae in bitvector theory to precisely represent symbolic values. However DIVINE produced a few wrong results in the competition, these should not be possible in theory and likely stem from implementation errors in the verification tool.

Our compilation-based approach has allowed us to increase modularity of the tool. It is easy to change the representation of symbolic values, the verification algorithm and even the entire verifier while preserving the transformation. Another upside is that the implementation of symbolic operations is subject to checks performed by the verifier.

On the other hand, the current implementation is only a proof of concept. Our primary goal was to show that a compilation-based approach may compete with interpretation-based approaches even though it increases the size of the verified program and therefore possibly also verification complexity. Currently, the transformation can only handle scalar values, hence verification of programs with symbolic memory is not yet possible.

3 Tool Setup and Configuration

The verifier archive can be found on the SV-COMP 2019 page[2] under the name DIVINE-SMT. In case the binary distribution does not work on your system, we also provide a source distribution and build instructions at https://divine.fi. muni.cz/2019/sv-comp-smt.

It is usually sufficient to run divine as follows: `divine check --symbolic --svcomp TESTCASE.c`. This command runs DIVINE with the SMT-based representation of symbolic data described in this paper and with SV-COMP-specific instrumentation.

For SV-COMP benchmarks, additional settings are handled by the `divine-svc` wrapper.[3] The only option used for DIVINE-SMT is `--32` for 32 bit categories. The wrapper sets DIVINE options based on the property file and the benchmark. In particular, it enables symbolic mode if any nondeterminism is found, sequential mode if no threads are found, and it sets which errors should be reported based on the property file. It also generates witness files. More details can be found on the aforementioned distribution page.

DIVINE participates in all categories, but it can only produce non-unknown results for the error reachability and memory safety categories.

4 Software Project and Contributors

The project home page is https://divine.fi.muni.cz. Many people have contributed to DIVINE, including Petr Ročkai, Henrich Lauko and Vladimír Štill. DIVINE is open source software distributed under the ISC license.

References

1. Beyer, D.: Automatic verification of c and java programs: Sv-comp 2019. In: Beyer, D., Huisman, M., Kordon, F., Steen, B. (eds.) TACAS 2019, Part III. LNCS, vol. 11429, pp. 133–155. Springer, Cham (2019)
2. Cadar, C., Dunbar, D., Engler, D.: KLEE: unassisted and automatic generation of high-coverage tests for complex systems programs. In: Operating Systems Design and Implementation, pp. 209–224. USENIX Association (2008)

---

[2] https://sv-comp.sosy-lab.org/2019/systems.php.
[3] To be found in the main directory of the binary archive, or in the `tools` directory of the source distribution. Usage: `divine-svc DIVINE_BINARY PROP_FILE [OPTIONS] TESTCASE.c`.

3. Komuravelli, A., Gurfinkel, A., Chaki, S.: SMT-based model checking for recursive programs. In: Biere, A., Bloem, R. (eds.) CAV 2014. LNCS, vol. 8559, pp. 17–34. Springer, Cham (2014). https://doi.org/10.1007/978-3-319-08867-9_2
4. Lauko, H., Ročkai, P., Barnat, J.: Symbolic computation via program transformation. In: Fischer, B., Uustalu, T. (eds.) ICTAC 2018. LNCS, vol. 11187, pp. 313–332. Springer, Cham (2018). https://doi.org/10.1007/978-3-030-02508-3_17
5. Phan, Q.-S., Malacaria, P., Păsăreanu, C.S.: Concurrent bounded model checking. SIGSOFT Softw. Eng. Notes **40**(1), 1–5 (2015)
6. Ročkai, P., Štill, V., Černá, I., Barnat, J.: DiVM: model checking with LLVM and graph memory. J. Syst. Softw. **143**, 1–13 (2018)

ESBMC v6.0: Verifying C Programs Using k-Induction and Invariant Inference
(Competition Contribution)

Mikhail R. Gadelha[1]([✉]), Felipe Monteiro[2], Lucas Cordeiro[3], and Denis Nicole[4]

[1] SIDIA Instituto de Ciência e Tecnologia, Manaus, Brazil
m.gadelha@samsung.com
[2] Federal University of Amazonas, Manaus, Brazil
felipemonteiro@ufam.edu.br
[3] University of Manchester, Manchester, UK
lucas.cordeiro@manchester.ac.uk
[4] University of Southampton, Southampton, UK
dan@ecs.soton.ac.uk

Abstract. ESBMC v6.0 employs a k-induction algorithm to both falsify and prove safety properties in C programs. We have developed a new interval-invariant generator that pre-processes the program, inferring invariants based on intervals and introducing them in the program as assumptions. Our experiments show that ESBMC v6.0 using k-induction can prove up to 7% more programs when the invariant generation is enabled.

1 Overview

The k-induction algorithm is an effective verification technique implemented in various software model checkers with the goal of proving partial correctness over a large number of different programs and properties [1–3]. Typical k-induction-based verifiers use iterative deepening and repeatedly unwind the program to produce the verification results; its incremental nature means that it always finds the smallest falsification [2]. In SV-COMP'19, we have implemented a new interval-invariant generator that runs as a pre-processing step in ESBMC [4]. In this implementation, invariants based on intervals are automatically introduced in the program as assumptions and, although the implementation has some limitations in keeping track of the relations between variables (i.e., our abstract domain is non-relational), it significantly strengthens the k-induction algorithm results; in particular, we have observed that the use of invariants increases the number of correct proofs by about 7% over the SV-COMP benchmarks.

M. R. Gadelha—Jury member.

© The Author(s) 2019
D. Beyer et al. (Eds.): TACAS 2019, Part III, LNCS 11429, pp. 209–213, 2019.
https://doi.org/10.1007/978-3-030-17502-3_15

2   Verification Approach

ESBMC uses a k-induction algorithm [2] to verify and falsify properties over C programs. Let a given C program P under verification be a finite transition system M, where we define:

- $I(s_n)$ and $T(s_n, s_{n+1})$ as the formulae over program's state variable set s_i constraining the initial states and transition relations of M;
- $\phi(s)$ as the formula encoding states satisfying a required safety property;
- $\psi(s)$ as the formula encoding states satisfying the completeness threshold, i.e. states corresponding to termination. $\psi(s)$ will contain unwindings no deeper than the maximum number of loop-iterations occurring in the program.

Note that, in our notation, termination and error are mutually exclusive: $\phi(s) \wedge \psi(s)$ is by construction unsatisfiable; s is a deadlock state if $T(s, s') \vee \phi(s)$ is unsatisfiable.

In each step k of the k-induction algorithm, three checks are performed: the base case $B(k)$, the forward condition $F(k)$ and the inductive step $S(k)$ [2]. $B(k)$ is the standard *bounded model checking* and it is satisfiable *iff* P has a counterexample of length k or less:

$$B(k) = I(s_1) \wedge \bigwedge_{i=1}^{k-1} T(s_i, s_{i+1}) \wedge \bigvee_{i=1}^{k} \neg\phi(s_i). \tag{1}$$

The forward condition checks for termination, i.e. whether the completeness threshold $\psi(s)$ must hold for the current k. If $F(k)$ is unsatisfiable, P has terminated:

$$F(k) = I(s_1) \wedge \bigwedge_{i=1}^{k-1} T(s_i, s_{i+1}) \wedge \neg\psi(s_k). \tag{2}$$

No safety property $\phi(s)$ is checked in $F(k)$ as they were checked for the current k in the base case. Finally, the inductive condition $S(k)$ is unsatisfiable if, whenever $\phi(s)$ holds for k unwindings, it also holds after the next unwinding of P:

$$S(k) = \exists n \in \mathbb{N}^+. \bigwedge_{i=n}^{n+k-1} (\phi(s_i) \wedge T'(s_i, s_{i+1})) \wedge \neg\phi(s_{n+k}). \tag{3}$$

Here $T'(s_i, s_{i+1})$ is the transition relation after havocking the loop variables [2]. Through $B(k)$, $F(k)$, and $S(k)$, the k-induction algorithm at a given k is:

$$kind(P, k) = \begin{cases} P \text{ contains a bug,} & \text{if } B(k) \text{ is satisfiable,} \\ P \text{ is correct,} & \text{if } B(k) \vee [F(k) \wedge S(k)] \text{ is unsatisfiable,} \\ kind(P, k+1), & \text{otherwise.} \end{cases} \tag{4}$$

2.1   Invariant Inference Based on Interval Analysis

Our major new feature is a new interval invariant generator for integer variables; it computes for every integer variable a lower and an upper bound of possible values. These intervals are injected into the program as assumptions (constraints) to address a limitation of the k-induction: when trying to check $S(k)$, the inductive step may find spurious counterexamples if the $T'(s_i, s_{i+1})$ over-approximation is unconstrained. This is because we havoc the variables that are written in a loop, i.e. all loop variables are assigned non-deterministic values. The effect can be seen in Eq. (3): the inductive step checks if whenever ϕ holds for $k-1$ unwindings, it also holds in the current unwinding of the system. In Eq. (3), the state space is only constrained using the properties in the program; these are (usually) not strong enough to prove program correctness.

Several authors address this problem by generating program invariants to rule out unreachable regions of the state space, either as a pre-processing step where invariants are introduced in the program before verification [3], or during the verification itself [1,5]. Similarly to Rocha et al. [3], we perform a static analysis prior to loop unwinding and (over-)estimate the range that a variable can assume. In contrast to Rocha et al., we do not rely on external tools to infer polyhedral constraints (e.g., $ax + by \leq c$, where a, b, and c are constants and x and y are variables) over C programs. Instead, we implement a "rectangular" invariant generation based on interval analysis (e.g. $a \leq x \leq b$) as a pre-processing step of the verification, i.e., before the program is symbolically executed and the resulting formulae are checked by an SMT solver.

Here we use the abstract-interpretation component from CPROVER [6]. This implements an abstract domain based on expressions over intervals; these constraints associate each variable with an upper and lower bound. The algorithm starts by assuming an unbounded interval for each variable in the program and follows the reachable instructions from the `main` function while updates the intervals, merging them if necessary. When loops are found, an widening operation is applied, in order to accelerate the generation process [7].

Our tool generates new invariants $\varphi(s_n)$ and changes Eq. (3) to use them as assumptions during verification, such that the new inductive step is defined as:

$$S'(k) = \exists n \in \mathbb{N}^+.\ \varphi(s_n) \wedge \bigwedge_{i=n}^{n+k-1} (\phi(s_i) \wedge T'(s_i, s_{i+1})) \wedge \neg\phi(s_{n+k}). \qquad (5)$$

The k-induction algorithm of Eq. (4) now uses the inductive step from Eq. (5) to participate in all categories with C programs of SV-COMP'19.

3 Strengths and Weaknesses

We have observed that the use of invariants increases the number of correct proofs in ESBMC by about 7%. This, however, comes at a cost: due to bugs in the invariant generator, the number of incorrect proofs is trebled if these invariants are used. In particular, we do not track intervals of variables changed through pointers and nor if the intervals are defined in terms of other variables. For this we would need a relational analysis that can keep track of relations between variables. As a result, with the interval invariants enabled, ESBMC becomes a (better) *bug-finding* tool rather than one delivering proofs of guaranteed soundness.

In SV-COMP'19, ESBMC correctly claims 3556 benchmarks correct and finds existing errors in 1753. Sadly, it also finds unexpected errors for 14 benchmarks and fails to find the expected errors in another 41, which impacts its overall performance. The failures are mostly concentrated in the `MemSafety` and `ConcurrencySafety` categories and are mainly due to: (1) our non-relational abstract domain, (2) an internal bug in ESBMC (since corrected) which did not track variables going out of scope, and (3) an incomplete modelling of some *pthread* functions. ESBMC's performance has improved greatly since SV-COMP'18 (v4.60): the number of errors detected has increased by 36% and the number of correct-true results increased by 32%. The biggest improvements are reflected in the categories `ReachSafety` and `FalsificationOverall`.

4   Tool Setup and Configuration

In order to run our `esbmc-wrapper.py` script[1], one must set the architecture (*i.e.*, 32 or 64-bit), the competition strategy (k-induction, falsification or incremental BMC), the property file path, and the benchmark path, as:

```
esbmc-wrapper.py [-h] [-a {32,64}] [-p PROPERTY_FILE]
                 [-s {kinduction,falsi,incr}]
                 [benchmark]
```

where `-a` sets the architecture, `-p` sets the property file path, and `-s` sets the strategy, in this case, `kinduction` for k-induction.

Internally, by choosing the k-induction strategy, the following options are set for every property when executing ESBMC-kind: `--no-div-by-zero-check`, which disables the division by zero check (required by SV-COMP); `--k-induction`, which enables the k-induction; `--floatbv`, which enables floating-point SMT encoding; `--unlimited-k-steps`, which removes the upper limit of iteration steps in the k-induction algorithm; `--witness-output`, which sets the witness output path; `--force-malloc-success`, which sets that all dynamic allocations succeed (also an SV-COMP requirement); and `--interval-analysis`, which enables the invariant generation. In addition, ESBMC-kind sets further options depending on the property that needs to be checked: `--no-pointer-check` and `--no-bounds-check` for reachability verification; `--memory-leak-check` for memory verification; and `--overflow-check` for overflow verification. The Benchexec tool info module is named `esbmc.py` and the benchmark definition file is `esbmc-kind.xml`. For SV-COMP'19, ESBMC-kind uses Boolector v2.4.1 [8] and competes in all categories with C programs.

5   Software Project

The ESBMC source code is available for downloading at https://github.com/esbmc/esbmc, while self-contained binaries for ESBMC v6.0 64-bit can be

---

[1] https://gitlab.com/sosy-lab/sv-comp/archives-2019/blob/master/2019/esbmc-kind .zip.

downloaded from https://github.com/esbmc/esbmc/releases. ESBMC is publicly available under the terms of the Apache License 2.0. Instructions for building ESBMC from source are given in the file BUILDING (including the description of all dependencies). ESBMC is a joint project with the Federal University of Amazonas (Brazil), University of Southampton (UK), University of Manchester (UK), and University of Stellenbosch (South Africa).

References

1. Beyer, D., Dangl, M., Wendler, P.: Boosting k-induction with continuously-refined invariants. In: Kroening, D., Păsăreanu, C.S. (eds.) CAV 2015. LNCS, vol. 9206, pp. 622–640. Springer, Cham (2015). https://doi.org/10.1007/978-3-319-21690-4_42
2. Gadelha, M.Y.R., Ismail, H.I., Cordeiro, L.C.: Handling loops in bounded model checking of C programs via k-induction. STTT **19**(1), 97–114 (2017)
3. Rocha, W., Rocha, H., Ismail, H., Cordeiro, L., Fischer, B.: DepthK: a k-induction verifier based on invariant inference for C programs. In: Legay, A., Margaria, T. (eds.) TACAS 2017. LNCS, vol. 10206, pp. 360–364. Springer, Heidelberg (2017). https://doi.org/10.1007/978-3-662-54580-5_23
4. Gadelha, M.R., Monteiro, F.R., Morse, J., Cordeiro, L.C., Fischer, B., Nicole, D.A.: ESBMC 5.0: an industrial-strength C model checker. In: ASE, pp. 888–891. IEEE/ACM (2018)
5. Malík, V., Martiček, Š., Schrammel, P., Srivas, M., Vojnar, T., Wahlang, J.: 2LS: memory safety and non-termination. In: Beyer, D., Huisman, M. (eds.) TACAS 2018. LNCS, vol. 10806, pp. 417–421. Springer, Cham (2018). https://doi.org/10.1007/978-3-319-89963-3_24
6. Kroening, D.: CProver Manual (2018). http://www.cprover.org/cprover-manual/. Accessed Feb 2019
7. Yamaguchi, T., Brain, M., Ryder, C., Imai, Y., Kawamura, Y.: Application of abstract interpretation to the automotive electronic control system. In: Enea, C., Piskac, R. (eds.) VMCAI 2019. LNCS, vol. 11388, pp. 425–445. Springer, Cham (2019). https://doi.org/10.1007/978-3-030-11245-5_20
8. Niemetz, A., Preiner, M., Biere, A.: Boolector 2.0 system description. J. Satisfiability Boolean Model. Comput. **9**, 53–58 (2015)

JayHorn: A Java Model Checker
(Competition Contribution)

Temesghen Kahsai[1], Philipp Rümmer[2(✉)], and Martin Schäf[3]

[1] The University of Iowa, Iowa City, USA
[2] Uppsala University, Uppsala, Sweden
philipp.ruemmer@it.uu.se
[3] SRI International, Menlo Park, USA

Abstract. JayHorn is a model checker for verifying sequential Java programs annotated with assertions expressing safety conditions. JayHorn uses the Soot library to read Java bytecode and translate it to the Jimple three-address format, then converts the Jimple code in several stages to a set of constrained Horn clauses, and solves the Horn clauses using solvers like SPACER and Eldarica. JayHorn uses a novel, invariant-based representation of heap data-structures, and is therefore particularly useful for analyzing programs with unbounded data-structures and unbounded run-time. JayHorn is open source and distributed under MIT license (https://github.com/jayhorn/jayhorn).

1 The JayHorn Approach

JayHorn is a model checker for verifying the absence of assertion violations in sequential Java programs by automatically inferring program annotations that are sufficient to witness program safety. Annotations are quantifier-free formulas in first-order logic modulo relevant theories like LIA. The choice of annotations is inspired by refinement types [1] and liquid types [7], and consists of:

- for each method m, a pre-condition `pre_m` defining conditions under which the method can be invoked, and a post-condition `post_m` stating the effect of the method in terms of the method parameters, the method result, possible exceptions, and certain ghost variables encoding the state of the heap;
- for each control location l, a state invariant `loc_l` describing the possible values of local variables that are in scope;
- for each class C, an instance invariant `inv_C` describing possible values of object fields and the dynamic object type.

The sufficiency of annotations is characterized by a set of constrained Horn constraints expressing that state invariants in a method body are ensured by the method pre-condition and preserved by all statements in the method body, that methods establish their post-conditions, and that updating the fields of an object preserves the instance invariant `inv_C`; more details are provided in [4]. Given the complete set of conditions on the annotations, the actual annotation inference

© The Author(s) 2019
D. Beyer et al. (Eds.): TACAS 2019, Part III, LNCS 11429, pp. 214–218, 2019.
https://doi.org/10.1007/978-3-030-17502-3_16

can be carried out with the help of off-the-shelf Horn solvers, like SPACER [5], which uses a variant of PDR/IC3, and Eldarica [3], which uses CEGAR.

The representation of heap data-structures using instance invariants in general over-approximates the program behavior, since instance invariants have to hold for the possible states of *all* objects of some class (as well as all elements of encoded arrays), at *any* point during program execution, and they cannot refer to local variables or to fields of other objects. The encoding (and JayHorn) is therefore incomplete, and it is easy to construct correct Java programs that cannot be verified using any choice of annotations [4]. To prevent incorrect answers, JayHorn applies a counterexample validation step whenever the generated Horn clauses are found to be unsatisfiable (see Sect. 2).

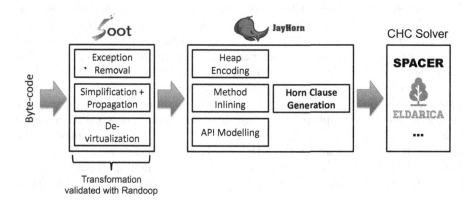

Fig. 1. Architectural overview of JayHorn.

2   Architecture of JayHorn (Fig. 1)

Program Transformations: In its default configuration, JayHorn takes Java byte-code as input and checks if Java `assert` can be violated. JayHorn accepts any input that is supported by the Soot framework [8]: Java class files, Jar archives, or Android apk. For code that is not annotated with `assert` statements, Jay-Horn also provides an option to guard possible `NullPointerExceptions`, `Array-IndexOutOfBoundsExceptions`, and `ClassCastExceptions` with assertions.

Soot is used to translate Java bytecode to the simplified Jimple three-address format, followed by a set of transformations to further simplify a program, among them elimination of exception handling and implicit exceptional control-flow; replacement of `switch` statements by `if` statements; and de-virtualization of method calls in the input program. We can test the correctness (or soundness) of these steps by comparing input/output behavior of the original and transformed code. Since this step is crucial for the soundness of the overall system, we employ Randoop [6] to automate this test.

On the simplified input program, JayHorn performs one abstraction step to eliminate arrays, again implemented as a bytecode transformation in Soot.

Arrays in Java are objects, so there are a few subtleties that makes it harder to handle them. For example, access to the `length` field of an array is not a regular field access but a special bytecode instruction. To simplify the later generation of Horn clauses, we transform arrays into real objects, and introduce a `get` and `put` method to access the array elements.

The next step is the replacement of all heap accesses with `push/pull` instructions that copy all fields of an object in a single step to/from local variables [4], preparing the ground for the later representation of heap using invariants. The placement of `push/pull` is optimized to use as few statements as possible, this way reducing the size of generated constraints, and minimizing the effect of later over-approximations.

Horn Clause Generation: The transformed simplified Java program is then encoded as a set of constrained Horn clauses, using uninterpreted predicates to represent the annotations from Sect. 1. The encoding is mostly standard, and follows the rules given in [2]. The `push/pull` instructions are replaced with assertions and assumptions of the corresponding instance invariant `inv_C` [4].

In order to mitigate incompleteness due to the instance invariants, JayHorn implements number of refinements of the basic encoding, extending the set of programs that can be captured using instance invariants. *Flow-sensitive* instance invariants rely on a separate static analysis to determine which `pushes` a `pull` instruction can read from, and can this way distinguish different object states. *Vector references* enrich references with additional information about an object, for instance the dynamic type, the allocation site, or values of immutable fields.

Counterexample Validation: Since the encoding of programs using instance invariants over-approximates program behavior, there is a possibility of spurious assertion violations. JayHorn therefore implements a separate counterexample validation step with a precise, but bounded representation of heap (i.e., an under-approximate program encoding). This step is applied when the encoding with instance invariants leads to an inconclusive result. If neither over-approximate nor under-approximate encoding are able to infer a conclusive result, JayHorn reports UNKNOWN as overall verification result.

3   Weaknesses and Strengths

Weaknesses: The development of JayHorn is ongoing, and at this point several key Java features are not fully supported yet, including (i) strings; (ii) enums; (iii) bounded integer data-types; (iv) floating-point data-types; (v) reflection and dynamic loading; (vi) concurrency. The JayHorn model of the Java API is rudimentary, so that JayHorn assumes arbitrary behavior for most API functions. Some parts of JayHorn also need more optimization to reduce the run-time of the tool, in particular some of the program transformation steps. The Horn encoding could be optimized to use fewer relation symbols with smaller arity.

Strengths: Due to way heap is encoded, JayHorn is particularly suitable for the analysis of relatively shallow properties of programs with unbounded iteration, unbounded recursion, or unbounded heap data-structures; examples illustrating the capabilities of JayHorn are given in [4].

SV-COMP 2019: The mentioned features make JayHorn a relatively bad match for the Java benchmarks used in SV-COMP 2019, which are predominantly regression tests checking the correct handling of language features and of the Java string API. A large fraction of the benchmarks (the MinePump family) relies on correct handling of enums, and could therefore not be solved by JayHorn. Only a few of the SV-COMP benchmarks contain unboundedness in the form of loops, recursion, or heap data-structures.

JayHorn gave a wrong answer for two benchmarks in the competition. The program UnsatAddition02 was incorrectly classified as correct (true), since Jay-Horn assumes unbounded integers. synchronized was incorrectly reported to be incorrect (false) due to an incomplete model of the synchronized construct, JayHorn does not support concurrency yet.

The results in the competition are overall promising, but do not represent a typical application scenario of JayHorn. The JayHorn team plans to address this for 2020 by submitting further benchmarks to SV-COMP, and by completing Java support of JayHorn, in particular fully supporting strings.

4   Download and Use of **JayHorn**

JayHorn is fully implemented in Java, and uses the libraries mentioned in Fig. 1. The version submitted to SV-COMP 2019 is JayHorn version 0.6.[1] In the configuration used in the competition,[2] JayHorn only applies the Horn solver Eldarica. Since Eldarica is itself implemented in Scala, this means that no native code was used in JayHorn in the competition. The Benchexec tool info module is called jayhorn.py and the benchmark definition file jayhorn.xml. JayHorn competes in the Java category.

To run JayHorn 0.6, it is enough to download the Jar file jayhorn.jar from the link below, and run it on bytecode:

```
wget https://raw.githubusercontent.com/jayhorn/jayhorn/devel/ \
  jayhorn/src/test/resources/horn-encoding/classics/UnsatMccarthy91.java
wget https://github.com/jayhorn/jayhorn/releases/download/v0.6/jayhorn.jar
mkdir tmp
javac UnsatMccarthy91.java -d tmp
java -Xss40m -Xmx3000m -jar jayhorn.jar -inline-size 10 -solution -j tmp
```

---

[1] https://github.com/jayhorn/jayhorn/releases/tag/v0.6.
[2] Java options -Xss40m -Xmx3000m, JayHorn options -inline-size 10.

Acknowledgement. We are grateful for contributions to JayHorn by Daniel Dietsch, Rody Kersten, Huascar Sanchez, and Valentin Wüstholz. The development of JayHorn is funded in parts by AFRL contract No. FA8750-15-C-0010, NSF Award No. 1422705, by the Swedish Research Council (VR) under grants 2014-5484 and 2018-4727, and by the Swedish Foundation for Strategic Research (SSF) under the project WebSec (Ref. RIT17-0011).

References

1. Freeman, T., Pfenning, F.: Refinement types for ML. In: PLDI, pp. 268–277. ACM, New York (1991)
2. Grebenshchikov, S., Lopes, N.P., Popeea, C., Rybalchenko, A.: Synthesizing software verifiers from proof rules. In: PLDI, pp. 405–416. ACM (2012)
3. Hojjat, H., Rümmer, P.: The ELDARICA Horn solver. In: Bjørner, N., Gurfinkel, A. (eds.) FMCAD, pp. 1–7. IEEE (2018)
4. Kahsai, T., Kersten, R., Rümmer, P., Schäf, M.: Quantified heap invariants for object-oriented programs. In: LPAR-21. EPiC, vol. 46, pp. 368–384 (2017)
5. Komuravelli, A., Gurfinkel, A., Chaki, S.: SMT-based model checking for recursive programs. Form. Methods Syst. Des. **48**(3), 175–205 (2016)
6. Pacheco, C., Ernst, M.D.: Randoop: feedback-directed random testing for Java. In: OOPSLA, pp. 815–816. ACM, New York (2007)
7. Rondon, P.M., Kawaguchi, M., Jhala, R.: Liquid types. In: Gupta, R., Amarasinghe, S.P. (eds.) PLDI, pp. 159–169. ACM (2008)
8. Vallée-Rai, R., Hendren, L., Sundaresan, V., Lam, P., Gagnon, E., Co, P.: Soot - a Java optimization framework. In: CASCON (1999)

JBMC: Bounded Model Checking
for Java Bytecode
(Competition Contribution)

Lucas Cordeiro[1]([✉]) [iD], Daniel Kroening[2,3] [iD], and Peter Schrammel[2,4] [iD]

[1] University of Manchester, Manchester, UK
lucas.cordeiro@manchester.ac.uk
[2] Diffblue Ltd., Oxford, UK
[3] University of Oxford, Oxford, UK
[4] University of Sussex, Brighton, UK

Abstract. JBMC is a bounded model checking tool for verifying Java bytecode. It is built on top of the CPROVER framework. JBMC processes Java bytecode together with a model of the standard Java libraries. It checks a set of desired properties, such as assertions and absence of uncaught exceptions, under given bounds on loops, recursion and data structures. Internally, it uses the same bounded model checking engine as its sibling tool CBMC and discharges the generated verification conditions with the help of MiniSAT 2.2.1.

1 Overview

JBMC is a bounded model checker based on Boolean Satisfiability (SAT) and Satisfiability Modulo Theories (SMT), which allows the verification of Java programs [3]. JBMC inherits memory model, symbolic execution engine and SAT/SMT backends of its sibling tool CBMC [2]. In particular, JBMC consists of a frontend for parsing Java bytecode and a Java operational model (JOM), which is an exact but verification-friendly model of the standard Java libraries. Thus, JBMC supports Java bytecode and can verify programs that make use of classes, inheritance, polymorphism, arrays, bit-level operations and floating-point arithmetic using CBMC's verification engine.

JBMC can reason about array bound violations, unintended arithmetic overflows, and other kinds of functional and runtime errors. However, as with other bounded model checkers, JBMC is in general incomplete, i.e., can only be used to find property violations up to a given bound k but not to prove properties, unless we know an upper bound on the depth of the state space by checking whether all loops have been fully unrolled; this is accomplished by inserting a so-called *unwinding assertion* at the end of each loop and recursion to check for termination.

JBMC natively supports MiniSAT as its main solver to discharge verification conditions (VCs) and check for their satisfiability, but can also be used with other incremental SAT solvers such as Glucose. For SV-COMP 2019, however, JBMC

D. Beyer et al. (Eds.): TACAS 2019, Part III, LNCS 11429, pp. 219–223, 2019.
https://doi.org/10.1007/978-3-030-17502-3_17

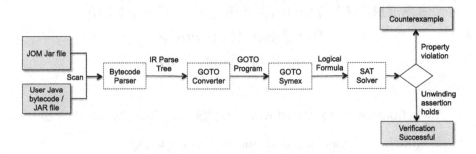

Fig. 1. JBMC architecture. Grey rectangles represent input and output while white rectangles represent the JBMC main verification steps.

does not use incremental bounded model checking to verify Java programs with (multiple) loops, i.e., it does not check the VCs in iteration $k + 1$ by building upon the work done for iteration k [5].

2   Architecture

JBMC's architecture is illustrated in Fig. 1. JBMC accepts Java bytecode class files or JAR files as input together with the JOM to parse the Java bytecode and translate it into the CPROVER control-flow graph representation, which is called a GOTO program; this transformation simplifies the Java bytecode representation (e.g., replacement of *switch* and *while* by *if* and *goto* statements) as well as lowering of exceptional control flow.

The GOTO Symex component performs a symbolic execution of the program, which thus handles dynamic memory allocation, encoding of virtual method dispatch, unrolling of the loops and unfolding of recursive method calls. In particular, JBMC uses two functions that compute the constraints C (i.e., assumptions and variable assignments) and properties P (i.e., built-in and user-defined assertions); it automatically generates safety conditions that check for null dereference, array bounds errors, type cast errors and other kinds of functional and runtime errors. Both functions accumulate the control-flow predicates at each program point and use these predicates to guard both the constraints and the properties, so that they properly reflect the Java bytecode's semantics. JBMC's VC generator then derives the VCs from these; the resulting bit-vector formula (i.e., $C \wedge \neg P$) is then passed on to the configured SAT solver to check for satisfiability. If this formula is *satisfiable*, then JBMC produces a counterexample; otherwise, if the formula is *unsatisfiable*, then a successful verification result is reported.

3   Features

JBMC uses an abstract representation of the standard Java libraries, called the Java operational model (JOM), which consists of simplified models of the most common classes from *java.lang* and a few from *java.util*; these models remove verification-irrelevant performance optimizations (e.g., in the implementation of container classes), exploit declarative specifications (using **assume** statement) and functions that are built into the CPROVER framework (e.g., for array and string manipulation).

JBMC also implements a solver for strings to determine the satisfiability of a set of constraints involving strings [4]. Specifically, our string solver implements a decision procedure for string operations that are typically used by Java programs, such as concatenation, search, extract and conversions to other data types. This decision procedure uses incremental SAT solving to lazily instantiate quantifiers.

JBMC also provides API classes that allow users to define non-deterministic verification harnesses and stub functions as used in the SV-COMP benchmarks. The API[1] contains such methods for primitive data-types (e.g. **nondetDouble()**) and *strings* (e.g. **nondetString()**). The API also provides an **assume**(*condition*) method, which advises JBMC to ignore paths that do not satisfy a user-specified condition. JBMC is able to check for array bounds, division by zero, unintended arithmetic overflows, runtime errors in Java (e.g. illegal memory access) and user-specified assertions.

Current development efforts include improving support for regular expressions, multi-threaded programs and enabling output of VCs using the SMT-LIB format to be checked by SMT solvers such as Z3, CVC4, Boolector, MathSAT and Yices.

4   Strengths and Weaknesses

JBMC does not produce any incorrect result for any of the Java verification tasks available in SV-COMP 2019 [1]; it correctly claims 139 benchmarks correct and finds existing errors in 192. However, JBMC crashes (and returns unknown) in 37 benchmarks due to time or memory exhaustion, or due to missing models of the Java standard library. JBMC can handle most Java basic features (e.g., inheritance, polymorphism and exceptions) and strings manipulations (but *regexes* are not fully supported yet). However, JBMC's concurrency support is still limited and there is no support for Java 8 lambdas, reflection and Java Native Interface (JNI). As its sibling CBMC, JBMC can only prove bounded programs unless an upper bound is known on the depth of the state space, which is not generally the case. Lastly, our JOM does not cover the entire Java standard library.

---

[1] https://github.com/diffblue/java-models-library/blob/master/src/main/java/org/sosy_lab/sv_benchmarks/Verifier.java.

```
1  import org.sosy_lab.sv_benchmarks.Verifier;
2  public class Main {
3    public static void main(String[] args) {
4      String arg = Verifier.nondetString();
5      float floatValue = Float.parseFloat(arg);
6      String tmp = String.valueOf(floatValue);
7      assert tmp.equals("2.50");
8    }
9  }
```

Fig. 2. Illustrative Java code extracted from SV-COMP 2019 (`StringValueOf08`).

5 Tool Setup

The competition submission is based on JBMC version 5.10.[2] For the competition, JBMC is called from a wrapper script.[3] The wrapper script compiles the .java source files in the given benchmark directories and then invokes the jbmc binary repeatedly with increasing values for the unwinding bound until the property has been refuted (answering false) or the program has been fully unwound without finding a property violation (answering true). See the wrapper script for the relevant command line options given to JBMC. As an example, we can run the JBMC wrapper script to check for a reachability property in the program shown in Fig. 2 by executing the following command:

```
./jbmc --propertyfile <path-to-sv-benchmarks>/properties/assert.prp
    <path-to-sv-benchmarks>/java/jbmc-regression/StringValueOf08
```

where `assert.prp` indicates the specification to be verified for `StringValueOf08`. Note that this program invokes in line 4 a non-deterministic method (*Verifier.nondetString();*) to produce an arbitrary string value; this method is provided by SV-COMP in org.sosy_lab.sv_benchmarks.Verifier. The JOM (core-models.jar) is also part of the submission archive. If a verification task uses a Java library method that is not part of the JOM then the wrapper script returns unknown. The Benchexec tool info module is called jbmc.py and the benchmark definition file jbmc.xml. The competition submission of JBMC uses MiniSAT 2.2.1 as SAT backend. JBMC competes in the Java category.

6 Software Project

JBMC is maintained by Peter Schrammel together with numerous contributors[4] from the community. It is publicly available under a BSD-style license. The source code is available at http://www.github.com/diffblue/cbmc in the jbmc directory. Instructions for building JBMC from source are given in the file COMPILING.md.

---

[2] Executable available at https://gitlab.com/sosy-lab/sv-comp/archives/tags/svcomp19.

[3] Can be built from https://github.com/diffblue/cprover-sv-comp/tree/svcomp19.

[4] https://github.com/diffblue/cbmc/graphs/contributors.

References

1. Beyer, D.: Automatic verification of C and Java programs: SV-COMP 2019. In: Beyer, D., Huisman, M., Kordon, F., Steffen, B. (eds.) TACAS 2019. LNCS, vol. 11429, pp. 133–155. Springer, Cham (2019)
2. Clarke, E., Kroening, D., Lerda, F.: A tool for checking ANSI-C programs. In: Jensen, K., Podelski, A. (eds.) TACAS 2004. LNCS, vol. 2988, pp. 168–176. Springer, Heidelberg (2004). https://doi.org/10.1007/978-3-540-24730-2_15
3. Cordeiro, L., Kesseli, P., Kroening, D., Schrammel, P., Trtik, M.: JBMC: a bounded model checking tool for verifying Java bytecode. In: Chockler, H., Weissenbacher, G. (eds.) CAV 2018. LNCS, vol. 10981, pp. 183–190. Springer, Cham (2018). https://doi.org/10.1007/978-3-319-96145-3_10
4. Li, G., Ghosh, I.: PASS: string solving with parameterized array and interval automaton. In: Bertacco, V., Legay, A. (eds.) HVC 2013. LNCS, vol. 8244, pp. 15–31. Springer, Cham (2013). https://doi.org/10.1007/978-3-319-03077-7_2
5. Schrammel, P., Kroening, D., Brain, M., Martins, R., Teige, T., Bienmüller, T.: Incremental bounded model checking for embedded software. Formal Aspects Comput. **29**(5), 911–931 (2017)

Java Pathfinder at SV-COMP 2019
(Competition Contribution)

Cyrille Artho[1]([⊠]) and Willem Visser[2]

[1] EECS, KTH Royal Institute of Technology, 100 44 Stockholm, Sweden
artho@kth.se
[2] Department of Computer Science, University of Stellenbosch,
Stellenbosch, South Africa
visserw@sun.ac.za
https://people.kth.se/~artho/

Abstract. This paper gives a brief overview of Java Pathfinder, or jpf-core. We describe the architecture of JPF, its strengths, and how it was set up for SV-COMP 2019.

Keywords: Java Pathfinder · Software model checking ·
Java program analysis

1 Verification Approach

Java Pathfinder (JPF) is a framework for Java bytecode analysis [13]. At the core of the system is an explicit-state model checker [4], often just called JPF (but officially called jpf-core). This core can be extended to allow a variety of other analyses, most notably there is an extension for doing symbolic execution, called Symbolic Pathfinder [9]. Here however we focus only on the core system, i.e., on the explicit-state model checker.

JPF is a mature system with its first version released in the late 1990s. It was first open-sourced by NASA in 2004 and since around 2016 it is a community project hosted on GitHub [12]. It is based around the core algorithms for doing on-the-fly explicit state model checking, similar to SPIN. Unlike SPIN however, it does not support temporal logic property checking by itself. Instead, this functionality can be added as an extension; the core system used here only checks for uncaught exceptions (which include assertion violations).

2 Software Architecture

The main architectural component of JPF is a Java virtual machine (JVM), implemented in Java. This component supports functionality for executing bytecode as well as backtracking over already executed code. Additionally a fingerprint of each state of the JVM (using hash-compaction [5]) is stored to allow

---

C. Artho—Jury member.

D. Beyer et al. (Eds.): TACAS 2019, Part III, LNCS 11429, pp. 224–228, 2019.
https://doi.org/10.1007/978-3-030-17502-3_18

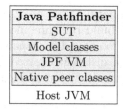

Fig. 1. Architecture of JPF

state-matching and to keep the analysis linear in the size of the state-space of the program being analyzed. Another optimization to allow for the efficient analysis of concurrent programs is a form of partial-order reduction that groups bytecode together in a transition as long as they cannot have any visible effect on other threads. Note that both the hash-compaction and the implementation of partial-order reduction (JPF group instructions that can only have a local effect into the same transition, but this is based on heuristics) used can cause behaviours to be missed during analysis and for this reason JPF is only a bug-finding tool, not a verification tool.

At its core, JPF treats any source of non-determinism as a choice; common choices are scheduling choices and non-deterministic choices over a range of values, e.g., whether a network is available or not [3]. In the context of SV-COMP, symbolic inputs were always treated as entirely non-deterministic choices when using jpf-core.

Java Pathfinder itself is written in Java and therefore runs on the standard JVM, called *host JVM* (see Fig. 1). The system under test (SUT) is run inside the JPF VM, and cannot directly interact with the host VM. This allows JPF to capture the full address space of the program, and revert any changes in memory when backtracking the state of the SUT during the state space search. However, this approach cannot handle native methods, which execute unmanaged code (written in C or C++) that is not supervised by JPF. Changes to memory by native methods, or other side effects thereof, are not visible to JPF. To overcome this limitation, JPF allows *model classes* to be defined, which replace the standard library classes with custom code. With this mechanism, a class with native methods can be replaced with a Java-based model class that does not use native code. Such model classes are fully managed by JPF. Sometimes, though, it is necessary to access native code, for example, to perform input/output. To achieve this, JPF supports *native peer classes*, which are executed directly on the host VM. This means that any built-in library functionality (such as I/O) is available to native peer classes. Furthermore, native peers have access to low-level data structures inside the JPF VM, and thus can read and modify the state of model classes or any other classes that are managed by the JPF VM.

Java Pathfinder is highly extensible and modular. Its VM can handle different platforms and instructions sets (such as Java bytecode and Dalvik code for Android), use different state space exploration strategies and schedulers, and also allows listeners to receive notifications of program state changes or execution actions, allowing users to build run-time monitoring algorithms on top of JPF. JPF extensions are vital to expand its capabilities, and allow it to handle features like the verification of distributed systems [7,11], generating missing native code on the fly [10], or monitor temporal-logic properties [8].

3   Discussion of Strengths and Weaknesses of the Approach

As expected, JPF performed very well on examples with simple non-deterministic inputs such as Boolean parameters. In this case, the state space is small enough that an exhaustive search is easy, and there is no need to track path conditions (which are implemented by the Symbolic Pathfinder extension [9]). It is therefore also unsurprising that JPF did poorly in some cases where a constraint solver is required to analyze the full state space effectively. An example would be assert3 in the jbmc-regression suite where an error occurs when the input satisfies the constraint $i \geq 1000 \land i \leq 1000$. JPF will only enumerate the inputs for small ranges of values. Because the range of i is not directly specified, but indirectly derived through constraints, JPF does not analyze this variable and therefore misses this error. Finally, there were a few cases where JPF did not conclude its analysis due to missing model classes or native peers.

Java Pathfinder would really excel when analyzing simple to moderately complex concurrent applications, and applications using advanced functionality like input/output and network communication. In the 2019 benchmark set, no concurrent applications were present, so JPF is not fully utilized in this preliminary evaluation. The addition of networked applications would require additional configuration information, so it is therefore not clear how soon the benchmark suite can be extended with such additional, realistic applications. Examples that have been successfully verified by JPF in the past include a WebDAV client [2], and scp client [6], and HTTP servers [1,7].

4   Tool Setup and Configuration

Java Pathfinder is available on GitHub [12]; the submitted compiled version is archived under https://gitlab.com/sosy-lab/SV-COMP/archives-2019/blob/master/2019/jpf.zip.

Java Pathfinder (jpf-core) has no external dependencies; JUnit is necessary to run the unit tests, but not to build and use jpf-core.

JPF is compiled with `./gradlew build`.

We used the default values for all options, except that `cg.enumerate_random` was changed to `true` from the default configuration, because this option forces JPF to explore all possible values for random choices.[1] This setting was necessary

---

[1] JPF will explore all outcomes for Boolean choices, and a set of predefined corner cases for choices on integers.

to enable JPF to explore non-deterministic inputs. It is not enabled by default because JPF is normally used to analyze concurrency.

JPF participated in all Java benchmarks.

5 Software Project and Contributors

The project is managed by the Java Pathfinder group. Contact person is Cyrille Artho (artho@kth.se). JPF is available under the Apache License, version 2.0 and hosted on GitHub [12].

Acknowledgements. We thank all contributors who have participated in the development of JPF over the last 20 years.

We would also like to thank Peter Schrammel and Dirk Beyer for their support, and for providing the scripts and configuration files for the competition.

References

1. Artho, C., Hagiya, M., Potter, R., Tanabe, Y., Weitl, F., Yamamoto, M.: Software model checking for distributed systems with selector-based, non-blocking communication. In: Proceedings of the 28th International Conference on Automated Software Engineering (ASE 2013), Palo Alto, USA, pp. 169–179. IEEE Computer Society (2013)
2. Artho, C., Leungwattanakit, W., Hagiya, M., Tanabe, Y., Yamamoto, M.: Cache-based model checking of networked applications: from linear to branching time. In: Proceedings of the 24th International Conference on Automated Software Engineering (ASE 2009), Auckland, New Zealand, pp. 447–458. IEEE Computer Society (2009)
3. Artho, C., et al.: Using checkpointing and virtualization for fault injection. IJNC **5**(2), 347–372 (2015)
4. Holzmann, G.: The SPIN Model Checker. Addison-Wesley, Boston (2004)
5. Holzmann, G.J.: An analysis of bitstate hashing. Formal Methods Syst. Des. **13**(3), 289–307 (1998). https://doi.org/10.1023/A:1008696026254
6. Leungwattanakit, W., Artho, C., Hagiya, M., Tanabe, Y., Yamamoto, M.: Model checking distributed systems by combining caching and process checkpointing. In: Proceedings of the 26th International Conference on Automated Software Engineering (ASE 2011), Lawrence, USA, pp. 103–112. IEEE Computer Society (2011)
7. Leungwattanakit, W., Artho, C., Hagiya, M., Tanabe, Y., Yamamoto, M., Takahashi, K.: Modular software model checking for distributed systems. IEEE Trans. Softw. Eng. **40**(5), 483–501 (2014)
8. Lombardi, M.: jpf-ltl (2013). https://bitbucket.org/michelelombardi/jpf-ltl. Accessed 11 Jan 2019
9. Pasareanu, C.S., Visser, W., Bushnell, D.H., Geldenhuys, J., Mehlitz, P.C., Rungta, N.: Symbolic PathFinder: integrating symbolic execution with model checking for Java bytecode analysis. In: Proceedings of the 28th International Conference on Automated Software Engineering (ASE 2013), pp. 391–425 (2013). https://doi.org/10.1007/s10515-013-0122-2

10. Shafiei, N., Breugel, F.V.: Automatic handling of native methods in Java PathFinder. In: Proceedings of the 2014 International SPIN Symposium on Model Checking of Software, SPIN 2014, pp. 97–100. ACM, New York (2014). https://doi.org/10.1145/2632362.2632363

11. Shafiei, N., Mehlitz, P.: Extending JPF to verify distributed systems. ACM SIG-SOFT Softw. Eng. Notes **39**(1), 1–5 (2014)

12. The Java Pathfinder Group: jpf-core (2019). https://github.com/javapathfinder/jpf-core. Accessed 11 Jan 2019

13. Visser, W., Havelund, K., Brat, G., Park, S., Lerda, F.: Model checking programs. Autom. Softw. Eng. J. **10**(2), 203–232 (2003)

PeSCo: Predicting Sequential Combinations of Verifiers
(Competition Contribution)

Cedric Richter[(✉)] and Heike Wehrheim

Department of Computer Science, Paderborn University, Paderborn, Germany
cedricr@mail.upb.de, wehrheim@upb.de

Abstract. PESCO is a tool for predicting a (likely best) sequential combination of verifiers on a given verification task and then running it. The approach is based on machine learning, more precisely on learning *rankings* of verifiers on verification tasks (where the ordering of verifiers is based on the SV-COMP scoring schema). The learning part employs Support Vector Machines; as base verifiers we use CPACHECKER in 6 different configurations.

1 Verification Approach

Composing verification techniques in sequence has in the past been a promising approach in the annual software verification competition SV-COMP. Especially in 2018[1], the software verification framework CPACHECKER [3], using a composition of analyses, was able to outperform competitors in category ReachSafety. However, the analysis sequence is often predefined and fixed. In other words, a problem instance might pass through a sequence of unsuccessful verification configurations until it is processed by the right technique or exceeds a time limit.

Our competition contribution utilizes the sequential setting of CPACHECKER (more precisely, of CPA-SEQ), but *predicts* the order of verification tools viz. configurations. For this, we applied an extension of our rank prediction approach introduced in [7]. Basically, for a given verification task we predict an ordering of CPACHECKER configurations, and then sequentially run these configurations. Configurations are ordered with respect to their (likely) performance on the verification task.

The prediction employs machine learning. For the learning, we extract *features* of verification tasks via an encoding of programs as graphs combining concepts of control-flow and program dependence graphs with abstract syntax trees. Features represent certain graph substructures of programs, where the depth of substructures considered is configurable.

---

[1] sv-comp.sosy-lab.org/2018/results/results-verified/.

C. Richter—Jury member.

D. Beyer et al. (Eds.): TACAS 2019, Part III, LNCS 11429, pp. 229–233, 2019.
https://doi.org/10.1007/978-3-030-17502-3_19

To obtain the execution order for a new problem instance, the *Ranking by pairwise comparison* (RPC) [9] framework is employed utilizing *kernelized Support Vector Machines* (SVM) [11] as base learners. By employing SVMs, we are able to choose a kernel function[2] (similar to Weisfeiler-Lehman kernels [12]) that is specifically designed for graph substructures. However, the function proposed in [7] needed to be computed between the input instance X (the graph of a verification task) and *every* training sample Y, which can be quite costly in practice. As a consequence, we have re-implemented this approach and now compute Weisfeiler-Lehman-based features of *single* graphs. This significantly improves the performance of prediction.

2   Software Architecture

Our tool contribution PESCO embeds a `Planning` step in the `restart` algorithm employed in the verification framework CPACHECKER [3]. The `restart` algorithm [10] is used in a sequential combination of verifiers to let the next verifier start on already computed (partial) results of previous verifiers, in particular when the previous verifier could not solve the verification problem. However, instead of executing a fixed list of verification techniques, our algorithm plans an execution order dependent on the verification task to be solved. Our approach consists of the following steps.

Training. To train our rank predictor, we employ rankings obtained by executing 5 CPACHECKER configurations on the verification tasks of SV-COMP 2018. Similar to CPA-SEQ [10] from 2018, we use *Value Analysis* [5], *Value Analysis + CEGAR* [5], *Predicate Analysis* [4], *k-Induction* [1] and *Bounded Model Checking* [6]. In addition, we introduced and carried out training with a special `UNKNOWN` configuration. This extension will allow our prediction procedure to cut off an analysis when it will most probably fail.

Planning. As can be seen in Fig. 1, we utilize the preprocessor and control flow automaton (CFA) construction implemented in CPACHECKER. Instead of passing the CFA directly to an analysis, we first query our rank prediction process. The prediction process starts by building an intermediate graph representation. This is followed by a feature extraction and the final ranking procedure (details in [7]). If a prediction is not achievable in a certain time frame, we fall back to the standard CPA-SEQ.

Execution. After planning a sequential composition, we can apply the analyses in the given order. If an analysis fails or exceeds its time limit, we switch to the next configuration. On reaching the `UNKNOWN` configuration, we exit the verification sequence. Instead of leaving the overall process, specialized techniques will be applied in the following situations: For recursive programs we facilitate *Block Abstraction Memoization* (BAM) [8,13] and *Binary Decision Diagrams* (BDD) [2] are used for concurrent programs. Witnesses are written as generated by the verifiers.

---

[2] Kernels are similar to a similarity functions between feature vectors.

Despite the fact that our implementation is only dependent on Java 8, we need MathSAT 5^3 to run individual configurations. Furthermore, parser frontend for C programs are used according to CPACHECKER.

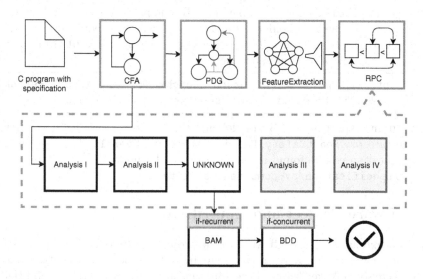

Fig. 1. Architecture of PeSCo implemented within CPACHECKER. The dotted box represent the Restart Algorithm enhanced by our rank prediction. Hence, Analysis II receives partial results of Analysis I for a restart of the verification. The rank prediction utilizes the control flow automaton extended by data and control dependencies (PDG).

3   Strengths and Weaknesses

In contrast to traditional compositional approaches, PeSCo adapts to the given tasks. As a result, our tool is able to decrease the runtime by skipping techniques that do not fit to the given verification task. More importantly, the adaptation allows us to omit analyses which introduce failures. Consequently, PeSCo improves the number of correct results in a given time frame.

Nevertheless, learning the optimal ranking requires time and introduces uncertainty to the verification process. Experiments on 1148 tasks in *ReachSafety-ECA* show that optimal rankings on a large number of *similar* programs with *different* requirements are difficult to predict. Still, the results of SV-COMP 2019 show that PeSCo can effectively verify a number of C programs in that category.

Due to the prediction process, PeSCo is furthermore limited to the configurations that occur during training. Since we trained our predictor with the version of CPACHECKER employed in SV-COMP 2018, we perform slightly worse than the improved 2019 version of CPA-SEQ.

---

³ mathsat.fbk.eu.

4   Tool Setup and Configuration

PESCO is fully integrated in the official source code of CPACHECKER. Thus, it can be downloaded as a fork: https://github.com/cedricrupb/cpachecker. We use Revision b8d6131 for the competition. To compile the tool, ant should be executed on the checkout folder. After this step, our tool requires Java 8 and MathSAT 5 as external tools. To verify a test program, CPACHECKER is executed with the following command line:

```
$ scripts/cpa.sh -svcomp19-pesco -benchmark -heap 10000M -stack
    ↪   2048k -timelimit 900s -spec prop.spc program.c
```

For programs expecting a 64 Bit model, add the parameter -64. PESCO participates in category ReachSafety, Falsification and Overall. The corresponding specification can be found in the checkout folder under config/specification/sv-comp-reachability.spc.

5   Software Project and Contributors

Being an extension of the CPACHECKER project, PESCO is developed as an open-source project by a research group from Paderborn University. Contributors were so far Mike Czech, Marie-Christine Jakobs, Cedric Richter and Heike Wehrheim. We would furthermore like to thank Eyke Hüllermeier for machine learning expertise and his contribution to the prediction process. We aso thank the CPACHECKER team for allowing us to use their tool.

References

1. Beyer, D., Dangl, M., Wendler, P.: Boosting k-induction with continuously-refined invariants. In: Kroening, D., Păsăreanu, C.S. (eds.) CAV 2015. LNCS, vol. 9206, pp. 622–640. Springer, Cham (2015). https://doi.org/10.1007/978-3-319-21690-4_42
2. Beyer, D., Friedberger, K.: A light-weight approach for verifying multi-threaded programs with CPAchecker. In: Electronic Proceedings in Theoretical Computer Science, no. 233, pp. 61–71 (2016)
3. Beyer, D., Keremoglu, M.E.: CPACHECKER: a tool for configurable software verification. In: Gopalakrishnan, G., Qadeer, S. (eds.) CAV 2011. LNCS, vol. 6806, pp. 184–190. Springer, Heidelberg (2011). https://doi.org/10.1007/978-3-642-22110-1_16
4. Beyer, D., Keremoglu, M.E., Wendler, P.: Predicate abstraction with adjustable-block encoding. In: Proceedings of the 2010 Conference on Formal Methods in Computer-Aided Design, pp. 189–198. FMCAD Inc. (2010)
5. Beyer, D., Löwe, S.: Explicit-state software model checking based on CEGAR and interpolation. In: Cortellessa, V., Varró, D. (eds.) FASE 2013. LNCS, vol. 7793, pp. 146–162. Springer, Heidelberg (2013). https://doi.org/10.1007/978-3-642-37057-1_11
6. Clarke, E., Kroening, D., Lerda, F.: A tool for checking ANSI-C programs. In: Jensen, K., Podelski, A. (eds.) TACAS 2004. LNCS, vol. 2988, pp. 168–176. Springer, Heidelberg (2004). https://doi.org/10.1007/978-3-540-24730-2_15

7. Czech, M., Hüllermeier, E., Jakobs, M., Wehrheim, H.: Predicting rankings of software verification tools. In: Baysal, O., Menzies, T. (eds.) Proceedings of the 3rd ACM SIGSOFT International Workshop on Software Analytics, SWAN@ESEC/SIGSOFT FSE 2017, pp. 23–26. ACM (2017). https://doi.org/10.1145/3121257.3121262

8. Dangl, M., Löwe, S., Wendler, P.: CPACHECKER with support for recursive programs and floating-point arithmetic. In: Baier, C., Tinelli, C. (eds.) TACAS 2015. LNCS, vol. 9035, pp. 423–425. Springer, Heidelberg (2015). https://doi.org/10.1007/978-3-662-46681-0_34

9. Fürnkranz, J., Hüllermeier, E.: Preference learning and ranking by pairwise comparison. In: Preference Learning, pp. 65–82 (2010). https://doi.org/10.1007/978-3-642-14125-6-4

10. Löwe, S., Mandrykin, M., Wendler, P.: CPACHECKER with sequential combination of explicit-value analyses and predicate analyses. In: Ábrahám, E., Havelund, K. (eds.) TACAS 2014. LNCS, vol. 8413, pp. 392–394. Springer, Heidelberg (2014). https://doi.org/10.1007/978-3-642-54862-8_27

11. Schölkopf, B., Smola, A.: Learning with Kernels: Support Vector Machines, Regularization, Optimization, and Beyond. MIT Press, Cambridge (2001)

12. Weisfeiler, B., Lehman, A.: A reduction of a graph to a canonical form and an algebra arising during this reduction. Nauchno Technicheskaya Informatsia **2**(9), 12–19 (1968)

13. Wonisch, D., Wehrheim, H.: Predicate analysis with block-abstraction memoization. In: Aoki, T., Taguchi, K. (eds.) ICFEM 2012. LNCS, vol. 7635, pp. 332–347. Springer, Heidelberg (2012). https://doi.org/10.1007/978-3-642-34281-3_24

Pinaka: Symbolic Execution Meets Incremental Solving
(Competition Contribution)

Eti Chaudhary[ID] and Saurabh Joshi[✉][ID]

Department of Computer Science and Engineering,
Indian Institute of Technology Hyderabad, Kandi, India
{cs17mtech11029,sbjoshi}@iith.ac.in

Abstract. Many modern-day solvers offer functionality for incremental SAT solving, which preserves the state of the solver across invocations. This is beneficial when multiple, closely related SAT queries need to be fed to the solver. Pinaka is a symbolic execution engine which makes aggressive use of incremental SAT solving coupled with eager state infeasibility checks. It is built on top of the CProver/Symex framework. Pinaka supports both Breadth First Search and Depth First Search as state exploration strategies along with partial and full incremental modes. For SVCOMP 2019, Pinaka is configured to use partial incremental mode with Depth First Search strategy.

Keywords: Symbolic execution · Incremental solving · Software bug detection

1 Verification Technique

Pinaka extends symbolic execution with incremental solving coupled with eager infeasibility checks. A pure symbolic execution [6] engine builds a logical formula representing a potential execution path using symbolic values which may then be passed on to theorem-provers/solvers. An UNSAT outcome from the solver implies that the verification condition will not be violated along that path, whereas a SAT outcome provides a scenario leading to failure of an assertion during an execution along that path. The number of paths in a program blow-up exponentially as the number of branches increases. Pinaka, being a single-path symbolic execution engine, never merges two paths (i.e., diamonds). It employs eager infeasibility checks to avoid unnecessary exploration. Rather than making queries to the solver only when a path encounters an assertion, a query is made everytime a branch is encountered to check its feasibility. Infeasible branches are not explored further. These eager checks help Pinaka tremendously in reducing its search efforts. Pinaka is further powered by incremental solving [5] offered by

---

E. Chaudhary—Jury Member.

D. Beyer et al. (Eds.): TACAS 2019, Part III, LNCS 11429, pp. 234–238, 2019.
https://doi.org/10.1007/978-3-030-17502-3_20

many state-of-the-art solvers such as MiniSAT [3]. Incremental Solving greatly benefits our technique by reducing the overhead encountered due to eager infeasibility checks. Pinaka has Depth First Search (DFS) and Breadth First Search (BFS) as its search strategies. It offers two different modes of operation: Partial Incremental (PI) Mode and Full Incremental (FI) Mode.

In PI mode, a single solver instance is maintained along a search path. In the event that a branch is encountered, only a partial path is encoded from the current point to the previous point from which a query was made along the current path. For example, in Fig. 1, a query would be made at b_1. If both s_1 and s_2 are feasible, s_2 is put in a queue and the current solver instance is used to further explore the path starting from s_1. When b_2 is encountered, only the path from s_1 to b_2 is encoded and added in the current solver instance before making a query. If both the branches at b_2 are infeasible, a new solver instance is created and a path from the initial state to another symbolic state (e.g., s_2) in the queue is encoded and the path along that symbolic state is explored further. Essentially, a new solver instance is created every-time a backtrack happens. Using BFS in PI mode is very memory consuming because for every symbolic state in the queue, a corresponding solver instance is retained. Running Pinaka with this combination is not recommended.

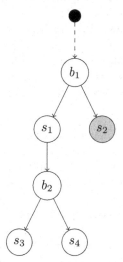

Fig. 1. Branching state in a program graph

In FI mode, a single solver instance is retained throughout. In Fig. 1, if $b_1 \rightarrow s_1$ is a feasible branch, a new activation variable $a_{b_1 s_1}$ is created. Let $\phi_{b_1 b_2}$ be the encoding of the path from b_1 to b_2. When b_2 is encountered, $a_{b_1 s_1} \Rightarrow \phi_{b_1 b_2}$ is added in the solver, and $a_{b_1 s_1}$ is added as an assumption to enforce the path. Since the underlying SAT solvers integrated with Pinaka do not allow *popping of a stack*, upon backtrack, $\neg a_{b_1 s_1}$ is set as an assumption to disable the constraints generated by this fragment of the path.

FI mode is beneficial when the input program does not have too many paths. Otherwise, the solver becomes quite slow over time with a large memory footprint. For a large program with too many paths, the benefit of a lower memory footprint and speed of PI mode outweighs its overhead of instantiating a new solver instance on every backtrack.

Loops are handled just like branches. Consider the program fragment given in Fig. 2. Assume that along some path where $(x_1 = 1) \land (y_3 = -1)$ the loop is encountered. Branch $x_1 >= 3$ is infeasible along this path and will not be explored. Since $x_1 < 3$ is feasible, it is explored further by unrolling this iteration on-the-fly. Therefore, the path will further add $y_3 < 0$. Since it is feasible, $x_2 = x_1 + 1$ is added and feasibility of $x_2 < 3$ will be checked. After one more unrolling $x_3 < 3$

```
while(x<3)
{
    if (y < 0 )
    { x=x+1; }
}
```

Fig. 2. Handling loops

will be found infeasible, thus guaranteeing termination of the loop along this path. Note that, along a path having $y_3 = 2$, the loop will be non-terminating for that path. In this case, Pinaka may not terminate. Function calls, including recursion, are handled in a similar fashion by inlining a call on-the-fly. Therefore, even though Pinaka provides an option of --unwind NUM to specify an unwinding limit, it does not mandate that a loop unwinding limit is specified. If a user-given unwinding limit is not sufficient to reach an assertion violation, it declares the program as *safe*, which may be unsound. To ensure soundness, we run it without any loop unwinding limit. For *unsafe* programs, upon encountering the first assertion violation, Pinaka terminates and reports a failure. For *safe* programs, however, Pinaka terminates only if all the paths of the program are terminating.

2   Architecture

Pinaka 0.1 is built upon the CProver [2]+ Symex [10] framework[1]. Taking a *C* program as input, it makes use of CProver framework APIs to convert the input C program to a GOTO program. CProver APIs further come into play for pre-processing of GOTO-programs, witness generation, transformation passes such as setting the rounding-mode for floating-point operations, handling complex data types, etc. Pinaka implements PI and FI mode and eager infeasibility checks along with BFS/DFS exploration. Apart from DFS, none of those features are present in Symex [10]. Additionally, we make use of our forked version of the Symex repository in which we fix many bugs, especially for handling recursive procedures and ternary operators. As of now Pinaka only supports some MiniSAT-like solvers (i.e., Glucose [4], MapleSAT [7]) and not SMT solvers. Once a program has been verified, a verification successful/failed outcome is generated along with the appropriate witness (Fig. 3).

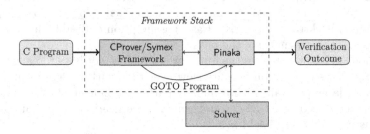

Fig. 3. Architectural overview of Pinaka

---

[1] Note the specific Symex version used on which Pinaka is built.

3   Strengths and Weaknesses

Modulo the soundness of the CProver/Symex framework and the back-end solver, Pinaka's technique is sound. In addition, if CProver/Symex do not have any over-approximation in modeling the C constructs, then a bug reported by Pinaka would indeed be a bug.

   As explained in Sect. 1, Pinaka can potentially be non-terminating if for some input value there is a non-terminating path. However, termination of verification process guarantees the termination of the underlying program (modulo the approximations introduced in modeling by CProver/Symex) *if* the program is declared *safe* by Pinaka. A notable strength of Pinaka lies in its speed. A majority of Pinaka's verification outcomes were obtained under a mere limit of 10 s. A clear display of the same can be seen in the ReachSafety-Floats category, where Pinaka came in second with 1500 s CPU time [9], as compared to other tools that share a similar score but require 4 to 10 times more CPU time.

   One major weakness of the current version Pinaka is a lack of techniques for loop invariants. Even with eager infeasibility checks and incremental solving, there is still a need for more loop-directed abstraction based approaches. Furthermore, support for handling multi-dimensional arrays is still lacking.

4   Tool Setup and Configuration

Pinaka 0.1 is available for download at https://github.com/sbjoshi/Pinaka. The repository contains a description of Pinaka's working along with all the necessary configuration files required to run Pinaka SVCOMP style. All the instructions are listed in a stepwise manner in the README.md file. Although Pinaka is built on top of the CProver/Symex framework, the binary itself is sufficient and the tool does not require any additional pre-requisites. Pinaka has been tested on Ubuntu 18.04.

   Pinaka 0.1 submitted for SVCOMP 2019 runs DFS in PI Mode as for SVCOMP benchmarks we found this combination the best. No loop unwinding limit was specified to retain soundness. For SVCOMP'19 [1,9] it uses Glucose-Syrup (Glucose-4.1) [4] as its solver back-end. Tool's default search strategy, i.e., DFS may be overridden by providing `--bfs` option. Similarly, a default of FI mode may also be overridden by providing `--partial-incremental` option. Other additional options may be explored from the `--help` menu. The set of global parameters passed to the tool are: (1) `--graphml-witness`: to specify the witness file to be generated, (2) `--propertyfile`: to specify the property file, (3) `--32/--64`: to define the architecture to be used. Pinaka 0.1 participated in all ReachSafety subcategories *except* ReachSafety-Sequentialized, and also participated in NoOverflows and Termination meta-categories in SVCOMP 2019.

5   Software Project and Contributors

Pinaka is a result of very heavy code rewriting and refactoring of VerifOx [8] (developed by Saurabh Joshi) with a lot of feature additions and bug fixes. Pinaka is developed at Indian Institute of Technology, Hyderabad, India. It is available at https://github.com/sbjoshi/Pinaka under BSD License. The authors acknowledge the financial support from DST, India under SERB ECR 2017 grant.

References

1. Beyer, D.: Automatic verification of C and Java programs: SV-COMP 2019. In: Beyer, D., et al. (eds.) TACAS 2019, Part 3. LNCS, vol. 11429, pp. 133–155. Springer, Cham (2019)
2. CPROVER homepage. http://www.cprover.org. Accessed 10 Feb 2019
3. Een, N., Sörensson, N.: Minisat v2. 0 (beta). Solver description, SAT race 2006 (2006)
4. Glucose's homepage. http://www.labri.fr/perso/lsimon/glucose/. Accessed 10 Feb 2019
5. Hooker, J.N.: Solving the incremental satisfiability problem. J. Logic Program. **15**(1–2), 177–186 (1993)
6. King, J.C.: Symbolic execution and program testing. Commun. ACM **19**(7), 385–394 (1976)
7. Maplesat homepage. https://sites.google.com/a/gsd.uwaterloo.ca/maplesat/. Accessed 10 Feb 2019
8. Mukherjee, R., Joshi, S., Griesmayer, A., Kroening, D., Melham, T.: Equivalence checking of a floating-point unit against a high-level c model. In: FM (2016)
9. SVCOMP 2019 results. https://sv-comp.sosy-lab.org/2019/results/results-verified/. Accessed 4 Jan 2019
10. Symex repository. https://github.com/diffblue/symex/tree/9b5a72cf992d29a905 441f9dfa6802379546e1b7. Accessed 10 Feb 2019

Symbolic Pathfinder for SV-COMP
(Competition Contribution)

Yannic Noller[1], Corina S. Păsăreanu[2,3], Aymeric Fromherz[2],
Xuan-Bach D. Le[2], and Willem Visser[4(✉)]

[1] Humboldt-Universität zu Berlin, Berlin, Germany
[2] Carnegie Mellon University Silicon Valley, Moffett Field, USA
[3] NASA Ames Research Center, Mountain View, USA
[4] Stellenbosch University, Stellenbosch, South Africa
visserw@sun.ac.za

Abstract. This paper describes the benchmark entry for Symbolic
Pathfinder, a symbolic execution tool for Java bytecode. We give a brief
description of the tool and we describe the particular run configuration
that was used in the SV-COMP competition. Furthermore, we comment
on the competition results and we outline some directions for future
work.

1 Verification Approach

Symbolic Pathfinder (SPF) is a program analysis tool for Java bytecode; the
tool is based on *symbolic execution*. In this approach, programs are executed
on symbolic inputs representing multiple concrete inputs. Values of variables
are represented as numeric constraints, generated from the analysis of the code
structure, i.e. conditionals and other statements in the program. These constraints are then solved using different constraint solvers (both off-the-shelf and
built-in-house) to generate test inputs that are guaranteed to reach those parts
of the code.

The current implementation handles the following:

- Inputs of type boolean, int, long, float, double
- Input data structures, using *lazy initialization* [5]
- Preconditions [5]
- Multi-threading (via Java PathFinder exploration)
- Mixed symbolic/concrete execution mode [9]
- Symbolic arrays [3]
- Inputs of type String – work in progress [1].

SPF can also be used for probabilistic analysis by leveraging model counting
over symbolic constraints [2,4], and for automated program repair [6,7]. Most
recent work explores combinations of SPF with AFL-style fuzzing [8] and further
differential analysis for regression problems.

© The Author(s) 2019
D. Beyer et al. (Eds.): TACAS 2019, Part III, LNCS 11429, pp. 239–243, 2019.
https://doi.org/10.1007/978-3-030-17502-3_21

2   Software Architecture

SPF is described in detail in a journal article [10] (however, as it is an active project, it is being updated with new features all the time). We depict the current tool architecture in Fig. 1. The input to the tool is a Java bytecode program and a configuration file that specifies different options for analysis (as discussed below). The output is a set of test sequences that execute different paths through the code. The output also lists the errors that were found (e.g. exceptions, assert violations) together with various statistics about the analysis.

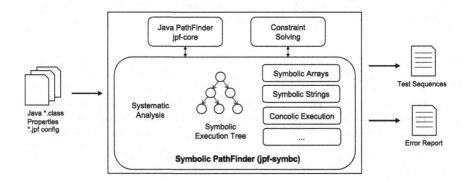

Fig. 1. Symbolic PathFinder overview.

Symbolic execution is implemented by a "non-standard" interpretation of bytecodes. The symbolic information is propagated via *attributes* associated with program variables, operands, etc. The analysis can start from any point in the program and it can perform mixed concrete/symbolic execution. SPF relies on jpf-core's search engine to explore different paths through the code. The default search strategy is depth-first search. State matching (as implemented in jpf-core) is usually turned off during symbolic execution.

SPF uses several constraint solvers and decision procedures, most notably Z3 and Z3bitvector, which are available from https://github.com/Z3Prover/z3. SPF implements both incremental and non-incremental constraint solving.

3   Discussion of Strengths and Weaknesses of the Approach

The competition results are provided on the SV-COMP website. The results indicate that SPF outperforms the other tools in terms of correct answers (337), cpu time (1300 s) and energy (13000 J). However, SPF also reported 6 incorrect results, which penalized the overall final score. While the incorrect true results are due to the bounded nature of the analysis, the incorrect false results are due mainly to the string analysis, with the exception of one result which was due to an error in jpf-core which has since been corrected. The string solver was incorrectly specified and tested (i.e. the path to the string solver is hard coded in the current implementation but we provided no string solver for the competition).

In the future we plan to test SPF on the competition string examples using either ABC or Z3str and to robustify the implementation. We also plan to contribute to the competition by adding more interesting benchmarks, particularly related to input data structures.

4 Tool Setup and Configuration

Symbolic PathFinder is available at https://github.com/SymbolicPathFinder/ jpf-symbc. It requires Java 8 and Java PathFinder, which available at https:// github.com/javapathfinder/jpf-core.

For this competition we used the version with the timestamp *Mon Nov 19 09:51:16 CET 2018*, which refers to the date when we pulled the artifacts from the GitHub repository and generated the jpf-symbc jar archive.

To run SPF, the user needs to download Symbolic PathFinder and Java PathFinder (default branches) and create a file `.jpf/site.properties` in the home directory. The `site.properties` file should contain the following lines (the users should modify to point to the location of `jpf-core` and `jpf-symbc` on their computer):

```
jpf-core = ${user.home}/workspace/jpf-core
jpf-symbc = ${user.home}/workspace/jpf-symbc
extensions = ${jpf-core},${jpf-symbc}
```

The user then creates a `*.jpf` configuration file (described in detail below). For the competition we modified the SPF tool to handle the non-deterministic constructs required by the competition.

4.1 Example Configuration

We give here an example configuration that can be used to run the SPF tool; this is the default configuration, that we used in the competition. The explanation for the different options is given in parenthesis.

- `target=test.Main` *(specify the target application)*
- `classpath=/..` *(path to your class example)*
- `sourcepath=/..` *(path to the source of your example)*

- `symbolic.dp=z3bitvector` *(specify the decision procedure)*
- `symbolic.bvlength=64` *(specify the bitvector length)*

- `symbolic.min_int=-100` *(specify various min max values)*
- `symbolic.max_int=100`

- `symbolic.min_double=-100.0`
- `symbolic.max_double=100.0`

- `symbolic.debug=true` *(print debug information)*
- `search.depth_limit=15` *(specify search limit)*

- `symbolic.lazy=on` *(handling symbolic arrays)*
- `symbolic.arrays=true`

- `symbolic.strings=true` *(specify string analysis)*
- `symbolic.string_dp=ABC` *(specify string solver).*

SPF also has the option of running the constraint solving incrementally. Note however that we did not use the string solving and the incremental solving options in the competition as we did not have enough time to prepare and test those features, as we were entered late in the competition.

5   Software Project and Contributors

Information about the project and contributors can be found at the project webpage: https://github.com/SymbolicPathFinder/jpf-symbc. For more information please contact the authors of this paper.

References

1. Bang, L., Aydin, A., Phan, Q., Pasareanu, C.S., Bultan, T.: String analysis for side channels with segmented oracles. In: FSE 2016, Seattle, WA, USA, 13–18 November 2016, pp. 193–204 (2016)
2. Filieri, A., Pasareanu, C.S., Visser, W.: Reliability analysis in symbolic PathFinder. In: ICSE 2013, San Francisco, CA, USA, 18–26 May 2013, pp. 622–631 (2013)
3. Fromherz, A., Luckow, K.S., Pasareanu, C.S.: Symbolic arrays in symbolic PathFinder. ACM SIGSOFT Softw. Eng. Notes **41**(6), 1–5 (2016)
4. Geldenhuys, J., Dwyer, M.B., Visser, W.: Probabilistic symbolic execution. In: ISSTA 2012, Minneapolis, MN, USA, 15–20 July 2012, pp. 166–176 (2012)
5. Khurshid, S., PǍsǍreanu, C.S., Visser, W.: Generalized symbolic execution for model checking and testing. In: Garavel, H., Hatcliff, J. (eds.) TACAS 2003. LNCS, vol. 2619, pp. 553–568. Springer, Heidelberg (2003)
6. Le, X.-B.D., Chu, D.-H., Lo, D., Le Goues, C., Visser, W.: JFIX: semantics-based repair of Java programs via symbolic PathFinder. In: ISSTA 2017, pp. 376–379 (2017)
7. Le, X.-B.D., Chu, D.-H., Lo, D., Le Goues, C., Visser, W.: S3: syntax- and semantic-guided repair synthesis via programming by examples. In: ESEC/FSE 2017, pp. 593–604. ACM, New York (2017)
8. Noller, Y., Kersten, R., Pasareanu, C.S.: Badger: complexity analysis with fuzzing and symbolic execution. In: ISSTA 2018, Amsterdam, The Netherlands, 16–21 July 2018, pp. 322–332 (2018)

9. Pasareanu, C.S., Rungta, N., Visser, W.: Symbolic execution with mixed concrete-symbolic solving. In: ISSTA 2011, Toronto, ON, Canada, 17–21 July 2011, pp. 34–44 (2011)
10. Pasareanu, C.S., Visser, W., Bushnell, D.H., Geldenhuys, J., Mehlitz, P.C., Rungta, N.: Symbolic PathFinder: integrating symbolic execution with model checking for java bytecode analysis. Autom. Softw. Eng. **20**(3), 391–425 (2013)

VeriFuzz: Program Aware Fuzzing
(Competition Contribution)

Animesh Basak Chowdhury, Raveendra Kumar Medicherla[(⊠)],
and Venkatesh R

Tata Research Development and Design Centre, Pune, India
raveendra.kumar@tcs.com

Abstract. VeriFuzz is a program aware fuzz testing tool, which combines the power of feedback-driven evolutionary fuzz testing with static analysis. VeriFuzz deploys lightweight static analysis to extract meaningful information about program behavior that can aid fuzzing based test-input generation to achieve coverage goals quickly. We use constraint-solver to generate an initial population of test-inputs. VeriFuzz could generate the maximum number of counterexamples for reachsafety category benchmarks in SV-COMP 2019 and in Test-Comp 2019 [16]. (All the terms in typewriter font are competition specific. See [15].)

1 Introduction

VeriFuzz is a coverage driven automated test-input generation tool based on *grey-box* fuzzing [5]. The idea of grey-box fuzzing is to use lightweight instrumentation to observe behaviors exhibited during a test run. This information is used while fuzzing for new test-inputs that might exhibit new behaviors. For VeriFuzz, the behavior of interest is code coverage. VeriFuzz relies on evolutionary algorithms to generate newer test-inputs from an initial population of test-inputs. Central to an evolutionary algorithm is the *selection* of *best-fit* candidates from a *population* and generate offspring by applying *crossover* and *mutating* operations on them. The newer offspring are checked for their *fitness* against a goal. The population evolves by adding the fit offspring to the existing population. In an automated testing, a candidate test-input plays the role of an individual in a population. The new test-inputs are generated from a selected test-input by repeatedly applying mutation operations, for example, by flipping byte at a random position. The fitness of a generated test-input is determined by the code coverage during its run [11,18].

State-of-the-art grey-box fuzzers such as afl-fuzz [19], though simple to use, have several key shortcomings. (a) The fuzzer is aware of neither the program structure nor the input structure. This leads to the generation of a large set of redundant test-inputs with respect to code coverage. (b) For programs that

---

R. K. Medicherla—Jury Member.

© The Author(s) 2019
D. Beyer et al. (Eds.): TACAS 2019, Part III, LNCS 11429, pp. 244–249, 2019.
https://doi.org/10.1007/978-3-030-17502-3_22

does *complex* validations on their input, the fuzzer finds it hard to generate a test-input that satisfies such validation conditions [13]. Finding a suitable initial population of test-inputs for such programs requires the analysis of validation conditions. (c) For programs with unbounded loops, the fuzzer may get *stuck* forever without generating any new test-inputs. There are several approaches proposed in the literature to address some of these shortcomings [1,7,12,13]. However, all these approaches address each concern separately.

2   Our Approach

In order to alleviate the problems described in Sect. 1, our approach analyses and transforms the subject program. The analysis information is then passed to the enhanced mutation engine of afl-fuzz for fuzzing the transformed program. The following are the key steps of our approach.

Efficient Instrumentation: To measure the coverage due to a run on a test-input, the subject program is *instrumented*. However, instrumentation adds a significant overhead to the program execution, impacting the fuzzer's execution speed. We have optimized the instrumentation overhead by placing the probes either true or false branches of each conditional statement in the program. Our scheme is efficient to implement and preserves the coverage measure though it is sub-optimal than instrumentation schemes proposed in literature [7].

Loop Bounding: Certain class of programs, for example, reactive programs, during their execution, either does not terminate or crash upon reaching the *error location*[1]. In order to handle such non-terminating programs, our approach transforms the program loops by replacing the condition in their loop heads with a known bound. This bound is increased dynamically during the fuzzer run till it finds an input that can take program execution to an error location or the budgeted time elapses.

Novel Initial Test Population Generation: Grey-box fuzzers find it hard to generate test-inputs that can take program execution to cover the program blocks that are guarded by complex checks [10,13]. If the initial test-input population can take program execution through some of the complex checks, fuzzing such inputs is *likely* to generate test-inputs that can pass through other complex checks [17]. In order to create such initial test-input population, our approach first flattens the program by unrolling the loops up to a certain bound. Then, a program path is chosen that contains such complex checks and path constraints are generated along that path. The constraints are solved to create an initial test-input population.

Program Analysis to Assist Mutation: For programs that read input only within restricted range values, it is possible to fine-tune the fuzzer's mutation operators to choose values within this restricted ranges. In order to determine

---

[1] Program statement where error function __VERIFIER_error() is called.

the ranges of input values that can reach the error locations, our approach statically determines the input value ranges of the program using k-path interval analysis [9]. For a given program, this analysis determines the conservative over approximate ranges of input values that may reach any given program point. We have enhanced the mutation engine of the fuzzer such that it accepts the input value ranges at the error location in the program and generates inputs that have values within the given ranges.

Algorithmic Selection of Strategies: All the aforementioned techniques are generic enough to use across the programs. However, in order to optimize the given resource budgets in the competition, we have selectively applied a subset of techniques to a specific class of programs. For example, loop bounding technique is applied to programs where syntactic unbounded loop structures are detected. In order to identify and map the best performing set of techniques to all benchmark programs, we have grouped them into a finite set of classes and formulated it as *multi-label classification* problem. The classifier model is developed using a non-parametric supervised learning based approach [6]. The model has been trained using nine syntactic structures of a C program and a subset of techniques as classification labels. The benchmark programs from SV-COMP 2018 [14] were used as training and validation set. We have used the decision tree classifier for this multi-label classification [2].

3   Tool Architecture and Flow

Figure 1 shows the architecture of the VeriFuzz tool. It consists of a fuzzing engine and an analysis engine. The core fuzzing engine is built on top of the state-of-art grey-box fuzzer afl-fuzz v2.52b [19]. The program analysis, instrumentation and transformation components of the analysis engine are implemented using the PRISM, a TCS in-house program analysis framework [8]. The initial input generation component uses CBMC v5.10 [3] as path-constraint solver. The program classification component uses an offline trained model and scikit-learn v.0.19.2 to access the model. The implementation is in C, Java, and Python languages.

The input to the tool is a program P and a safety property ϕ. In the first step, the syntactic features are extracted and the class of the program is determined using a program classification module. This class information is used in subsequent steps. In the second step, the program P_i is generated using an instrumentation and transformation module. This step also emits the transformed programs for `witness generation` (P_w) and initial test-input generation modules. In the next step, the program is analysed to determine input ranges. These input ranges are used to formulate the fuzzing engine parameters F_i. Subsequently, initial test-input population T_i is generated using the initial input generation module. The fuzz engine is then invoked with P_i, F_i, and T_i as inputs.

As a first step of the fuzzing engine, the program P_i and a harness program that implemented `__VERIFIER_*` functions are compiled together using `gcc` to generate the executable program P_e. The core fuzzer begins with T_i as its initial

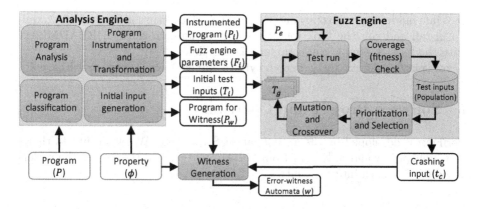

Fig. 1. VeriFuzz architecture.

population, executes P_e, and measures the coverage. A test-input from the population is selected and mutated several times to generate newer test-inputs T_g. The program P_e is repeatedly executed with each test-input $t_g \in T_g$ and coverage is measured. The fitness check step compares the code coverage due run on each t_g with the historical code coverage and determines whether t_g should be added to the population or not. This process is repeated until the core fuzzer finds a crashing test-input t_c that causes the program run to reach the error location or the time budget is elapsed. The t_c and P_w are passed to a witness generation program to generate error-witness.

4   Strengths and Weaknesses

The core strength of VeriFuzz is its ability to find a test-input that can cause the program execution to reach the error locations quickly. The tool participated both in SV-COMP and Test-Comp [16]. In SV-COMP, VeriFuzz could identify 1264 out of 1458 reachsafety FALSE benchmarks with 67 s as mean time per verification task. Whereas in Test-Comp, it could identify bugs in 592 out of 636 benchmarks. VeriFuzz could generate test-inputs that can, on an average, cover 70% branches in 1720 benchmarks.

VeriFuzz explores the concrete program paths randomly and redundantly due to its evolutionary approach. Therefore it may not always discover a test-input that cause the execution to reach an error location.

5   Tool Configuration and Setup

The VeriFuzz tool for testing SV-COMP benchmarks is available at the URL https://gitlab.com/sosy-lab/sv-comp/archives-2019/blob/master/2019/verifuzz .zip. Its Test-Comp 2019 variant is available at the URL https://gitlab.com/sosy-lab/test-comp/archives-2019/blob/master/2019/verifuzz.zip.   The benchexec tool-info module is verifuzz.py and the benchmark description file is verifuzz.xml. To install and run the tool, follow the instructions provided in README.txt with the tool. A sample run command is as follows:

```
./scripts/verifuzz.py --propertyFile unreach-call.prp example.c
```

6   Software Project and Contributors

VeriFuzz is developed by the authors at TCS Research. We would like to thank B. Chimdyalwar and S. Kumar from VeriAbs [4] team for the help in the understanding of k-path interval analysis.

References

1. Böhme, M., Pham, V.T., Nguyen, M.D., Roychoudhury, A.: Directed greybox fuzzing. In: Proceedings of the 2017 ACM SIGSAC Conference on Computer and Communications Security (CCS), pp. 2329–2344. ACM (2017)
2. Chen, T., Guestrin, C.: XGBoost: a scalable tree boosting system. In: Proceedings of the 22nd SIGKDD International Conference on Knowledge Discovery and Data mining (KDD), pp. 785–794. ACM (2016)
3. Clarke, E., Kroening, D., Lerda, F.: A tool for checking ANSI-C programs. In: Jensen, K., Podelski, A. (eds.) TACAS 2004. LNCS, vol. 2988, pp. 168–176. Springer, Heidelberg (2004). https://doi.org/10.1007/978-3-540-24730-2_15
4. Darke, P., et al.: VeriAbs: verification by abstraction and test generation. In: Beyer, D., Huisman, M. (eds.) TACAS 2018. LNCS, vol. 10806, pp. 457–462. Springer, Cham (2018). https://doi.org/10.1007/978-3-319-89963-3_32
5. DeMott, J., Enbody, R., Punch, W.F.: Revolutionizing the field of grey-box attack surface testing with evolutionary fuzzing. BlackHat and Defcon (2007)
6. Demyanova, Y., Pani, T., et al.: Empirical software metrics for benchmarking of verification tools. Form. Meth. Syst. Des. **50**(2–3), 289–316 (2017)
7. Hsu, C.C., Wu, C.Y., Hsiao, H.C., Huang, S.K.: INSTRIM: lightweight instrumentation for coverage-guided fuzzing. In: Symposium on Network and Distributed System Security (NDSS), Workshop on Binary Analysis Research (2018)
8. Khare, S., Saraswat, S., Kumar, S.: Static program analysis of large embedded code base: an experience. In: Proceedings of the India Software Engineering Conference (ISEC) (2011)
9. Kumar, S., Chimdyalwar, B., Shrotri, U.: Precise range analysis on large industry code. In: Proceedings of the 2013 9th Joint Meeting on Foundations of Software Engineering, pp. 675–678. ACM (2013)
10. Lemieux, C., Sen, K.: FairFuzz: a targeted mutation strategy for increasing grey-box fuzz testing coverage. In: Proceedings of the 33rd ACM/IEEE International Conference on Automated Software Engineering, pp. 475–485. ACM (2018)
11. McMinn, P.: Search-based software testing: past, present and future. In: 2011 IEEE Fourth International Conference on Software Testing, Verification and Validation Workshops (ICSTW), pp. 153–163. IEEE (2011)
12. Rawat, S., Jain, V., et al.: VUzzer: application-aware evolutionary fuzzing. In: USENIX security (2017)

13. Stephens, N., Grosen, J., et al.: Driller: augmenting fuzzing through selective symbolic execution. In: Proceedings of the Network and Distributed System Security Symposium (NDSS) (2016)
14. SV-COMP 2018 Benchmarks: (Commit - f2996ff). https://github.com/sosy-lab/sv-benchmarks/releases/tag/svcomp18
15. SV-COMP, Test-Comp: Definitions and Rules (2019). https://sv-comp.sosy-lab.org/2019/rules.php, https://test-comp.sosy-lab.org/2019/rules.php
16. TOOLympics 2019: Competetion on software testing (Test-Comp). TACAS 2019 (2019). https://test-comp.sosy-lab.org/2019/
17. Wang, J., Chen, B., Wei, L., Liu, Y.: SkyFire: data-driven seed generation for fuzzing. In: 2017 IEEE Symposium on Security and Privacy (SP), pp. 579–594. IEEE (2017)
18. Wegener, J., Baresel, A., Sthamer, H.: Evolutionary test environment for automatic structural testing. Inf. Softw. Technol. **43**(14), 841–854 (2001)
19. Zalewski, M.: American fuzzy lop. http://lcamtuf.coredump.cx/afl/

VIAP 1.1
(Competition Contribution)

Pritom Rajkhowa$^{(\boxtimes)}$ and Fangzhen Lin

Department of Computer Science and Engineering,
The Hong Kong University of Science and Technology,
Clear Water Bay, Kowloon, Hong Kong
{prajkhowa,flin}@cse.ust.hk

Abstract. VIAP (Verifier for Integer Assignment Programs) is an automated system for verifying safety properties of procedural programs with integer assignments and loops. It is based on a translation from of a program to a set of first-order axioms with quantification over natural numbers, and currently makes use of SymPy as the algebraic simplifier and the SMT solver Z3 as the theorem prover. Our first version of the system competed at SV-COMP 2018. This paper describes VIAP 1.1, a new version that makes use of our newly developed recurrence solver. As a result, VIAP 1.1. is able to verify many programs that were out of reach for the older version VIAP 1.0.

Keywords: Automatic program verification · First-order logic ·
Mathematical induction · Recurrences · SMT · Arithmetic

1 Introduction

VIAP (Verifier for Integer Assignment Programs) is an automated system for verifying safety properties of procedural programs with integer assignments and loops. It translates a given program to a set of first-order axioms with natural number quantification using an algorithm proposed by Lin [1]. An earlier version of VIAP competed at SV-COMP 2018, and is described in [2,3]. A key feature of Lin's translation is that loops are translated to a set of recurrence relations. Then, VIAP simplifies those axioms by using a Python library for symbolic computation systems, *SymPy* [4], to compute the closed-form solutions of recurrence relations. *SymPy* is equipped with function *rsolve()* to compute closed-form solution of recurrence relation. The translation of the loop body generates recurrence relations which are either simple non-conditional, conditional or mutual in nature. But *rsolve()* can find the closed form solution only for certain class of simple non-conditional recurrence relations. This motivated us to design a recurrence solver (RS) that goes beyond what the *rsolve()* function can do in *SymPy*, and integrate it with our system. The new system, VIAP 1.1, is the one that will compete at this year's SV-COMP. VIAP 1.1 continues to use *SymPy* for simplifying algebraic expressions, and the SMT solver Z3 [5] as

© The Author(s) 2019
D. Beyer et al. (Eds.): TACAS 2019, Part III, LNCS 11429, pp. 250–255, 2019.
https://doi.org/10.1007/978-3-030-17502-3_23

the underlying theorem prover without ever explicitly generating loop invariants. Because of the new recurrence solver, VIAP 1.1 can solve many more benchmarks that were previously out of the reach of VIAP 1.0.

To illustrate how our system works, consider the simple program below:

```
int x=0,y=0;
while (x<100) { if (x < 50){ y++; } else { y--; } x++; }
assert(y==0);
```

With some simple simplifications, the translation outlined in [1] would generate the following axioms:

$$x_1 = x_2(N), y_1 = y_2(N),$$
$$\forall n.x_2(n + 1) = x_2(n) + 1, x_2(0) = 0,$$
$$\forall n.y_2(n + 1) = ite(x_2(n) < 50, y_2(n) + 1, y_2(n) - 1), y_2(0) = 0,$$
$$\neg(x_2(N) < 100), \forall n.n < N \rightarrow x_2(n) < 100.$$

Here, x_1 and y_1 denote the output values of x and y, respectively, and $x_2(n)$ and $y_2(n)$ denote the values of x and y during the n-th iteration of the loop, respectively. The conditional expression $ite(c, e_1, e_2)$ has value e_1 if c holds and e_2 otherwise. Also N is a natural number constant, and the last two axioms say that it is exactly the number of iterations the loop executes before exiting.

There are two recurrence relations in the above axioms. Both the recurrence relations are passed to RS. It first solves $x_2(n)$ which yields the closed-form solution $x_2(n) = n$ which can then be used to simplify the recurrence relations for $y_2(n)$ into

$$y_2(0) = 0, \ y_2(n + 1) = ite(n < 50, y_2(n) + 1, y_2(n) - 1).$$

Then RS tries to solve the above simplified conditional recurrence relations, and returns the following closed-form solution:

$$y_2(n) = ite(0 \le n < 50, n, 50 - n).$$

After computing the closed-form solutions for $x_2()$ and $y_2()$ by RS, VIAP eliminates them, and produces the following axioms:

$$x_1 = N \wedge y_1 = ite(0 \le N < 50, N, 100 - N), N \ge 100),$$
$$\forall n.n < N \rightarrow n < 100.$$

The translation of assertion results $y_1 == 0$. With this set of axioms, SMT solvers like Z3 can then be made to prove the assertion. Similarly, when an assertion like `assert(y==1)` is made to prove using above set of axioms, then Z3 will return following counterexample:

$$[y_1 = 0, N = 100, x_1 = 100].$$

Using this counterexample, VIAP constructs the violation witness.

2   VIAP Architecture

VIAP is implemented in Python 2. VIAP has been developed in a modular fashion, and its architecture is layered into two parts:

- **Front-End:** The system accepts a program written in C (C99 language) as input and translates it to first order axioms. The recurrence solver solves the recurrence relations generated during the translation if closed-form solutions are available.
- **Back-End:** The system takes the set of translated first-order axioms and translates all the axioms to equations compatible with Z3 (Version 4.5) by pre-processing them using *SymPy* (Version 1.1.1). Then the proof engine applies different strategies and tries to prove post-conditions in Z3 [2].

Translation. Given a program P, and a language X, our system generates a set of first-order axioms denoted by Π_P^X that captures the changes of P on X. Here, a language means a set of functions and predicate symbols. For Π_P^X to be correct, X needs to include all program variables in P as well as any functions and predicates that can be changed by P. The axioms in the set Π_P^X are generated inductively on the structure of P. The algorithm is described in detail in [1] and an implementation is explained in [2]. The inductive cases of translations are given in the table provided in the supplementary information[1]. We have extended our translation programs with arrays; the extension is described in detail in [3].

Recurrence Solver (RS). The main objective of this module is to find closed-form solutions of recurrence relations generated from the translation of the loop body. Our recurrence solver (RS)[2] takes a set of recurrence relation(s) and other constraints, returns a set of closed-form solutions it found for some of the recurrences and the remaining recurrences relations and constraints simplified using the computed closed-form solutions. It uses *SymPy* [4] (V 1.1.1) as the base solver. The RS classifies input recurrence relation(s) into three major categories (1. non-conditional 2. mutual and 3. conditional recurrences relation) and applies the following corresponding sub-solver and tries to find closed form solution(s).

- The Non-Conditional Recurrence Solver (*NCRS*): RS applies this sub solver to the non-conditional recurrence relation(s) of the form of either

$$X(n+1) = f(X(n), n),$$

where $f(x, y)$ is a polynomial function of x and y
or

$$X(n+1) = X(n) + f(n) + A_1 F_1(n) + \cdots + A_k F_k(n),$$

where $f(n)$ is a polynomial function in n, A_i's are constants, and F_i's are function symbols.

---

[1] https://github.com/VerifierIntegerAssignment/VIAP_ARRAY/blob/master/ Document/Inductive_Translation.pdf.

[2] https://github.com/VerifierIntegerAssignment/recSolver.

– The Mutual Recurrence Solver (MRS): RS applies this sub solver to a set $\boldsymbol{\sigma}$ of the mutual recurrence relations where each $\sigma \in \boldsymbol{\sigma}$ is the form of

$$X_i(n+1) = A * (X_1(n) + \ldots + X_h(n)) + C_i, \qquad \text{for } 1 \leq i \leq h,$$

where A and C_i are constants.
– The Conditional Recurrence Solver (CRS): RS applies this sub solver to conditional recurrence relation(s) of the form

$$X(n+1) = ite(\theta_1, f_1(X(n), n), ite(\theta_2, f_2(X(n), n) \ldots, f_{h+1}(X(n), n))),$$

where $\theta_1, \theta_2, \ldots, \theta_h$ are Boolean expressions, and $f_1(x,y), f_2(x,y), \ldots, f_{h+1}(x,y)$ are polynomial functions of x and y.

Instantiation: Instantiation is one of the most important phases of the pre-processing of axioms before the resulting set of formulae is passed on an SMT-solver according to some proof strategies. The objective is to help an SMT solver like Z3 to reason with quantifiers. There are two strategies (1) Instantiating arrays and (2) Instantiating array indices applied to an array element assignment that occurs inside a loop. More details are provide in the supplementary information[3].

Proof Strategies: As the semantics of P are precisely encoded as Π_P^X, the goal is to prove that $\alpha \wedge \Pi_P^X \models \beta$, where α is a set of assumption(s) and β is the set of assertion(s) to prove. We work in a refutation-based proof schema, i.e., in order to prove that a formula is valid in a background theory T, we show that $\alpha \wedge \Pi_P^X \wedge \neg\beta$ is T-unsatisfiable. In VIAP, we implemented two different strategies whose details can be found in our previous work [2].

3   Strength and Weaknesses

VIAP supports user assertions, including reachability of labels in the C-code. In SV-COMP 2019, these checks are only enabled for ReachSafety-Arrays, ReachSafety-Loops and ReachSafety-Recursive sub-categories of ReachSafety category. VIAP translates a program to a set of axioms and then uses off-the-shelf systems like SymPy and Z3 to prove properties about the program. The advantage (strength) of this approach comes with a clean separation between the translation (semantics) and the use of the translation in proving the properties (computation). The translation part is stable. But as more efficient provers become available, the capabilities of the system improve. This is seen in our newer version of VIAP that we entered in this year's competition: by having a more powerful system for computing closed-form solutions of recurrences, the new system becomes more efficient and can prove many properties that our

---

[3] https://github.com/VerifierIntegerAssignment/VIAP_ARRAY/blob/master/Document/TranslatonInsRules.pdf.

previous system were not able to. However, VIAP provides little or no support for translation and reasoning about dynamic linked data structures or programs with floating points. We are working in the direction to strengthen our front- and backhand to handle all types of the program so that we can participate in all the sub-categories of ReachSafety in the future edition of SV-COMP. The SVCOMP'19 results show that VIAP can effectively verify a number C programs from those categories. VIAP came in first in the ReachSafety-Arrays and ReachSafety-Recursive sub-category. The major disadvantage of the method which translates loop body to the recurrence relation is that if they failed to find closed form solution, then they unable to find suitable invariant as a result they failed to complete the proof. When VIAP fails to come up with a closed-form solution, it falls back to simple induction using Z3. There is clearly a need of better way to do induction and we are working on it. In terms of closed-form solution, in general it is undecidable whether a recurrence has a closed-form solution or not.

4   Tool Setup and Configuration

The version of VIAP (version 1.1) submitted to SV-COMP 2019[4] is provided as a set of binaries and libraries for Linux x86-64 architecture. The options for running the tool are:

```
./viap_tool.py  --spec=SPEC INPUT
```

SPEC is the property file, and INPUT is a C file. The output of VIAP is "VIAP_OUTPUT_True" when the program is safe. When a counterexample is found, it outputs "VIAP_OUTPUT_False" and a file named *errorWitness.graphml* that contains the witness of error-path is generated in the VIAP root folder. If VIAP is unable find any result it outputs "UNKNOWN".

5   Software Project and Contributors

VIAP is an open-source project, mainly developed by Pritom Rajkhowa and Professor Fangzhen Lin of the Hong Kong University of Science and Technology. We are grateful to the developers of Z3 and *SymPy* for making their systems available for open use.

Acknowledgments. We are very thankful to the anonymous reviewers for their helpful comments on an earlier version of this paper.

---

[4] https://gitlab.com/sosy-lab/sv-comp/archives-2019/blob/master/2019/viap.zip.

References

1. Lin, F.: A formalization of programs in first-order logic with a discrete linear order. Artif. Intell. **235**, 1–25 (2016)
2. Rajkhowa, P., Lin, F.: VIAP - automated system for verifying integer assignment programs with loops. In: Jebelean, T., Negru, V., Petcu, D., Zaharie, D., Ida, T., Watt, S.M. (eds.) 19th International Symposium on Symbolic and Numeric Algorithms for Scientific Computing, SYNASC 2017, Timisoara, Romania, 21–24 September 2017, pp. 137–144. IEEE Computer Society (2017)
3. Rajkhowa, P., Lin, F.: Extending VIAP to handle array programs. In: Piskac, R., Rümmer, P. (eds.) VSTTE 2018. LNCS, vol. 11294, pp. 38–49. Springer, Cham (2018). https://doi.org/10.1007/978-3-030-03592-1_3
4. SymPy Development Team: SymPy: python library for symbolic mathematics (2016)
5. de Moura, L., Bjørner, N.: Z3: an efficient SMT solver. In: Ramakrishnan, C.R., Rehof, J. (eds.) TACAS 2008. LNCS, vol. 4963, pp. 337–340. Springer, Heidelberg (2008). https://doi.org/10.1007/978-3-540-78800-3_24

Author Index

Printed in the United States
By Bookmasters